THE CAMBRIDGE HISTORY
OF
ENGLISH LITERATURE

VOLUME VI

THE DRAMA TO 1642

PART TWO

The Cambridge History

of

English Literature

Edited by

A. W. Ward, Litt.D., F.B.A.

Master of Peterhouse

and

A. R. Waller, M.A.

Peterhouse

Volume VI

The Drama to 1642

Part Two

New York: The Macmillan Company

Cambridge, England: at the University Press

1933

Copyright, 1917
by
The Macmillan Company

Published, March, 1917

Reprinted four times, 1920-1927
Reissued, October, 1931
Cheap Edition, October, 1933
Reprinted November, 1933.

PRINTED IN THE UNITED STATES OF AMERICA
BY THE FERRIS PRINTING COMPANY

CONTENTS

CHAPTER I

BEN JONSON

By ASHLEY H. THORNDIKE, M.A., Ph.D. (Harvard), Professor
of English in Columbia University, New York

CHAPTER II

CHAPMAN, MARSTON, DEKKER

By W. MACNEILE DIXON, M.A. (Dublin), Litt.D. (Glasgow),
Professor of English Language and Literature in the
University of Glasgow

CHAPTER III

MIDDLETON AND ROWLEY

By ARTHUR SYMONS

Contents

CHAPTER IV

THOMAS HEYWOOD

By A. W. WARD, Litt.D., F.B.A., Master of Peterhouse

CHAPTER V

BEAUMONT AND FLETCHER

By G. C. MACAULAY, M.A., late Fellow of Trinity College, University Lecturer in English

CHAPTER VI

PHILIP MASSINGER

By EMIL KOEPPEL, Professor of English Philology in the University of Strassburg

Contents

CHAPTER VII

TOURNEUR AND WEBSTER

By C. E. VAUGHAN, M.A., Balliol College, Oxford, Professor of English Literature in the University of Leeds

CHAPTER VIII

FORD AND SHIRLEY

By W. A. NEILSON, M.A. (Edinburgh), Ph.D. (Harvard), Professor of English in Harvard University

CHAPTER IX

LESSER JACOBEAN AND CAROLINE DRAMATISTS

By the Rev. RONALD BAYNE, M.A., University College, Oxford

Contents

CHAPTER X

THE ELIZABETHAN THEATRE

By HAROLD CHILD, sometime Scholar of Brasenose College, Oxford

CHAPTER XI

THE CHILDREN OF THE CHAPEL ROYAL AND THEIR MASTERS

By J. M. MANLY, M.A., Ph.D. (Harvard), Professor of English in the University of Chicago

CHAPTER XII

UNIVERSITY PLAYS

By F. S. BOAS, M.A., Balliol College, Oxford, LL.D. (St. Andrews), late Professor of English Literature in Queen's College, Belfast, and late Clark Lecturer, Trinity College

Contents

CHAPTER XIII

MASQUE AND PASTORAL

By the Rev. RONALD BAYNE, M.A.

CHAPTER XIV

THE PURITAN ATTACK UPON THE STAGE

By J. DOVER WILSON, M.A., Gonville and Caius College, Lecturer in English Literature at the Goldsmiths' College, University of London

The Cambridge History of
· English Literature

CHAPTER I

Ben Jonson

BEN JONSON the man is better known to us than any of his literary contemporaries. Drummond's record of his conversations has preserved an unkindly but vivid picture of his manners and opinions; and, indeed, his egoism made everything that he wrote partly a portrait of himself. Almost every contemporary reference to him has added something personal and characteristic. We hear of his quarrels, his drinking-bouts, his maladies and his imprisonments, as well as of his learning and his theories of literary art. We know him as the huge galleon of Fuller's account, "built far higher for learning, solid but slow in his performances," engaging in those memorable wit combats at the Mermaid tavern with that "English man-of-war," Shakespeare, who "took advantage of all winds by the quickness of his wit and invention"; and, again, as the autocrat of those later lyric feasts of Herrick's reminiscence, where each verse of his "outdid the meat, outdid the frolic wine." His humours, his dissipations, his prejudices make distinct and human for us the main interests of his life. Huge of body, bibulous and brawling, he yet loved Latin as heartily as canary, and could write the tenderest epitaph as well as the grossest epigram. Laborious and pertinacious, he rode his hobbies hard, confusing his scholarship with pedantry and his verse with theory; but few have ever served learning and poetry with so whole-hearted a devotion.

Since the days of Fuller, Jonson's personality and work have rarely been discussed or even mentioned without reference to his "beloved master" Shakespeare. The myth of his devouring jealousy of Shakespeare, supported by Chalmers and Malone, was demolished by Gifford nearly a century ago. But the facts about which the dispute was waged may be again recalled, because of the light that they throw on Jonson's character and friendships. That he criticised Shakespeare is known from the remark to Drummond that Shakespeare wanted art and from the well known passage in *Discoveries*. It also seems likely, from a reference in *The Returne from Pernassus*,[1] that, in the famous "war of the theatres," Shakespeare and Jonson were on opposite sides. In addition, there are scattered about the works of Jonson various remarks directed against Shakespeare's plays—especially, the ridicule of chronicle history plays, like *Henry V*, in the prologue to *Every Man in His Humour*, the remark on "tales, tempests, and such like drolleries" in *Bartholomew Fayre* and the petulant gird at *Pericles* in the *Ode to Himself*. In each of these instances, Jonson is defending one of his own plays and censuring a dramatic fashion contrary to his own practice and hostile, in his opinion, to the best interests of the drama. While it would be absurd to regard Jonson as representative of a dramatic theory and practice at all points opposed to Shakespeare, we shall find his plays representative of carefully considered views which imply a close criticism of much in Shakespeare and the contemporary drama.[2] His criticism of Shakespeare was based on a definite literary creed and methods, and not on jealousy or personal feeling. On the contrary, we have abundant tradition of his close friendship with Shakespeare, and we have the appreciative as well as discriminating passage in *Discoveries*, together with the generous eulogy prefixed to the folio, to testify to Jonson's admiration of his friend's plays, as "not of an age, but for all time." No other of Shakespeare's contemporaries has left so splendid and so enthusiastic an eulogy of the master.

Of Sidney, Spenser, Drayton, Beaumont and Donne, Jonson has likewise left us words of sharp censure and of ardent praise. With regard to Beaumont, Donne, Fletcher, Chapman, Bacon and others, as in the case of Shakespeare, he has mingled praise of their work with protestations of personal affection. With Marston, to whom, for a time, he was most bitterly hostile, he came to a full reconciliation. In all his relations with his

---

[1] Part II, act IV, sc. 3.
[2] Cf. Jusserand, J. J., "Ben Jonson's Views of Shakespeare's Art," in *Works of Shakespeare*, 1907, vol. x, pp. 297–321.

literary rivals, we see a man, vain, assertive, arrogant, quick to censure, strong in his loves and hates and always ready for a fight, but also one whose quarrels often ended in friendships, and who was loved and admired by the worthiest of his time. His boasting and carping could not conceal his sturdy honesty of intellect and heart and his generous admiration for high merit in either art or conduct.

The events of his life,[1] apart from his writings, can here be traced only in meagre outline. He was born in Westminster in 1572 or 1573, and "poorly brought-up," working, probably, at the trade of his step-father, a bricklayer. In spite of poverty, however, he was sent to Westminster school, where Camden, his life-long friend, was master. He did not enter either university,[2] although, later, he received honorary degrees from both; and the details of his life for a decade after he left school are unknown. He married, possibly in 1592, a wife "curst but honest"; had several children, none of whom survived him; enlisted and served a time in Flanders; and, in 1597, is found employed as both actor and playwright by Henslowe. He must have already won considerable reputation as a dramatist, for, in 1598, Meres, in his *Palladis Tamia*, mentions him as one of the six most excellent in tragedy. On 22 September, 1598, he killed a fellow actor, Gabriel Spencer, in a duel. His goods were confiscated and he was branded with a T; but he escaped capital punishment by pleading benefit of clergy. While in prison, he became a Roman Catholic; but, twelve years later, he returned to the church of England.

In the same year, 1598, and according to a letter of Sir Toby Matthew to Dudley Carleton, just before the duel with Spencer, Jonson's *Every Man in His Humour* was acted with great success by the Chamberlain's men, Shakespeare's company. The

[1] The chief recent authorities for the life of Jonson are Fleay, F. G., *English Drama*, 1559–1642, 2 vols. 1891; *Ward, A. W.*, vol. II, pp. 298 ff.; Herford, C. H., art. in *Dict. of Nat. Biogr.*; Castelain, M., *Ben Jonson, l'Homme et l'Œuvre*, 1907. See, also, Small, R. A., *The Stage Quarrel between Ben Jonson and the so-called Poetasters*, 1899. A life by Gregory Smith is promised in the English Men of Letters Series.

[2] Certain indications—they cannot be called evidence—in favour of the supposition that Jonson, about 1590, was resident for a short time at St. John's college, Cambridge, are discussed by J. Bass Mullinger in *The Eagle*, vol. XXV (1904).

tradition, preserved by Rowe, that the play was accepted through Shakespeare's efforts, may be founded on truth, but, manifestly, is erroneous in particulars. The play marks the beginning of a revolutionary movement in dramatic methods and the institution of a new species, the comedy of "humours." It is an important turning point in the course of the Elizabethan drama, and furnishes an announcement of Jonson's programme for the rest of his dramatic career. In the half-dozen years, however, which immediately followed its production, Jonson failed to write any comedy of comparable merit or of equal popular success. He seems to have been a sort of free lance, writing now for one company and now for another;[1] and the carrying out of his programme for reforming the drama was hindered both by the necessity of suiting the immediate stage demand, and by quarrels with his fellow dramatists Munday, Marston, Dekker and, possibly, Shakespeare. *Every Man out of His Humour*, acted 1599 by the Chamberlain's men, carries on the comedy of humours without dramatic success; *Cynthia's Revels* and *Poetaster*, both acted in 1600 and 1601 respectively by the children of the chapel, are interesting as satires rather than as dramas. They were concerned with the famous stage quarrel between Jonson and his foes.[2] Probably, there was some personal satire in the earlier of these plays, and its successor attacked Marston and Dekker, calling forth Dekker's rejoinder, *Satiro-mastix*. Jonson seems to have replied to Dekker only in his *Apologetical Dialogue*, withdrawn after it had been once on the stage, and appended to the first edition of *Poetaster*. In this, Jonson refused to carry the quarrel further, and promised to forsake comedy for tragedy. In 1598–9, he was also writing for Henslowe's companies, both in collaboration and alone, on plays not now extant, and, in 1600–1, he prepared for Henslowe additions to *The Spanish Tragedie*, presumably those of the edition of 1602. Two other

---

[1] The attempt to trace him back and forth from one company to another has led Fleay and his followers into many errors.

[2] The most satisfactory account of this conflict is given by Small, R. A., *op. cit.* An interpretation opposed to Small's is held by Fleay, Penniman, J. H., *War of the Theaters*, 1897, and Schelling, F. E. They are in general agreement; especially in giving Jonson's enmity for Daniel a large importance. Penniman and Schelling identify Matthew in *Every Man in His Humour* with Daniel. (See also below as to *Bartholomew Fayre*.)

plays, *The Case is Altered* and *A Tale of a Tub* (in an early form), belong to this period.

In *Sejanus*, acted by Shakespeare's company in 1603, Jonson carried his theories of dramatic art into tragedy. The "war of the theatres" was now over, and his reconciliations were made with his enemies; furthermore, the accession of James I brought him acceptable employment—for an entertainment at Althorp, and, in collaboration with Dekker, for the royal progress in London. Jonson seems to have been living at this time with lord d'Aubigny and to have won the patronage of several men of prominence; but, apparently, he had made enemies as well as friends at court. In connection with *Sejanus*, he was accused by the earl of Northampton of papacy and treason; and, in connection with *Eastward Hoe*, 1604/5, he was imprisoned with his collaborators, Marston and Chapman. Letters by Jonson and Chapman, recently discovered by Bertram Dobell,[1] probably refer to this later imprisonment.[2] Jonson, though fearing the loss of his ears, apparently escaped without punishment.

The year 1605, moreover, marked not only the escape from these difficulties but the beginning of Jonson's happiest days. His *Masque of Blacknesse* was the first of the long series with which he delighted the court of James; and his comedy *Volpone* achieved a triumph both in London theatres and upon its presentation at the two universities. The ensuing decade was Jonson's prime. He produced his four masterly comedies: *Volpone* in 1605 or 1606,[3] *The Silent Women* (*Epicoene*) in 1609, *The Alchemist* in 1610 and *Bartholomew Fayre* in 1614; and his tragedy *Catiline* in 1611; he wrote nearly all the important masques for the court, and won increasing favour with his patrons and the king; and, at the Mermaid tavern, which beheld his wit-combats with Shakespeare and the meetings vividly described by Beaumont, he gained recognition as a leader among London poets and wits. Of his occupations outside literature, we know little, except that he was employed in connection

---

[1] *The Athenæum*, March–April, 1901; reprinted in F. E. Schelling's ed. *Eastward Hoe.*

[2] For a different opinion and a summary of all the evidence, see Castelain, *Ben Jonson*, appendix C, p. 901.

[3] Fleay and Holt, L. H., Jr., *Mod. Lang. Notes*, 1905, find evidence for dating the play early in 1606, probably in March.

with the discovery of the gunpowder treason, and, in 1613, was tutor to Ralegh's son in France.

In 1616, there appeared a folio edition of his works, carefully edited,[1] including his entertainments, masques and plays (except *The Case is Altered*) already produced, with collections of poems entitled *Epigrams* and *The Forest*. This edition set an example for the recognition of the drama as literature. In the same year, his play *The Divell is an Asse* was acted; and, in 1618, he made a pedestrian expedition to Scotland, where he was entertained by the *literati* of Edinburgh, and was a guest of the poet Drummond of Hawthornden who proved an unadmiring Boswell. On his return, he spent some time at Oxford, where he met with the welcome due to him as a scholar and a poet. In 1616, he had been granted a pension of a hundred marks, and, later, he received the reversion to the mastership of the revels; but he did not live to enjoy the benefits of that lucrative office. This was an era of great prosperity for Jonson. James considered the question of making him a knight; his masques continued to be received with great favour at court; and he was able to withdraw entirely from the public stage. At the Apollo room in the Devil tavern he had established a new court of wits, whither young poets thronged to hail him as oracle. Outside literary circles as within, his friends included the greatest and worthiest of the time—Camden, Selden, Clarendon, Falkland, d'Aubigny, the Pembrokes and the Cecils.[2] Clarendon tells us that "his conversation was very good and with men of most note."

The later years of Jonson's life brought many misfortunes. All his books and several manuscripts of unpublished works were burnt in 1623,[3] the year in which the Shakespeare folio appeared, introduced by Jonson's fine tribute. Within a few years, he was suffering from paralysis and dropsy, and had

---

[1] Probably edited by Jonson 1611–12. The later masques are edited less carefully. See Fleay, vol. I, p. 349; Castelain, p. 46.

[2] See lists of persons mentioned in his work, Fleay, *Biog. Chron.* vol. I, pp. 335–340.

[3] See his *Execration upon Vulcan* for a list of lost works: a translation of *Ars Poetica*, with a commentary from Aristotle, an English grammar, a poetical narrative of his journey to Scotland, a poem in three books on the rape of Proserpine, a history of Henry V, philological collections of twenty-four years and "humbler gleanings in divinity."

become much bed-ridden. After an interval of nine years he now again essayed the public stage; but his comedies, *The Staple of Newes*, acted in 1625, *The New Inne*, in 1629, *The Magnetick Lady*, in 1632, and the revised *Tale of a Tub*, in 1633, were either failures or only partial successes. With the accession of Charles I, Jonson seems, for a time, to have lost favour at court; and, later, a quarrel with the architect Inigo Jones led to loss of employment as a writer of masques. Jonson's appeals to the king, however, brought a gift of one hundred pounds in 1629, and, later, the increase of his pension from a hundred marks to a hundred pounds, together with the grant of an annual butt of canary. He succeeded Middleton in the office of city chronologer in 1628, and, when he was deprived of this because of neglecting his duties, the king obtained his restoration in 1635. In 1631, after an interval of six years, he wrote two court masques; and, in 1633 and 1634, he prepared two entertainments for the king at the earl of Newcastle's. On 6 August, 1637, Jonson died. He was buried in Westminster Abbey; the troublesome times that ensued prevented the erection of a monument in his memory; but the inscription of a chance admirer upon his grave has proved unforgettable: "O rare Ben Jonson!"

Among his unpublished manuscripts were a collection of miscellaneous poems entitled *Underwoods*, *Timber: or Discoveries: made upon men and matter*, a translation of *Ars Poetica*, a fragment of a tragedy *The Fall of Mortimer*,[1] the *English Grammar* and an unfinished pastoral *The Sad Shepherd*.[2] These were included in the second folio edition of his works, published in 1640. A collection of memorial verses, edited by Bryan Duppa, bishop of Winchester, appeared in 1637/8, under the title *Jonsonus Virbius*, and contained eulogies from the most famous men of the time.

Even a brief summary of Jonson's life indicates its importance in the history of literature. The forty years of his

---

[1] *The Fall of Mortimer* was completed by William Mountfort and published in 1731. Later, in 1763, it was revived, acted and published with a satirical dedication by Wilkes to Bute. Schelling, *Eliz. Drama*, vol. I, p. 306, apparently connects Jonson's fragment with the non-extant play mentioned by Henslowe.

[2] Published as completed by Waldron, F. G., 1783. See Greg's reprint in Bang's *Materialien*, vol. XI, 1905.

literary career were marked by varied and influential activity in both prose and verse, in other forms as well as the drama, and as a critic no less than as a creator. Four or five of his plays won immediate recognition as masterpieces of realistic comedy; his tragedies, also, were regarded as models; and his masques were not the least important source of his contemporary reputation. As a scholar, he was highly regarded; as a writer of occasional verse, he was the laureate of James and Charles and the leader of the younger poets of the early seventeenth century; as a critic, seeking the reform of abuses and the definition and maintenance of standards of literary art, he exercised an influence comparable to that of Dryden or Samuel Johnson on later generations. During the major part of his career, he was a sort of literary dictator, encouraging or restraining the literary endeavours of his fellow craftsmen, by means of his conversation as much as of his published writings. Though Jonson was often opposed to prevailing fashions, no other writer so comprehensively represents the course of English literature from the end of the sixteenth century to the outbreak of the civil war.

Of the significance of his criticism, we can now form an idea only through a study of the fragmentary comments in his *Discoveries, Conversations with Drummond*, prologues and prefaces, taken in connection with his actual poetic and dramatic practices. A reconstruction of that criticism, therefore, can be only hypothetical and partial, and must be concerned, mainly, with his own work in the drama. But it should be observed that, in the main, his career was a consistent application of certain fundamental views of literary art. These comprised a high estimation of the dignity and value of literature, a complete acceptance of classical authors as the great models and, also, a clear recognition of the high opportunity and great achievement of English poetry and drama. Further, Jonson believed in a painstaking, laborious and self-conscious art, dictated, in some measure, by standards and rules as well as by individual genius or caprice. He worked with the precepts and definitions of *Poetics* and *Ars Poetica* for guides, and he desired judgment and approval only from those acquainted with these standards. Hence, at times, he was rigid in adhering to rules, given overmuch to imitation of the classics and slow to accept modern achievement when it seemed foreign to ancient law and precedent. He demanded a workmanship that laboured over details, and he was suspicious of eccentricity, incongruity, or fantasy, whether in figure and rhythm, or in structure and treatment. In an age of romanticism, he was, in some degree, a classicist and a realist—the former, in his reverence for the masterpieces of Greece and Rome, in his view of art as imitating nature by means of fixed forms and regularised methods and in his insistence on restraints and proprieties; the latter, in his fidelity to details, and in his preference, whether in theme or expression, for the actual rather than the splendid, the usual rather than the adventurous and the general rather than the fantastic.

Jonson's non-dramatic writings include two unfinished works in prose, both in the nature of compilations. His *English Grammar*[1] has little interest for anyone to-day; *Timber, or Discoveries*, however, contains miscellaneous observations of striking pith and eloquence and the matter for an essay on style or literary art. Swinburne, in a successful effort to recall *Discoveries* to general appreciation, devoted the major part of his *Ben Jonson* (1889) to praise of this production, declaring, with characteristic extravagance, that it outweighs in value all the dramatic works, and is, in comparison with Bacon's *Essays*, superior "in truth of insight, in breadth of view, in vigour of reflection and in concision of eloquence." When the attention of scholars was directed to the book, the extent of its indebtedness to Latin writers became gradually apparent. Jonson's sub-title, "made upon men and matter: as they have flow'd out of his daily Readings; or had their refluxe to his peculiar Notion of the Times," had always been accepted as describing a sort of commonplace book, in which citations from his reading and original observations were mingled; but investigation has reduced the original element to a minimum. Schelling was the first to trace a large number of borrowings; Spingarn and others added to the list; which, recently, Maurice Castelain has so extended that it seems to include nearly everything in the book.[2] A few observations on contemporaries remain

---

[1] Ed. Waite, Alice W., New York, 1909.
[2] Cf. *ante*, Vol. IV, p. 398, and see *ibid.* p. 594, for a list of writings in which the sources of *Discoveries* have been investigated. To these should be added Briggs, W. D., *Mod. Lang. Notes*, Feb., 1908.

wholly Jonson's, and the impress of his individuality is apparent even in direct translation. The book also shows the
opinions that he selected and shared, and the wide range of
his reading, especially in later classical writers, such as Seneca,
Pliny and Quintilian, and in renascence scholars, Erasmus, the
Scaligers, Lipsius and Heinsius.

In his non-dramatic poetry, Jonson rarely attains high
excellence. A large portion belongs to the class headed "miscellaneous" in collected editions, and is of interest rather for the
information which it supplies as to his friends and patrons,
and for its satirical pictures of contemporary life, than for any
charm of verse. Few of the odes, epistles and epigrams show
aught but careful writing, but there are also few that can be
praised unreservedly or read with delight. The *Epigrams*
(1616) are characteristically coarse; and some of the satirical
sort recall the persons of his comedies; as those on alchemists,
Lieutenant Shift, Court Worm, Sir Voluptuous Beast, or Lady
Would Be. Others are laudatory in praise of Camden, Donne
or Sylvester, or the poet's noble patrons, or the king. Perhaps
the best of these is that on Lucy countess of Bedford.[1] But the
only epigram that has been widely remembered is the beautiful
epitaph on the child actor, Salathiel Pavy. The fifteen poems
that compose *The Forest*, taken as a whole, are of a higher
order than the *Epigrams;* but, except the immortal "Drink
to me only with thine eyes,"[2] none, to-day, has much interest
beyond what is historical. In spite of occasional fine lines,
their style is fatally marred by that stiffness with which Swinburne justly charges Jonson's verse. *To Penshurst*, written
in heroic couplets, is one of the best—sober, dignified, adequate.
The lyric note is absolutely wanting in most. A vocabulary
that seems purposely prosaic and realistic, an absence of
figures, correctness and sanity of expression—these are the
qualities of Dryden's verse; but Jonson's has neither Dryden's
animation nor his melody.

This description, in general, also applies to *Underwoods*,[3] a

---

[1] Fleay attempts to date the individual epigrams, vol. I, pp. 316–322.

[2] Richard Cumberland, in *The Observer*, No. 74, was the first to point out
that this lyric is a free translation from Philostratus.

[3] The famous epitaph on the countess of Pembroke, now usually included
in *Underwoods*, was first printed as Jonson's in the edition of Peter Whalley

much larger collection, not published until after Jonson's death. Two groups begin the collection—the first of devotional pieces, and the second of love poems forming *A Celebration of Charis*. The miscellaneous poems that follow include the charming *A Nymphs Passion*, the graceful *Dreame*, a long series of eulogistic verses—the best and most famous of which is the poem to Shakespeare, a sonnet to lady Mary Wroth and several epistles, of which that entitled *An Epistle to a Friend, to perswade him to the Warres (Master Colby)* (xxxii),[1] in terse, vigorous couplets, may be instanced as representative of Jonson's satirical verse at its best. A series of four elegies (lvii–lx) in regard to a lover's quarrel is quite different from the rest of the poems, and quite in the manner of Donne. The second of these (lviii), indeed, appeared in the 1633 edition of Donne's poems, and, doubtless, should be assigned to him. But if this be given to him, why not the other three?[2] It is true that reminiscences of Donne are found elsewhere in *Underwoods*, and that Jonson may have been writing in direct imitation; but the four poems deal with the same subject and, apparently, express the feelings of the same lover. The remaining poems in *Underwoods* include *An Execration upon Vulcan*, one of the best of the occasional poems; the elaborate and regular Pindaric ode on the death of Sir H. Morison, which contains the beautiful strophe beginning

> It is not growing like a tree
> In bulke, doth make men better bee . . . ,

and the curious *Eupheme; or, the faire fame . . . of . . . Lady Venetia Digby*, which begins with "the dedication of her cradle" and rises to its height in "the picture of the mind":

> Thou entertaining in thy brest
> But such a Mind, mak'st God thy Guest.

(1756). Weighty, though by no means decisive, evidence that it was written by William Browne is given by Bullen, A. H., in his article on Browne in *Dict. of Nat. Biogr.* (Cf. *ante*, Vol. IV, p. 143, where it is assigned to Browne.)

[1] The numbering follows Cunningham's edition.

[2] Castelain, pp. 801–4, would give these to Donne. See, also, Swinburne, p. 106; Fleay, *Biog. Chron.* vol. I, pp. 326, 328; and E. K. Chambers's edition of Donne, vol. I, p. 241 and vol. II, p. 307. Cf., on this subject, *ante*, Vol. IV, p. 240.

The impression made by Jonson's non-dramatic poetry, as a whole, falls far short of that produced by the half-dozen short lyrics which, alone, have survived in men's memories. These have a unique and happy grace, a sure touch of immortality. And the two songs, *To Celia* ("Drink to me only with thine eyes") and "Goddess excellently bright,"[1] have the allurement of Elizabethan poetry at its best. On the other hand, the great majority of his poems are lacking in melody, charm, or distinction. They are the work of a forerunner of classicism, of one who departs from Spenser, and looks forward to Dryden. The frequent choice of occasional subjects, the restriction to definite forms, the prevalence of satire—all tend toward pseudo-classicism. Moreover, as Schelling has shown the character of the versification, the use of the rimed couplet, the prosaic vocabulary, the avoidance of *enjambement*, the fixed caesura, point the same way. That Jonson's verse was very influential in advancing the change in poetic taste, can, however, hardly be maintained. Doubtless, his preaching and precepts had something to do with promoting a tendency toward classicism; but the tribe of Ben—Carew, Cartwright, Suckling, Herrick and others—did not profit largely from their master's practice. Herrick, who most imitated him, greatly excelled him; and his general influence was not comparable to Spenser's or to Donne's.[2]

His plays fall into well defined classes: masques, comedies and tragedies, with the addition of the unfinished pastoral, *The Sad Shepherd*. As the pastoral and the masque are treated elsewhere in this work,[3] Jonson's contributions to these two dramatic types must be very briefly noticed here. *The Sad Shepherd*,[4] probably, represents an attempt of his last years to revise and complete for the stage (then addicted to pastorals) a play written, in part, many years before. Whenever his

---

[1] The refrain of Hesperus's song in *Cynthia's Revels*, act v, sc. 3.

[2] More will be said concerning Jonson's lyric verse in the chapter on Caroline lyrics in Vol. VII.

[3] See *post* Chap. XIII.

[4] Probably it is not identical with the lost *May Lord*, but was written, in part, before Jonson's visit to Drummond. See Fleay, vol. I, pp. 379–381; Greg, *The Sad Shepherd*, in Bang's *Materialien*, 1905, vol. XI, p. XVIII; Schelling, *Eliz. Drama*, vol. II, pp. 166–8. For discussion of the play, see, also, Greg, W. W., *Pastoral Poetry and Pastoral Drama*, 1906.

little excursion to Arcadia was first planned, it has since succeeded in carrying many readers thither. It is another of
those delightful surprises in Jonson's work, not unlike the
trouvaille of the "Queen and huntress" hidden in the impene-
trable jungle of *Cynthia's Revels*. Among later comedies, *The
Sad Shepherd* is like a breeze in a drowsy lecture-room. Its
Arcadia is called Sherwood and is inhabited by Robin Hood
and his merry men, but it has visitors from the fantastic
Arcadia of the pastorals, and others from fairyland; and it most
resembles the rural England of Jonson's observation. The
plan of bringing together Robin Goodfellow and Robin Hood,
Maudlin the witch of Paplewick and Aeglamour the sad, was
ingenious. And Jonson managed to write about little fishes
without making them talk like whales. He evidently had
collected a formidable array of data in regard to fairies, folklore, rustic terms and habits; but, as he wrote, sweet fancy,
for once, shared with realism in guiding his pen. No other of
his plays can be read from beginning to end with such genuine
refreshment.

Less refreshing are the masques,[1] with which Jonson
delighted both the pleasure-loving court and the pedantic king.
The *libretti* of these splendid entertainments are rather flavour-
less, without the music, dancing and spectacle. To the elaboration of these compositions, however, Jonson devoted his
ingenuity and learning, his dramatic and lyrical gifts in prodigal effort. Moral allegory, classical myth, English folklore,
with realistic and satirical pictures of contemporary life, were
all summoned to provide novelty, grandeur, or amusement as
might be desired. For the masque, as for other forms, Jonson
conceived definite rules and restrictions; but he was bound,
of course, to respond to the desires of his royal patrons. Remembering the limitations and conditions, we must allow that
his work in these masques displays in full all the remarkable
talents which he exhibited elsewhere. The anti-masques gave
opportunity for comic scenes, in which persons similar to those
of his comedies find a place. The spectacular elements called
for the play of fantastical invention, such as Jonson denied to
his regular dramas. And the songs gave a free chance for
lyrical verse. It must be said, however, that neither in drama-

[1] See under Soergel, Brotanek and Evans in the bibliography.

tic nor lyric effects is there supreme excellence. No lyric
in all the forty masques is unforgettable, and few rise above a
mediocre level of adequacy. But Jonson virtually invented
and perfected the court masque in its Jacobean form. Its
history is mainly the record of his contributions.

We turn now to by far the most important division of
Jonson's writings, the comedies and tragedies which he wrote
for the popular theatres. At the beginning of Jonson's
dramatic career, however, we are confronted by a lack of data.
What were the plays that, by 1598, had gained him praise as
one of the best writers of tragedy? None survives; but there
are some hints that his early work did not differentiate itself
from that of his fellow dramatists. From 1597 to 1602, he
wrote at least one play a year for Henslowe, none of which
could have been a comedy of humours. These include an
unnamed play of which he made the plot; *Hot Anger Soon Cold*,
which he wrote with Porter and Chettle; *Page of Plymouth*, a
domestic tragedy on the story of a murder of 1581, in collaboration with Dekker; a tragedy, *Robert II King of Scots*, with
Dekker and Chettle; and another tragedy, *Richard Crookback*.
At the time when he was writing this last play, he was also
engaged on additions to *The Spanish Tragedie*. In spite of
definite external evidence, these have sometimes been denied to
Jonson because of their theme and style.[1] The style is not,
indeed, like that of his later plays; but we may fairly assume
that it is not unlike that which he was employing on domestic
and historical tragedies.[2] Splendidly imaginative in phrasing
and conception, rehabilitating the old Hieronimo, giving his
madness and irony new truth and new impressiveness, the
"additions" far surpass in imaginative power most of the
contemporary attempts at tragedy which they rivalled. But
they imply an unhesitating acceptance of the whole scheme
of the old revenge play at which Jonson was wont to scoff.
Further evidence that his early work was romantic rather than
realistic may be found in the romantic elements of *The Case is
Altered*, and in the Italian scene and names with which *Every*

---

[1] Castelain, Appendix B, pp. 886–901. Cf., as to these additions, *ante*,
Vol. V, Chap. VII *ad fin.*

[2] See Symonds, J. A., *Ben Jonson*, English Worthies Series, and *Shakespeare's Predecessors*, on the "romantic tone" in Jonson's early work.

Man in His Humour was first decked. Of plays still earlier
than those named, we may surmise that, whether realistic or
romantic, tragic or comic, they conformed to the fashions of
the time. Jonson was serving his dramatic apprenticeship
and writing the kind of plays demanded; but he early showed
that imaginative power which gave him high rank among his
fellows, at least in tragedy.

The presentation of *Every Man in His Humour* apparently
marked a change of plan on his part and his devotion to a new
propaganda. By 1598, the drama was long out of its swaddling
clothes. Since the union of poetry and the theatre on the
advent of Marlowe, ten years earlier, the importance of theatres
in the life of London had been rapidly increasing, and the drama
had been gaining recognition as a form of literature. Marlowe,
Kyd, Peele, Greene, Lyly and others, as well as Shakespeare,
had played important parts in creating a drama at once national, popular and poetical. On the whole, this dramatic
development, while breaking away from classical models and
rules, had established no theory or criticism of its own. It had
resulted from the individual innovations of poets and playwrights, who strove to meet the demand of the popular stage
through the dramatisation of story. The main divisions of
tragedy and comedy were recognised, and a third, the chronicle
history, created; and there were various species corresponding
to the initiative of individuals, as a Marlowe type of tragedy
or a Lyly type of comedy; but there were no accepted laws for
any species, and hardly any restrictions or principles guiding
the presentation of narratives on the stage.

To those acquainted with classical drama, these tragedies,
comedies and histories offered much that was absurd and lawless. Frequent change of place, long duration of time represented, absence of a unified plan or coherent structure, mingling
of farce and tragedy, of clowns and kings, lack of definite
aesthetic or ethical aims, seemed errors that could find little
palliation. The matter was as objectionable as the form, for
it was similarly unrestricted. As Sidney asserted, dramatists
did not always distinguish a dramatic fable from a narrative,
and they brought any matter whatsoever into their plays.
They did not mirror nature or imitate life, they merely told
impossible stories. The impulses that had found freest

expression in the popular drama were, indeed, romantic.
Marlowe, Greene, Shakespeare and the rest had been inspired
to give the thrills and glory, the wonder and sentiment of life.
They had dealt with remote places, idealised persons, marvellous adventures, conquests and vicissitudes; they had not
attempted an orderly analysis of history or a rationalised
imitation of the life of their own day.   The drama was romantic, in the sense that it ran counter to the theory and practice
of the Greeks and Latins, and, also, in the sense that it departed from a veracious representation of actuality.   Inevitably, criticism cried for classical form and a realistic
presentation of life.

While the main tendency was toward romanticism, neither
classicism nor realism had, by any means, been lacking in the
earlier drama, particularly in comedy.   In tragedy, classicism
had been driven from the stage to the closet; but, in comedy,
Plautus and Terence were still largely followed as models.
The Plautian model, early anglicised in *Ralph Roister Doister*,
had notable copies in Lyly's *Mother Bombie* and Shakespeare's
Comedy of Errors.   Moreover, not only its stock characters, its
clever servants, parasites, misers, braggart soldiers and so on,
but, also, its general scheme of a series of tricks brought about
through disguises, had come to be widely adopted in the English
drama.   This scheme lent itself readily to realism and formed
the basis for most comedies of intrigue or manners, and of some
romantic plays.   Another species of comedy, the satirical, may
be traced back to moralities, and found an important early
representative in the plays of Wilson.[1]   Again, sheer farce,
often Plautian in scheme, naturally took realistic themes,
and plays of English domestic manners were not uncommon.
In addition to these incompletely defined species, there was a
good deal of realistic comedy mingled with the various types
of romantic drama.   Tragedy, however gruesome, usually
admitted some realistic farce; romantic comedy had its servants, drunkards, constables and clowns; and chronicle history delighted in the elbowing of its monarchs by humorous
persons from low life.   Falstaff and his crew were already
on the stage, and they certainly betokened the keenest scrutiny
of London manners.   In fact, the Elizabethan drama had

[1] As to Robert Wilson, see Vol. V, Chap. XIII.

always devoted itself to the representation of contemporary manners as well as to romantic story. It had delighted not only in the heroisms, villainies and aspirations of romantic vision, but, also, in the absurdity, frivolity and grossness of daily actuality.

What Jonson intended was to recall comedy from its romantic entanglements and to restore it to its ancient province. In 1598, he was a playwright seeking success on the public stage, and trained in its conventions and practices. Neither at that time nor at any other did he plan plays that should break from the popular theatres and become academic or closet affairs. His purpose was to alter his own practices, and to reform the stage; and he represented the critical tendencies already exist-ing: first, a reaction from the absurdities of current forms secondly, a recourse to classical standards as a cure for law-lessness; and, lastly, the establishment of a realistic and satirical comedy on a rational plan. The first two positions were those of Sidney's *Apologie*, which must have potently influenced Jonson; the third was being promoted by contemporary dramatists, especially by the comedies of his friend Chapman. Chapman's earliest romantic comedy *The Blinde begger of Alexandria*, 1598, acted about 1596, was immediately followed by *An Humerous dayes Myrth*, realistic in matter and, apparently, preceding *Every Man in His Humour*, and then by his *Al Fooles* (acted about 1599), a play both Terentian and Jonsonian. Similarly, Middleton's early romantic comedies, *The Old Law* and *Blurt Master-Constable*, were soon followed by a series of realistic comedies of manners; and the romance of Marston's *Antonio and Mellida* (acted 1598 or 1599) was followed by the satire of his *Malcontent* (acted 1601). Moreover, a series of formal satires by Marston, Donne and Hall had vogue in the years 1597–9. But, to whatever extent Jonson was anticipated by Chapman, and to whatever extent his attitude was due to the same immediate influences that acted on his fellows, there is no doubt that he was leader in a movement which gave to realistic and satirical comedy a new importance, or that, of the early representative plays of this class, *Every Man in His Humour* was the masterpiece. Its famous pro-logue[1] sets forth a definite programme. It protests especially

---

[1] Not printed until the folio of 1616, but probably connected with an early

against chronicle history plays, discards tragedy and romance,
implies an observance of the proprieties and promises

> deeds, and language, such as men do use:
> And persons, such as comedy would choose,
> When she would show an image of the times,
> And sport with human follies, not with crimes.

The play, happily, is free from the laboriousness that often
results from devotion to a theory. The plot, of Jonson's own
invention, deals with tricks played upon the elder Knowell and
the jealous Kitely, involving the exposure of various humours
and ending happily with the marriage of young Knowell and
Kitely's sister. The term "humour," then applied to any
oddity of manner, is used to designate the prevailing traits of
a number of distinctly defined characters, illustrative of London manners.[1] The braggart soldier, the clever servant, the
avaricious and jealous husband, the gay young men and even
the gulls, are all, obviously, suggested by the common types in
Plautus; to whom, also, are due the plot of tricks and the device
of disguises. Nevertheless, both plot and persons are developed with abundant originality and represent Jonson at his
best. Bobadill, indeed, is almost the very greatest of Jonson's creations, and is distinct from the other representatives
of *miles gloriosus* which preceded and followed him in the
Elizabethan drama. Whenever he appears, there is more than
mere satire or farce—an amazing and sustained *vis comica* that
reaches its culmination in the great scene[2] in which he meets
with discomfiture. The play is written mainly in terse and
pointed prose, only the two old men and the ladies using blank
verse. One superb purple patch, the defence of poetry, Jonson
ruthlessly cut out in the revised edition.

In comparison with *Every Man in His Humour*, Jonson's
comedies for the next few years do not exhibit any advance. A
large portion of his work, including the additions to *The
Spanish Tragedie* and other plays for Henslowe, shows a return
to old ways. The comedy entitled *The Case is Altered* hardly

---

presentation of the play. At all events, it represents opinions similar to those
set forth in *Every Man out of His Humour*.

[1] Cf., as to the origin and application of the term, *ante*, Vol. IV, Chap. XVI.
[2] Act IV, sc. 5.

belongs to the class of humoristic comedies. Never admitted by Jonson among his collected works, it may be a revision of an earlier play; at least, it was not approved by his later standards. Though Plautian in plot and introducing personal satire on Munday, it is romantic in tone, with its scene in Milan and its element of averted tragedy.

The comedy of humours was carried on in *Every Man out of His Humour*. A vainglorious knight, a public jester,[1] an affected courtier, a doting husband and others exhibit their humours and are finally forced out of their affectations through the agency of Macilente, who, also, is cured of his besetting envy. In the induction, Asper, representing Jonson himself, presents the play in a long conversation with two friends, who remain on the stage to serve as an expository chorus. Jonson announces a highly satirical and moral purpose, akin to that of *Vetus Comoedia*:

> I will scourge those apes
> And to these courteous eyes oppose a mirror,
> As large as is the stage whereon we act;
> Where they shall see the time's deformity
> Anatomised in every nerve and sinew,
> With constant courage, and contempt of fear.

Jonson's induction and comments show how conscious was his art, and how carefully considered his aims. He exhibits his knowledge of the history and rules of classical comedy; but, at the same time, he declares,

> I see not then but we should enjoy the same license, or free power to illustrate and heighten our invention, as they did; and not be tied to those strict and regular forms which the niceness of a few, who are nothing but form, would thrust upon us.

To this extent, he declares for the national tradition; but he rejects the conventions of romantic comedy,

> of a duke to be in love with a countess, and that countess to be in love with the duke's son, and the son to love the lady's waiting maid; some such cross-wooing with a clown to their servingman.

---

[1] Fleay (*Chronicle History*, vol. I, p. 97), Herford, Penniman and Schelling identify Carlo Buffone with Marston; but see Small's discussion, *op. cit.*

He succeeds in removing all elements of romance from his plot;
but what remains, while "familiarly allied to the time," has
little dramatic merit. The comedy is long-winded, and
didactic, rarely either rapid or amusing. The faults that
beset all Jonson's subsequent comedies, even the best, are manifest: an over-elaboration of uninteresting characters, and a
too detailed exposure of folly.

Cynthia's Revels resembles *Every Man out of His Humour*
in its general plan of a group of would-be gallants and ladies
whose follies are exposed to ridicule and shame through the
efforts of a censor representing the author's attitude. The
devices of gods, a masque, an echo dialogue, the fountain of
self-love and—to some extent—the gallants and pages, remind
one of the plays of Lyly, which had recently been revived.
Apparently, it was with these suggestions from Lyly and his
Aristophanic scheme that Jonson set at work on his court
entertainment. He also introduced personal satire (perhaps
already used in *Every Man out of His Humour*), though the only
part that can with much confidence be identified is that of
Anaides, which Dekker promptly took to himself. In spite
of the evident care taken in construction and phrasing, the
play is inordinately tedious, with the exception of the lively
induction. All the persons bathe in the fountain of self-love,
but, in the end, find restoration in the well of knowledge.
In the epilogue, Jonson forestalls the obvious taunt that he
has mistaken the fountain, and proclaims of the play:

> By God 't is good, and if you like 't, you may.

Jonson's arrogance had occasioned enmities with his fellow
dramatists. In *Poetaster*,[1] he undertook their castigation.
The scene is placed in Rome; the story of Ovid's love for Julia is
introduced; and the satirical scheme is not unlike that in the
preceding comedies—a voluble captain, an actor, a beggar poet
and an affected gallant come in for exposure, and Vergil and
Horace (Jonson) are the censors. In the end, Demetrius
(Dekker) and Crispinus (Marston) are tried for calumniating

---

[1] Act III, sc. I is based on Horace's ninth satire of book I; and there are
other imitations of Horace, Lucian and Homer. See Koeppel, E., *Quellenstudien*, 1895; Small, *The Stage Quarrel*, pp. 25–27, and Mallory's ed. of the
play, Yale Studies, 1905.

Horace, and to Crispinus is administered a purge which causes
him to vomit up a prodigious vocabulary. Probably, other
personal references were intended in addition to those indicated, but they are not discernible now. Jonson seems to
have been attempting a further extension of comedy on Aristophanic lines, satirical allegory, praise of himself and direct
personal satire.

Jonson now deserted comedy for a time. His additions to
The Spanish Tragedie and the non-extant *Richard Crookback*
were acted within the next two years. In connection with
Sejanus (acted 1603),[1] we may consider *Catiline* (acted 1611)
as representing Jonson's contribution to tragedy; *The Fall of
Mortimer* is only a fragment, and, apparently, was intended
to be even more classical than *Catiline*.

In these two plays, Jonson attempted in tragedy a reform
similar to that which he had striven for in comedy. He sought
to treat Roman history with scholarly accuracy and to ex-
emplify upon the public stage what he regarded as the essential
rules of tragic art. Such representations of Roman history as
Lodge's *The Wounds of Civill War*, or the still more incongruous
medley of Heywood's *Lucrece*, must have excited in him even
greater condemnation than did the English chronicle plays.
We know that Shakespeare's *Julius Caesar* provoked a sneer
or two from Jonson,[2] though its dramatisation of Plutarch's
portraits apparently excited his emulation and suggested much
in his treatment of Sejanus and Catiline. Mere spectacle
and farce disappear, and events are treated in accord with a
well thought-out theory of historical tragedy. But Jonson's
theory proved hampering; while his effort to secure fidelity to
the historical authorities led him to encumber *Sejanus* with an
absurd paraphernalia of notes, and to transcribe large portions
of Cicero's orations into *Catiline*. And, as he was forced to
confess, the historical material and the style of action demanded
by the audiences of the day did not readily lend themselves to
the restrictions of classical rules.

[1] In the address prefixed to the 1605 quarto of *Sejanus*, Jonson acknow-
ledges the share of "a second pen" in the play as first written and acted, for
which he had substituted his own work in the published play. This "so
happy a genius" has been indentified as Chapman among other dramatists;
but there is no evidence to support these conjectures.

[2] *Bartholomew Fayre*, act II, sc. I.

His plays, it must be remembered, were intended for the public stage, and are not to be classed with closet dramas like those of Fulke Greville and William Alexander. Jonson had already contributed to current popular forms of tragedy, and he started with these as a basis, attempting to rebuild them into something more like classical models. His cardinal error was his acceptance of the belief of the classicists that the essential difference between epic and dramatic fable lay in the observance of the three unities and similar proprieties. In *Sejanus* he gave up unity of time, but kept that of place; he retained the comic scenes of the courtesan, but avoided any grotesque mixture of the comic and the tragic. He omitted battles, jigs and spectacles, and secured a coherent and carefully integrated development of the main action. In *Catiline*, which he boldly proclaimed a "dramatic poem," he adopted the Senecan technique of an introductory ghost and a segregated chorus. In both plays, he was following both humanistic and popular practice in choosing for his themes the evil effects of ambition resulting in conspiracy and civil war.

When we consider the self-imposed restrictions by which he was bound, his achievement must seem remarkable. His interest lay largely in characterisation, and in this resides the chief merit of the plays. Jonson, to be sure, never learned Shakespeare's art of transforming incidents and events into terms of a spiritual conflict. His method is rather that of exposition, each scene illustrating and emphasising some trait without securing much illusion of life. Yet the chief persons, Sejanus and Tiberius, Catiline and Cicero, are thoughtfully conceived and faithfully represented. Moreover, the minor characters are depicted with care and even with vivacity, so that the picture of Roman life carries a strong impression of truthfulness, due to the whole-hearted concentration of Jonson's imagination upon his task as well as to his painstaking study of authorities. In their interpretation of historical characters, his tragedies resemble those of his friend Chapman; but he lacks Chapman's extraordinary eloquence. Jonson's style, especially in long speeches, is too often rhetorical, and rarely displays great beauty or dramatic power. Yet it is masterly in its way, competent to its purposes and free from obscurity or over-ornamentation. The two tragedies, however, in spite of their excellences, must be regarded as representing another failure to turn popular English tragedy back into the classical mould.

Jonson's return to comedy after *Sejanus* was made in 1604/5, in collaboration with Chapman and Marston, in *Eastward Hoe*. No success has attended any endeavour to disentangle the contributions of the three authors, and their co-operation was probably very intimate.[1] It seems likely that Jonson aided largely in plan and suggestion, and that comparatively little of the prose text was by him.

The four comedies which followed rank with *Every Man in His Humour* as his masterpieces. They are all comedies of humours; but each is a peculiar development of the type. In *Volpone*, the Plautian model appears only in the use of the clever servant as the mainspring of the action, and of entanglements based on the trickster-tricked type of plot. The subject and persons, however, are different from those usual in either Latin or English comedy.[2] Volpone, a miser and sensualist, works on the greed of his acquaintances, and, by false reports of his sickness and death, excites their hopes of inheriting his fortune, and lures them into all kinds of abominable knavery. A shameless lawyer, a father who disinherits his son in order to satisfy his own greed and a wittol who offers his wife in return for an inheritance, are the chief dupes; while Sir Politick Would Be, a foolish English traveller, and his affected wife, who quotes Plato and knows of *Pastor Fido* and "Montaignié," play lesser parts. The play has little mirth; but it is a vigorous exposure of greed and iniquity. Its purpose is not amusement but satire, its subject not folly but vice, its protagonist not the managing servant but his master, a monster of villainy. Utterly bad men are common in Elizabethan tragedy, and are found, occasionally, in comedy. But nowhere else, unless in Iago, has vice been drawn with such fulness of detail and yet with such consistency as in Volpone. No tragic elevation lends majesty to the theme. The play depicts human mean-

---

[1] Cf. *post*, Chap. II, and see the edition of this play by Schelling, F. E., (Belles Lettres Series), 1903.

[2] As to the actual source, Lucian's *Dialogues of the Dead*, v–ix, see Adams, J. Q., *Modern Philology*, vol. II, p. 289 (1905), and Browne, W. H., *Modern Language Notes*, vol. XXI, p. 113 (1906).

ness, unrelieved by any greatness of purpose or unselfishness
of passion.   It presents men as beasts, with the greed of swine,
the craft of foxes and the rapacity of wolves.

Plot, characters and blank verse, unusually vigorous and
flowing, all show Jonson at his best; and he was justly proud, as
he boasted in the prologue, of having written in five weeks a
comedy that observed the laws of time, place and persons, and
swerved from no needful rule.   In the dedication to both
universities, he excuses the punishment of the vicious in comedy,
defending himself by the example of the ancients, and still more
because "it is the office of a comic poet to imitate justice, and
instruct to life."   This is interesting as an adumbration of
Rymer's "poetic justice," and as an expression of the purpose
of Jonson's satiric comedy.   Other passages in this same
dedication give noble expression to the aims at which his
art had now arrived,

to reduce not only the ancient forms, but manners of the scene, the
easiness, the propriety, the innocence, and last, the doctrine, which
is the principal end of poesie, to inform men in the best reason of
living.

It must be confessed, however, that Jonson's vainglorious proclamation of reform exhibits an insolent disregard of his great
predecessors and contemporaries.   He promises

the maturing of some worthier fruits; wherein, if my muses be true
to me, I shall raise the despised head of poetry again, and stripping
her out of those rotten and base rags wherewith the times have
adulterated her form, restore her to her primitive habit, feature,
and majesty, and render her worthy to be embraced and kist of all
the great and master-spirits of our world.

The Silent Woman[1] is much less intent on moral castigation
than is *Volpone*, and, also, much merrier.   Its plot is farcical,
dealing with the entrapping of Morose, who hates noise, into
marriage with Epicoene, who turns out to be a noisy tartar,
and, after Morose has forgiven his nephew, proves to be a boy.
Sir Dauphine, the nephew, and his friends, are the wits; Daw,
La Foole and the Ladies Collegiates, the butts of their jests.

---

[1] The edition of the play by Aurelia Henry, Yale Studies, 1906, discusses
suggestions for this play in Libanius and Plautus.

There is abundant satire of the manners and affectations of the day; but the skilfully complicated action depends on numerous disguises, and does not rise above the level of admirable farce.

In *The Alchemist*,[1] Jonson essays another large canvas of tricksters and gulls. Subtle, the alchemist, Dol Common and Face, a housekeeper, have set up their snares in the house of Face's master. Hither come an extraordinary procession of gulls, whose very names are enough to recall the lifelike characters—Dapper, a lawyer's clerk; Abel Drugger, a credulous tobacco man; Sir Epicure Mammon, a voluptuary with a Micawber-like gift of eloquent anticipation; Pertinax Surly, a doubting Thomas; Tribulation Wholesome and Ananias, two brethren of Amsterdam, who make an effort to serve both God and Mammon, without forgetting the weaker brethren; Kastrill, a foolish heir and Dame Pliant, his sister, a widow. One after another, they expose their folly and greed, and add to the fun and entanglement, until the master of the house returns and joins with Face to keep the spoils, including the widow, and to lock the doors on dupers and duped. Perhaps in no other play has Jonson so completely succeeded in accomplishing what he intended as he has in this. There are no tiresome excursuses, as in *Volpone* and *Bartholomew Fayre;* in everything, he uses "election and a mean." The entire play is in blank verse, which is most skilfully adapted to the rapid dialogue or to the orations of Tribulation and Sir Epicure. The language is varied, idiomatic and precise; the style, finished and animated. The ingenuity of the plot, which Coleridge ranked among the three most perfect in literature, the liveliness of the action and the delineation of manners, harmonise in a work which, of its kind, could hardly be bettered. The satire on alchemy, which was not without daring in the days of Simon Forman, flavours the fun without destroying it; and the picture of Elizabethan London is without an equal, unless it be in *Bartholomew Fayre.*

In the presentation of manners and character *Bartholomew Fayre* may, indeed, be held to outrank even *The Alchemist.* In many respects, however, its inferiority is palpable. It is

---

[1] On the relation of *The Alchemist* to *Il Candelaio* of Giordano Bruno, see a note by Child, C. G., in *The Nation*, 28 July, 1904. See, also, Schelling, *Eliz. Drama*, vol. I, pp. 540, 541.

unwieldy in structure; its fun is often gross and farcical; and it is overcrowded with persons and incidents. There are thirty speaking parts and many supernumeraries. Nowhere else, perhaps, in literature, have so many people been so vividly presented in a three hour entertainment as here. The usual pair of witty friends, a pompous judge bent on reform, a proctor who has written a puppet show,[1] a foolish widow, a puritan zealot, Cokes, a booby, and his man Waspe, mingle in the fair with a cutpurse, a ballad singer, a tapster, a bawd, a bully and that Falstaffia of the stews, Ursula the pig woman. The trouble here, as in other plays by Jonson, is that every character is worked out with elaborate detail. If some of the subordinate parts were removed, and others reduced in proportion, the play, doubtless, would be improved. Certainly, much of Littlewit's puppet play could be spared. But all the personages mentioned, and as many more, are drawn not only with painstaking exactness, but, also, with unflagging animation. A play which unites such masterpieces of comic characterisation as justice Overdo, Cokes and Zeal-of-the-land Busy, together with much uproarious fun, must, surely, be accounted an amazing achievement of comic invention.

In the amusing induction, Jonson protests against the attribution of personal satire to the play, and against the tendency of the public to judge everything by their old favourites, such as *Jeronimo* and *Andronicus*. His protests, in fact, are directed at the whole field of romantic drama, and include scoffs at *A Winter's Tale* and *The Tempest*.

If there be never a servant-monster in the fair, who can help it, he [the author of *Bartholomew Fayre*] says, nor a nest of antiques? he is loth to make nature afraid in his plays, like those that beget tales, tempests, and such like drolleries, to mix his head with other men's heels; let the concupiscence of jigs and dances reign as strong as it will amongst you; yet if the puppets please any body, they shall be intreated to come in.

"The concupiscence of jigs and dances," to which he also alludes in the address "To the Reader" prefixed to *The Alchemist*, seems to refer to the introduction of dances and other elements

---

[1] Littlewit is identified by Fleay, Penniman and Schelling with the poet Daniel.

from court masques into comedy, as in *A Winter's Tale*, *The Tempest* and other contemporary plays. Jonson, always a precisian, preferred to keep his masques and comedies separate. It seems clear that he intended to make *Bartholomew Fayre* an example of pure realism. Perhaps for this reason he wrote it, like *Epicoene*, wholly in prose, remarkable for its clearness and flexibility, admirably suited to the different speakers and imitative of the manners of the time. Characters and incidents, also, are freer from imitation of Plautus or Aristophanes than are those of any other of his comedies, though the usual scheme of gulls and knaves is preserved and amplified. Further removed from classical models than his other comedies, nevertheless, it is Aristophanic in the breadth and liveliness of its mirth and in its unhesitating realism. Original in its scheme and subject, daring in its invention, it marks the highest development of the comedy of humours as a national type. The kind of comedy which it presents has continued in prose fiction, in Fielding, Smollett and Dickens; but, since the Elizabethan period, our theatre has never permitted such robust fun and so unvarnished a presentation of the absurdities of human nature.

The Divell is an Asse betrays a flagging invention, as was to be expected after the prodigal expenditure of the four preceding comedies. The machinery of the devils is not very happy. Pug, a lesser devil, is despatched by Satan to do some mischief; but his stupidity renders his expedition unsuccessful, and, indeed, leaves it without effect on the action of the play. Jonson, apparently, planned to enlarge his collection of gulls by proving the devil one; but the result of this humorous conception is merely to add another stupid and uninteresting person to the *dramatis personae*. The other characters are more or less repetitions of those in earlier plays, though the chief gull, Fitzdottrel, who aims to become "Duke of Brownlands" through taking part in a project for draining the waste lands of the kingdom, gives rise to plenty of humour. The satire is lively, especially that on the exorcism of supposed evil spirits, and that on projectors and projects—among which is one for "serving the whole state with toothpicks." Mrs. Fitzdottrel is drawn with more sympathy than is common in the case of Jonson's female characters, and all the characters are, as usual, carefully differentiated. But the comic entanglements are cumbersome, and the play moves heavily.

Nine years intervened before the appearance of Jonson's next comedy, *The Staple of Newes*. Though his prologue is as boastful as ever, yet, in the induction and the intercalary scenes, there are indications that he felt the uncertainty of his powers and was driven back to the stage by want. He went to Aristophanes for a model, composing an allegorical satire based on *Plutus*, from which and from *The Wasps* he borrowed certain passages. The main allegory of Pecunia, Pennyboy, Mortgage and the rest, is tiresome; but the secondary plot, dealing with the Staple-of-News office, has excellent satire and fun. So, too, has the scheme of the Canters' college. But the details of the plan are not fused into a dramatic whole. More than any play since *Cynthia's Revels*, this production lacks the movement and verisimilitude indispensable in comedy.

The remaining comedies come near to deserving Dryden's harsh criticism: "mere dotages." *The New Inne* was incontinently damned at its first representation, and published two years later (1631) by Jonson with an angry address to the reader. The improbable plot, dependent on the disguises of Lord Frampul as an inn-keeper, his wife as a vulgar Irish beggar and their second daughter as a boy, deals, mainly, with the winning of the elder daughter by Lord Lovel, thanks to two elaborate orations on love and valour before a mock court of love. The play aims at taking advantage of the current interest in "platonism" fostered at court by the queen;[1] and both the platonic Lady Frampul and her suitor are treated sympathetically. But the platonic addresses are dull; and so, indeed, is the low comedy supplied by Fly, Bat Burst, Sir Glorious Tipto and others. The failure of the play called forth Jonson's ode "Come, leave the loathèd stage"; but one's sympathies incline to remain with the audience. Four years later, *The Magnetick Lady: Or Humors Reconcil'd* attempted a continuation and conclusion of the series of comedies of humours begun thirty-five years before. A marriageable young niece of the magnetic lady is constituted the "centre attrac-

---

[1] On this topic, see Fletcher, J. B., "Précieuses at the Court of Charles I." in *The Journal of Comparative Literature*, vol. 1, p. 125.

tive, to draw thither a diversity of guests, all persons of different humours, to make up his [the author's] perimeter." This
plan is carried out in a half-hearted way, though with the
usual elaborate attention to details, and explanatory intermez-
zos. But, while the acts conform to the laws of *protasis*,
epitasis and *catastasis*,[1] there is no life or wit. *A Tale of a
Tub* was acted in the same year. Various references to the
queen make it likely that the play was first written about 1597;
but the satire on Inigo Jones as In and In Medley must have
been incorporated in the 1633 revision. The separation of the
early crudities and the later dotages is now impossible. The
action, of the trickster-tricked variety, deals entirely with
rustics, and presents considerable ingenuity and possibility
of fun. The characters, however, are all beneath interest,
and the whole treatment reveals neither fresh nor worthy
impulse.

Two additional plays, which, on some seventeenth century
authority, have been ascribed in part to Jonson, probably owe
little or nothing to his pen. *The Widdow*, published (1652)
as by Jonson, Fletcher and Middleton, was, probably, wholly
by Middleton.[2] *The Bloody Brother* (entered in the Stationers' register, 1639, as by "B. J.," and printed in 1640 as by
"B. J. F.") is, undoubtedly, in part by Fletcher.[3] Jonson's
share can hardly have extended beyond the second scene of
act IV.

Jonson's qualities as a dramatist, with regard to which
there is general critical agreement, have, perhaps, been sufficiently indicated. His wide and penetrating observation of
manners, whether of city or of court, and his ingenious and
systematic construction of plots are obvious merits. But
the great excellence of both his tragedies and his comedies is
their delineation of character. This is conditioned less than
in other Elizabethan dramatists by the story, but more by
classical models and rules, as in his observance of the unities,
or his fidelity to historical authorities, or his copying of the

---

[1] Cf. act I, *ad fin.*   [2] See *post*, Chap. III.

[3] See Chap. V, and cf. Fleay, F. G., *The English Drama*, vol. I, pp. 203–5,
and Oliphant, E. F., *Eng. Studien*, vol. XV, pp. 353–5. Concerning the
anonymous Latin comedy *Querolus* as the source of the scene (IV, 2) attributed to Jonson, see Garnett, R., *Mod. Phil.* vol. II, p. 491.

Plautian plan and types. It is also conditioned by his method of making each person the illustration of one trait or humour, and by his disposition to substitute description for drama, and satire for fact, and to exaggerate his satire into farce. Thus, in *Every Man in His Humour*, only Bobadill represents the complete transformation of a type into an individual; and, in *Bartholomew Fayre*, the individualisation follows the broad lines of caricature. Again, each person is set forth with such distinctness of detail that, while it aids visualisation, it often distracts from the interest of situation. Only in *The Alchemist* is there an entire absence of this impeding garrulity. Akin to this defect are Jonson's over-use of the long monologue after the fashion of classical models, the heaviness and coarseness which his realism often gives to his vocabulary and his thoroughness, which refuses to let go person, speech, or situation until it is absolutely exhausted. Yet, in spite of all these limitations, Jonson's comic characterisation remains among the greatest achievements of the English drama, because of its clearness and certainty, its richness of humour and its dramatic veracity. A. W. Ward is justified in giving him preeminence in the highest species of comedy, that "in which everything else is subordinated to the dramatic unfolding of character."

What most discourages the reader of Jonson is the absence of charm. Jonson was certainly not incapable of depicting noble passions or of writing winsome verse; but in his plays he resolutely refused to attempt either. This refusal, in marked contrast with the practice of his fellow Elizabethans, is precisely the negative side of his most positive characteristics. He did not write of passions, but of follies—not of fairyland, but of London; he often deliberately preferred prose to poetry, and he always restrained poetry to his subject. If poetry must, at times, have freedom, it must, at times, have restraint; if, at times, it may soar on fancy's wing or evoke glorious or appalling habitants for our reflection, at other times it may well cling to the actualities of daily existence. Comedy, of all forms of literature, has its duties in the street or tavern as well as in Arden or on the sea-coast of Bohemia. Jonson found neither charm nor heroism in London streets, though both were unquestionably there. He found neither the truth and passion that lay at the heart of puritanism nor the joy and fancy that stirred the light-hearted moods of Fletcher, Shirley, or Herrick. But he mirrored what he saw of men and manners with an untiring fidelity, heightened and coloured his picture with a hearty and virile humour and interpreted it by a sound and censorious morality. Imaginative idealism, characteristic of the Elizabethan age and its literature, had another and a greater master; but interest in the depiction and criticism of the actual life of the day—an interest essential to vitality in the literature of any age, and manifest in the golden days of the Armada as well as in degenerate Jacobean times—had its chief exponent in Jonson.

His influence, commanding in his own day, has continued down to the present. His comedies were imitated so soon as they appeared; witness *Everie Woman in her Humor* (1609, acted by 1600). Beaumont and Fletcher studied in his school, as *The Woman Hater*, written by the former,[1] testifies; and Marston, Middleton and Chapman profited from his example. Of later dramatists, Field, Randolph, Cartwright, Nabbes and May—to name no others—employed Jonson's methods and wrote plays in his manner. The comedy of humours became, in fact, an established model, which few later writers altogether disregarded. All realistic comedy owned its influence, and reminiscences of its most effective scenes and types of character found their way into every kind of drama. There were other leaders in realistic comedy, Middleton in particular, who may be said to have set an example of a less satirical, less moral, but hardly less Plautian, representation of London manners. But Jonson continued through his lifetime the chief advocate and exemplar of serious realism.

After the Restoration, Jonson's reputation, for a time, increased. Dryden's praise was echoed by Dennis and others, especially by those who were most eager to see neo-classical rules and models prevail in the theatres. Both his tragedies and his comedies were held in high esteem. The former were revived, but did not long hold the stage. The latter found a warm welcome on the stage and maintained themselves there during the long period when Shakespeare's romantic comedies failed to please. *Bartholomew Fayre* disappeared (1731),

[1] See below, Chap. v.

even before *As You Like It* returned to the stage (1740), and, of *Volpone*, *The Silent Woman* and *The Alchemist* [1] not one has outlasted the eighteenth century on the public boards. The last three were revived by Garrick, who also brought out a revision of *Every Man in his Humour*. That play continued on the stage well into the nineteenth century.

Jonson's influence, moreover, has been felt in the novel as well as in the drama. His plays have been constantly read and have always encouraged a study of the absurdities of character and the incongruities of manners. Fielding and Smollett were conscious of their incentive, and Dickens, who knew them well and himself acted Bobadill, must, to no inconsiderable extent, have been indebted to their suggestion. Not only are there specific resemblances, as between Zeal-of-the-land Busy and Stiggins, but Dickens's comic invention and characterisation are often strikingly Jonsonian in method and effect. Whether Jonson's comedies are ever again revived on the stage or not, they are likely to continue long to encourage in fiction a frank and searching presentation of foible and folly.

---

[1] A droll, *The Empiric* (1676), and a farce, *The Tobacconist* (1771) were based on *The Alchemist*. A satirical tragedy, *The Favourite*, based on *Sejanus*, appeared in 1770.

CHAPTER II

Chapman, Marston, Dekker

AMBITIONS are naturally fired in an age of unusual achievement in any field of human activity, and men of every variety of genius or talent, however unfitted to command success in it, are drawn to the glittering arena. Many men were dramatists in 1600 whose gifts were not conspicuously dramatic, and whose instincts in another epoch would hardly have driven them to the service of the stage. Of these, George Chapman was an example. He was a poet; but his muse did not point him towards the theatre, and, had she designed him for drama, she would have delayed his birth. For, in 1600, when Jonson was about twenty-seven and Dekker thirty, Chapman was already forty years old. He was twenty-eight when Marlowe's *Tamburlaine* was produced, and thus did not in early youth, nor until his mind had already taken its mould, come under the dramatic influences or inspiration which formed Shakespeare and the greater playwrights. Nor is it even certain that he was greatly interested in drama till within five years of the close of the century. He did not serve a youthful apprenticeship to the theatrical art, and he never learnt to think in any character but his own.

We gather from one of his early poems (*Euthymiae Raptus*) that Chapman was born in or near Hitchin in Hertfordshire, and, from the title-page of his *Homer*, that his birth year was 1559. It is frequently said that he studied at both universities, but there is no certain evidence that he was at either. Wood asserts that he spent some time at Oxford, in 1574 or thereabouts, "where he was most excellent in the Latin and Greek tongues, but not in logic or philosophy," and that he left without taking a degree. Of his personal affairs for the next

twenty years, we know nothing.   It is not improbable that he
travelled, and a passage in one of his poems suggests that, like
Jonson, he may have served in the Netherlands.   As a man of
letters, his first appearance, apparently, was made in a volume
of poetry, *The Shadow of Night*, when he was thirty-five.
From this time, he was busy as poet and dramatist until 1614,
and seems to have achieved reputation and gained distinguished friends, though he gathered little wealth.   Meres
speaks of him in 1598 as a renowned scholar, tragedian and
comedian.   We know that he found a patron in the earl of
Essex, and that, after the earl's execution in 1601, he was
befriended by prince Henry, to whom he was appointed "server
in ordinary."   The prince encouraged him in his work of
translating Homer, and appears to have promised him a pension; but he died in 1612, and Chapman received no further
royal favours.

> To all times future this time's mark extend,
> Homer no patron found, nor Chapman friend.

In 1605, he had shared with Marston and Jonson the displeasure
of the authorities for the satire in *Eastward Hoe* on the Scottish
king's needy followers, and had suffered imprisonment.   Again,
in 1608, he narrowly escaped punishment for an unhappy reference to the French queen in *The Conspiracie, And Tragedie
of Charles Duke of Byron*, which roused the indignation of the
French ambassador.   From 1614, Chapman appeared less
frequently as an author, and he died in no very prosperous
circumstances in 1634.   He was buried in St. Giles's in the
Fields (Habington, in his *Castara*, speaks of his tomb as without
the church), and a monument by his friend Inigo Jones, to
whom he had dedicated his translation of Musaeus, was then
erected to his memory, as "a Christian Philosopher and
Homericall Poett."
    It is difficult to escape the conviction that Minto was correct
in his identification of Chapman with the "rival poet" of
Shakespeare's *Sonnets;* and it has been argued with great force
and ingenuity[1] that the rivalry here indicated may be traced
elsewhere in the work of both authors, and that the note of
anger in the strain of invective which frequently appears in

---

[1] *Shakespeare and the Rival Poet*, by Arthur Acheson, 1903.

Chapman's poems and prefaces, hitherto interpreted in his favour as the natural scorn of a great artist for inferior work, was the outcome of bitter personal resentment at the success of the unlettered Shakespeare and was directly aimed at him. According to this view, *The Amorous Zodiac*, in the 1595 volume of poems, is the poem indicated by Shakespeare in his twenty-first sonnet; Holofernes, in *Love's Labour 's Lost*, is a satirical portrait of Chapman in reply to his malevolent attacks, and *Troilus and Cressida* an elaborate castigation of Chapman's extravagant laudation of Homer, his praise of Greek ideals and his contempt of all poets who were not his equals in scholarship. Though not proven, the thesis cannot be lightly dismissed.

We are told that Chapman was a student of the classics who made little progress in philosophy; but his earliest works exhibit him rather as a metaphysician in verse than as a disciple of the canons of ancient art. Passages in *The Shadow of Night* (1594) and in *Ovid's Banquet of Sauce*, containing *A coronet for his Mistress Philosophy*, *The amorous Zodiac* and other poems (1595), may be praised with justice; but they will never be widely read. In the dedication of the second volume he disclaims all ambition to please the vulgar—"The profane multitude I hate, and only consecrate my strange poems to those searching spirits, whom learning hath made noble and nobility sacred." Yet, even among "searching spirits," some reluctance to return to poems in the main so warped and obscure as these may well be found. Better work was to come. In his continuation of Marlowe's *Hero and Leander* (1598), Chapman not unworthily completed an incomparable fragment, and, in *The Tears of Peace* (1609), dedicated to his young patron, prince Henry, he reaches his happiest moods as an original poet. By *Andromache Liberata* (1614), he added nothing to his reputation. The subject was an unfortunate one—the marriage of the earl of Somerset and Frances Howard, the divorced lady Essex—and was treated in so enigmatic a manner as to make necessary a subsequent prose justification of its aims and intentions. Distinction of mind and intellectual vigour are apparent in all Chapman's work; but, though he may occasionally soar, he never sings, and his finest verses possess gnomic and didactic, rather than lyric, quality. When

it emerges from the entanglements amid which the current
of his reflections is usually split, his poetry can be as limpid as
it is stately.   But not often do we hear such music as when he
tells us that Fletcher's *Faithfull Shepheardesse*

> Renews the golden world and holds through all
> The holy laws of homely Pastoral,
> Where flowers and founts and nymphs and semi-gods
> And all the Graces find their old abodes.

Though Chapman was well known as a dramatist in 1598,
only two plays by his hand are extant which were produced
before that date—*The Blinde begger of Alexandria* (printed
1598) and *An Humerous dayes Myrth* (printed 1599), probably
the play mentioned by Henslowe as *The comodey of Umers* in
1597.   Both are comedies; but neither deserves any particular
notice, though the first appears to have been successful on the
stage, and the second contains one or two characters drawn
with some cleverness and spirit.   *Al Fooles* (printed 1605),
another comedy, was first produced under the title *The World
runs on Wheels*, and displays a surprising advance in dramatic
technique.   The plot, partly borrowed from Terence, is ingenious and excellent, and makes a good framework for a satirical
sketch of humours developed through amusing situations in
the manner of Jonson.   As a writer of comedy, here, and in
Eastward Hoe (to be noticed later), where, however, he had
collaborators, Chapman appears to the greatest advantage.
When dealing with lighter themes, he condescended, though
with apologies, to write an uninflated style; and, however
he may himself have preferred the heightened and fantastic
rhetoric of his tragedies, they are indisputably inferior in
construction and far less natural in tone than the dramas he
affected to despise.

For four or five years after the opening of the seventeenth
century, Chapman, doubtless because he was occupied with
the continuation of his translation of Homer, contributed nothing to dramatic literature.   By 1605, he had, evidently,
resumed his connection with the theatre; for two plays were
printed in the following year—*The Gentleman Usher* and
Monsieur D'Olive.   In the first of these, Chapman threw his
chief strength into a romantic love episode introduced into

the comic scheme of the play, and succeeded in imparting to it an intensity and sweetness foreign to his character and talent. *Monsieur D'Olive* opens strongly; but the main plot is subsequently obscured by the shifting of the centre of interest to the character who gives his name to the piece. This cleverly conceived and diverting town gull, whose wit and coolness in a trying situation are pleasantly rendered, at once spoils the play as a work of art and keeps it alive as an entertainment. Later in his career, Chapman wrote two more comedies—*May-Day* (printed 1611), shown by Stiefel to be an adaptation of the *Allesandro* of Allesandro Piccolomini, and *The Widdowes Teares* (printed 1612)—and took part with Shirley in a third, *The Ball* (printed 1639). The last named owes little to Chapman,[1] and neither of the others rises to anything approaching excellence. *The Widdowes Teares*, the idea of which is borrowed from Petronius, is not altogether wanting in power and has some characteristic passages, but entirely fails to arouse interest in its characters or admiration for the contrivance of the action.

His translations apart, Chapman's fame rests upon his tragedies founded on French history, of which *Bussy D'Ambois* (printed 1607) and *The Revenge of Bussy D'Ambois* (printed 1613) have always and rightly received most attention. The subjects here chosen were singularly adapted to display the qualities of his genius, never impressive save on an elevated stage. *Bussy D'Ambois* was by far the most successful of his dramas, its popularity being due, in part, to its revival of recent history, in part to the character and career of the chief figure, formed by nature for an invincible hero of romance, and in part to the glowing rhetoric which certainly rises in places to pure and impassioned poetry. Some entries in Henslowe suggest that *Bussy D'Ambois*, and not Marlowe's *Massacre at Paris*, as Collier thought, may have been the play for which payments were made in 1598;[2] but, if we assign to it so early a date as this, we must allow a revision after the death of Elizabeth, who is spoken of as the "old Queene." The sources of this drama have not been precisely determined—De Thou's

---

[1] Cf. *post*, Chap. VIII.

[2] Cf. Greg's *Henslowe's Diary*, part II, pp. 198, 199, and *Henslowe Papers*, p. 120, note.

Historiae sui temporis and Rosset's *Histoires Tragiques*, from which it was supposed that the author derived his incidents, were not published in 1607—and Chapman, therefore, must have had recourse to contemporary accounts. The part of Bussy was acted by Nathaniel Field. A revised version of the play by Thomas D'Urfey was produced on the stage of the Theatre Royal in 1691. For *The Revenge of Bussy D'Ambois* and the tragedies *The Conspiracie, And Tragedie of Charles Duke of Byron* (printed 1608), he drew directly from a translation of Serres's *Inventaire Général de l'Histoire de France* by Edward Grimeston, published in 1607.[1] Grimeston supplemented Serres, whose narrative ends in 1598, from Matthieu's *Histoire de France* and other contemporary writers.

In his first tragedy, the court of Henry III is employed as a frame for the full length portrait of the brilliant adventurer, Bussy, whose love affair with Tamyra, countess of Montsorry, betrayal to her husband and last stand when encircled by his enemies, make an admirable drama of the heroic and melodramatic type. It is successful in a style thoroughly Elizabethan (the antithesis of the classic), in which violent scenes and extravagant rhetoric mingle with profound reflection and magnificent outbursts of poetry—a strange compound of the fantastic and forbidding with the noblest and most inspiring elements in art. Dryden, in his famous depreciation of this play, went too far:

I have sometimes wondered in the reading [he said] what has become of those glaring colours which amazed me in *Bussy D'Ambois* upon the theatre; but when I had taken up what I supposed a fallen star, I found I had been cozened with a jelly; nothing but a cold dull mass, which glittered no longer than it was shooting; a dwarfish thought, dressed up in gigantic words, repetition in abundance, looseness of expression, and gross hyperboles; the sense of one line expanded prodigiously into ten; and to sum up all, incorrect English, and a hideous mingle of false poetry and true nonsense; or, at best, a scantling of wit, which lay gasping for life, and groaning beneath a heap of rubbish. A famous modern poet used to sacrifice every year a Statius to Virgil's manes; and I have indignation enough to burn a *D'Ambois* annually to the memory of Jonson.

[1] *Bussy D'Ambois* and *The Revenge of Bussy D'Ambois*, ed. by Boas, F. S., 1905.

We have here a typical example of Restoration feeling and criticism. Chapman exhibits in excess precisely those Elizabethan qualities which a later age found Gothic and barbaric. The faults of the romantic school are all present in an exaggerated degree. But Dryden overlooked the fiery energy, the imaginative splendours and rich suggestiveness of phrase and imagery which were its glory, and beside which the undeniable excellences of his own age of literature seem the cold and lifeless offspring of uninspired labour. *The Revenge of Bussy D'Ambois* (printed 1613), written after an interval during which Chapman had produced his Byron tragedies, though inferior as a drama for the stage, is stronger in its reflective passages and contains by far the most interesting and profound of Chapman's character studies. This is Clermont d'Ambois, a brother of the dead Bussy invented by the dramatist who is incited by Bussy's ghost, as Hamlet is by his father's spirit, to undertake the mission of revenge. Clermont, the "senecal man," who, like Hamlet, is of a speculative habit of mind and disinclined towards violence, only after delays accomplishes his task, and, in the end, dies by his own hand. *The Revenge* is suffused with memories of Shakespeare's play, to which, undoubtedly, it owes its plan and many of its episodes, while Clermont's philosophy is largely drawn from Epictetus. It is somewhat remarkable that this drama, the interest of which is centred in a true philosopher moving amid the intrigues and violences of a renascence court, makes him the faithful follower of the infamous duke of Guise, whose portrait, as given us here, is no less flattering than it is unhistorical—a piece of perversity certainly not calculated to commend the play to reformation England.

If high intellectual interest and authentic eloquence sufficed to constitute a dramatic masterpiece, *The Conspiracie, And Tragedie of Charles Duke of Byron, Marshall of France* might give Chapman rank among great playwrights. But we have here rather "a small epic in ten books or acts" than a drama. The verse runs more smoothly, however, than in the Bussy plays, the poetry is less pestered with the cloudy turbulence of his "full and heightened style," and nowhere does Chapman win more completely upon his reader. In his next tragedy, *Caesar and Pompey* (printed 1631), he turned from contemporary to classical history, and, standing on scholar's ground, might have been expected to derive powerful inspiration from his theme, but the design is feebly handled, and he fails, as before, to communicate movement to the action or vitality to the *dramatis personae*. Only the oratorical passages, especially those placed in the mouth of Cato, can be read with much pleasure.

The remaining plays of Chapman were not published during his lifetime. In *Chabot Admirall of France* (printed 1639), for which materials were drawn from Pasquier's *Les Recherches de la France*, he had the assistance of Shirley, and it seems fruitless to attempt the task of partitioning their respective contributions. *Revenge for Honour* (printed 1654), an eastern tale of which the scene is laid in Arabia, may have been written by Chapman; but the play is by no means in his usual manner, and it is difficult to believe that, in his old age, he could have assimilated the style of the later dramatists. (A play printed for the same publisher and entitled *The Paraside, a Revenge for Honour* was entered in the register (1653) as by Henry Glapthorne.) Neither play possesses any great distinction, though some critics have found in the variety of incident and portraiture in the last named drama reason for assigning to it a high place among Chapman's works. It is certainly superior to *Alphonsus Emperour of Germany* (printed 1654), also ascribed to Chapman on more slender grounds. The intimate knowledge of the German language and German life displayed by the author has been variously explained. Either Chapman spent some time in Germany, or he was assisted by some unknown writer intimately acquainted with the language and customs of that country. There remains the possibility that he had no hand in it. Zeal for Chapman's reputation might easily be better expended than in the attempt to prove this play his. *Sir Gyles Goosecappe* (printed 1606), an anonymous play, has been ascribed to Chapman or a disciple by several critics, on internal evidence of method and manner. Two of his plays, never printed, were destroyed in manuscript by Warburton's cook, *The Yorkshire Gentlewoman and her Son*, and *Fatal Love*, a French tragedy. Jonson told Drummond that "next himself, only Fletcher and Chapman," both of whom "he loved," "could make a masque." Only one such composition by Chapman is extant, *The memorable Masque of the two honourable Houses or Innes of Court; the Middle Temple, and Lyncolnes Inne*, performed at Whitehall in 1614. Probably he wrote others; the merits of this piece afford insufficient warrant for Jonson's compliment. While it would be absurd to deny the presence of masculine force and fervid poetry in Chapman's best tragedies, it would be mere irony to claim for him fine sensibility or delicate discrimination in the portrayal of character. He is not great either in invention or construction, and, though his work abounds in wise sayings, moral apophthegms and high pitched sentiments, and though the talent for observation is not absent, there is an invincible coarseness in his fibre. The comedies show all men either as deceivers or deceived; his tragic heroes are often little more than the embodiment of physical energy and tenacious will; pathos he never attains; and he seems to have been incapable or undesirous of painting the portrait of a lovable woman. Chapman's immense pretensions and determination to storm Parnassus hardly win our allegiance. Nor need we pay homage to his scholarship, though reputed as vast. He was overburdened not so much by the weight of his learning as by a mistaken sense of its importance and authority. Approach him first by way of his original poems and dramas, and it will not easily prove practicable to find the measure of the man. Like Milton writing in prose, he is using, as it were, his left hand. But approach him first under the spell of Homer, who was "angel to him, star and fate," when both genius and character are sublimated, and he will be known for what he is. In Chapman's view, Homer was not only emperor among the poets, he was the greatest of men and philosophers. "Of all books extant in all kinds, Homer is the first and best . . . out of him, according to our most grave and judicial Plutarch, are all Arts deduced, confirmed, or illustrated." At this shrine, he burns continual incense, and he would seem to have conceived himself as directly inspired by the spirit of his great original. It was impossible, indeed, that, out of the Elizabethan age, should issue a version of Homer marked by the Homeric qualities of simplicity and directness, nor does Chapman so much translate Homer as reproduce his narrative with a certain divine ardour. He describes it as "an absurd affectation in the interpretation of any author to turn him word for word," and disclaimed in his own case any such intention. In Chapman, the bright equable stream, that reflected sun and stars and open heaven, dashes through the chasms and ravines of a mountain country. The stately breadth and sweeping curve and quiet eddy are lost, but speed and volume and majesty remain. The famous version deserves its fame.[1]

"Our Homer-Lucan," as Daniel styled him, did not appear as a translator till he was nearly forty years old. The first instalment of his labours, *Seaven Bookes of the Iliades of Homere* (I and II and VII to XI), was published in 1598, and dedicated to the earl of Essex. In 1609 were published the first twelve books, dedicated to prince Henry, and the completed *Iliad*, without date (books I and II having been rewritten) about 1611. It appears from his own statement that he wrote the last twelve books in fifteen weeks. The metre, a fourteen-syllabled riming couplet, one of the oldest English measures, was a sixteenth century favourite, and had been employed in a translation of ten books of Homer, from a French version, in 1581, by Arthur Hall. Chapman's *Achilles Shield*, "translated out of" the eighteenth book, in the heroic couplet, and prefaced by an epistle attacking Scaliger, was also published in 1598. The first twelve books of the *Odyssey* in the heroic couplet appeared in 1614, with a dedication to the earl of Somerset, and the second twelve within another year. The *Works and Days* of Hesiod was next undertaken and completed in 1618. In 1616, both the *Iliad* and the *Odyssey* were issued in a folio entitled *The Whole Workes of Homer, Prince of Poets*, and, with *Batrachomyomachia*, the *Hymns* and the *Epigrams* in 1624, the first complete translation of Homer into English was made, and the author could say, "The work that I was born to do is done."

Like the pyramid of Caius Cestius, it was planned as "a refuge for his memory"; to Homer's keeping Chapman committed his name and fame. And to Homer he owes his reputation, as to his long companionship with Homer he owed his chief happiness in life. In the presence of that mighty shade, he forgot his quarrel with the world, the cloud of anger that sat upon his brow dispersed and his soul had peace.

[1] See, for further remarks on Chapman's *Homer*, Vol. IV, Chap. I, pp. 24, 25.

John Marston, a man of good Shropshire family and son of John Marston, a member of the Middle Temple, was probably born, and certainly educated, in Coventry. Italian blood on his mother's side (she was the daughter of an Italian physician, Andrew Guarsi) helps us to understand some features of his genius and character which distinguished him among his fellows and made him at the same time a typical representative of his age. He was admitted to Brasenose college, Oxford, and graduated in 1593. Marston began his literary career as a satirist, changed his muse and entered the dramatic field in the last year of the sixteenth century, but deserted the theatre for the church in 1607. He was presented to the living of Christchurch in Hampshire, and married the daughter of a clergyman, William Wilkes, chaplain to James I. Ben Jonson sarcastically observed to Drummond that "Marston wrote his father-in-law's preachings, and his father-in-law his comedies." A collected but incomplete edition of his plays was published in his lifetime by William Sheares (1633), who speaks of him as "now in his Autumn and declining age," and "far distant from this place," but claims for him a position among the best poets of his time. He made no demands of his own upon the attention of posterity. When he died in 1634, he was buried beside his father in the Temple church, "under the stone," says Wood, "which hath written on it *Oblivioni Sacrum.*" Marston was thus faithful to the sentiment which, in derision of the ambition of most poets, induced him, in his earlier life, to dedicate his works to forgetfulness.

> Let others pray
> For ever their faire poems flourish may;
> But as for mee, hungry Oblivion
> Devour me quick, accept my orizon.

In any estimate of Marston, it ought to be remembered that he suffered from no illusions—

> Farre worthier lines, in silence of thy state,
> Doe sleep securely, free from love or hate.

And, again, "He that thinks worse of my rimes than myselfe, I scorn him, for hee cannot: he that thinks better is a foole." As man of letters, Marston embarked at once upon "a troubled sea of noises and hoarse disputes." In 1598, he published two volumes, *The Metamorphosis of Pygmalion's Image, And Certain Satires*, and, later, *The Scourge of Villanie*, dedicated "to his most esteemed and best beloved Selfe," crossing blades with Hall, who, with some arrogance, had claimed the title of father of English satire:

> I first adventure: follow me who list,
> And be the second English satirist.

This unedifying duel has been dealt with in a previous chapter of the present work, and need not detain us here.[1] Marston had now achieved something of a reputation. He is mentioned by Meres, in his *Palladis Tamia* (1598), among the chief English satirists, and, in *The Returne from Pernassus* (acted in 1601), he is addressed by the title "Kinsayder," under which he had written a note in *The Scourge of Villanie*. Here, his portrait is boldly drawn as "a ruffian in his style," who "backs a proper steed" and "cuts, thrusts and foins at whomsoever he meets." No sooner had he joined the ranks of the dramatists than he set about him in the same deliberately aggressive fashion, "his shield hung ever in the lists." In the famous "war of the theatres," a war in which most of the dramatists of the day were involved, Marston's name is unceasingly prominent. He aimed an occasional shaft at Shakespeare, as in the parody (in *The Scourge of Villanie*)

> A man, a man, a Kingdom for a man,

or the line in *The Malcontent*

> Illo, ho, ho, ho! arte there, old Truepenny?

but his chief violence was directed against Jonson. "He had many quarrels with Marston," said Jonson, of himself, to Drummond, "beat him and took his pistol from him, wrote his *Poetaster* on him; the beginning of them were that Marston represented him on the stage." Jonson represents himself as patiently sustaining the "petulant styles" of his enemies "on every stage" for three years, and, at last, unwillingly forced into rejoinder. It is sometimes argued—on slender evidence, however—that Marston's first attack on Jonson was made

---

[1] Cf. *ante*, Vol. IV, Chap. XVI, pp. 379, 380; and bibl. p. 587.

not in a play but in *The Scourge of Villanie*, under the name "judicial Torquatus." But Jonson, at least as early as 1598, had expressed some of his literary judgments upon the stage. Daniel, in his opinion, "a good honest man, but no poet," had been publicly ridiculed in *Every Man in His Humour*, and the noble parts which Jonson assigned to himself—Asper in *Every Man out of His Humour*, Crites in *Cynthia's Revels*, Horace in *Poetaster*—no less than his unflattering portraits of enemies, naturally provoked and suggested reprisals. We need not wonder that he was facetiously saluted by Dekker in his "three or four suites of names," "Asper, Criticus, Quintus, Horatius, Flaccus." Theatre-goers familiar with the characteristics, literary and personal, of the popular dramatists were, probably, amused by these personal rivalries, assaults and counter assaults, and pleasure to the audience brought profit to the authors. So, at least, we gather from Jonson's remarks in *Poetaster:*

> What they have done 'gainst me,
> I am not moved with: if it gave them meat,
> Or got them clothes, 't is well: that was their end.
> Only amongst them, I am sorry for
> Some better natures, by the rest so drawn
> To run in that vile line.

In 1599, a play was performed at court, probably by the boys of Paul's, which carried on the practice of staging contemporary authors, and, in the personage of Chrisoganus, "Master Pedant" and "translating scholler," who is advised, "goe, get you clothes," the audience of the day probably recognised the most learned of the dramatic circle, Jonson, who "excelled in a translation," and was famous no less for his scholarship than for his shabby garments. This play, *Histrio-Mastix*, based on an earlier drama, possibly by Chapman, was directed against adult players, perhaps with special reference to the Chamberlain's company, and authors who wrote for it, of whom Jonson was one, and the evidence is strongly in favour of Marston's responsibility for the greater share in its production. Jonson, when, for the first time, he attacks Marston in *Every Man out of His Humour*, selects for derision words used in this play as well as in Marston's *Scourge of Villanie*, and, in the opinion of some critics, presented him as Carlo Buffone, "a most fiend like disposition," "a public scurrilous and profane jester . . . who will swill up more sack at a sitting than would make all the guard a posset." We are told that "he will sooner lose his soul than a jest, and profane even the most holy things to excite laughter." The identification, however, is far from certain, and Carlo may have been intended for a certain Charles Chester, a familiar city character. Attempts have been made to identify various other characters in the play with well known contemporaries of Jonson—Fastidious Brisk with Daniel, Fungoso with Lodge and Sordido with Henslowe—but with more ingenuity than success. So far, Dekker had not been in the battle. Before this date, he and Jonson had been collaborators and may have been friends. Some critics have thought Emulo a portrait of Jonson; but nothing could be more inapplicable to that sturdy shabby scholar than a description such as this—

My brisk spangled baby will come into a stationer's shop, call for a stool and a cushion, and then asking for some Greek poet, to him he falls, and then he grumbles God knows what, but I 'll be sworn he knows not so much as one character of the tongue.

In *Jacke Drums Entertainment*, an anonymous play performed in 1600 by the children of Paul's, in which Brabant Senior, "the censurer," is probably a portrait of Jonson, and Sir Edward Fortune may be intended for Edward Alleyn, there is again evidence of Marston's hand, his rhodomontade and fustian vocabulary, and these are ridiculed in *Poetaster*. "The new poet Mellidus" was probably a representation of the author himself. Jonson had already returned to the charge in *Cynthia's Revels*, where Dekker has been thought to be staged for the first time as Anaides, and where, most probably, Marston is pilloried as Hedon:

> The one a light voluptuous reveller,
> The other a strange arrogating puff,
> Both impudent and arrogant enough.

Both are represented as engaged in a plot against Crites, who, they agree to give out, is a plagiary, "all he does is dictated from other men," and "the time and place where he stole it" is known. Anaides is described as one "who will censure or discourse of anything, but as absurdly as you would wish. His fashion is not to take knowledge of him that is beneath him in clothes. He never drinks below the salt." He has a voice like the opening of some justice's gate or a postboy's horn, "a great proficient in all the illiberal sciences." "He will blaspheme in his shirt. The oaths which he vomits at one supper would maintain a town of garrison in good swearing a twelve month." We hear from him that, in argument with Crites, "because I could not construe an author I quoted at first sight, he went away and laughed at me." Anaides revenges himself by describing Crites as smelling of "lamp-oil with studying by candle-light." The Amorphus of this play may be Anthony Munday, who "walks most commonly with a clove or pick-tooth in his mouth," and is "more affected than a dozen waiting women." He will "usurp all the talk, ten constables are not so tedious," and he has been "fortunate in the amours of three hundred forty and five ladies, all nobly, if not princely descended." The epilogue to *Cynthia's Revels* connects this play with Marston's *Antonio and Mellida*. The actor who pronounced it had injunction from the author

> I 'll only speak what I have heard him say:
> By God, 'tis good, and if you lik't, you may.

The epilogue to *Antonio and Mellida* enters armed and re-marks: "I stand not as a peremptory challenger of desert, either for him that composed the Comedy, or for us that acted it; but as a most submissive suppliant for both." To the armed epilogue of Marston's play succeeded the armed pro-logue of *Poetaster* (1601), Jonson's most elaborate attack upon his detractors, where Marston is Crispinus, Dekker Demetrius. Hedon, in *Cynthia's Revels* is supposed, by some critics, to be Dekker; but it seems more probable that as "a dresser of plays about the town here," "one of the most over-flowing rank wits in Rome," he appears for the first time upon the stage as Demetrius. *Poetaster* doubtless presents other portraits of contemporaries; Virgil, a complimentary picture, may have been intended either for Shakespeare or Chapman. The pill which Caesar permits Horace to administer to Cris-pinus forces him to disgorge a number of Marston's fustian

words, which offended Jonson's taste; and both he and Demetrius are sworn never again "to malign, traduce or detract the
person or writings of Quintus Horatius Flaccus, or any other
eminent man." The reply to *Poetaster* was entrusted by the
aggrieved fellowship to Dekker, and his *Satiro-mastix* was produced in 1601. It seems certain that Jonson knew of the intention to reply to *Poetaster*, and that Dekker was to share in it, for
the part of Demetrius looks like an afterthought. He is introduced as a stranger in the third act "hired to abuse Horace, and
brings him in a play." The controversy is carried on by the
author of *Satiro-mastix* in a light, pleasant and facetious vein.
Dekker cleverly introduces some of Jonson's own characters
and even improves that of the swaggerer Tucca, and, while
this play falls far short of *Poetaster* in construction, its mockery
is more genial, its humour more subtle and sparkling and the
management of the whole is marked by a delightful air of
irresponsibility. Jonson is charged with having "arraigned
two poets against all law and conscience." There are a
number of jocose references to his personal appearance, his
scholar's pride, his slow methods of composition, his early
trade as a bricklayer, his military service in the Netherlands,
the duel in which he killed his adversary. The "humourous
poet" is "untrussed," and condemned to wear a crown of
nettles. He is no longer to swear he will hang himself if he
thinks any man could write as well as he, nor to enter the
gallery when his comedies are performed, and there make
vile and bad faces at every line to make men have an eye to
him and make the players afraid.

Besides, you must forsweare to venter on the stage, when your
play is ended, and to exchange curtezies, and complements with
Gallants in the Lordes roomes, to make all the house rise up in
Armes, and to cry that's Horace, that's he, that's he, that's he,
that pennes and purges Humours and diseases.

And, again, "when your plays are misse-likt at Court, you shall
not crye Mew like a Pusse-cat, and say you are glad you write
out of the Courtier's Element." "We come," says Crispinus,
"like your Phisitions, to purge

Your sicke and daungerous minde of her disease."

In yet another play was Jonson made the target of satirical jest, Marston's *What You Will*, probably written (1601) before *Poetaster* and revised later. But, while some investigators identify Jonson with Lampatho and Marston with Quadratus, others reverse the portraits. The evidence is somewhat conflicting; yet, if Marston intended anything but general satire, it would harmonise with all we know of him that he should here introduce his old *nom de plume* of Kinsayder, and thus present himself as Lampatho. He engages in a hectoring match with Quadratus, who abuses him as "a ragged satirist," "an envy-starved cur," "a libertine"; but Marston, who "presented his poetry to Detraction," was indifferent to abuse, and prepared to invent and discharge it against himself with the same zest that he hurled it at others.

> Then do but rail at me—
> No greater honour craves my poesy.

With this play the famous *poetomachia* comes to an end. In the same year, we find Marston collaborating with Jonson in *Love's Martyr*, and, with Chapman and Jonson, three years later, in *Eastward Hoe*. He also dedicated to Jonson his *Malcontent—Benjamino Jonsonio poetae elegantissimo gravissimo, amico suo, candido et cordato*—and, in an equally generous strain, praised his *Sejanus* in 1605—

> For never English shall, or hath before
> Spoke fuller graced.

The chief interest to-day of this ancient literary logomachy, waged on the boards of the Elizabethan theatre, lies in the personalities which assist us to envisage men with whose works we are familiar, and the attempt to identify in the plays the authors represented finds its justification in our natural curiosity to know these celebrities in their habits as they lived. Here, as elsewhere, we are baffled by the elusive personality of Shakespeare, for of the man in whom our interest is deepest no certain identification is possible, and the most plausible critical conjectures lack convincing quality. Wellbred in *Every Man in His Humour* may be Shakespeare, so may Posthast in *Histrio-Mastix*, Amorphus in *Cynthia's Revels*, Planet in *Jacke Drums Entertainment*, Ovid or Virgil in *Poetaster*, William Rufus,

"learning's True Maecenas, poesy's king," in *Satiro-mastix*.
But for the passage in the anonymous *Returne from Pernassus*
(1601) we might be spared all speculation with respect to the
part played by him in the theatrical wars and conclude that he
was never at any time found in either camp. Yet the speech
of Kemp to Burbage in that play draws conjectures like a
magnet and is encrusted with speculation.

Few of the university pen plaies well, they smell too much of
that writer *Ovid* and that writer *Metamorphosis*, and talke too much
of *Proserpina* and *Juppiter*. Why heres our fellow *Shakespeare*
puts them all downe, I and *Ben Jonson* too. And that *Ben Jonson*
is a pestilent fellow, he brought up *Horace* giving the Poets a pill,
but our fellow *Shakespere* hath given him a purge that made him
beray his credit.

The "purge" has been held to be the play of *Troilus and Cressida*, which would make the characters Thersites and Ajax
Marston and Jonson. But, until we understand *Troilus and
Cressida* better, it is wise, perhaps, to regard the "purge" as
nothing more than Shakespeare's triumph as a popular dramatist over the ablest and most celebrated of his contemporaries.
Yet, if Shakespeare eludes us, we learn some interesting particulars about others of the dramatic group. Marston's hair
(he is Rufus) and thin legs are a subject of continual mirth; if
he desire to be a poet, he is advised "to change his hair"; "he is
proud of his gentle birth," " a gentleman parcel-poet," "your
legs do sufficiently show you are a gentleman born, sir; for a
man borne upon little legs is always a gentleman born." Of
Jonson we hear that, as Drummond also tells us, he was a
great lover and praiser of himself—"Thou lovest none," says
Tucca, "neither wisemen nor fools but thyself"; Demetrius
speaks of his "arrogancy and his impudence in commending his
own things"; we hear of his shabby clothes—"that Judas
yonder that walks in rug"; his "rocky face," "a very bad face
for a soldier," a face "puncht full of oylet-holes like the cover
of a warming pan,"

the most ungodly face . . . it looks for all the world like a rotten
russet-apple, when 'tis bruised. It's better than a spoonful of
cinnamon-water next my heart, for me to hear him speak; he sounds

it so i' th' nose, and talks and rants . . . like the poor fellow under Ludgate . . . its cake and pudding to me to see his face make faces, when he reads his songs and sonnets,

his slowness in composition, "Will he bee fifteene weekes about this Cockatrice's egge too?" Other identifications are very precarious. Of Daniel, if Fastidious Brisk and Hedon be Daniel, as some suppose, we are told that he will "creep and wriggle into acquaintance with all the brave gallants about the town," "a light voluptuous reveller," a "rhyme-given" rascal who utters "sonnets by the gross," and will "overflow you half a score or a dozen at a sitting," "a neat, spruce, affecting courtier, one that wears clothes well, and in fashion; practiseth by his glass, how to salute," who "believes rich apparel hath strange virtues" and "had three suits in one year made three great ladies in love" with him,

has a rich wrought waistcoat to entertain his visitants in, with a cap almost suitable. His curtain and bedding are thought to be his own; his bathing tub is not suspected. He loves to have a fencer, a pedant and a musician seen in his lodging a-mornings.

While some of the satire in these descriptions may have been ill-natured, it is hard to believe that much of it was more than stage exaggeration of the good-humoured banter which passed between rivals at their actual meetings in tavern or ordinary.

Marston's dramatic activity was confined to about eight years in a lifetime of fifty-eight.

We may take it that the reference in Henslowe's diary to a "new poet" Maxton or Mastone, in 1599 referred to the author of *Antonio and Mellida*, his first play, acted in 1600. The first part deals with "the comic crosses of true love," the second, *Antonios Revenge*, with a world of vice and passion. Here, as elsewhere, Marston displays at moments a flash of tragic grandeur, but as often falls away into bombast and mere verbal gesticulation. It is impossible to deny to him in tragedy something of Marlowe's passion and Webster's solemn splendour, yet, whether through haste, or carelessness, or deficiency in taste, he is unable to maintain the heights to which he occasionally attains. Scenes and passages, such as Lamb selected, do not unfairly represent his power, but, when read as a whole, the dramas from which they are taken prove disappointing. Furious or monstrous characters, like duke Piero in the play under notice, or Isabella in *The Insatiate Countesse*, artificial rhetoric and the absence of reasonable construction, may not have alienated the sympathies of spectators who delighted in *The Spanish Tragedie*, but they distress and repel the modern reader. The source of *Antonio and Mellida*—probably an Italian story— is not known, but the drama belongs to the well known "blood and thunder" species, and irresistibly reminds us of Kyd's famous play and, necessarily, also of *Hamlet*. In the second part, we have the familiar ghost who clamours for revenge, the device of the dumb-show and the horrors of mutilation as well as death, repeated from *The Spanish Tragedie*. It is clear that Marston was a student of Seneca and knew Shakespeare's work, for there are quotations from *Thyestes* and reminiscences of *Richard II* and *Richard III*. Marston's first play, which was produced when he was twenty-four, bears all the signs of youth and must be described as a patch-work of such violent scenes as delighted the groundlings, entirely destitute of unity or skill in characterisation.

A marked advance is apparent in *The Malcontent*. Of this comedy, there exist two editions of 1604, one of which ascribes the authorship of the play to Webster and the augmentations to Marston. That it is chiefly Marston's work is clear, how-ever, from the preface, in which he expresses regret that scenes invented merely to be spoken should be printed for readers, but concludes that the least hurt he can receive is to do himself the wrong. Here, again, we have an Italian story, of which the source is unknown; but we are once more reminded of *Hamlet* in the person of the hero, and of *Richard III* in the villain Mendozo. The malcontent, a banished duke, returns in dis-guise to his former court. Like Hamlet's, "his own soule is at variance within herselfe," and, under the guise of a mad hu-mour, he contrives to speak the bitterest home truths. The situation has great possibilities, of which, perhaps, the fullest advantage is hardly taken; but Marston had already learnt important lessons in stagecraft and the delineation of character. In the cynical hero, we find depicted a type of mind somewhat akin to that of the author, and the humour of the piece is of the satirical variety which he himself appears most to have affected.

The Dutch Courtezan, published in 1605, shows a further advance in the handling of plot and character. There are scenes both serious and comic which revive memories of Beatrice and her cousin, and of Dogberry and the watch, in *Much Ado about Nothing;* both the men and women are fairly drawn and contrasted; the secondary plot—in part borrowed from the last novel in *The Palace of Pleasure*—with the knavish tricks of Cockledemoy, makes excellent fooling. The prologue apologises for the "slight hastie labours in this easie play" and declares that it was meant not for instruction but delight. It needs no apology, however, and, though charged by Antony Nixon (*The Black Year*, 1606) with "corrupting English conditions," only the sourest of moralists could feel resentment against the author of the comedy, one of the cleverest and most amusing of its time. It was revived late in the seventeenth century, with the alterations of Betterton, the actor, under the title *The Revenge, or The Match in Newgate.*

The Dutch Courtezan, though a capital play, is surpassed by *Eastward Hoe*, but, since the drama was written in conjunction with Chapman and Jonson, the entire credit for this brilliant and delightful performance cannot be claimed for Marston. While it might not be difficult to assign with some confidence certain scenes to each of these writers, the attempt exactly to apportion their respective contributions would lead to a succession of unverifiable conjectures. All must share in the praise due to it, as all were partakers in the misfortune to which it led. It was written shortly after the accession of James I to the throne of England, and contained sarcastic references to the multitude of needy Scottish adventurers who came south with their king, and many of whom successfully claimed place and fortune. Stage jesting at the expense of Scottish men and manners had been complained of to lord Burghley by the English agent at the Edinburgh court in 1598, and it had now become possible to deal with it. Attention was called by Sir James Graham, who may himself have been glanced at in the play, to a passage in the third act, in which captain Seagull remarks:

But as for them [the Scots] there are no greater friends to Englishmen and England, when they are out on't, in the world.

than they are. And for my part, I would a hundred thousand of
'hem were there, for we are all one countrymen now, ye know, and
we should find ten times more comfort of them there than we do
here.

The consequences of the mild freedom of comment which the
dramatists here allowed themselves was related by Ben Jonson
to Drummond—

He was dilated by Sir James Murray to the King, for writing
something against the Scots, in a play *Eastward Hoe*, and voluntarily
imprisoned himself with Chapman and Marston, who had written
it amongst them.   The report was, that they should then [have] had
their ears cut and noses. After their delivery, he banqueted all
his friends; there was Camden, Selden and others; at the midst of
the feast his old mother dranke to him, and shew him a paper which
she had (if the sentence had taken execution) to have mixed in the
prisson among his drinke, which was full of lustie strong poison, and
that she was no churle, she told, she minded first to have drunk of
it herself.

Some copies of the play, of which several editions appeared in
1605, omit the matter complained of, and other slight variations
are to be found in the extant copies. A version by Tate was
acted in 1685 under the title *Cuckold's Haven, or An Alderman
no Conjurer*. As a picture of city life, *Eastward Hoe* has no
superior in our dramatic history. The old goldsmith Touchstone, with his wife and daughters, and the idle and the indus-
trious apprentice, form an admirable and life-like group, which
instantly engages interest and attention. The reckless and
extravagant Sir Petronel Flush, burning to repair his fortunes
and escape his creditors by a treasure seeking voyage to
Virginia, and ravished by Seagull's account of its wealth, declares:

I tell thee, golde is more plentiful there than copper is with us
. . . all the chaines with which they chaine up their streets are
massie gold; all the prisoners they take are feterd in gold; and for
rubies and diamonds, they go forth on holydayes and gather 'hem
by the sea-shore.

This adventurer, with his companions, gives the authors an
admirable opportunity for depicting the shifty society of the
city which lives by its wits, and a vivid contrast is thus fur-

nished to the household of the honest tradesman. The plot
is complicated by intrigue, and well managed, the action has a
lively movement and the conclusion contrives "to reconcile
us to ourselves and to human nature." Few Elizabethan
comedies can be praised so unreservedly as this.

"Comedies are writ to be spoken, not read; remember the
life of these things consists in action," remarks the author in
the preface to his play entitled *Parasitaster, Or The Fawne*
(printed in two editions 1606), and certainly, though no doubt
fairly successful on the stage, this drama has no great literary
merit. The chief character, duke Hercules, appears in disguise at the court of Urbino, whither he has sent his son as an
ambassador of love, and the situation reminds us of *The Malcontent*. The heroine, Dulcimel, is of the type already portrayed in Crispinella (*The Dutch Courtezan*) and Rossaline in
Antonio and Mellida, the gay, sparkling and vivacious damsel,
who holds her own in the company of men. In Beatrice, the
sister of Crispinella, and in Mildred (*Eastward Hoe*) we have
another of Marston's favourite types of feminine character,
the good, simple girl, modest and affectionate. Marston is not
rich in female types, and if we add, to those mentioned, the
strong-willed passionate woman who appears in some of his
tragedies, we exhaust his range. The story is taken from the
third novel of the third day of *The Decameron;* but the idea is
an old one and had already been employed by Terence in his
Adelphi.

In *The Fawne*, Marston had promised shortly "to present a
tragedy which should boldly abide the most curious perusal."
But the tragedy, when it came, certainly belied the author's
promise. *The Wonder of Women Or The Tragedie of Sophonisba*
is the crudest of Marston's performances. The story, told by
Livy and other historians, has been frequently dramatised—in
English by Lee (1706) and Thomson (1730); in French by
Corneille (1663), and in German by various hands. Sophonisba
herself is rendered not without force and skill, but, for the
rest, the play is a singularly feeble attempt to do justice to a
powerful tragic theme. The witch Erichto and the scenes in
which she appears are almost ludicrous in their failure to produce
the intended impression of mystery and horror. It is difficult
to understand how the author could have believed the piece

to possess any literary quality; it is easy to see that he has over-
leaped the limits of his power.

Marston's last play, *The Insatiate Countesse* (printed 1613),
does not appear in the 1633 edition of his works, and in an
extant copy of 1631 its authorship is assigned to William
Barkstead.   It is generally, and, no doubt, correctly, assumed
that this was the actor William Barkstead, author of two
poems—*Mirrha, the Mother of Adonis* (1617) and *Hiren, or
the Faire Greeke* (1611).   Two of the best lines in the play are
found in the first named poem—

> Night, like a masque, is entered heaven's great hall
> With thousand torches ushering the way.

Of tragedies assigned to Marston, this contains the most
interesting work, but much of it, clearly, is by another hand.
The text is corrupt, and it seems probable that Marston devised the plot (taken from the fourth and fifteenth novels of
Bandello and reproduced in *The Palace of Pleasure*), that he
wrote the first draft and that the play was then completed by
Barkstead, and finally printed without revision from a stage
copy.   Marston, evidently, was attracted by Shakespeare and
Shakespeare reverberates through this play.   It echoes *Hamlet*,
Julius Caesar, *Macbeth*, *Richard II* and *Henry IV;* but some
of these echoes may be due to the player Barkstead's unconscious memories.   The subject of the drama—the unbridled
passions of Isabella, countess of Swevia, and her dealings with
her many lovers—is too remote from nature and modern life to
command our sympathy; but there are scenes which it is impossible to read without a thrill of admiration.   Webster
alone has excelled them in their own kind, while passing through
the same dark region of things violent and forbidding, lust,
cruelty, madness and death.   A Latin pageant for the visit of
king Christian of Denmark to England in 1606 and an entertainment for a visit of the countess of Derby to her son-in-law,
lord Huntingdon, complete the list of Marston's extant works,
unless, with Collier, we attribute to him the amusing *Mounte-
bank's Masque*, performed in 1616.

The texture of Marston's genius was singularly unequal, and
he constantly promises more than he performs.   In comedy only

can it be truly said that he achieved success, yet in his more
ambitious and less successful work there resides an arresting
quality. When we are about to condemn unreservedly, he
flashes into unexpected splendour; when we lay down the
book, his characters refuse to be altogether dismissed into the
limbo of forgotten things. Marston, as he himself tells us, was
powerfully "enticed with the delights of poetry," and confesses
that, "above better desert," he was "fortunate in these stage
pleasings." As a young man, he essayed what all young men of
talent were essaying, the highest reaches of a most difficult art.
Nor was his measure of success inconsiderable, for we are told
by Wood that he was "in great renown for his wit and ingenuity in 1606." Yet it was at this time, while still a young man
and on the very threshold of fame, that he resolutely turned
away to take up the unexciting routine of parish business. Too
little notice has been taken of this remarkable renunciation, and
Marston's character too much obscured by the unrelieved emphasis laid upon the heady violences of his satirical youth and
his extravagances of diction and humour in the theatrical wars.
He outgrew these affectations and absurdities; but, at the
same time, he outgrew the passion for distinction. There
seems no good reason to doubt the sincerity of his own statements,—"of men of my own addiction I love most, pitie some,
hate none"; "I have ever more endeavoured to know myself
than be known of others"—and, without hesitation, we may
ascribe his neglect of his "unfenced reputation," and his
retirement from the pursuit of fame, to his having deliberately
"esteemed felicity a more solid contentment," and readily
responded to the summons, when life's current ran less tur-
bulently, of "his bosom friend, good Epictetus," to the quiet
meadows and sober pleasures of philosophy.

Thomas Dekker, in whose case, as in that of many of his
contemporaries, we possess no certain record of the facts of his
life, was born and bred in London—"thou beautifullest daughter of the two united Monarchies! from thy womb received
I my being; from thy breasts my nourishment." He spoke of
himself as "old" in 1628, of his "three score years," a vague
phrase, in 1637; and we may take it he was born, or not long
in the world, in the year 1570. The first mention of Dekker,

as author of a book called *Phaeton*, appears in Henslowe's diary in 1597, and his name appears again in 1599, when he is associated with Chettle, an experienced playwright, in the production of a play entitled *Troilus and Cressida* In the same year, he received various payments for other pieces of work. And, though the popular narrative poem *Canaan's Calamitie* (1598), signed T. D., is, probably, Deloney's and not Dekker's, it is evident that he was early involved in the multifarious literary activities to which his life appears to have been devoted without cessation. Of his parentage and education, we know nothing, but it is improbable that he was ever a student at either of the universities. Since the theatre of the time offered the only remunerative career to poetical talents, to the theatre Dekker betook himself; but his energies, stimulated by necessity, overflowed into other channels. Plays, pageants, pamphlets followed each other with amazing rapidity. Yet, despite all his labours, early in life he made acquaintance with the misfortunes which dog the steps of poverty. In 1598, Henslowe provided forty shillings to secure his release from the "Counter in the Poultrey," and we are told by Oldys that he was in prison from 1613 to 1616, and "how much longer he could not tell." It has been conjectured, not without probability, that his phrase "the Bed in which seven years I lay Dreaming" (*Dekker his Dreame*, 1620) has reference to this unhappy period. Some letters to Alleyn which have been preserved prove that he was several times befriended by that open-handed actor. For the rest, we know that Dekker was married before 1594, and that his last book was printed in 1637. Here the story ends; but, if the details of his private life, like those of Shakespeare, are hidden in the cloud, his work, like Shakespeare's, offers an ample field for the study of the author's personality. Many of his writings of which the titles survive have been lost, and others, doubtless, have perished with them; yet so much remains that, even in the absence of personal knowledge of the man, it is possible to estimate his genius and character with unusual precision. To the mental energy and literary facility of Defoe, he added the unpractical temperament, the genial kindliness, the happy heart of Goldsmith. Of the Elizabethan playwrights, excluding Shakespeare, he is not the greatest, but he is the most lovable, not the most learned but the most sympathetic; he was not the most skilful craftsman among them, but he possessed the most natural vein of inspiration. Dekker "was a rogue," said Jonson; but we are not prepared to believe it of so sweet and so good-humoured a disposition as his. There is no such mirror of contemporary Elizabethan and Jacobean life and ways as is offered us in the works of Dekker.[1] In his natural sympathies and in his choice of subjects, he clings more closely to his own country than any dramatist of his age. No writer since Chaucer, with whom Dekker may fruitfully be compared, has painted so many essentially English pictures of men and manners in so natural and realistic a style. In his first extant play, the comedy entitled *The Shomakers Holiday* (printed 1600), his admirable talent and characteristic interests are displayed. The rise in fortune of the jovial and honest shoemaker, Simon Eyre, gives the poet opportunity to depict the life of the London he knew—rich in shifting scenes of love, intrigue, commerce and domestic doings. The canvas is crowded with portraits of tradesmen, apprentices, aldermen, courtiers, their wives, daughters and sweethearts, a motley procession surging through the streets, each elbowing the other in shop and tavern. No dramatist of the day supplies so vivid and humorous a spectacle of the city world which lay around him—the world for which his plays were written—as Dekker. In the same year was printed *The Pleasant Comedie of Old Fortunatus*, a drama in which the poet in Dekker emerges rather than the observing humorist. As in the well known fifteenth century romance, Fortunatus meets lady Fortune, and, of her gifts—"wisdom, strength, health, beauty, long life and riches"—a choice among which is offered him, he selects riches, and receives a purse which is never empty however much may be withdrawn from it. His travels after his unwise choice, and his unhappy fate, with that of his sons, make up the story of the play. The theme is simple, the construction somewhat rambling; but much of the poetry is exquisite. It was, perhaps, revised for a performance at court. Dekker never surpassed these early dramas. His rapid, careless methods betrayed him, and, though he preserved to the last something of the sweetness of fancy, the quickness

---

[1] See Vol. IV, Chap. XVI, pp. 401–407, where his contributions to pamphlet literature are discussed at length. See also Vol. IV., bibl. pp. 596–598.

of invention and the lightness of touch for which he is justly
famed, he constantly offends against the stricter canons of art
which require unity of design, coherence and precision in
construction and character. In these and other plays, Dekker
followed Shakespeare in the mingling of prose and verse.
Where prose serves his purpose, as in the humorous scenes of
ordinary life, he employs it freely, exchanging it for verse where
a deeper key of feeling, a higher pitch of passion or sentiment is
reached, passing into rimed verse in tender or pathetic passages.
The singing note is heard throughout his best work, and to the
charming lyrical vein in his genius we owe such perfect songs as
the familiar

> Art thou poor, yet hast thou golden slumbers,

where the melody breaks into a child-like overflow of almost in-
articulate joyful emotion. After *Satiro-mastix*, already referred
to, in which he took up arms against Jonson, Dekker reverted to
a more congenial sphere in *The Honest Whore*. Although he
had been one of the "screaming grasshoppers held by the wings"
of Jonson's *Poetaster*, Dekker, in his reply, had exhibited no
malevolence, nor did he return to the attack. In the first
part of *The Honest Whore* (printed 1604), Middleton, as proved
by an entry in Henslowe, had a share; the second and superior
part is wholly Dekker's (printed 1630), and indisputably a
masterpiece as well in execution as invention. The father of
Bellafront (whose return to virtue makes the point of the
action) is one of the most interesting characters in Elizabethan
fiction, and the conception would have done honour to any
dramatist. Orlando Friscobaldo, as Hazlitt wrote in his admirable appreciation, is one of the characters who "raise,
revive and give a new zest to our being." Bellafront's husband Matheo, is an equally life-like portrait of the unprincipled
libertine whose vices are due as much to lack of brain as lack
of heart. No single play by Dekker more worthily represents
him, or better reflects the blend of humour, pathos and poetry
which made the man. But he was never a sure artist. In *The
Whore of Babylon* (printed 1607), we have a play without merit,
whose only interest lies in some few passages descriptive of
London manners and fashions, and in its exhibition of protestant and patriotic sentiment, displayed in references to queen

Elizabeth, under the name of Titania, to the Armada and to the *Drake*,

> Who from their rivers beat their water fowl,
> Tore silver feathers from their fairest swans,
> And plucked the Halcyon's wings that rove at sea.

If It Be Not Good, the Divel is in it (printed 1612) is a sufficiently extraordinary title for a worthless dramatic fantasy, based upon *The Pleasant History of Friar Rush* (1567), which presents a bewildering group of human and superhuman beings, from Ravaillac and Guy Faux to Pluto and Charon. If, to these last named works, we add *Match mee in London* (printed 1631) and *The Wonder of A Kingdome* (printed 1636), neither of which add much to Dekker's laurels, we exhaust the list of plays which can with any confidence be assigned to his unassisted pen. But there remain a number of dramas to which he was a contributor and of some of which, perhaps, he was the chief architect. The habit of collaboration, "the noble practice of the times," in which Elizabethan playwrights freely indulged, left to criticism numerous problems not yet solved—many, no doubt, never to be solved. Dekker had partners, good and bad, in various theatrical ventures. We know that Middleton had a share in the first part of *The Honest Whore*, and a share, almost certainly the largest, in *The Roaring Girle* (1611), whose heroine, Moll Cutpurse, masquerades as a London gallant; we know that Webster took part in the composition of *West-Ward Hoe* and *North-Ward Hoe*, comedies of intrigue, and *The Famous History of Sir Thomas Wyat* (all printed 1607), possibly an unfinished or unskilful attempt to recast an older historical play on the subject of lady Jane Grey in two parts, both mentioned by Henslowe. We find Massinger's name associated with Dekker's in connection with *The Virgin Martir* (printed 1622) and, though the comic scenes and the characters of Dorothea and Angelo have been claimed for Dekker, the conception and framework of the play may, without injustice, be assigned to the younger dramatist.[1] *The Pleasant Comodie of Patient Grissill*, printed anonymously in 1603; but, in all probability (though Jonson may have had a hand in a revision), rightly assigned, on the evidence of certain entries

---

[1] See *post*, Chap. VI.

in Henslowe, to Chettle, Haughton and Dekker, is generally believed to owe its two beautiful lyrics and much of its merit to the most celebrated of its three authors.[1] *The Witch of Edmonton* (printed 1658), a fine play, raises some very difficult questions. The witch scenes, in which an aching spirit of human sympathy appears, and the tender character of Susan, have been very generally allotted to Dekker, but Mother Sawyer is by some critics thought to have been a creation of Rowley. The first act, the plan and general management of the piece, indisputably belong to Ford.[2]   To Ford, also, may, without hesitation, be assigned a large part, probably the last two acts at least, in *The Sun's-Darling: A Moral Masque* (1656), which, perhaps, is a hasty revision of Dekker's *Phaeton*. Another masque by the same authors, entitled *The Fairy Knight* (licensed in 1624), has not come down to us, and we know the names of a number of other dramas in which Dekker assisted or was assisted by Jonson (*Robert the Second*, and *Page of Plymouth*), by Drayton (*The Civil Wars in France*) and by Haughton and Day (*The Spanish Moor's Tragedy*, identified by some critics with *Lusts Dominion*, at one time ascribed to Marlowe, but not published till 1657).   There are passages in *Lusts Dominion* which certainly suggest Dekker, and, whether we identify it or not with the last drama, we may grant it as possible that he had a hand in it.   *The magnificent Entertainment: Given to King James* (1603), in which Jonson joined, and to which Middleton contributed a speech, and various civic pageants, are evidence of contemporary appreciation of Dekker's versatile talent, but possess no serious literary interest.

Quick, impulsive sympathies and a deep vein of humanity were the qualities beyond price in Dekker's dramatic equipment, and to these good gifts of nature the muses added their authentic inspiration.   "A priest in Apollo's temple many years," as he said, his place and honours were acknowledged by his own age and remain unchallenged.   The "poetry enough for anything," of which Lamb spoke, was joined in Dekker to an amazing and unflagging interest in life, without touch or trace of weariness or cynicism.   It would be absurd to claim for him the intellectual range, the sure-footed judgment or unerring taste of the great masters, and perilous to assert that

---

[1] See *ante*, Vol. V, Chap. XIII.   [2] See *post*, Chap. VIII.

his faults became him; yet, from his very artlessness, there shines a charm denied to better considered and far more perfect work. By the way of unaffected simplicity, Dekker almost captured greatness, and, while some of his fellows have secured a larger share of the admiration of posterity, he has crept into its more affectionate remembrance. If we incline to criticise his haste and carelessness, we ought to remember that he wrote "with the printer's devil and the bailiff always at his elbow," and we may well be astonished not so much at the demerits as at the wealth and value of his performance. "The right happy and copious industry" which, in Webster's estimate, placed "Master Dekker" beside "Master Shakespeare," is a tribute from a critic who knew what excellence was, and against what mighty currents men must struggle to attain it. As a humorist, London was his province, a sufficient field. Sinful humanity did not lie beyond his pale, but the sunny breadth of mind which was his, while he retained reverence for the things that call for reverence, transforms and transfigures the world, and we are the more reluctant to dismiss it as merely common and unclean. Dekker's satire is without sting, for, while he laughs, he loves, and is honest without being angry. He only among the men of his time seems to have recognised the whole hardness of the fate of the poor, and to have ranged himself on the side of distressed persons, maltreated animals, misjudged, lonely and eccentric members of society.

For the student of Elizabethan social life, Dekker's prose is even more important than his plays. There are no surviving documents so rich in material for the reconstruction of its manners and fashions as these vivid and entertaining pamphlets. Of some of these an account has been given in a previous volume of the present work.[1] Both in *The Wonderfull Yeare* (1603) and in *A Rod for Runawayes* (1625), which also deals with appalling incidents of the plague and upbraids those who fled from the city in its need, Dekker anticipates Defoe in the realism and force of his descriptions, not unmingled in the former work with certain grimly humorous narratives, designed, as he said, "like a merry Epilogue to a dull Play, to shorten the lives of long winter's nights, that lie watching in the

---

[1] See the passages in Vol. IV, Chap. XVI, and bibl., to which reference has already been made.

dark for us." *Worke for Armorours, or the Peace is broken*
(1609), with its motto, "God help the Poor, the rich can shift,"
allegorises the eternal conflict of classes in the war of the rival
queens, Money and Poverty, and the perplexed social problems of our own no less than Dekker's day are poignantly
presented. Here, again, Dekker refers to "the purple whip of
vengeance," the plague, and its effects on the city life. Like
many others, the poets and players are in evil case, the playhouses are closed, their flags and bushes taken down, the muses
more sullen than monkeys,

no good doing in these dayes but amongst Lawyers, amongst
Vintners, in Bawdy houses and at Pimlico. There is all the Musick
(that is of any reckning), there all the meetings, there all the mirth,
and there all the money.

Among incidental descriptions which give interesting glimpses
into the city's life is that of the bear pit, "the Dogges, like so
many Divels inflicting torments upon it," in which savage
entertainment was included sport with a blind bear, not baited
by dogs, but whipped "till the blood ran down his old shoulders" by "a company of creatures that had the shapes of men
and faces of christians."

Methought [says Dekker] this whipping of the blinde Beare,
moved as much pittie in my breast towards him, as ye leading of
poore starved wretches to the whipping posts in London (when they
had more neede to be releeved with foode) ought to move the hearts
of cittizens, though it be the fashion now to laugh at the punishment.

Dekker's prose is not always faultless, but it is clear to any
student of Shakespeare or of Elizabethan literature in general
that what Arnold called "the victory of the prose style, clear,
plain and short" was already won by our dramatists before the
advent of Dryden, the virtues of whose prose were derived from
his studies in their school. At his best, Dekker is as simple and
lucid and direct as any later writer. Take this, from the complaint of Paules steeple in *The Dead Tearme* (1608)—

The Marriner there called mee his sea-marke, for to him I stood
as a watch-tower to guide him safely to our English shore. No
sooner did the traveller by land see me but his heart leaped for
joy, and the wearisomnesse of his way seemed to go from him,

because he knew he was in sight of the most goodly Cittie which he loved.

Dekker his Dreame (1620) (to which was prefixed a woodcut representing the poet asleep in bed) is a mixture of prose and verse, which opens with an apocalyptic vision of the end of all things and the last judgment, and describes the author's progress through the infernal regions. It reveals an intense and vivid consciousness of the guilt and peril of sin but is singularly devoid of the natural grace and distinction of another religious book, *Fowre Birds of Noahs Arke* (1609). This is a very remarkable collection of prayers, distinguished by a deep spirit of devotion, exquisite feeling and perfection of phrasing. There is probably no prayer book in the language from a single hand which can bear comparison with this for simplicity and beauty.

CHAPTER III
Middleton and Rowley

I T is believed that Thomas Middleton was born in London
about 1570; he died there, and was buried at Newington
Butts on 4 July, 1627. The known facts about his life
are that he married a daughter of one of the six clerks in chancery, and had a son in 1604; that he was city chronologer from
1620 till the time of his death, when he was succeeded by Ben
Jonson; that, in 1624, he was summoned before the privy
council, with the actors who had played in his *Game at Chesse*,
and, it appears, put in prison at the instigation of Gondomar,
the Spanish ambassador; and that, in 1619, Ben Jonson spoke
of him to Drummond of Hawthornden as "a base fellow."
This hard saying may, after all, have been meant as no more
than a literary criticism. The words are: "that Markham
(who added his English Arcadia) was not of the number of
the Faithful, *i.e. Poets*, and but a base fellow. That such were
Day and Middleton." This might mean no more than that, to
Jonson, Middleton's art or verse seemed "base," in the sense of
pedestrian, or going on a low level. Nothing more was said
about him by anyone of consequence, except a passing word
from Scott, before the appearance, in 1808, of Lamb's *Specimens
of English Dramatic Poets*. Lamb gave copious and carefully
chosen extracts from his plays, and said almost all the essential
things about him; Leigh Hunt followed, picking up the one grain
left over by Lamb; and, in 1860, Dyce brought out a complete
edition of the plays, which was re-edited and extended by
Bullen in 1885.

Of William Rowley, there has never been any edition, and
we know even less of him than of Middleton. It is conjectured
that he was born about 1585 and died some time after 1637,

the year of his marriage. He was an actor in various companies, and is supposed to have revised plays for new performances. For the most part, he collaborated with other playwrights, especially with Middleton; and the finest work of both Middleton and Rowley was done in this collaboration. Rowley's chief play, *Alls Lost by Lust*, has never been reprinted from the scarce original edition of 1633. Besides the plays, he published, in 1609, *A Search for Money; or, the Lamentable Complaint for the Loss of the Wandering Knight, Monsieur L'Argent*, a pamphlet in the manner of the time full of crude realistic satire, written in his abrupt, lean and straightforward prose.

The earliest work attributed to Middleton is an endless composition in six-lined stanzas called *The Wisdom of Solomon Paraphrased*, published in 1597. The dedication to lord Devereux, and an address, wanting in some copies, "To the Gentlemen-Readers," are both signed Thomas Middleton, and we can but hope that it was someone else of the same name. Addressing critics as Momus and Zoilus, the writer regrets, not quite truthfully, "I lack a scarecrow," and bids them "if you gape for stuffing, hie you to dead carrion carcases, and make them your ordinaries." But no better fare is provided, and a sufficient scarecrow has been set up over this unploughed field by every subsequent editor. The task, if he really endured it, must have effectually cured Middleton of any further inclination for preaching. "O weak capacity of strongest wit!" he laments, and with justice; yet, two years afterwards, he seems to have attempted satire with no less futility than sermonising. *Micro-cynicon. Six Snarling Satyres*, published in 1599, has been attributed to Middleton for no more certain reason than the signature "T. M. Gent," following the introductory *Defiance to Envy* with which the writer, in imitation of Hall, introduces his first and only book of satires. They are weakly imitated from Marston.

> My pen's two nebs shall turn into a fork,
> Chasing old Envy from so young a work,

the writer threatens; but the threat could not possibly have been needed. The "snarling Muse" that "now thundered rhyme" thus feebly must have been beyond the reach of envy,

and has become too insignificant to need identification. But
Middleton was an unequal writer, and it is impossible to regard
even such bad work as this unlikely, because unworthy, to
have been written by him.

His mark is much more distinctly to be traced in two pamphlets published in 1604, signed "T. M." in their epistles to the
reader. The less interesting of these is *Father Hubburd's Tales*,
which contains a good deal of indifferent verse, no better than
Middleton's lyric verse usually is. Its main interest for us
is in the very kindly and regretful praise of Nashe, whom he
calls "honest soul," "too slothful to thyself," "cut off in thy
best blooming May":

> Drones eat thy honey: thou wast the true bee.

The tract is one of the allegorising satires of the time, written in
a slow narrative style, with abundant detail of the manners and
fashions censured, and a good deal of quite sober realism in the
descriptions and incidents. *The Black Book* is more extravagant and more pungent, and is like a sample of the raw material,
presented to us by the writer in his first self-conscious pose as
moralist. He parades as one "diving into the deep of this
cunning age" and bringing to light "the infectious bulks, of
craft, cozenage, and panderism, the three bloodhounds of a
commonwealth." He professes that his lively exposures are
meant for the warning and confirming of the "truly virtuous,"
and commends himself for "the modesty of my phrases, that
even blush when they discover vices and unmask the world's
shadowed villanies." The tale is put into the mouth of Lucifer,
who speaks his own prologue in a vigorous piece of blank verse
and rime, by way of response to Nashe's dedication of *Pierce
Penilesse* to "the high and mightie Prince of darknesse, Donsell
dell Lucifer, King of Acheron, Stix and Phlegeton, Duke of
Tartary, Marquesse of Cocytus, and Lord high Regent of
Lymbo." The pamphlet is done in Nashe's manner, and shows
a knowledge of its subject not inferior to Nashe's own. It
describes what may possibly have been Nashe's actual deathbed, seen by "the sullen blaze of a melancholy lamp that burnt
very tragically upon the narrow desk of a half-bedstead, which
descried all the pitiful ruins throughout the whole chamber."
It shows glimpses of "your twelve tribes of villany," engaged

in much the same machinations as in the plays; and the devil, having gone to and fro in London, "to gorge every vice full of poison," sits down to make out his last will and testament, leaving legacies "like ratsbane to poison the realm," in a catalogue of the more profitable of the vices. We see Middleton, for all his drawing of a moral, very interested and at home in the details of all that he denounces; preparing himself, deliberately or not, for his work as a writer of dramatic comedy.

It is quite possible that *The Mayor of Quinborough*, which was printed with Middleton's name in 1661, is the earliest play of his that we have; and quite possible that we have it only in a revised state. Such merit as there is in the play lies almost wholly in individual lines and passages, which stand out from a confused and rather hideous mingling of tragic bombast and strained farce. The dumb-show and choruses between the acts are not less immature than the horrors in action by which we can imagine Middleton to be trying to force himself to be tragic. No trace of Rowley is to be seen anywhere in the play, least of all in the comic scenes, which have distinct traces of the manner of Middleton. The whole play seems to be the premature attempt of a man, not naturally equipped for tragic or romantic writing, to do the tragic comedy then in fashion; and this attempt was probably continued in the plays, now lost, at which we know Middleton was working in 1602: *Caesar's Fall*, with Munday, Drayton and Webster; *The Two Harpies*, with the same and Dekker; and *The Chester Tragedy*. In *Blurt Master-Constable*, which belongs to the same year and is the first of his published plays, we see him recovering himself after his false start, and setting off spiritedly on the comedies of intrigue which were to form the first division of his work. The prose has become alive, and swift of foot; the dialogue slips easily from prose into verse and back again; the action, and the unchastened tongues, gallop. Middleton has found a theme and a technique; and to these he will be almost wholly faithful for the long first half of his career, the fifteen years of comedy.

That is, unless we are to believe, on the strength of a dubious allusion, that Middleton, before writing *The Mayor of Quinborough*, wrote *The Old Law*, or part of it, and that Massinger and Rowley, who would both have been too young to have collaborated with him at the time, added large portions

later. Of Massinger, though he may conceivably have revised it at a much later date than that of its original production,
there is no trace in the play;[1] but of Rowley the traces are
unmistakable, not so much in the actual writing of the comic
parts as in the whole conception of the main scenes and characters. In a sense the play is the preparation for *A Faire
Quarrell* (1617), which both wrote together; it seems to mark
the beginning of the collaboration, and of that new influence
which came into Middleton's work with Rowley. It is in these
two plays that we find, for the first time, that "exquisiteness
of moral sensibility" which Lamb divined in the one, and that
"delicacy of perception in matters of right and wrong" which
he distinguished in the other.

From 1602, the date of *Blurt Master-Constable*, to 1617, the
date of *A Faire Quarrell*, almost the whole of Middleton's work
is in farcical comedy, at once realistic and satirical. It is to the
early part of this period that a play is generally attributed into
whose authorship no one would have troubled to enquire if it
had not been published as "written by W. S." *The Puritane*
is still printed among what are called the "doubtful plays" of
Shakespeare. When Swinburne says that it is "much more
like Rowley's than like Middleton's worst work" he is strictly
correct; but he is not to be taken to mean that Rowley wrote it.
There is nothing sufficiently individual in the play to give so
much as a solid starting-point for conjecture. Compare it
with the worst of Middleton's comedies, *The Famelie of Love*,
and it will be found that, in that tedious satire, there is at
least some intention, though it is now mainly lost to us; we
have here the realist's attempt to show up the dulness of dull
people by making them speak and act no more nimbly than was
natural to them. The parody, apparently, is so close that we
can mistake it for the original. But the diction, though creeping, is not ignoble; it is like the fumbling of a man on an
instrument which he is on the way to master. The fumbler of
The Puritane will get no further.[2]

In 1604, Middleton had some, but no very considerable,
share in *The Honest Whore* of Dekker, so far as his manner can be
traced there; and, seven years later, we find him collaborating

---

[1] Cf. *post*, Chap. vi.

[2] As to *The Puritane*, cf. *ante*, Vol. V, Chap. x.

again with Dekker in *The Roaring Girle*, though here, also, what is finest in the play seems to be Dekker's. Apart from these two divergences, and an occasional masque or pageant, done to order, Middleton's course is direct, and his main concern, as he defines it later, in commending *The World tost at Tennis* to the reader and understander, is to be "neither too bitterly taxing, nor too soothingly telling, the world's broad abuses." In a prefatory address to the "comic play-readers" of *The Roaring Girle*, he is still more explicit.

"The fashion," he says, "of play-making I can properly compare to nothing so naturally as the alteration in apparel; for in the time of the great crop-doublet, your huge bombasted plays, quilted with mighty words to lean purpose, was only then in fashion: and as the doublet fell, neater inventions began to set up. Now, in the time of spruceness, our plays follow the niceness of our garments; single plots, quaint conceits, lecherous jests, drest up in hanging sleeves: and those are fit for the times and the termers. Such a kind of light-colour summer stuff, mingled with divers colours, you shall find this published comedy."

The early comedy of Middleton is as light, rancid and entertaining as anything in Elizabethan drama. It is irresponsible rather than immoral, and does not exactly recommend, or approve of, the trickeries and debaucheries which it represents in a lifelike way, under improbable conditions. Yet the writer is no more careful of his ethical than of his other probabilities, and takes little trouble to keep up any consistency in the minds or morals of his agile puppets. His aim is at effect, and he rarely fails in his aim. Even when we do not believe in the persons, and do not care about the upshot of the action, we are almost constantly enlivened, and, willingly or unwillingly, carried along.

The main material of his comedy is in the acts and moods of the human animal. The idea of sex dominates the whole Elizabethan drama; here, however, it is not a terror, a fascination, or a sin, but an occupation. A passage in *The Phoenix* might be applied to almost any of these plays:

> What monstrous days are these!
> Not only to be vicious most men study,
> But in it to be ugly; strive to exceed
> Each other in the most deformed deed.

Is it a merit in Middleton that he shows us vice always as an ugly thing, even when he seems to take pleasure in it, and to forget to condemn it? The "beggarly fools and swarming knaves," to use a phrase of his own, who traffic in souls, bodies and possessions throughout the travesties, confusions and "familiar accidents which happen in town," are set agog by no moralist, but by so keen and unprejudiced an observer of the human comedy that, for the most part, they come out in their naked colours, almost against his intention. And, as he lets vice peep through all cloaks and stand self-condemned, so he shows us a certain hardly conscious "soul of goodness in things evil." There is true and good human feeling in some of the most shameless scenes of *Your five Gallants*, where a whole lost and despised world of "strange devils and pretty damnable affections" is stirred up into plausible action. They take place where there is "violet air, curious garden, quaint walks, fantastical arbours, three back-doors, and a coach-gate," in a "music-school" or Maison Tellier of the period, and the very names of the characters are hardly quotable. The humanity is accidental, and comes from absolute knowledge of a world where "every part shoots up daily into new subtlety; the very spider weaves her cauls with more art and cunning to entrap the fly." Middleton, though the spider preoccupies him, and lends him a web for spinning, puts the fly, too, into the pattern.

If we seek a reason for the almost universal choice of brothels and taverns as favourite scenes of Elizabethan comedy, we shall find it partly in a theory, taken over from Latin and Italian drama, that this was the proper province of the comic muse. The accidents of a player's or professional writer's life gave opportunities for knowledge of just that world into which he was naturally thrust. The Elizabethan audience was accustomed from the first to the two extremes of noble tragedy and brutal comedy. This violent contrast appealed to a taste always hungering and thirsting for strong meat and strong drink. Puritan limits had not yet fixed themselves; they were but divined as a thing one could be aware of and mock at. At the same time, the stage was not exactly respected; it had no character to keep up. Thus, the dramatist, being as free as a modern French caricaturist to make his appeal in the most direct way, to the animal through the animal, had no hesitation in using the gross material at hand grossly. In the more serious dramatists, we get no more than painful attempts to please a taste which Middleton must have found it easy to gratify. He was no dreamer; he was not a poet in the instinctive irrepressible sense in which Dekker, for instance, was a poet; and he shared a love which was common to Dekker and to others at that time, for mean adventures of loose people in cities, knaves who gulled and fools who were gulled, sharpers and, outside cities, highwaymen and gipsies. His eyes were open to every folly of fashion or freak of religion; he knew his law and his lawyers, and he saw their capabilities for entertainment; he had all the terms of astrological and other cant at his fingers' ends, and realised the savour of the oddities of popular speech. It was easy for him to set these people talking as they would really talk, or with just that heightening which his sense of pungent and appropriate words gave him; and he could set scene after scene galloping across the stage, without taking more trouble than his public demanded as to making his plots consistent or probable, so long as they went at full speed along familiar ways; not caring, most of the time, to create individual characters, but relying upon the effect of vividly realised moods, or people very much alive for a given moment. A character so ripely developed as Sir Bounteous Progress in *A Mad World, My Masters* is rare among these nimble types and instances of fixed follies or ascertained "humours."

We remember Midleton's comedies, not for their separate characters, but for their brace of gallants, their "school" of wantons, their clash of cozener with cozener, their ingenuities of deceit, the "heat of fury" of their entangled action. We remember single scenes, of a marvellous and sometimes cruelly comic reality, like the deathbed of Dampit the drunkard in *A Trick to catch the Old-one*, or that other death scene in *A Chast Mayd in Cheape-side*, where an old sinner makes his exit in grotesque and frightened repentance, while the man and woman whom he may be supposed to have most wronged remember the fact for the first time, as they foresee the stopping of their shameful revenue. Here, as often in Middleton, irony comes out of the mere faithfulness with which he sets before us exactly what would happen at such a moment. His plays are full of these paradoxes of event, which it is the custom to call unpleasant—and which, sometimes, certainly are unpleasant, when the playwright seems to be unaware that some hideous piece of villainy is being set to rights (so far as relative justice is concerned) by a trick of "virtue" hardly less pardonable.

If Bullen is right in his conjecture that *The Widdow* (a play published in 1652 as a "lively piece, drawn by the art of Jonson, Fletcher, and Middleton") belongs to about this date, though revised later, it would seem to be curiously innocent, for a play by Middleton, notwithstanding all its vivid banter and thieves' foolery. In how many plays of this period could the characters say to one another at the close, without irony, "Be good" and "Be honest," as two of the characters do in this? Jonson is for nothing in it, unless as a passing influence; but it is hard to see why Fletcher might not have been the reviser, as well as the writer of one or two of the songs. But the main part, unmistakably, is Middleton's, and it is, perhaps, in this play that the romantic element first shows itself among the incidents and actualities of knavery.

It took Middleton a long time to recognise, as a dramatist, that there was such a thing as honour, even in transactions which he felt it his business to watch from the knaves' point of view because that view was the one which would best entertain his audience. He chose stories, persons and surroundings for their immediate stage effect making them as real and amusing as he could, scene by scene; and it was so rarely that it occurred to him to temper the trickeries of his plots by some honest motive that we find him confusing moral values without due indication of his being aware of it. There is no doubt that he wrote hastily, and with ease, and a man who writes hastily and with ease for the stage will readily sacrifice a point of conscience to a theatrical solution. Once, in *The Roaring Girle*, some frank and convincing honesty comes into the bad company, and has the best of it there. But how much of what gives a pleasant quality to that play is Middleton's, though the play is not less astir than the others with his usual crew and company?

Though the work of each overlaps occasionally, there can be little doubt of the main shares of Middleton and Dekker in *The Roaring Girle*.[1] It was Dekker, undoubtedly, who

---

[1] For the view, according to which the larger part of this play was Middleton's, see *ante*, Chap. II.

Middleton the possibility of that passionate note, by which drama becomes not only drama but poetry?

If, as has been conjectured, *The Old Law* leads the way from the farcical comedies to the tragic comedies like *A Faire Quarrell*, it is in that play that the influence of William Rowley may be first distinguished; and it is impossible not to connect it with the change which came about in the work of Middleton, a change from work almost wholly comic, and of the city kind, to work partly tragic and partly comic in a higher and more romantic sense. We find Rowley's name beside Middleton's on the title-pages of *The Old Law*, *A Faire Quarrell*, *The World tost at Tennis*, *The Spanish Gipsie* and *The Changeling*: most, that is, of the finest of Middleton's later work, with only the two exceptions of *Women beware Women* and *A Game at Chesse*. The manner and measure of this collaboration is not so easy to discover as may at first sight appear. It is his faults that are most obvious in Rowley, his dissonant verse, his over-strained speech, his incapacity for construction, something jagged and uneven in his whole work; and it is only gradually that critics are beginning to realise that these defects are not the essential part of him. His plays have had the not unnatural misfortune to be chaotically printed; verse and prose never clearly distinguished from one another; and some of them are only to be found in a few rare copies of the original editions. It is difficult to be certain of his exact share in many plays to which, rightly or wrongly, his name is appended. One thing is certain: that the plays written by Rowley and Middleton together are finer than any of the plays written by either separately. And it is almost equally certain that Rowley's share in the work was not confined to those scenes or passages in which his actual hand can be distinguished in the versification, but that there was a further and closer collaboration of a kind which no tests of style or versification can ever disentangle. We have seen Middleton working alone, and, to some extent, with Dekker; we shall see him, at the end of his career, again working alone. We have now to consider what is discoverable about Rowley, in such work as he did by himself or in company with others, before we can hope to arrive at any conclusion in regard to the work in which he is the companion of Middleton.

The plays published under Rowley's name or initials are: *A*

new Wonder, A Woman never vext, 1632; *Alls Lost by Lust,*
1633; *A Match at Midnight,* 1633; and *A Shoo-maker a Gentleman,* 1638.   Of these, *A Match at Midnight* has little resemblance to any of his known work while it has a close resemblance
to the early work of Middleton.   It goes with something of the
rapidity of the wild and whirling comedies of about the time of
Your five Gallants, but would add more credit to an imitator
than to Middleton.   Here, as elsewhere, Rowley, in his capacity of actor, may have made slight changes for acting purposes,
which would account for the use of his initials.   There is no
reason for supposing that he had even so much as that to do
with *Fortune by Land and Sea,* published, in 1655, as by Heywood and Rowley, or with *The Thracian Wonder,* attributed
to Webster and Rowley by Kirkman in 1661.   There is little
more probability in the same publisher's attribution to the same
writers of *A Cure for a Cuckold,* which he brought out in the
same year.   Kirkman's word is valueless as evidence, and
there is nothing in the play of which we can say with much
probability that it is by either Webster or Rowley.   Only the
slow and thoughtful quality of some of the verse gives any real
suggestion of Webster; and verse of Webster's kind is quite
possible to imitate.   The drearily comic prose is done after the
pattern of the time, and there is nothing in it distinguishable
from similar hackwork. whether done by Rowley or by others
for the day's wage.[1]

In *The Travailes of The three English Brothers,* published in
1607, with a dedication signed "John Day, William Rowley,
George Wilkins," it is easy, but not very profitable, to trace the
share of Rowley.   He probably put in Zaripha, the Shylock of
the play, and wrote some of the more pompous blank verse and
of the coarser verbal fooling.   In *The Maid in the Mill,*
licensed to Fletcher and Rowley on 29 August, 1623, and played
at the Globe with Rowley as one of the actors, his share and
Fletcher's are quite distinct, and they are divided pretty
equally.   Rowley's verse, by the side of the winged verse of
Fletcher, seems somewhat crabbed and abstract, and the prose
(interspersed with Fletcher's songs) somewhat cold and
laboured.   In *The Witch of Edmonton,* published in 1658 as "a

---

[1] Cf., as to the indications of a co-operation by Webster in this play, *post,*
Chap. VII.

Tragi-Comedy By divers well-esteemed Poets; William Rowley, Thomas Dekker, John Ford, etc.," where Dekker and Ford are both equally evident, in their direction of the two main currents, the share of Rowley is difficult to make out, and could hardly have been considerable. There remains *The Birth of Merlin*,[1] which was published in 1662 as by Shakespeare and Rowley. Langbaine tells us that "William Rowley was not only beloved by those great men, Shakespeare, Fletcher, and Jonson, but likewise writ, with the former, *The Birth of Merlin*." The share of Shakespeare need not be discussed here; the play is crude and lumpish; it is stilted and monotonous in the verse, gross and tame in the prose. It would be pleasant to think that Rowley had no more to do with it than Shakespeare; but it is difficult to be positive in the matter after reading *A Shoo-maker a Gentleman*.

This incongruous and incoherent piece is a tragic farce, which has never been reprinted[2] from the execrable first edition of 1638, where the printer, in his address to "the honest and high-spirited gentlemen of the never decaying art, called the gentle craft," admits with some candour: "I know it may come short of that accurateness both in plot and style that this witty age doth with greater curiosity require"; yet excuses it, on the ground "that as plays were then, some twenty years ago, it was in the fashion." It is a sad jumble of cobblers, kings, "a wise virgin in Wales" and a Juliet's nurse; at one moment, "an angel ascends out of the well and after descends again," at another, there is drinking of blood, and we hear in detail of tortures endured in war; the language varies from "Moulting tyrant, stop thy scandalous breath," used by quarrelling kings, to "Clapperdudgeon" and "Knipperdolin," flung as pet names by the cobbler at his wife. The few good lines which we come across at rare intervals are almost cruelly wasted; the farce which submerges them is a mere desperate attempt at comic realism.

On the title-page of *A new Wonder*, Rowley is described as "one of his Majesties Servants"; he is mentioned among the principal actors in *The Maid in the Mill;* in *The Inner-Temple Masque*, he played Plumporridge; and, in the list of persons in

[1] As to *The Birth of Merlin* and its relation to Middleton's *The Mayor of Quinborough*, see *ante*, Vol. V, Chap. x.
[2] See bibliography, p. 483.

Alls Lost by Lust, we are told that Jaques, "a simple clownish
gentleman," was "personated by the poet." In the plays
which he wrote in collaboration with Middleton, his hand has
been most generally traced in the comic underplots, and, sometimes, as a disturbing element there, working for hardly
more than the ears of the groundlings. In the low peasants'
humour, earthy and almost animal, over which he takes much
trouble in all these plays, sometimes making it really droll,
always making it emphatic and telling, there seems to have
been something which he really cared to do, perhaps because it
was what he could represent best on the stage. In the two
chief plays which he wrote by himself, he wove comic prose not
ineffectively into more serious substance; but in *A Shoo-
maker a Gentleman*, and, indeed, in most of the work done with
Middleton, it stands out in sharp contrast. And this is the
more curious, as we shall find unmistakable signs of a very
different kind of influence exercised by him upon precisely
that serious substance.

For it is not as a comic poet that Rowley is most himself, or
most admirable. Of his two remaining plays, one is a heroic
tragedy and the other a pathetic domestic comedy; and we find
in both, very differently exhibited, the same qualities of sincerity and nobility, often turning to uncouthness or exaggeration,
but never, as in Middleton, losing the moral sense, the honesty
of insight. The action in each is strained beyond probability,
and in one becomes barbarous, in the other artificial; the verse
follows the action, and halts not only through the treasons of a
more than usually treacherous printer. Yet, as the verse is
but an emphasis upon profoundly felt speech, so the action
rests always on a strong human foundation.

In *Alls Lost by Lust* (which deals with a subject made more
famous by Landor in *Count Julian*), Rowley shows himself
poet by his comprehension of great passions, his sympathy
with high moods, and by a sheer and naked speech, which can
grasp filth or heroism with equal strength. He has no measure, though sometimes constraint; no subtlety, though he will
set consciences or clowns arguing in terms of strange pedantry;
no sentiment, though he has all the violences of direct emotion;
and he says what he wants to say and then stops. He has no
ease or grace, and often labours to give point to his humour and

weight to his serious utterances. The kind of verse that characterises him at his best is

> Thy soul is a hired lackey towards hell,

and he can sharpen it thus:

> Time's ancient bawd, opportunity,
> Attends us now, and yet our flaming blood
> Will scarce give leave to opportunity.

Often he will go beyond the bounds of natural speech, not on a carrying imagination, but under the dragging weight of an emphasis which eloquence can do better without. In some of Blake's drawings of naked men with prodigious muscles, sweeping beards and frantic eyes, the intense imitation of emotion has gone further than nature can support. Just so does some of the tragic speech in Rowley falter through defects of mere force. "Rough Rowley, handling song with Esau's hand," as Swinburne has called him in a significant line, sets himself to construct imagery, and does it, sometimes with splendour, but a splendour prolonged to extinction. Thus, he will develop a figure after this manner:

> We'll make so high to quench their silver moons
> And on their carcases an isthmus make
> To pass their straits again and forage them.

Both in fun and in earnest, he plays on words, and is capable of writing "My heart's triangled," as Donne might have done, and of distinguishing the number and position of the points. More often he does it in this wholly Elizabethan manner:

> My honoured friends,
> What we all thought to have borne home in triumph
> Must now be seen there in a funeral,
> Wrecked honour being chief mourner; here's the hearse
> Which we'll all follow.

Even his "virgin martyrs," like Jacinta, who act nobly, are sometimes set talking with horrible detail, as, like Jacinta they spit at their tormentors and wish

> that my tongue
> Were pointed with a fiery Pyramis
> To strike thee through.

It is impossible for him to realise, even in his Dionysia, who dies
with some of the ecstasy of Shakespeare's Cleopatra, that a
woman can be lascivious without talking like a courtesan. His
men can say memorable things, in which there is some of the
passion of meditation; but, however well he knew "what kind
of thing a man's heart" is, he did not know how to give continuously adequate speech to those passions of whose habitation
there he was aware.

In *A new Wonder*, of which the scene lies in London, and
which shows us the strange vehement passions, both petty
and ardent, of business men, their small prides and large resolu-
tions, we have a speech more easily on the level of the occasion,
whether in this heightened way:

> Then be not angry, gentle sir,
> If now a string be touch'd, which hath too long
> Sounded so harshly over all the city;
> I now would wind it to a musical height;

or whether the unrelenting father in prison repels his son with
the direct cry:

> Ha! what art thou?　Call for the keeper there,
> And thrust him out of doors, or lock me up.

Here, as elsewhere, the language is sometimes injured by emphasis, yet there is nothing of Middleton's aim at point and
cleverness, but a speech vividly, and sometimes grossly, natural,
which sticks close to the matter. Its comedy is a kind of
literalness, and so is its pathos; both are crammed with fine
substance, thoughtful humour and thoughtful pity, with that
simple acceptance and rendering of things as they are which
Lamb noted in the play with much satisfaction. It is of this
play that he says: "The old play-writers are distinguished by
an honest boldness of exhibition, they show everything without
being ashamed." Here, there is coarseness and there is clumsi-
ness, but there is no flaw in the essential truthfulness and
reality of the contest in hearts, in which a natural human
charity has its way with invincible softness.

Now, if we begin to look for the influence of Rowley upon

Middleton, we shall find it not so much in the set scenes of low comedy which he inserted among Middleton's verse, as in a new capacity for the rendering of great passions and a loftiness in good and evil which is not to be recognised as an element in Middleton's brilliant and showy genius, and which hardly survives the end of his collaboration with Rowley. The whole range of subject suddenly lifts; a new, more real and more romantic world (more real and more romantic because imagination, rather than memory, is at work) is seen upon the stage; and, by some transformation which could hardly have been mere natural growth, Middleton finds himself to be a poet.

That Middleton learnt from Rowley, or did, with his help, more than either of them could do by himself, is evident for the first time clearly in *A Faire Quarrell*. The best part of the actual writing is not Rowley's. Middleton was a man of flexible mind, and we find in him everywhere a marvellous tact of matching his matter and manner. Never, in his wild comedies, does he bring in false heroics; he can keep on a due actual level beyond any dramatist of his time; and, when a great human moment comes to him, and has to be dealt with, he rises easily, and is no less adequate. He does not rise of himself—his material compels him, he is obedient to it, and, as it would seem, awake to a fiercer impulse like Rowley's. It is certain that Rowley could not have written the two great captain Ager scenes as they stand; but it is equally certain that, with all his promptness of response to an emotion, Middleton could not have begun to render, at such a moral height, such an "absolute man," without some spiritual aid or lift from Rowley. When there, when started, he drew his poetry, as he was wont to do, directly from his subject, and the natural emotion of it; and made a great scene where a weak one would have been contemptible. Can nature and poetry go further together, poetry hardly distinguishable from the direct speech of nature, so warmed is it by human breath? Captain Ager's last words to his mother shine like fire and cut like steel, and are mere plain words with no more rhetoric in them than in this line, which strikes straight:

I never shall have need of honour more.

In the scene of the duel, when all this fire in the man's soul is out, the tamer verses are not less absolute in their disheartened speech:

> What shall be done in such a worthless business
> But to be sorry, and to be forgiven;
> You, sir, to bring repentance, and I pardon?

That the writing, in the two great scenes of captain Ager, is Middleton's, and owes nothing in form, whatever it may owe in substance, to Rowley, can be proved beyond doubt by a mere reading over together of two speeches, one in this play, one in a play so wholly and characteristically Middleton's as *A Chast Mayd in Cheape-side*—the speech of captain Ager, which begins

> Mine? think me not so miserable,

and ends

> Without which I 'm ten fathoms under coward,
> That now am ten degrees above a man,
> Which is but one of virtue's easiest wonders;[1]

and the speech of Sir Walter which begins

> O death! is this
> A place for you to weep?

and ends

> this shows like
> The fruitless sorrow of a careless mother,
> That brings her son with dalliance to the gallows,
> And then stands by and weeps to see him suffer.[2]

The difference is all in the feeling; there is none in the phrasing.

But the difference in the feeling! There is no indication, in anything which Middleton has so far written by himself, that he was capable of conceiving a character like captain Ager, or of keeping such a character on a single level of high emotion. This Rowley could do, and it can scarcely be doubted that he was the "only begetter" of what he left to Middleton to develop. It is Rowley who writes the dedication, and it is evident that he takes much of the credit of the play to himself. "You see, sir," he says, "I write as I speak, and I speak as I am, and that 's excuse enough for me." His share in the actual writing, indeed, is almost too evident; there is cold, pedantic, sour and

---

[1] Act II, sc. I.　　　　　[2] Act V, sc. I.

crabbed prose, aping comedy, and, in the scene between Jane and the physician, a hard, reasoning kind of serious verse which jars singularly on the rich and copious verse of Middleton, in the finer parts of the play. Some of the worst of the mechanical fooling in prose was added in a second edition, and (the public being much the same in all ages) it was probably added because the original sample had given much satisfaction. Rowley worked for hire, and this is some of his hired work.

It was not long after the time of *A Faire Quarrell* that Middleton and Rowley collaborated together in the admirable and entertaining masque, *The World tost at Tennis*. For the most part, Middleton's masques are tame and tedious, without originality in the invention of lyrical quality in the songs. In one only, *The Inner-Temple Masque,* is there any natural gaiety, any real quaintness or humour; and, as we find Rowley's name among the actors, in the humorous peasant part of Plumporridge, may it not be conjectured that he had some share in the writing? His heavy tread is as distinctly heard through all the opening part of *The World tost at Tennis*, as Middleton's new voice is heard in the later part. Middleton rarely wrote a lovelier succession of cadences than in these lines spoken by Deceit to Simplicity:

> The world, sweetheart, is full of cares and troubles,
> No match for thee; thou art a tender thing,
> A harmless, quiet thing, a gentle fool,
> Fit for the fellowship of ewes and rams;
> Go, take thine ease and pipe; give me the burden,
> The clog, the torment, the heart-break, the world:
> Here 's for thee, lamb, a dainty oaten pipe.

And there is suavity, swiftness and a quaint fantastic colouring in the verse chattered against hypocrites and puritans by the Five Starches.

It was probably about the time when he was engaged on his masques that Middleton wrote *The Witch;* and this may well have been his first attempt at a purely romantic play. The versification is done with astonishing ease, in long, loose, rapid lines; and, in the witches' songs, there is not only a ghastly fancy awake, but something nearer to a fine lyric cadence than he ever caught before or since. It is through the interpolation, as it obviously was, of some of these lines in the very imperfect text of *Macbeth*, that a play in which the main action is almost a parody of the romantic drama has come to be looked upon as one of Middleton's chief works. The mere writing throughout is good; but the easy eloquent dialogue covers no more than the gaps and deformations of the main outline. The witches bring a new element into Middleton's work, a wild fancy, of which he had shown hardly a trace; in the rest of the play, he does but practise in the romantic manner. They stand in dim middle air, between the old vile pitiable crone of Dekker in *The Witch of Edmonton*, who is dreadfully human, and the "crowned empress of the nether clefts of hell" in *Macbeth*, who bears no resemblance to the other Hecate but in her name, and who is more dreadful because she is not human. But Lamb has said finally all that need be said on these fundamental differences.

After the experiment of *The Witch*, Middleton seems to have returned to his collaboration with Rowley, and it is to this period that we must assign the play by which both are now chiefly remembered, the tragedy called *The Changeling*. It is Rowley who begins the play, and thus introduces and characterises both Beatrice and De Flores. The germ of both is there, and the rest of the play is but its growth. But, even in this opening, there are distinct, though slight, traces of Middleton, as if collaboration had begun already. Middleton takes up the thread in the second act, and has both hands upon it in the third, though, at the end of the great scene, Rowley seems to snatch the whole web out of his hands and to twist it into an abrupt end. In all this part, mainly written by Middleton, there is a restraint never paralleled elsewhere in his work; nowhere else are words used with such fruitful frugality, or so much said in so little. And this bareness, this fierce reticence, lead up, with a stealthy directness, to that outbreak of evil joy when De Flores cries

> O this act
> Has put me into spirit!

and the modest murderess answers in astonishment

> Why, tis impossible thou canst be so wicked,
> Or shelter such a cunning cruelty
> To make his death the murderer of my honour!

The whole scene is written in words of white heat; Middleton has distilled into it the essence of his own genius and of the genius of Rowley; in Leigh Hunt's famous and revealing words concerning De Flores, it is "at once tragical, probable, and poetical" beyond almost any single scene in the Elizabethan drama—a scene unlike anything in Shakespeare, but comparable, not as poetry but as drama, with Shakespeare. And it is on the level of this great scene that the play ends, in a splendid horror, and it is Rowley who ends as he began the dreadful lives of De Flores and of Beatrice. Rowley's underplot and some of Middleton's intermediate action do what they can to deform a play which, but for them, would be a noble and complete masterpiece. Yet the single impression left upon our minds is scarcely affected by them. The play is De Flores, and De Flores seems to grow greater as he passes from one to the other of the two playwrights, as they collaborate visibly at his creation. This great creation is the final result and justification of Middleton and Rowley's work in common; for it is certain that De Flores as he is would never have been possible either to Rowley or to Middleton alone.

The Spanish Gipsie is generally put down almost as a whole to Middleton, and even Swinburne refuses to see the hand of Rowley in "the more high-toned passages." It seems possible that Rowley wrote a larger part of the play than Middleton, and not by any means only the gipsy scenes, with their jollity, dancing and crabbed ballad singing. The opening, no doubt, was actually written by Middleton; but it has a quality unusual in his work, and not unusual in the work of Rowley. It is as if Rowley stood behind Middleton, controlling him. Most of the prose, both when it goes creeping and tedious with Sancho and Soto, and when it overflows into doggerel and occasionally unsavoury snatches of song, has Rowley's manner and substance; but he is to be traced, also, in the slow and powerful verse which ends the third act, in lines like

> This is the triumph of a soul drowned deep
> In the unfathomed seas of matchless sorrow,

and in the whole attitude and speech of a father who speaks with the very accent of Julianus in *Alls Lost by Lust:*

> Teach me how I may now be just and cruel,
> For henceforth I am childless.

Rowley is heard, also, through much of the fourth act, though Middleton comes in unmistakably towards the end, and is the writer of the whole fifth act. The characters are distributed between them, and so charming a person as Constanza is decidedly at her best when she speaks through Middleton. The whole play is not made very probable, or meant to be so; it is a frank romance, with stage mysteries, some of them thrilling, like the wonderful opening scene, some, mere tricks of convenience; and there is a freshness and pleasantness about it which seem to show us Middleton in full and final acceptance of the romantic manner.

Yet it is difficult to assign to any other period the comedy of *Any Thing for a Quiet Life*, printed in 1662, and so badly printed that it is not easy to distinguish prose from verse, the more so as the one seems to be set to run in no very different measures from the other. It seems to be a late and only return to the earlier manner of the farcical comedies of city life, with shopkeeping scenes of the old random brilliance and the old domestic fooleries. Even more matter is crammed into it, and this even more hastily, and there is the old fierce vigour of talk. But, in two plays, published together in 1657, we see what seems to be almost the last mood of Middleton, after his collaboration with Rowley was at an end, and the influence, perhaps, not wholly evaporated. *More dissemblers besides Women*, which is characteristic of Middleton in its tangle of virtues and hypocrisies, its masquerade of serious meanings and humorous disguises, is written in verse of a lovely and eager quality, which bends with equal flexibility to the doings of "those dear gipsies" and to the good cardinal's concerns of conscience "in a creature that 's so doubtful as a woman." It is a particoloured thing, and has both beauty and oddity. But, in *Women beware Women*, we find much of Middleton's finest and ripest work, together with his most rancid "comic relief"; a stern and pitiless "criticism of life" is interrupted by foul and foolish clowning; and a tragedy of the finest comic savour ends in a mere heap of corpses, where

> vengeance met vengeance
> Like a set match, as if the plagues of sin
> Had been agreed to meet here all together.

"I 've lost myself in this quite," Middleton might say with the duke, and rarely has better material been more callously left to spoil. There is no finer comedy of its kind in the whole of Elizabethan drama than the scene between Livia, Bianca and the widow; and the kind is a rare, bitter and partly tragic one. The human casuistry is flawless; the irony is an illumination rather than a correction of reality. And these vile people are alive, and the vices in them work with a bewildering and convincing certainty. The technique of such scenes as that in which husband and wife flaunt their new finery at each other is not less than astonishing. All the meaner passions are seen in probable action, speaking without emphasis, in a language never too far from daily speech for the complete illusion of reality. There is not even the interruption of a mere splendour; no one speaks greatly or utters irrelevant poetry; here, poetry is the very slave and confidant of drama, heroically obedient. But the heights of *The Changeling*, the nobility of even what was evil in the passions of that play, are no longer attained. Middleton, left to himself, has returned, with new experience and new capacity, to his own level.

With one more experiment, and this a masterpiece of a wholly new kind, "the only work of English poetry," says Swinburne, "which may properly be called Aristophanic," the career of Middleton comes, so far as we know, to an end. *A Game at Chesse* is a satire, taking the popular side against Spain, and it was the Spanish ambassador Gondomar, the "Machiavel-politician" and Black Knight of its chess-board, who caused the suppression of the play, and the punishment of all concerned in it. It is the most perfect of Middleton's works, and it carries some of his most intimate qualities to a point they had not reached before. Banter turns into a quite serious and clear and bitter satire; burlesque becomes a severe and elegant thing; the verse, beginning formally and always kept well within bounds, is fitted with supreme technical skill to this new, outlandish matter; there are straight confessions of sins and symbolic feasts of vices, in which a manner acquired by the city chronologer for numbering the feasts and fastings of the city is adapted by him to finer use. We learn now how

> fat cathedral bodies
> Have very often but lean little soul,

and the imagery, already expressive, takes on a new colour of
solemn mockery.

> From this leviathan-scandal that lies rolling
> Upon the crystal waters of devotion,

is sometimes the language of the Black Knight, and sometimes

> In the most fortunate angle of the world
> The court hath held the city by the horns
> Whilst I have milked her.

Technique, in drama and verse alike, never flags; and the play is
a satire and criticism, no longer of city manners or of personal
vices, but of the nation's policy; and that it was accepted as
such, by the public and by the government of the time, is proved
by the fifteen hundred pounds taken by the actors in nine days,
and by the arrest of Middleton for what was really a form of
patriotism.

We have no record of anything written by Middleton during
the three remaining years of his life. *A Game at Chesse* is the
culmination of those qualities which seem to have been most
natural and instinctive in him, in spite of the splendid work of
another kind which he did with Rowley in *The Changeling*. His
genius was varied and copious, and he showed his capacity to do
almost every kind of dramatic work with immense vigour.   Life
is never long absent from the tangled scenes, in which a hetero-
geneous crowd hurries by, not stopping long enough to make us
familiar with most of the persons in it, but giving us an unmistakable human savour.   Few of the plays are quite satisfactory all through; there is almost always some considerable flaw,
in construction, in characterisation, or in aesthetic taste; yet
hardly one of them can be neglected in our consideration of the
dramatist's work as a whole.   In single scenes of tragedy
and of comedy (romantic comedy, the comedy of manners,
farce and satire) he can hold his own against any contemporary,
and it is only in lyric verse that he is never successful.   He
became a remarkable dramatic poet; but he was not born to
sing.   Poetry came to him slowly, and he had to disentangle
it from more active growths of comic energy.   It came to him
when he began to realise that there was something in the world
besides cheating shopkeepers and cozening lawyers, and the

bargains made between men and women for bodies, not souls.
With the heightening of emotion his style heightens, and as his
comedy refines itself his verse becomes subtler. In Middleton's work, the cry of De Flores

> Ha! what art thou that tak'st away the light
> Betwixt that star and me? I dread thee not:
> 'T was but a mist of conscience;

is almost unique in imagination. And it is drama even more
than it is poetry. His style is the most plausible of all styles
in poetry, and it has a probable beauty, giving an easy grace
of form to whatever asks to be expressed. It rarely steps
aside to pick up a jewel, nor do jewels drop naturally out of
its mouth.

CHAPTER IV

Thomas Heywood

IT is in writers of the second rank—and of these, with his abundant merit and attractive idiosyncrasy, Thomas Heywood unmistakably was—that we find it easiest to study the progress and expansion of the form of art practised by them. In the brief but often interesting addresses prefixed by Heywood to his plays, he was fond of referring to the changes in public taste which playwrights had been called upon to consult in the course of his own long experience; but he seems to care little about indicating his own preference for either old style or new, being manifestly as ready to fall in with the latter as he had been to put forth his best endeavours in the former. When commending to favour a drama depending for its effect entirely on character, situations and dialogue, and introducing

> No Drum, nor Trumpet, nor Dumbe show,
> No Combate, Marriage, not so much Today
> As Song, Dance, Masque, to bumbaste out our Play—

he hastens to add:

> Yet these all good, and still in frequent use
> With our best Poets.[1]

And, as with matter, so with form: recalling the time when rime was in fashion in plays and "strong lines were not lookt after," he takes occasion to observe that what is out of date now may come into fashion again "and sute well"—and, for himself, he is clearly quite ready to stop or rime his lines with his fellows.[2]

[1] Prologue to *The English Traveller*.
[2] Epilogue (to the Reader) to *The Royall King, and The Loyall Subject*.

He has no wish to criticise or to theorise, or to set himself up
as a representative of any special class or select sort of English
drama. Had he not, at the beginning of his twoscore or more
years of labours for the stage, dramatised both history and
historical romance in plays to which no bold prentice could listen
without breaking into rapturous applause and no citizen's
wife without dropping a sympathetic tear; and, as for "song,
dance and masque," had not Homer and Ovid and Apuleius
been alike laid under contribution by him for providing entertainments from which neither learned nor lewd would go home
unsatisfied? Even dramatic species to which he felt no personal
attraction—such as that comedy of "humours flash'd in wit"
which satirised types of humanity neither heroic nor attractive
—he declined to depreciate, merely urging those who cultivated
them not to eschew the treatment of other and loftier subjects:
the deeds of "great Patriots, Dukes and Kings," for the
memorising of which the English drama (some plays of his own
with the rest) had hitherto been notably distinguished.[1]

But, while Heywood, cheerfully suiting himself and his art
to a variety of dramatic genres, attained to virtuosity rather
than to supreme excellence in the chronicle history and the
romantic drama, and did as well as many others in the comedy
of manners and the mythological play, he associated his name
after a more intimate fashion with a species which had a character, and a future, of its own. This was the domestic drama,
which, on the background of ordinary family life, presents an
action of deep and commanding moral interest. Heywood was
not the inventor of the domestic drama, which is as thoroughly
English in its genesis and in a great part of its development as
the national historical drama itself, justly held in high honour
by him. Nor was it given to him, or to any of his contemporaries, to realise in the Elizabethan age the possibilities of
this species with a fulness comparable to that reached by others
—the comedy of manners, for instance. But he achieved
memorable and enduring results in a field in which few of his
fellow dramatists whose names are known to us made more
than tentative efforts, and to which the greatest of them ab-

---

[1] See the interesting prologue to *A Challenge for Beautie*, where the superiority of English historical plays to the dramatic efforts of other nations
is roundly asserted.

stained from turning his attention except, as it were, in passing.
The simplicity of·these works cannot be held to detract from
the honour due to the art which produced them, or to impair the
recognition implied in the fact that, in the history of European
literature, the name of Thomas Heywood is linked to those of
great writers, to some of whom it was probably unknown—
Steele and Richardson, Diderot and Lessing.

Thomas Heywood was born, somewhere about the year
1572, in Lincolnshire, where his family must have been of good
standing and repute.   We have it on his own authority that he
was at one time a resident member of the university of Cambridge, where he saw "tragedyes, comedyes, historyes, pastorals
and shewes, publicly acted," and "the graduates of good place
and reputation specially parted" in these performances.[1]   The
time-honoured tradition, which unfortunately it is impossible
to corroborate with the aid of either college or university
records, that he was a fellow of Peterhouse, rests on an explicit
statement made by the bookseller and actor William Cartwright not more than ten years after Heywood's death.[2]   But
it is practically certain that he never held a fellowship at Peterhouse, and, among the few incidental references to Cambridge
scattered through his writings, there is but one which introduces the name of the college to which he is said to have belonged—and that, it must be confessed, in no very helpful
way.[3]

By 1596, Heywood is mentioned in Henslowe's diary as
writing, or having written, a play; but as to the time and
circumstances of his taking up the twofold vocation of actor and
playwright we know nothing.   No link of any sort can have
existed between him and the "university wits," whose academi-
cal experiences and entrance into London life belong to the
preceding decade, and from whose arrogance and affectations he
was equally free.   He became connected in turn with several
companies of players—probably beginning with the Admiral's

---

[1] *Apology for Actors* (Shakespeare Society edition), p. 28.

[2] In the dedication prefixed to his edition of the *Apology*, published in 1658
under the title *The Actor's Vindication*.

[3] In *The Wise-woman Of Hogsdon*, act IV, Sencer, disguised as a pedant,
caps the assertion of "Sir Boniface" that he was "student in Brazennose" by
"*Petrus dormit securus:* I was Sir of Peeterhouse." Fleay promptly concluded that Heywood acted Sencer.

men at the Rose, and, in 1634, becoming a servant of the king
(Charles I).   While a sound patriot, Heywood seems to have
had no love for courts;[1] though he celebrated the glories of
the great queen in one of his early plays as well as in a history
of the trials of her youth, indited the praises of Anne of Denmark five years after he had attended her funeral and hailed
queen Henrietta Maria's hopes of motherhood in more than one
loyal prologue.   On the other hand, his attachment to the
city of London, though not, so far as we know, due to any
official or hereditary tie, was very strong and enduring, and
comprehended both the town and its inhabitants.[2]   He celebrated the erection of the Royal Exchange,[3] whose interior is
admirably described in a comedy generally attributed to him,[4]
and of "Crosbie House";[5] he wrote, as we shall see, a series
of mayoralty pageants for divers city companies and immortal-
ised their coats of arms as blazoned on the shields borne at
the siege of Jerusalem;[6] he commemorated the labours of the
docks.[7]   He held up to honour the name of a princely merchant
like Sir Thomas Gresham,[8] and, for the *flos juventutis*, the
prentices of the city, he always kept a warm corner in his heart.[9]
In short, he was a Londoner every inch of him; and, though
few of our Elizabethan dramatists have better pictured the
freshness of rural life, and the jollity of its sports and pastimes,
he recognised the perennial superiority of the vicinity of St.
Paul's, and was capable of contrasting, in a daring paradox,

> the toil and travell of the country
> And quiet gaine of cities blessednesse.[10]

[1] Compare with the general tone of *The Royall King, and The Loyall
Subject*, Wendoll's words on making his exit in *A Woman Kilde with Kindnesse*.

[2] Fleay's suggestion that Heywood was one of the Master Stationers is
hardly offered as more than a happy thought.

[3] *Part II of If you know not me*, etc.

[4] *The Fayre Mayde of the Exchange*.

[5] *Part I of Edward IV*.

[6] *The Foure Prentises*.

[7] His pamphlet on the royal ship *The Sovereign of the Seas* contains an
account of ship-building from Noah's ark downwards.

[8] *Part II of If you know not me*, etc.

[9] *The Foure Prentises* and *Part I of Edward IV; in Loves Maistresse*,
Vulcan has "cyclops and prentices" in his smithy.

[10] *Part II of If you know me not*, etc.

It may be added that the moral code of the citizens of London was not one with which Heywood can have been naturally inclined to quarrel; though, of course, in his latter days, he was obliged by his "quality" to retort upon "that most horrible *Histriomastix* and the bitter juice of that *Coloquintida* and *Hemlocke*, which can neither relish the peace of the Church nor Common-weale."[1] There is little to be found in his plays against puritans or puritanism,[2] and even in his *Apology* he abstains from those *Satirica Dictaeria* and *Comica Scommata*, which he declares to be contrary to his practice.[3]

Heywood's industry as a playwright was, beyond all doubt, extraordinary, though far from unparalleled. His often quoted statement, made in 1633,[4] that he had "either an entire hand, or at least a main finger" in two hundred and twenty plays, Fleay, rather perversely, has sought to interpret in the sense which the words assuredly will not bear, that this total included all the plays in which Heywood had acted during the thirty years (or thereabouts) in question—inasmuch as in most of these plays he had, no doubt, inserted "gag," while many of them had been altered by him. This, in Fleay's opinion, would warrant the conclusion that only about twoscore plays were actually written by Heywood, who is not known to have been a frequent collaborator with other playwrights. In 1633, however, Heywood's connection with the theatre had extended over at least thirty-seven years, and an average of half-a-dozen plays *per annum*, in which he was concerned as sole or joint author, or as reviser, is not inconceivable, if, together with the general character of his dramatic writings, which will be considered immediately, the spirit in which he composed them and the little care which he took of them, after their appearance on the stage, be taken into account.

Nothing is more certain than that he gave little or no thought to the destiny of his plays as "literature." He wrote them,

---

[1] "To the Reader," prefixed to *A Mayden-Head well lost.*

[2] In *Part II of If you know not me*, etc., the dishonest factor Timothy Thinbeard is said by his principal to have been "so pure of life that I would have trusted him with all I had." In *A Woman Kilde with Kindnesse*, Mrs. Frankford's seducer comments on her remorseful reflections: "Fie! fie! you talk too much like a puritan."

[3] "To the Reader," prefixed to *The Iron Age.*

[4] "To the Reader," prefixed to *The English Traveller.*

inprimis, no doubt, for a living, and, also, in obedience to that impulse towards dramatic production which was never more prevalent than in the period of his connection with the stage, but which is not necessarily the same thing as poetic inspiration. Manifestly, he loved the theatre, which was to him a world in itself,[1] as it is to many actors and to not a few playwrights whose sense of their importance in the world outside is too great to allow them to confess it. But this did not make him anxious to find new ways and methods for compassing old ends. Like his fellow dramatists, he was constantly on the look-out for interesting dramatic subjects, and he took them where he found them, setting to work, we may rest assured, without loss of time and accomplishing his task "all of a piece." To have finished his play and brought it on the stage, was enough for him: he was careless about printing, and, on at least one occasion, had to submit as well as he could to the appearance of a corrupt copy, taken down by some enterprising expert in stenography and "put in print (scarce one word trew)."[2] Such plays of his as he allowed to be published he sent forth "with great modesty and small noise," and, above all "singly," not "exposed to the publike view of the world in numerous sheets, and a large volume"—like Ben Jonson's "works," or Shakespeare's.[3] But, whether or not his rapidity of production was such as to expose him, as Fleay conjectures, to contemporary dramatic satire in the character of Posthaste[4]— whether or not we are to believe Kirkman's ingenious statement that he was in the habit of writing his plays on the back of tavern-bills (which, no doubt, would satisfactorily account for the loss of many of them)—whether or not, according to the same authority, he, for several years together, imposed on himself the rule of writing a minimum of a sheet a day—his rate of productivity cannot be said to be left unexplained. His pen was facile, because his mind was both fresh and ready, and because, to use a vigorous German colloquialism, he "sang

---

[1] He that denyes then theaters should be,
He may as well deny a world to me.
"The Author to his Booke "(*An Apology for Actors*).

[2] See prologue to *If you know not me*, etc.

[3] See the address "To the Reader" prefixed to *The Fair Maid Of The West* (printed 1631).

[4] In Marston's *Histrio-Mastix*.

as his beak had grown." Heywood's *naïveté* is, perhaps, the most delightful element in his genius, although the directness of expression to which it leads him frequently sins against refinement.

After Heywood had been an actor and a playwright for twelve years or more—possibly at an earlier date—he bethought himself of turning his proved ability as a writer, and the studies which he cannot have allowed to lie fallow since his Cambridge days, to what the age would deem a more strictly literary account. Beginning with a translation of Sallust (1608), he produced a long series of compositions, of which as complete as possible a list will be furnished elsewhere,[1] but which in no instance, with the exception of the *Apology for Actors*, and, perhaps, the historical narrative entitled *England's Elizabeth* (to be noticed below in connection with the play which he based upon it), have any special interest for a generation not so much addicted to useless learning as was the author's own. We therefore set aside his two long poetical productions, *Troicus Britannicus, or Great Britain's Troy*, which tells its tale *ab ovo* down to the pedigree of king James I, and the didactic *Hierarchy of the Blessed Angels*, equal at all events to the ornate promise of its title-page. On a similar encyclopaedic pattern he composed *Nine Books of Women*, reprinted after his death under the still more ambitious title *The General History of Women*. Posterity would probably consent to burn these compilations, if from their ashes could be produced the *Lives of all the Poets*, with which the author had made some progress and which began with "the first before Homer"—and may have ended with Shakespeare.[2] *The Lives and Acts of Nine of the most Worthy Women* (three Jews, three Gentiles and three Christians) savours, it must be confessed, more entirely of the bookmaker. In addition, Heywood was an indefatigable translator and paraphraser, and one of his lengthiest publications, *Pleasant Dialogues and Drammas* (of which the date of publication is 1637), consists,

---

[1] See bibliography.

[2] In *The Fayre Mayde of the Exchange*, generally attributed to Heywood, Bowdler, "a humerous gallant," says: "I never read anything but Venus and Adonis." "Why," replies the Cripple, "that's the very quintessence of love."

mainly, of versions of Erasmus, Textor and Lucian in heroic verse, and of Ovid in blank, together with a long (and disagreeable) dialogue reproduced from the *Maechden-Pflicht* of Vader Cats (1618). To these pieces are added a series of prologues and epilogues, with as many epitaphs, elegies, epigrams, acrostics and anagrams thrown in as a last search of the author's cupboards can have produced. This piece of bookmaking has scant interest for the literary student except in so far as it helps to illustrate the extraordinary influence of the *Colloquies* of Erasmus, which continued for more than a century after their original appearance, and which, as has been pointed out by the editor of the *Pleasant Dialogues*, is distinctly noticeable in the English drama of the Elizabethan and Jacobean ages.[1]

It cannot be said that the *Apology for Actors* (published in 1612) holds a very important place in the controversy between the stage and its adversaries, which is narrated in a later chapter of this volume, where Heywood's contribution to the contention is discussed with the rest.[2] Biographically, it interests us as giving proof not only of his learning, which is solid and firsthand, as well as varied and ready for use, but also of a natural moderation and courtesy which led him to abstain from all personalities. And, while we find him anxious for the good report of the profession to which he belonged, and which such men as himself and Alleyn—not to mention greater names—adorned, he at the same time shows a modesty harmonising with all that we know of him as a writer. In the double capacity of actor and playwright—for it is noticeable that he seems to have no wish to distinguish between the two functions—he describes himself as "the youngest and weakest of the nest wherein he was hatcht," and liable to the charge of presumptuousness for venturing to "soare this pitch before others of the same brood, more fledge, and of better wing" than himself.[3]

---

[1] See the introduction to W. Bang's edition, where Fleay's assumption that any of the pieces contained in the book had previously formed part of the *Five Plays in One* performed in 1597, is rightly rejected as hazardous.

[2] See *post*, Chap. xiv.

[3] Heywood's admiration of his chief fellow dramatists, and the kindly way in which these men spoke of one another, are illustrated by the well known lines in the *Hierarchy of the Blessed Angels*, cited in Collier's introduction to his edition of the *Apology for Actors*.

To his own plays he makes no reference or allusion in the course of his tract, except in the passage where he insists on the moral purpose of the drama:

> The unchaste are by us shewed in their errors in the persons of Phryne, Lais, Thais, Flora; and amongst us Rosamond and Mistresse Shore.

The most rigid of censors could not set up a more "respectable" standard of morality and regard for authority than that desired by the author of the *Apology;* though there is obviously a polemic meaning in his protest against the practice of putting "bitternesse" and "liberall invective" into the mouths of children—say of the chapel—"supposing their juniority to be a priviledge for any railing."

It has been concluded—though it cannot be proved—that from 1634-5 onwards Heywood ceased to write for the stage. His *Pleasant Dialogues and Drammas*, a miscellaneous collection of essays such as many a modern author has indulged himself by publishing towards the close of his career, was completed by 1637; and the last of the seven pageants which he produced from 1631 onwards, was for the year 1639. These compositions attest his cordial appreciations of the glories of the city under the auspices of haberdashers, ironmongers and drapers—"the dignity of Merchants," he exclaims with conviction, "who can tell?"[1] He seems to have still been living in 1641, when a *Life of Ambrosius Merlin*, compiled by him, appears to have been printed; indeed, he is spoken of, as if alive, so late as 1648, in *The Satire against Satirists*.[2]

It seems to agree best with Heywood's method of production to name his numerous dramatic works in their chronological sequence, so far as this can be ascertained or, with more or less probability, surmised, without, however, adhering to it with absolute rigidity. A classification of his plays could be attempted

---

[1] See *Porta Pietatis*.

[2] Introduction to *Apology*, p. VI. The passage is quoted in Pearson's reprint, vol. I, p. XXV:

> So may you come to sleep in fur at last
>
> .   .   .   .   .   .
>
> And Heywood sing your acts in lofty verse.

without much difficulty, if it were worth while; but he, at least, would certainly not have thought it so.

Priority of mention may, accordingly, be given to *The Foure Prentises of London. With the Conquest of Jerusalem*, though, possibly, it was preceded on the stage by one or both parts of *Edward IV*. In the earliest extant edition, which is dated 1615, the preface states the play to have been in the fashion "some fifteene or sixteene yeares agoe"; but Fleay has shown that there must have been an earlier edition in, or not long after, 1610, and that Heywood's play, probably, was the *Godfrey of Bulloigne* performed by the Admiral's men as early as July, 1594.[1] And, though Heywood certainly did not take the story of his play direct from Tasso, it must be considered a curious coincidence that, in 1594, Richard Carew's translation of five cantos of *Gerusalemme* appeared in print.[2] Whatever its immediate source, this play, which combines the crude compiling method of the early chronicle history with the violently symmetrical improbabilities of the popular romance, is primitive to the last degree. The four heroes of the piece, whom their sire, the "olde Earl of Bulloign" had, under stress of misfortune, apprenticed in London city, after taking service for the holy wars pass through divers strange adventures in divers lands till they meet at last before the "high wals of Hierusalem." Their sister, whose spirit equals theirs, follows her star to the same spot, disguised as a page; and a French lady, in love with one of the brothers, accompanies him in similar gear. After the victory has been won (to the cries of "A Syon! A Jerusalem!") each of the brothers obtains a crown—Godfrey preferring one of thorns—and the story ends in an accumulation of happiness. Presenter and dumb-show have helped on the epic movement of the action, hardly any attempt being made by the author to soar into poetry, though he abounds in classical allusions. But the simplicity of Godfrey's enthusiasm on beholding the

> sacred path our Saviour trod
> When he came riding to Hierusalem

---

[1] Cf. Fleay, *English Drama*, vol. I, p. 282. The difficulties in the way cannot, however, be ignored; see Greg. W. W., *Henslowe's Diary*, vol. II, pp. 166, 284. The indication noted by Collier that this was the play in which. in 1602, Wentworth Smith collaborated with Heywood is not convincing.

[2] Warton, vol. IV, p. 350.

is impressive; and the whole play must have told irresistibly upon "the Honest and High-spirited Prentises" to whom it was afterwards dedicated, and to whom Godfrey's accurate description of his own and his brother's military functions, which has a strong smack of the Artillery Garden, must have specially appealed.

In the amusing farce, *The Knight of the Burning Pestle*,[1] in which Beaumont and Fletcher ridiculed those very civic tastes which Heywood's play had sought to gratify, fun is incidentally made of *The Foure Prentises*, as well as of the plays which will be noted next, and of a drama entitled *The Bold Beachams* (Beauchamps), which, without good authority, has been attributed to Heywood.[2]

In the two plays, each of them in two parts, which next come under consideration, Heywood worked on the model of the old chronicle history pure and simple. Though doubt has been thrown on Heywood's authorship of the earlier of these plays, *King Edward IV*, on the ground of its superiority to the rest of the dramatist's earlier work,[3] it may confidently be accepted as his, in view of the general unevenness in the relative merits of his plays, and of the fact that, in its sentimental as well as its humorous scenes, the piece is in a vein thoroughly his own. *Edward IV*, which, after the full title[4] had been entered in the Stationers' register in 1599, was printed in the following year, makes no attempt at dramatic unity—for it can hardly be said to derive this from the personality of the city's favourite king, Edward of the "gadding eye." As has been pointed out by Schelling,[5] the two parts of the play contain "not less than five stories indifferently connected together by personages that fill *rôles* in two or more"—viz. the story of the bastard Falconbridge's siege of London, in which were possibly incorporated reminiscences of *The Siege of London*, a play revived by the Admiral's men in December, 1594, and in which the gallant flat-caps are not forgotten, while we meet with an original humorous figure in the person of the well-meaning but unintelligible

[1] Cf. *post*, Chap. v.

[2] See Fleay, *u.s.*, vol. I, p. 287.

[3] By Fleay, who, I think, is successfully controverted by Greg, *Henslowe's Diary*, vol. II, p. 173.

[4] See bibliography.   [5] Vol. I, pp. 282-3.

Maister Josselin; the diverting episode of Hobs the tanner of Tamworth, a figure borrowed from an old ballad, who accurately represents the indifference of the populace towards the question at issue in the wars of the Roses; the futile expedition of king Edward to France (in which Louis XI makes his first appearance on the English stage); the murder of the little princes in the Tower, a tragic tale told with homely pathos; and, lastly, the story of Jane Shore, which alone stretches from the first into the second part of the play. The long-lived popularity of this story, which, also, was taken from an old ballad, and which found its way again and again into English dramatic and epic literature,[1] needs no explanation. Heywood's treatment of the figure of the erring wife, whose goodness of heart is attested by her openness to melting charity, and by her sorrow for her sin, as well as that of the high-minded and forgiving husband, is full of fine feeling; and it is to be regretted that, near its close, the episode should be marred by the unnecessary fool's play of Jockie and Jeffrey, with which the dramatist thought it his duty to gratify his patrons. The minor character of Mistress Blague, Jane Shore's sunshine friend, is admirably drawn. As for the death of husband and wife, it is sentimental drama of the purest water, but none the less in its place for that.

As it stands, Heywood's other chronicle play, *If you know not me, You know no bodie:*[2] *Or, The troubles of Queene Elizabeth*, surreptitiously printed from a stenographic copy in 1605, and revived in 1631, near the time of the publication of the author's *England's Elizabeth,* is, so far as *Part I* is concerned, little better than a jumble of misprinted fragments. It is clear, at the same time, that this portion of the work must, at best, have been a crude *ad captandum* treatment of Elizabeth's experiences before her accession, following its text-book,

---

[1] As to Churchyard's *Shore's Wife* in *A Mirror for Magistrates*, cf. Vol. III, pp. 205 and 223. It is open to question whether Chettle and Day's play of *Shore* ("wherein Shore's wife is written"), acted in 1602, was an independent piece of work; in Rowe's *Jane Shore* (1714), which, at a recent date, was still to be seen on the stage, no trace of a connection with Heywood's play is apparent.

[2] The phrase, which the instincts of the publisher may be supposed to have suggested as a title, seems to have been used proverbially; in *Part I of Edward IV*, Hobs the tanner applies it to himself.

Heywood's own monograph *England's Elizabeth,*[1] in depicting the martyr-like rectitude of the Protestant princess who suffered *tanquam ovis* in adversity, and who, after her fortune had turned, received from the hands of the lord mayor her prize and palladium—an English Bible. What availed the double-dyed animosity of the ruthless Gardiner against a fortitude so innocent that even king Philip was loth to be unkind? Repeated dumb-shows and some very unsophisticated clownery helps on the action. *Part II*, which is much better preserved, was not better worth preserving. After a long and tedious treatment of the magnificence of Sir Thomas Gresham, and the reckless prodigality of his nephew Jack, we have, as a sudden episode, the attempt against the queen's life by William Parry (which was plotted in 1583–4);[2] whereupon, a chorus, professing to bridge the interval between 1585 and 1588, brings us to the year of the Armada. But nothing follows except a rather bald account of this climax of Elizabethan glories, finishing with a succession of "posts," recalling with a difference, the ἄγγελοι of the *Persae*. No doubt the whole of this production was brought out hurriedly soon after the death of the great queen, having to serve its purpose *tant bien que mal;* and, though it is not without details of interest and contains at least one passage of real poetic feeling,[3] it bears the fatal mark of haste.

A third dramatic composition of the same class which has been ascribed to Heywood is the play entitled *No-Body, and Some-Body. With the true Chronicle Historie of Elydure*, which was entered in the Stationers' register in 1606, and must have been performed before 1604. But, though Heywood's authorship seemed unquestionable to Fleay, stronger evidence

[1] Queen Elizabeth also figures as "the last of the three Women Worthies among the Christians" in Heywood's *Nine Most Worthy Women of the World*. *England's Elizabeth* was not published till 1609, a date that may account for the freedom with which certain actions of Henry VIII are narrated, though not, perhaps, for the contrast drawn (*s.a.* 1547) between the "sweet lady" Elizabeth's determination to remain unmarried, and what "may be said of women in general."

[2] This episode is also treated by Dekker in *The Whore of Babylon*.

[3] See Tawny-coat's apostrophe to the earth, out of which his spade is to procure his sustenance, beginning

Hard world, when men dig living out of stones. (*Part II.*)

than that which satisfied him[1] seems requisite before we burden the dramatist's reputation with this ascription. The main plot, taken from Geoffrey of Monmouth, of king Elidure's threefold accession to the British throne, is of the antique cast of *The True Chronicle History of King Leir;* the by-plot which gives its name to the play is an elaborate development of the grim old jest of Οὖτις, which savours of the personifications familiar to the moralities and, like them, has a satirico-didactic aim.[2]

To the same early period in his career in which Heywood produced examples of a species soon to become all but obsolete belongs a series of plays from his hand which in subject seem to associate themselves with the tastes of more learned audiences than those for which he had thus early shown himself ready to cater. But, in the preface to *The Iron Age*—the last of *The Four Ages* in which he dramatised a long series of classical myths from Saturn and Jupiter down to Ulysses, who, alone among the Greek kings banded against Troy, survives to speak the epilogue—he expressly tells us that these plays were

often (and not with the least applause) Publickely Acted by two Companies uppon one Stage at once, and have at sundry times thronged three severall Theaters, with numerous and mighty Auditories.

There is every reason for believing that *Parts I and II of Hercules*, performed by the Admiral's men as new plays from May, 1595, are, respectively, *The Silver Age* and *The Brazen Age* and Heywood's series;[3] but Fleay's daring identification of *Selio and Olimpio* (*Caelo et Olympo?*), performed by the same company in 1594, with *The Golden Age*, and his conjecture that *Troye*, performed by them in 1596, is *Part I*, or an earlier and shorter edition of both parts, of *The Iron Age*, must remain questionable. In any case, these plays are more invertebrate than the most loosely constructed of chronicle histories; and not only is the number of characters very great, but it might

---

[1] Viz. the spelling *ey* for *ay* or I, which he had observed to be peculiar to Heywood. It may be added that the references to games of cards (ll. 1523 ff.) recall a scene in *A Woman Kilde with Kindnesse*, and that the author of *No Body, and Some-Body* was evidently familiar with London.

[2] See the bibliography as to this play.

[3] See Greg's *Henslowe*, vol. ii, p. 175, and cf. *ibid.*, pp. 180 and 284.

seem as if, to any audience far away from Cam or Isis, even
the indefatigable exertions of "old Homer" as presenter and
chorus, aided by occasional dumb-shows, would have proved
inadequate. There is, no doubt, a good deal of life and stir
in the action—the amorous scenes, indeed, are often very highly
coloured—quite apart from the stimulus of occasional unexpected parallels[1] and a large amount of clowning. But
it is incontestable that these plays offer a significant measure
of the imaginative powers on which an Elizabethan dramatist
could reckon in his audience. Homer might safely venture in
Heywood's phrase, to unlock the casket of which the learned
kept the key; and there is something contagious in the opening
boast of the poet-magician, that he had "raised out of the
earth" the gods who served the playwright as his puppets.

Proceeding in chronological sequence, we now arrive, among
Heywood's extant undoubted plays, at a group in which the
earliest in date is his acknowledged masterpiece, *A Woman
Kilde with Kindnesse*. It should, however, be noted that, on
the strength of the occurrence of some Latin ribaldry, both in
The Wise-woman Of Hogsdon, which is probably Heywood's,
and in the popular *How a man may chuse a good Wife from a
bad* (published anonymously in 1602), Fleay confidently asserts
that the two plays must be by the same author. Some further
indications of Heywood's authorship of the second of the pair
might be sought in its general tendency and tone, and in at
least one touch of true human kindness in his best manner,[2]
as well as in the humour of Pipkin, which is very like that of
Heywood's clowns and especially like Roger's in *The English
Traveller;* but such resemblances, and perhaps one or two
others which might be pointed out, are not evidence, and there
is more tirade in this piece than is usual with Heywood; for the
rest, it is deftly constructed and contains a good deal of humour.

[1] Not only do Tytan and Saturn, in *The Golden Age*, irresistibly recall
Esau and Jacob; but, in *The Silver Age*, the audience is apprised that the
prolongation of night, which favours Jupiter on his visit to Alcmena, also
serves Joshua in his battle against the Canaanites. In *The Golden Age*, the
clown informs Jupiter (when in search of a father) that "the parish" ought not
to be troubled with him.

[2] The courtesan's sense of shame in taking the wronged wife's place at
table (act III, sc. 3). This play, which could not have been written without
a knowledge of the tomb scene in *Romeo and Juliet*, is printed in vol. IX
of Hazlitt's *Dodsley*.

In any case, when, in 1603 or earlier, Heywood produced *A Woman Kilde with Kindnesse*, which was first printed in 1607, he was not moving on untrodden ground.[1] The germs of the species which we call domestic drama, and to whose growth in English dramatic literature incidental reference has already been made in this volume and in its predecessor, are discernible in the realistic scenes introduced into the mysteries as novelties by way of relief, and in those interludes in which, as in the case of Ingelend's *Disobedient Child*,[2] a serious treatment of a realistic situation or plot was essayed. In due course, however, the choice of actions localised in English everyday life fell more or less into disuse, as the regular drama developed itself, and as themes derived from national history, on the one hand, or from classical and Italian sources, on the other, found favour with an age filled with high aspirations and eager for the glittering contents of the newly opened treasure house. But a reaction was not long in coming; as Heywood repeatedly hints, new subjects were a necessity for the stage; and, soon after the beginning of the last decade of the sixteenth century, and for several years in the seventeenth, there was a constant flow of plays dealing with actions taken from ordinary life, and coming home to men's business and bosoms with a directness alien both to *tragoedia cothurnata* and to half allegorical, half satirical comedy.

Nor was it a mere change of preference which accounts for the impetus given to the dramatisation of experiences, sorrows and consolations familiar to the country squires and town merchants and their wives and children in contemporary England. In a period of the national history when the middle classes were beginning to assert themselves in the social system of the country—a movement which it would be a mistake to regard as altogether identical with the striving of puritanism for ascendancy—it could hardly be but that room should have been found in the drama for exposition of the middle class point of

---

[1] On the subject of the domestic drama, compare the excellent chapter on the subject, *passim*, in *Schelling*, vol. I, and *Creizenach*, vol. IV, part I, pp. 237 ff. See, also, Greg's *Henslowe*, vol. II, pp. 204 ff., and Fleay, *passim*; and cf. a very striking dissertation by Singer, H. W., *Das bürgerliche Trauerspiel in England*, Leipzig, 1891, and the opening remarks in Eloesser, A., *Das bürgerliche Drama*, Berlin, 1898.

[2] Cf. Vol. V, Chap. v.

view, middle class morality and middle class humanity, as distinct from the historic pretensions of kings and nobles and prelates, from the easier social codes of palaces and castles and, again, from the violent impulses and freer ways of life habitual to an uninstructed populace. Shakespeare, whose muse was at home on the throne of kings, in the strife of battlefields, or in communion with nature in her moods of elemental agitation or of woodland calm, and who (save in so exceptional an excursion into a new field as *The Merry Wives*) looked upon civic life in a satirical humour, was not responsive to this movement, and, indeed, appears to have been very imperfectly aware of it. When domestic troubles are his dramatic theme, they are conflicts in heroic minds or tempests of romantic passion.[1] Jonson, and his school—including Middleton—on the other hand, treat such griefs and their agents or victims from the point of view of critical superiority. The large majority of Elizabethan plays which may be classed as domestic drama proper are anonymous; and, with the exception of Dekker, who produced powerful work of the kind in *The Honest Whore* (assuredly his in the main) and in many scenes ascribable to him in plays of joint authorship, Heywood, in many ways specially attracted and suited to this genre, is the only Elizabethan dramatist of note who attained to eminence in it.

The currents which united in the flow of Elizabethan domestic drama were of various origin: perhaps the largest in volume was that which set in earliest, and which cannot be more succinctly described than as that of the murder plays. The earliest of these and the most effective—inasmuch as in no other Elizabethan drama has realism of treatment so completely matched the terrors of incident and situation—was *Arden of Feversham*, published in 1592, but probably brought on the stage some six or seven years earlier;[2] one of the latest of the series was *A Yorkshire Tragedy*, acted and printed in 1608, and founded on a ballad commemorating a murder committed

---

[1] The very accessories of the dramatic catastrophe, as Singer aptly remarks, are lifted into an uncommon atmosphere, and Desdemona's handkerchief has a mysterious history of its own—

> dyed in mummy which the skilful
> Conserved of maidens' hearts.

[2] See Vol. V, Chap. x.

in 1604. This is also, in its way, a remarkably powerful piece;
but, unlike *Arden*, it is tinged with the sentimentality which
had become almost inseparable from domestic drama.[1] The
intervening murder plays include, with *A warning for Faire
Women* (printed in 1599)[2]—a notable play of its kind, in which
Shakespeare has been confidently, but on no satisfactory
grounds, held to have had "at least a finger"—a number of
pieces which have perished, and in which, among other dramatists, Chettle, Day, Haughton, Dekker, Jonson and Samuel
Rowley were in various combinations concerned.[3] To these
should be added, as rather later in date than the above-mentioned group, the extremely interesting *Witch of Edmonton*
(printed in 1658, but probably acted in 1621 or soon afterwards),
which was at first attributed to "Dekker, Ford, Rowley, etc.,"
and in which the hands of the first two of the authors named
can almost certainly be recognised.[4] All these murder plays
are, in their surroundings, confined to English middle class life;
but this fact, of course does not exclude the influence either of
the Italian domestic tragedies of real life which have been
described as "more horrible than anything in Ford or Webster,"[5]
or of Italian and other foreign fiction.

In occasional combination with the realistic appeal to the
sentiment of terror which gives much direct force to the murder
plays, the Elizabethan and early Jacobean domestic drama
also occupies itself with other motives, the operation of which
powerfully affects the course of human life and is most clearly

---

[1] See Vol. V, Chap. X.

[2] Rptd. in *The School of Shakspere*, ed. Simpson, R., vol. II, 1878.

[3] Chettle and Day wrote *Black Bateman of the North* (1598); Day and
Haughton, *Cox of Collumpton* (for date, cf. Greg, *Henslowe's Diary*, vol. II,
p. 207) and *Thomas Merry, or Beech's Tragedy* (1599?). This seems to have
been combined with an Italian version of the story of the Babes in the Wood
(which, apparently had been dramatised by Chettle and Day as *The Italian
Tragedy*, printed 1605, and thought by Greg (*u.s.* p. 210) to have possibly
been identical with *The Orphans' Tragedy*) into a play printed in 1601 under
the title of *Two Lamentable Tragedies*, as by an unknown, and possibly
fictitious, Robert Yarington (rptd. in *Old Plays*, ed. Bullen, A. H., vol. IV,
1882). Dekker and Jonson wrote *Page of Plymouth* (1599), as to the subject
of which cf. "Dramaticus" in *Shakespeare Society Papers*, vol. II (S. S. Publ.
1845); and Samuel Rowley *The Bristow Tragedy* (1602), the identification of
which with the comedy *The Faire Maide of Bristow* is more than doubtful.

[4] See below, Chap. VIII.

[5] Cf. Smith, P. L., *Life of Sir Henry Wotton* (1907), vol. I, p. 22.

perceptible when its conditions are least complicated and unusual. The faithful observance of the marriage tie and the
shameful neglect of it, parental love and the pangs inflicted by
filial ingratitude—such are the themes which frequently recur
in the dramatic literature of this period. The faithful wife
appears in *How a man may chuse a good Wife from a bad*, mentioned above, from which *The Faire Maide of Bristow*, possibly
by Day, printed in 1602, is imitated, though the story of the
latter play is thrown back into the reign of Richard I.[1]   *The
Miseries of Inforst Mariage*, by George Wilkins, printed in 1607,
in a measure varies the theme; but the pathos of the first two
acts loses itself in a picture of reckless despair which is neither
probable nor pleasing, and, though the sentimental element
reappears, it is effectually submerged by the most imbecile of
"happy endings."[2]   The graceless son plays his part in *The
London Prodigall*, noticed above among the plays attributed to
Shakespeare,[3] where the figure of the faithful wife also recurs
in the person of Luce, one of the many reproductions in the
English drama of the Patient Grissel type, which Chettle,
Dekker and Haughton brought on the stage by their treatment
of the famous romantic theme.[4]   It seems unnecessary to pursue
further in this place the development of English domestic
drama, though, among the abnormally conceived and artificially
constructed plays of the early Stewart period, there are not a
few in which the directness distinctive of the entire species
asserts itself either in the main action of the play or in particular
scenes, even when overspread by some rank exotic intrigue or
driven into the corner by the intrusion of some supernatural
fancy.[5]

A Woman Kilde with Kindnesse, which deservedly holds a
foremost rank among the classics of domestic drama, derived
its title, like several other of its author's plays, from a proverb
or proverbial phrase. The expression "to kill a wife with

---

[1] Edited by Quin, A. H. (?), Philadelphia, 1902.   See Brereton, J. Le
Gay, in *The Modern Language Review*, vol. III, p. 74 (cf.).

[2] Rptd. in vol. IX of *Hazlitt's Dodsley* (1874).

[3] See Vol. V, Chap. X.

[4] Cf. *ante*, Chap. II.   As to the "*Griseldis-Motiv*" in English drama, cf.
Gothein, M., "Die Frau im engl. Drama vor Shakespeare," in *Shakespeare
Jahrbuch*, vol. XL (1904), pp. 40 ff.

[5] Cf. Schelling, *u.s.* pp. 349 ff.

kindness" occurs in *The Taming of the Shrew*,[1] which must have been produced on the stage some six or seven years before the performance, by Worcester's men, early in 1603 (N. S.), of Heywood's play.[2] It was first printed, without having been entered in the register, in 1607; the third edition of the play, "as it hath been oftentimes acted by the Queen's" men, appeared in 1617. This popularity was due to no adventitious attractions; and the author was perfectly conscious of the simplicity of the means by which the desired dramatic effect had been achieved; in the words of his prologue it was

> a barren subject, a bare scene

which he presented—nothing more than a sad experience of everyday life, redeemed from the dreariness of its melancholy only, so far as the erring wife is concerned, by the pity of it, and by the nobility of soul which, in the very depth of his grief, the wronged husband proves capable of revealing. In the strength of its sentiment and the directness of its appeal to a more than fleeting sympathy lie the main causes of the effect which this play produces; but the skill with which its action is constructed and the chief situations are devised should not he overlooked. While the seducer falters long on the threshold of his crime, but, when he has once crossed it, drags on his victim relentlessly from transgression to transgression, she is caught in the toils half unawares, and, with an "O Master Wendoll O,"[3] is lost— to awake to bitter remorse even before the hour of discovery has come. The nocturnal return of the betrayed husband to his closed door is presented with admirable theatrical effect—it

---

[1] Act IV, sc. 1, 192.

[2] See the entry in Henslowe's diary *ap*. Greg, vol. II, p. 234. Later uses of the phrase "to kill with kindness" are noted in the present writer's edition of Heywood's play in the Temple Dramatists Series (1897). Other proverbial titles of plays by Heywood are, besides *If you know not me*, etc., those of the non-extant *The Blind eats many a Fly; Christmas comes but once a year; Joan and my Lady*. The following are some of the proverbs or proverbial phrases to be found in the dialogue of his extant dramas: in *A Woman Kilde*, etc. "comparisons are odious"; in *The Royall King*, etc. "thou canst have no more of the cat but his skin"; in *The Fair Maid Of The West* "Base is the man that paies"; in *The Golden Age* "cast your old cloak about ye"; in *The Wise-woman Of Hogsdon* "a cat may look at a king"; in *The English Traveller* "January and May."

[3] Compare with this electrical touch another, almost equal to it—Mistress Frankford to her lute: "We both are out of tune, out of tune" (act IV, sc. 3).

might, as has been said, almost be described as a "prose" reproduction of some of the terrors of *Macbeth*. The magnanimity of the husband—prefigured by that of Master Shore in the chronicle play—might, conceivably, have failed to come home to an Elizabethan audience, but for the picture of the broken-hearted and penitent woman in the last act, which wins over all hearts to an acknowledgment of her husband's kindness, and of the Power which overrules both human sorrow and human sin. The scene of the play is laid in the midst of English country life, characteristic features of which—fresh air and hawking in the morning, and a game at cards o' nights [1]—are reproduced without an effort, but with a realistic effect which materially helps to bring home the story of the tragedy enacted thus amidst familiar surroundings.

While a criticism of certain details in the main action of *A Woman Kilde with Kindnesse* seems unnecessary here, it cannot be ignored that, in this as in several other of his plays, Heywood should have felt himself obliged to contrive a by-plot which, instead of relieving tension, offends judgment. In the present instance, though we would not willingly lose the hawking scene out of which the subsidiary plot arises, we have to accept a pedestrian version of the story of *Measure for Measure*, with a solution such as might, possibly, have commended itself to the author of *Pamela*.[2]

If Heywood wrote *The Wise-woman Of Hogsdon*, a comedy which, though not printed, with his name, till 1638 cannot have been produced at a date much later than 1604,[3] no more striking instance is to be found of his versatility. It is true that this play opens with a gambling scene as true to life as the hawking scene in *A Woman Kilde with Kindnesse*, and that, later, it suddenly changes its manner into that of domestic drama—of the *comédie larmoyante* variety—so as to make the reckless young libertine who is the hero of the action exclaim:

Here's such wetting of Handkerchers, hee weepes to thinke of

---

[1] Heywood must be pardoned the allusive ingenuity of the card-playing scene, which probably pleased the taste of his patrons. Cf. the repeated allusions to the game of Maw in Dekker's *Match mee in London*, which Fleay thought identifiable with *The Set at Maw*, acted in 1594.

[2] As to Heywood's indebtedness to the queen of Navarre and Bandello for the double plot of this play, see *Creizenach*, vol. IV, part I, p. 264.

[3] See *Fleay*, vol. I, p. 291.

his Wife, shee weepes to see her Father cry.   Peace foole, wee shall
else have thee claime kindred of the Woman Kill'd with Kindnesse.

But Heywood is hardly likely to have introduced this half
sarcastic allusion into a play of his own, and the general
character of this comedy of manners is such as to make his
authorship doubtful, notwithstanding the mention in it, noted
above, of his Cambridge college.   *The Wise-woman Of Hogsdon*
is, at the same time, a play full of life and spirit, with a plot very
well managed in spite of its complications, between the two
Luces and a third young lady and the gay Young Chartley who
flutters round the trio, depending on the services of the evil
old intermediary, the avowed rival of Mother Bombie, Mother
Phillips of Bankside, and half a dozen other wise women and
procuresses.   Much fuller of humorously grotesque characters
than any known play of Heywood's, this play, at the same
time, exaggerates all the blemishes which elsewhere he shows
no similar eagerness to parade—a profusion of doggerel, of
bad puns and equivoques and of unequivocal obscenity.

The case is different with *The Fayre Mayde of the Exchange.*
With The pleasaunt Humours of the Cripple of Fanchurch, which,
though printed anonymously in 1607 and later, has been
usually attributed to Heywood, and upon which, treating it as
his, Charles Lamb bestowed high praise.   The present writer,
without accepting Fleay's conjecture that the play was written
by Machin, cannot persuade himself that Heywood was its
author.   Though the comedy offers a very lively picture of the
Royal Exchange (from a shop front point of view), there is
little else to convey the sense of freshness and originality which
few of Heywood's dramatic productions fail, in some respect, to
leave upon the reader.   The heroine Phillis fails to charm, and
her repartees exhibit her as a very second-rate Beatrice, while
her passion for the "noble" Cripple, who is magnanimous
enough to reject it, is not so much unpleasing as unconvincing.
Apart from the Cripple's loyalty to the city and the virtue of
its shopwomen (a touch of characteristic directness) there is
little to suggest Heywood; the wittiness of some of the passages
of the play, and the cleverly symmetrical construction of its
plot,[1] are merits not common in his dramas.

[1] In the actual close of the play, which leaves the arrest of Phillis's father

In *The Royall King, and The Loyall Subject*, which, though not printed till 1637, was, undoubtedly, of a relatively early date,[1] we have an indisputable piece of Heywood's workmanship. His muse took a lofty flight on this occasion, seeking renown in romantic drama. Like Fletcher's similarly named play, from which it altogether differs in treatment, Heywood's is founded on a novel by Bandello;[2] but the dramatist is clearly anxious that his localisation of the story in England should be express and explicit; so that it is difficult—though useless—not to speculate on the possibility of some personal application being intended. Yet the story of the play is wildly improbable, and before the long-suffering fidelity of the Marshal and his family even Patient Grissel's pales; in short, an impression of artificiality mars the total effect. Moreover, the action, as it were, begins over again, after it had seemed to have reached its height. In a word, though the diction, in the case of the principal plot, maintains a level unusual with Heywood, the conception is superior to its execution, and the by-plot, which essays to illustrate the commonplace saying that clothes make the man, is, as not unfrequently with Heywood, extravagant and in part offensive. This play, which, very possibly, was earlier than *A Woman Kilde with Kindnesse*, cannot claim to be ranked beside it.

The Rape of Lucrece, printed in 1609, but first produced soon after the accession of James I,[3] is, again, in a different style, if style of any sort can be ascribed to this odd medley of tragedy and vaudeville. As to the serious action, all that need be said is that the dramatist has contrived to provoke a strange thrill of mixed pity and terror by the picture of the house of Collatinus when the morning dawns on Tarquin's crime. It is here that he introduces the one exquisite lyric known to have

---

for felony without explanation or sequence, there must have been something wrong in the stenography.

[1] See the references to versification and costume in the epilogue. *Fleay* (vol. I, p. 300) insists that this play was an altered version of *Marshal Osric*, by Heywood and Wentworth Smith (performed by Worcester's men in 1602), brought out, in consequence of the success of Fletcher's *Loyal Subject*, soon after that play, probably at Christmas, 1633.

[2] Cf. Koeppel, E., *Quellenstudien zu den Dramen Ben Jonsons* (1895), appendix, pp. 133–5.

[3] See *Fleay*, vol. I, p. 292.

come from his pen.[1]   The other songs—a budget of what at
the present day would be called music hall ditties interspersed
in the action of this "true Roman tragedy" by Valerius, "the
merry Lord among the Roman peers"—are, in part, of antiquarian interest (such as the list of London taverns, and that
of the street cries of Rome); they reach the nadir of shameless
inappropriateness in the catch with which the merry lord,
Horatius Cocles and the clown "follow on," when the tragic
action is suspended at its height.

In *The Fair Maid Of The West*, printed in 1631, which is
undoubtedly and unmistakably Heywood's we have another
romantic comedy, but one in which the patriotic note sounds
clearly and the salt breeze of the sea blows to and from our
island shores. *Part I* of this dramatic Odyssey (which must
have been founded on some popular tale unknown to us)
begins with a delightfully vivid picture of English seaport life,
localised at Plymouth and dated by a dumb-show as at the
time of the expedition of Essex to the Azores. On the Hoe,
the gallant Spencer parts from the lovely Besse Bridges, the
pride of the Castle inn—he to sail for "Fiall," she to keep her
faith and fortune for him at Foy. Soon afterwards, we are
transported into the land of eastern romance, and, after divers
marvellous adventures—all redounding to the honour and glory
of Elizabethan England and her sailors—we leave the lovers
reunited as the honoured guests of king Mullisheg of Fesse.
Part II completes the story in three stirring acts, brimful of
lust, courage, sensitive honour and royal magnanimity, enough
in their combination to furnish forth an entire drama. But,
as in *The Royall King*, the author cannot leave well alone,
and, in acts IV–V, adds a further series of adventures in Italy,
beginning with a shipwreck, which must have gone near to
surfeit even an Elizabethan audience. But the English "spirit
and fire,"[2] and the kindly clowning of Clem, Besse's faithful
"drawer" and constant follower in east and west, hold out to
the end.

The English Traveller, printed in 1633, was probably acted

---

[1] "Packe cloudes away, and welcome day," etc.
[2] These bold Englishmen
   I think are all compos'd of spirit and fire,
   The element of earth hath no part in them.
                              Part II, act IV, *ad fin.*

in or about 1627; but the evidence on the subject is slight. The story of Geraldine is told by Heywood in his *History of Women*[1] as having "lately happened within" his "own knowledge"; but the attempts which have been made to identify the hero remain mere conjectures.[2] The main plot with which the young traveller is concerned turns on the idea which lies at the root of Heywood's finest dramatic designs—that, if to err is human, to forgive is what raises humanity beyond the earth. There is genius in the twofold capacity for thinking nobly and beyond the range of common minds, and for bringing home such thoughts to their comprehension and sympathy. The by-plot of this drama is derived from Plautus.[3]

A few words will suffice as to the remaining extant plays of which Heywood was sole author. Among these, *The Captives, or The Lost Recovered*, which was not printed until 1883, when Mr. A. H. Bullen discovered a copy of it in the British Museum, is, by external evidence as well as by that of style and manner, proved to be that entered as "by Hayward" in Sir Henry Herbert's office book under the date 1634. This romantic comedy exhibits the writer's patriotic spirit, as well as his love of the sea and its ways. The main story is taken from the *Rudens* of Plautus, several passages in which are translated in the play, but it seems to have reached the author through the Italian hand of Masuccio Salernitano. The underplot, which is derived from an old French *fabliau*, translated into an English jest-book and retold by Heywood in his *History of Women*,[4] recalls the scenes with the friars in *The Jew of Malta*, a play which Heywood worked up for representation before he published it in 1632, possibly himself introducing into it these very scenes.[5] Another romantic drama, *A Mayden-Head well lost* (printed in 1634, but acted some time

---

[1] Book IV, *A Moderne History of an Adulteresse*.

[2] See *Fleay's* endeavour (vol. I, p. 297) to find the original of the young Levantine traveller in George Sandys; and cf. the suggestion hazarded by Bang (*Materialien*, etc., vol. III, p. 376) that Young Geraldine was meant for Sir Peter Pindar, whom in a distich (*ibid.* p. 266) Heywood couples with St. Paul—"both travel'd."

[3] The *Mostellaria*. This part of the play introduces the celebrated fancy of *Naufragium joculare*, to which Heywood recurs in less elaborate fashion in *The Captives*, and which comes from the *Deipnosophia* of Athenaeus.

[4] Cf. Book V, *The Faire ladie of Norwich*.

[5] Cf. Kittredge, G. L., in *The Journal of Germanic Philology*, vol. II, p. 13.

earlier—it contains dumb-shows, but little rime) has little or nothing in it to redeem the offensiveness of its plot, one of the numerous versions of the story of *All's Well that Ends Well*, relieved by drollery very inferior to that of Parolles. *A Challenge for Beautie* (printed in 1636, and probably produced on the stage only a year or two earlier) is, in some respects, more characteristic of Heywood, and is, in truth, written throughout in a vein of the most blatant national self-consciousness.[1] The main argument of the piece, the pride of the Spanish-born queen who arrogantly sends forth one of her courtiers to find her superior if he can—of course he finds her in England—resembles an Arabian night's tale, but the loss of the fair Hellena's ring in a washhand-basin is a trivial expedient. The by-plot of Ferars and Valladolid's rivalry, which ends in the discovery that the lady adored by both is the sister of the Englishman, is extremely theatrical but not the least satisfactory. Finally, the latest of Heywood's plays in date of production is, probably, *Loves Maistresse: Or, The Queens Masque*, performed in 1633, and again in the following year at Denmark house on the king's birthday, and printed in 1636. This dramatic entertainment, into which Fleay has read the signs of a theatrical quarrel between Apuleius (Heywood) and Midas (Christopher Beeston), cannot have given much pleasure even to the instructed except in some pretty passages,[2] especially in the earlier scenes dealing with the story of Cupid and Psyche; to the uninstructed, it must have seemed a shapeless jumble of mythological learning. Heywood lacked the lyrical gift needed to animate an effort of this nature; and Midas, who repeatedly declines to see out the play, may be pardoned for finding consolation in the dances.

Thus, passing by Heywood's seven pageants (1631–9), to the civic enthusiasm of which reference has already been made, we come, in conclusion, to two plays in which he collaborated with other writers. Of these, *Fortune by Land*

---

[1] "Of all the Christians this arme e'er stay'd," says the Turkish captain, "you come the neerest men? What country?" "England," replies Ferars as if he could have been mistaken for a "Diego" or a mounseer.

[2] The fine lines

> Oh griefe, that silver haires should crowne his head
> By whom the Muses are dishonourèd

are, probably, a reminiscence of Spenser.

and Sea was not printed till 1655, as the joint production of
Thomas Heywood and William Rowley (both of whose names
were mis-spelt on the title-page); but it belongs to a far earlier
date—possibly 1607-9, when both dramatists were included
in queen Anne's company.[1] The strong hand of William
Rowley may be discernible in this piece, which has a firmer
texture than is usual with his fellow playwright, and it may
(or may not) have been that hand which gave dramatic
form to the adventures and sentiments of the pirates
Clinton and Walton (the purser), apparently long-lived
favourites of the public—for pirates and patriots were not so
very far apart in that spacious age. In substance, however,
it is a domestic drama in Heywood's most characteristic
manner, while it bears witness once more to his love of the sea.
The admirable opening—a tavern brawl, the bloody ending of
which forms the starting point of the action[2]—resembles that
of Heywood's masterpiece; the troubles of Old Forrest are
treated with gentle pathos; and the very humours of the clown
are tinged with the kindliness which can relieve even tomfoolery.

The late Lancashire Witches was printed in 1634 as the joint
work of Thomas Heywood and Richard Brome. But the story
of the play was based, in part, upon an account, published
by T. Potts in 1613, of the doings of certain Lancashire
women, of whom twelve had suffered death as witches in the
previous year; and it is possible that Heywood was the author
of a play much earlier than that put on the stage in 1634. In
this year, another "discovery" of witches had attracted public
attention, and the principal witness in this case (who appears
in the play as the boy) had been brought up to London. This
ingenuous creature afterwards confessed that his evidence
before the Lancashire magistrates had been suborned, and the
accused, unlike their unfortunate predecessors in 1612, were pardoned. But the authors of *The late Lancashire Witches* cannot
be acquitted on the charge that they had, *pendente lite*, done

---

[1] Cf. *Fleay*, vol. I, p. 294; where see, also, as to the verse account of the
two pirates, first entered in the Stationers' register in 1586. The form of the
play, in which there is a great deal of rime, favours the assumption of an
early date.

[2] Barron Field, in his edition of the play, rightly points out that the degra-
dation of the disinherited eldest son and his wife to the position of farm labour-
ers may not have seemed unnatural to an Elizabethan audience.

their utmost to intensify public feeling against "witches"—whether or not their play was furbished up from an earlier piece written by one of them.[1] This makes it difficult to peruse with patience the regulation in this drama of the superstitious fictions which did twelve unhappy women to death—the "ridings" through the air and the unholy assemblies, together with the mischievous interference at a wedding feast and other rites. Yet, in this farrago of half realistic nonsense, it is possible to discern the elements of effective domestic drama, and the touching scene in which Master Generous seeks to redeem his misguided wife from her evil practices breathes a spirit akin to that which animates some of the finest passages in Heywood's dramatic work.

The above, necessarily compendious, review of the extant writings of this dramatist may have gone some way to make good the conclusion that the flexibility of his talent as well as his indefatigable industry enabled him to hold his own in dramatic species so diverse as the chronicle history, the romantic drama and the comedy of manners. In addition, he achieved at least one masterpiece in domestic drama—a species in which his sincerity and directness, together with a pathetic power springing from a manly, candid and generous nature, found their most congenial expression; while several other of his plays may, at least in part, be regarded as having contributed to this artistic growth. While he possessed the gift of genuine pathos, he was incapable of lending words to passion; his satiric gift was small, and he rarely sought to exercise it, his wit and humour moving more or less within conventional bounds, though his clowns are by no means invariably tedious. He was not strong in the art of construction, and the total effect of several of his plays suffers from the by-plots with which he thought it incumbent on him to eke out their main action; but he was singularly skilful both in devising most effective dramatic situations, and in providing for his plays a background —usually disclosed in an excellent opening—which gave to them individuality and variety. He was devoid of any lyric vein,

---

[1] See the present writer's account of the play in *English Dramatic Literature*, vol. II, p. 575; and cf. the late James Crossley's *Introduction* to Potts's *Discoverie of Witches*, etc. (Chetham Society's Publications, vol. VI, 1845), where will be found much learning on the subject.

though the popular sympathies by which he was stirred might
have seemed likely to move him to song—for patriotism, both
national and civic, was second nature to him.   Few features
are more striking in him than the love of learning which he
had brought with him from Cambridge and which he nourished
by lifelong application.   But from drying up into a pedant he
was preserved by the many-sidedness of his intellectual interests, and by the freshness of spirit that was in him.

A "prose Shakespeare" Heywood deserves to be called
only in so far as he, too, could, on occasion, probe the depths
of human nature, touching with the wand of poetic imagination
what seemed to him of interest in the homely figures and everyday experiences of contemporary life.   When he imitated
Shakespeare, as in passages of his plays he did more or less
unconsciously,[1] this was only in the way of business.   He was
not the man to dream of donning the armour of Achilles, any
more than to aspire to an enduring fame—though of such as
is his due meed he is not likely to be deprived.

---

[1] One or two of these passages may be noted here:

A horse! a horse!   (*Part II of If you know not me*, etc.)

What seek ye from the throne?
                        That in which Kings
Resemble most the Gods: Justice.   (*A Challenge for Beautie*, act v.)

And hand to hand in single opposition.   (*Fortune by Land and Sea*,
    act II.)

CHAPTER V

Beaumont and Fletcher

THE collection of plays with which the names of Beaumont and Fletcher are traditionally associated constitutes the most important body of dramatic work which was produced by the successors of the Elizabethans, that is to say, by those dramatists whose activity belonged wholly to the Stewart period. With this new generation, a new fashion had come in. The genuinely national interest in the drama which especially characterised the last fifteen years of Elizabeth had, to a great extent, passed away, and the taste of the court had become gradually more and more the prevailing influence. This tendency had outwardly expressed itself, nearly at the beginning of the reign of James I, in the fact that all the companies of actors in London then came to be directly under the patronage of the royal family, while the production of plays was, at the same time, subjected to the control of the master of the revels; and, as the older generation of dramatists disappeared, the new fashion showed itself more and more in the character of the plays produced. Ben Jonson's inductions are full of protests against the taste of the day in drama, and especially against the growing tyranny in the matter of criticism exercised by gallants who occupied seats on the stage and assumed the right to damn a play at their pleasure; but he found himself helpless to modify the prevailing fashions. The court of James I had lost the chivalrous aspirations of the earlier time, and the moral corruption which had been held in check, at least to some extent, by noble ideals, had become alarmingly prominent in the life of the upper classes of society. Shallowness and frivolity characterised the manners of the court, even where these were not tinged with gross vices, and a certain superficial brilliancy had taken the place of more estimable qualities. Such a society was naturally disinclined to serious reflection upon the issues of human life, and Shakespearean tragedy was both too wide and too deep for its sympathies. It was, perhaps, a perception of this change of conditions, rather than any marked change in his own genius or temperament, that led Shakespeare to abandon tragedy during the latest years of his connection with the stage, and to entertain his public with dramatic romances. However this may be, a definite preference was manifested, in the period which was then beginning, for that hybrid form of drama which became specially characteristic of the English stage—tragicomedy; in which serious matters are dealt with, but a tragic solution is avoided. Closely connected with this want of moral earnestness was the demand for theatrical entertainments which did not make any serious appeal to the intellect; and, hence, on the one hand, the exaggerated love of pageantry, which was gratified by the magnificence of the masques presented at court, and, on the other the growing preference, even of the better portion of the audiences at the playhouses, for plots full of interesting events and surprising turns of fortune, rather than such as were developed naturally from situations and characters: the result being a comparative neglect of character interest, and a disregard for the principle of artistic unity.

But, apart from the general relaxation of moral and intellectual fibre which was indicated in these tendencies, there were far more serious evidences of moral decadence. The manners of society had not yet sunk to the prosaic level of profligacy which characterised the period of the Restoration, and the feeling for poetry and romance had not altogether departed; but the court standard of morals with regard to the relations of men and women was decidedly low, and false notions of loyalty and honour, to a great extent, had established themselves in the higher classes of society. In these respects, there is no reason to doubt that the drama of the period reflected the prevailing fashions. Themes of love and honour are those in which an artificial society of this kind is chiefly interested, and it is these which it desires to see dealt with upon the stage. The moral standard of the drama is apt to be the same as that of the community for which it is composed; and where false ideals of conduct in regard to chastity and honour prevail in a society, we may reasonably expect to find them reflected in the drama which is patronised by it.

The tastes of the society which had its centre in the court of James I were, in fact, very faithfully provided for in the series of dramas which have come down to us under the names of Beaumont and Fletcher; and that these should have been better liked upon the stage than those of Shakespeare ought not to be matter for surprise. In the former, poetry and romance were found in combination with the code of manners and the standard of morals which prevailed among gentlemen; the spectator was entertained by a lively succession of events, contrived with consummate stage-craft to produce the most interesting situations and the most pleasurable surprises, and by a considerable variety of characters, for the most part well sustained, though very deficient in depth and truth to nature when compared with Shakespeare's; while, at the same time, the language was a model of lucidity and purity, altogether free both from tasteless conceits and from the obscurity to which a style either highly figurative or overloaded with thought is liable. Moreover, in the comedies, the audience was interested and delighted by a new style of wit in conversation, which was recognised as just that kind of brilliancy which every courtier would wish to display, and beside which "the old Elizabeth way" seemed clumsy and old-fashioned.

> Shakespeare to thee was dull, whose best wit lies
> I' the ladies' questions and the fools' replies,
> Old-fashion'd wit, which walk'd from town to town
> In trunk-hose, which our fathers call'd the clown.

So William Cartwright, a fellow poet and dramatist, addressed Fletcher; and Dryden was only repeating a commonplace when he said, comparing Beaumont and Fletcher with Shakespeare, that "they understood and imitated the conversation of gentlemen much better, whose wild debaucheries and quickness of wit in repartees no poet can ever paint as they have done." The morality of their plays, bad as it may seem to us in some cases, was by no means looked upon as a just ground of complaint by their contemporaries. On the contrary, the moral improvement to be gained from them is one of the points insisted upon by their panegyrists:

> Vices which were
> Manners abroad, did pass corrected there;
> They who possessed a box and half-crown spent
> To learn obsceneness, returned innocent.

We find here, fully developed for the first time, a species of stage entertainment which is rather an acted romance than a drama in the strict sense of the word; without the intensity of tragedy, but with more emotional interest and a more poetical style of expression than is proper to comedy. The poetical comedy of Shakespeare's middle period had been, to some extent, of this kind; and the species was exemplified further in the work of his latest period, in *Cymbeline*, *Pericles*, *The Tempest* and *The Winter's Tale*. Even by Shakespeare, the line between tragedy and comedy, in some instances, is doubtfully drawn, and reconciliations are huddled up when a tragic solution seems rather to be required—as, for example, in *Measure for Measure* and in *Cymbeline;* and still more is this the case with Beaumont and Fletcher. The name "tragicomedy" is applied usually to about a third of the whole number of their plays, and is equally applicable to a good many more, which are commonly called tragedies or comedies. In fact, the great majority of the plays in this collection are of the intermediate class to which the term "dramatic romance" is properly applicable, whether they have or have not a tragic catastrophe; and it was this kind of drama that was especially agreeable to the taste of the more aristocratic playgoer. In dramas of this type we may say that variety of incident was aimed at rather than unity of design, diffuseness took the place of concentration, amorous passion became almost the only dramatic motive and the conflict of emotions was of less importance than the romantic interest of situation. The impression made upon the mind of the reader of this large collection of plays is one of astonishment at the richness and variety of dramatic invention which they display; but it is seldom that he is able to commend one of these dramas without very serious reserves, either moral or artistic. The merit belongs usually to particular scenes in a drama rather than to the drama as a whole; and, in cases where there is no ground for criticising the conduct of the design, it is often found that the plot deals with morbid or doubtful situations.

In spite, however, of these general characteristics, it is not the case that the collection which passes under the names of Beaumont and Fletcher is strictly homogeneous, and it is certain that some of the differences which we observe between one portion of it and another arise from diversity of authorship. An attempt, therefore, must be made to distinguish the personalities of the principal contributors.

Of Beaumont and Fletcher as individuals, we know little, except what we can gather from their works. John Fletcher, the elder of the two, born in 1579, was the son of a clergyman, Richard Fletcher, then minister of Rye in Sussex, and afterwards successively dean of Peterborough, and bishop of Bristol, Worcester and London. This "comely and courtly prelate," who had the misfortune to fall out of favour with queen Elizabeth because of a second marriage, died in 1596, leaving a large family very poorly provided for. The poets Giles and Phineas Fletcher were sons of his younger brother, first cousins of the dramatist. John Fletcher was educated at Bene't (Corpus Christi) college, Cambridge, and probably began rather early to write for the stage. At what time his literary association with Beaumont began must remain uncertain. Dryden tells us that *Philaster* was the first play that brought them into esteem, "for before that they had written two or three very unsuccessfully." Each may have written plays separately in this early period; but, when their connection was formed, it was of a more intimate and permanent character than any other of those partnerships which were frequent in the history of the Jacobean drama—being based upon personal friendship rather than upon any merely occasional purpose. They lived together "on the Bankside, not far from the Play-house," and are reported to have carried their friendship so far as to have had all things in common. It is, perhaps, worthy of note that there are several passages in Fletcher's later work which seem to be reminiscences of such a friendship as this. After Beaumont left off writing for the stage, Fletcher worked either by himself or in conjunction with other dramatists, and particularly with Massinger. He died, of the plague, in 1625, and was buried in St. Saviour's, his parish church. The testimony of Fletcher's contemporaries is to the effect that he was very sparkling and brilliant, as good as a comedy in himself, and that his attitude towards the public was distinguished both by modesty and by self-respect. Jonson loved him and "was proud to call him son," distinguishing him as one of the few living writers "besides himself" who could make a masque.[1] His ceaseless activity in the production of plays, and his readiness to co-operate with various dramatists in supplying the needs of the stage, suggest the idea that he was dependent for his livelihood upon the theatre; but both he and Beaumont were gentlemen by position, and had probably seen more of fashionable society than most of their fellow dramatists.

Francis Beaumont was the youngest son of Sir Francis Beaumont of Grace-dieu in Leicestershire, one of the justices of the common pleas, and brother of John Beaumont, author of *Bosworth Field*. He was born probably in 1585, was educated at Broadgates hall (afterwards Pembroke college), Oxford, and was entered as a member of the Inner Temple in the year 1600. A long poem, after the model of Marlowe's *Hero and Leander*, entitled *Salmacis and Hermaphroditus*, which was published anonymously in 1602, was afterwards attributed to him; but the evidences of authorship are by no means conclusive. He became acquainted with Jonson very early, and wrote a copy of verses in 1605, "To my dear friend Master Ben Jonson, upon his Fox" (that is, the comedy *Volpone*), in which he declared that to Jonson alone the English stage owed the rules of dramatic art. He paid a similar compliment to two subsequent plays, *The Silent Woman* and *Catiline;* and in all these pieces he expressed a contemptuous opinion of public taste. On one occasion, while staying in the country, he wrote to Jonson a poetical epistle, in which the doings at the Mermaid are alluded to in the well known lines,

> What things have we seen
> Done at the Mermaid, etc.

and Jonson replied in verses which testify respect as well as affection. A tradition reported by Dryden tells us that Beaumont was

[1] There are no independent masques attributed to Fletcher, but several are to be found in the plays to which he contributed, as *The Maides Tragedy* and *The False One*.

so accurate a judge of plays, that Ben Jonson, while he lived, submitted all his writings to his censure, and 't is thought used his judgement in correcting, if not contriving, all his plots.

In the freedom of his conversations with Drummond, Jonson let fall the remark that "Francis Beaumont loved too much himself and his own verses." Fletcher also, as we have seen, was on terms of friendship with Jonson; and the two young dramatists may have become acquainted with one another through him. We shall see, however, that Beaumont produced at least one play, *The Woman Hater*, independently of his future partner, and in this the influence of Jonson is distinctly predominant. The verses of Beaumont on the stage failure of Fletcher's *Faithfull Shepheardesse*, probably in 1609, again express much contempt of popular judgment. On the marriage of the princess Elizabeth, early in 1613, the inns of court prepared masques, to be presented at Whitehall, and Beaumont supplied that which was provided by the Inner Temple and Gray's inn. This masque is dedicated to Sir Francis Bacon, solicitor general, as one who had "spared no time or travel in the setting forth, ordering and furnishing" of it. Beaumont was himself married, apparently about two years before his death, to Ursula, daughter of Henry Isley, of Sundridge in Kent; and from this time his relations with Fletcher must have been less intimate, and he may then have given up writing for the stage. He died in March, 1616, a few weeks before Shakespeare, and was buried in Westminster abbey, in a place not far from the tombs of Chaucer and Spenser. He wrote several occasional poems, besides those already mentioned, including elegies on lady Markham, lady Penelope Clifton (a daughter of Sidney's Stella) and the countess of Rutland (Sidney's daughter); but none of them rise above mediocrity, and they are disfigured by examples of false taste, from which the author's dramatic work is free. Among his intimates was Drayton, who speaks of the two Beaumonts and of Browne as his dear companions,

> Such as have freely told to me their hearts,
> As I have mine to them.

A certain amount of interest was taken by the succeeding generation in apportioning the qualities of genius displayed in the Beaumont and Fletcher dramas between these two leading authors of them. Some, it is true, adopted the convenient, but wholly uncritical, notion, that Beaumont and Fletcher were so absolutely alike, that it was a matter of indifference whether they were regarded as one author or as two, there being a complete "consimility of fancy" between them; but, in general, we note the acceptance of the conclusion which Pope has made familiar, namely, that Fletcher contributed the wit and Beaumont the judgment, and that Beaumont's function was to check the overflowings of Fletcher's genius. It was natural that, as Fletcher ruled the stage for a long period after his partner's death, the chief positive merit should be attributed to him by the generation for whose tastes he had successfully catered, and that to Beaumont, whose separate personality was little known, and whose genius, in fact, was more nearly allied than that of his friend to the spirit of the former age, should be assigned the negative function of criticism. So far as the claim to superior judgment may be taken to imply a more truly artistic conception of dramatic art, it is probable that it should be admitted in favour of Beaumont; but the idea that his work consisted chiefly of criticism must be rejected. It is noticeable that, in the only copy of commendatory verse which claims to date from the time of Beaumont's death, we hear nothing of his critical activity, but of

> those excellent things of thine,
> Such strength, such sweetness couch'd in every line,
> Such life of fancy, such high choice of brain.

Moreover, the writer of this, John Earle, does not think it necessary even to mention the name of Fletcher, while attributing *Philaster*, *The Maides Tragedy* and *A King and no King* to Beaumont alone. This, no doubt, is the result of a personal partiality; but we must remember that the verses written later, for the folio of 1647, were, for the most part, equally affected by partiality in the other direction, and, in general, these later compositions can only be relied upon as evidence of the vague impressions prevailing in the public mind in the age which succeeded the death of Fletcher.

The statements of publishers as to the individual or joint authorship of particular plays are scanty and untrustworthy.

Four only were printed in Beaumont's lifetime—*The Woman Hater*, *The Faithfull Shepheardesse*, *The Knight of the Burning Pestle* and *Cupid's Revenge*—and, of these, two appeared anonymously, while two, *The Faithfull Shepheardesse* and *Cupid's Revenge*, were ascribed to Fletcher alone, the latter, no doubt, wrongly. Five more were printed during the lifetime of Fletcher, *The Scornful Ladie*, *A King and no King*, *The Maides Tragedy*, *Philaster* and *Thierry and Theodoret*. Of these, *The Scornful Ladie*, *A King and no King* and *Philaster* were ascribed to Beaumont and Fletcher, the other two being anonymous; but there is no probability that these publications were, in any instance, made with Fletcher's authority, and the publisher of *A King and no King* in 1619 was, apparently, unaware that one of the authors to whom it was ascribed was dead. Most of the above-mentioned dramas were reprinted, and a few more were added to the list of published plays, before the death of Massinger, who, as we shall see, contributed largely to the Beaumont and Fletcher collection; and it has been argued that the mention of Beaumont upon the title-page of any quarto published before 1639 proves, at least, that the play was originally produced before Beaumont's death. But it is evident that this kind of reasoning is very unsafe. In 1647, five years after the closing of the theatres, Humphrey Moseley, the bookseller, brought out a folio which professed to contain all the plays of Beaumont and Fletcher that had not hitherto been printed, with the exception of one, of which the copy had been mislaid. Moseley declared that it had been his intention to print Fletcher's works by themselves, but he had finally decided not to separate him from Beaumont. It is probable that he could not have done so if he had desired; but the publication of this folio produced a protest in verse (which might much better have been in prose) from Sir Aston Cokayne, against the general ascription to Beaumont of plays in which, for the most part, he had no share; and, since nearly all the dramas in the composition of which Beaumont was concerned had already been printed and were, consequently, excluded from this edition, it cannot be denied that the complaint was well founded. He added that his old friend Massinger had contributed to some of the newly printed plays, but that, for the most part, they were "sole issues of sweet Fletcher's brain." The same complaint is contained in an epistle to his cousin Charles Cotton, who, as being "Fletcher's chief bosom friend," ought to have seen that justice was done to him by the printers. The main importance that these protests have for us consists in the incidental statement about Massinger, whose name had not hitherto been publicly mentioned in connection with the plays of Beaumont and Fletcher; and one of the most interesting and trustworthy results of modern criticism has been to establish, on metrical and other grounds, the extent to which this dramatist collaborated with Fletcher. With regard to Beaumont, our conclusions are, in detail, more uncertain; and possibly, in some cases, plays in which he had a share have been subsequently altered or rewritten, so as partly to obliterate the traces of his hand. A good deal of labour and ingenuity has been expended in the endeavour to solve, by critical methods, the very intricate problems of authorship which present themselves, and it has been found possible to arrive at a tolerably clear idea of the main characteristics of Beaumont's work as distinguished from that of his partner.[1] In certain particular cases, however, there remains much uncertainty, and opinions of very various kinds have been maintained with a confidence of assertion which is by no means justified by the available evidence. When a critic, with no external evidence of authorship before him concludes that a certain play was originally written by Beaumont, afterwards revised by Fletcher and finally rewritten by Middleton, he is evidently dealing in mere guesswork. On the other hand, these investigations have, undoubtedly, been accompanied by a more accurate and systematic study than had previously been made of the individual marks of style by which the dramatists of the period are distinguished, and have, doubtless, helped towards a clearer perception of the true value of metrical tests, as well as of the dangers of a too-mechanical application of them.

The general result of criticism seems to be as follows. It is probable that, of the fifty-two plays which have commonly passed under the joint names, at least one belongs to Beaumont alone, and that in some eight or nine others he co-operated

---

[1] The progress made in recent times may be estimated partly by the remark of Hallam in 1843, that no critic has perceived any difference of style between the two dramatists (*Literature of Europe*, vol. III, p. 98).

with Fletcher, taking, usually, the leading part in the combination; that Fletcher was the sole author of about fifteen
plays, and that there are some two-and-twenty, formerly
attributed to the pair conjointly, in which we find Fletcher's
work combined with that of other authors than Beaumont,
besides five or six in which, apparently, neither Fletcher nor
Beaumont had any appreciable share. To the general total
may be added *Henry VIII*, by Shakespeare and Fletcher,
which is commonly regarded as Shakespeare's; *A Very Woman*,
which passes under the name of Massinger, but in which
Fletcher, probably, had a share; and *Sir John van Olden Barnavelt*, by Fletcher and Massinger, which remained unprinted till
quite recently. Among the dramatists with whom Fletcher
worked after the retirement of Beaumont, by far the most
important place is taken by Massinger, who has a considerable
share in at least sixteen plays, and who in justice ought to have
been mentioned upon the title-page of the collection. There
is evidence, also, of the occasional co-operation of Fletcher with
Jonson, Field, Tourneur, W. Rowley and, perhaps Daborne.

It is evident that any investigation which may be made of
the separate styles of Beaumont and Fletcher must, in the first
instance, be based upon those plays which may reasonably be
attributed to Fletcher alone, and these, in fact, will be found
to supply a tolerably satisfactory criterion. The metrical style
of Fletcher is more unmistakably marked than that of any
other dramatist of the period. Its most obvious characteristic
is the use of redundant syllables in all parts of the line, but
especially at the end. So much is this the practice with him,
that, out of every three of his lines, usually two, at least, have
double or triple endings, and even this proportion is often far
exceeded. No other writer has anything like this number
of feminine endings: in a play of 2500 lines, while Massinger,
who approaches Fletcher most nearly in this respect, might,
possibly, have as many as 1200 double or triple endings, and
Shakespeare, in his latest period, as many as 850, Fletcher
would normally have at least 1700, and might not impossibly
have as many as 2000; and his marked preference for this form
of verse is emphasised by the fact that very often the feminine
ending is produced by the addition of some quite unnecessary
word, such as "sir," "lady," "too," "now," introduced,

apparently, for this sole purpose. A characteristic feature, also, of Fletcher's double endings, though not peculiar to him, is that the redundant syllable is occasionally a word of some weight, which cannot be slurred over, *e.g.*

> As many plagues as the corrupted air breeds,

or

> Welcome to the court, sweet beauties! Now the court shines.

The use of redundant syllables elsewhere than at the end of the line is also very frequent, so that the number of syllables in Fletcher's verse ranges, in comedy at least, from ten to fifteen or more.

These peculiarities of rhythm were deliberately adopted for dramatic purposes. Fletcher was quite capable of writing blank verse of the usual type, and in his pastoral drama, *The Faithfull Shepheardesse*, we have nearly two hundred lines of blank verse with not more than ten double endings, and with hardly any superfluous syllables in other parts of the line. For his ordinary dramatic work, however, he chose a form which, in his opinion, was better suited for dramatic expression. The object aimed at was to make the line more loose and flexible and to gain an effect of ease and absence of premeditation. No mouthing is possible in this verse, no rounding off of a description or sentiment with a period; all is abrupt and almost spasmodic, apparently the outcome of the moment. The quick and lively action of the later English stage, with its easy assumption of the ordinary speech of gentlemen, thus developed a metre which could supply the place of prose in the lightest interchange of fashionable repartee.

With this freedom in the matter of syllabic measure, Fletcher combines a singular absence of free movement from verse to verse. His lines, for the most part, are "end-stopped," that is to say, they have usually a marked final pause, so that each verse tends to become an independent unit of expression, and the running-on of the sentence from line to line is comparatively rare. The free distribution of pauses in the verse, which is naturally connected with a periodic structure of sentence, is thus seriously restricted, and the intention of excluding, so far as possible, the more rhetorical form of expression, and favouring the use of short sentences of simple structure, is evident. This, no doubt, conduces to clearness, and the effect of discontinuity, which is obtained by coincidence of pause with the end of the loosely constructed line, helps, perhaps, to suggest a spontaneous development of thoughts from the circumstances of the moment. But these advantages are dearly bought by the tiresome monotony which the system involves, a monotony which is only, to some extent, relieved by variation of the position of the internal pause and by the frequent use of the so-called "lyric" caesura. It is by the combination of the double ending with the stopped line that Fletcher's verse is chiefly distinguished from that of Massinger. Jonson's later verse exhibits, to some extent, the same combination as Fletcher's, and must, to some extent, have been influenced by it. The informal character of Fletcher's verse structure enabled him to dispense entirely with prose in his later work; but it must not be assumed that he never used it at any period. He seems to have almost always avoided rime in his ordinary dramatic verse; employing it occasionally, however, at the end of a scene.

Fletcher's metrical style, generally, is intimately associated with his endeavour to achieve a more lively and dramatic presentation of thought. Shakespeare, in his later work, to a great extent discarded the periodic structure of the sentence, and adopted what we may call the disjointed style, as more dramatic; but his method was altogether different from that of Fletcher. Instead of strengthening the end pause, he, to a great extent, abolished it, and attained his object by methods which, in the hands of an inferior writer, would have altogether disorganised the verse. Indeed, a comparison of Fletcher with Shakespeare generally would tend chiefly to emphasise the difference of their styles. Shakespeare's unequalled rapidity of imagination makes him concise even to obscurity, especially in his later work; he more and more abounds in metaphor; finding no leisure to do more than indicate his comparisons; and this pregnant brevity carries with it extraordinary force. Fletcher, on the other hand, notwithstanding the rapidity of action in his dramas, is inclined to move slowly in the expression of thoughts and feelings. "He lays line upon line, making up one after the other, adding image to image so deliberately that we see where they join. Shakespeare mingles everything, he runs line into line, embarrasses sentences and metaphors; before one idea has burst its shell, another is hatched and clamorous for disclosure."[1] But this very quality of Fletcher's style, this clear presentation of ideas and images in due succession, was likely to make him the more popular of the two poets upon the stage, and helps, in some measure, to account for the fact that, in the latter part of the seventeenth century, two of "Beaumont and Fletcher's" plays were acted for one of Shakespeare's or Jonson's.

In the plays which there is good reason to attribute partly or entirely to Beaumont, characteristics of style appear that are quite different from those which we have noticed in Fletcher's work. We find here a type of verse which rather resembles that of Shakespeare's middle period, with a small proportion of double endings, few redundant syllables in other parts of the verse, no marked tendency to pause at the end of the line, but a measured eloquence, and a certain rounded fulness of rhythm, which lend themselves well to poetical narrative and description. With this, there are tolerably frequent instances of occasional rime at the end of speeches and, also, elsewhere, and a free use of prose as the language of ordinary conversation. In verse passages, instead of a succession of short sentences, we notice a tendency, rather, to complex structure, and to enlargement by repetition or parenthesis, though without any failure in lucidity, and usually with a faultless balance of clauses. Such sentence and verse structure as we have in the following passage is quite alien to Fletcher's style:

> It were a fitter hour for me to laugh,
> When at the altar the religious priest
> Were pacifying the offended powers
> With sacrifice, than now. This should have been
> My rite, and all your hands have been employ'd
> In giving me a spotless offering,
> To young Amintor's bed, as we are now
> For you. Pardon, Evadne; 'would my worth
> Were great as yours, or that the king, or he,
> Or both, thought so! perhaps he found me worthless:

[1] Lamb, *Specimens of the Dramatists.*

> But till he did so, in these ears of mine
> These credulous ears, he pour'd the sweetest words
> That art or love could frame.[1]

In addition to the more external marks of style, we note in these plays a feature which is hardly to be found in any of Fletcher's admitted work, namely, the element of burlesque or mock-heroic. *The Woman Hater*, which abounds in this form of humour, is now generally assigned to Beaumont alone, and *The Knight of the Burning Pestle* is admitted to be either entirely, or almost entirely, his.

Apart from these, the dramas which, upon critical grounds, can, with confidence, be attributed to the joint authorship of Beaumont and Fletcher are the following: *The Scornful Ladie*, *Philaster*, *The Maides Tragedy*, *A King and no King*, *Cupid's Revenge*, *The Coxcombe* and *Four Plays in One*. A few others, as *Wit At severall Weapons*, *The Nice Valour*, *Loves Cure* and *The Little French Lawyer*, have been assigned partly to Beaumont, not so much on the evidence of style, as because it has been thought that, in their original form, they date from a time when Beaumont and Fletcher were working in partnership. But the assumption of an early date for these plays is extremely doubtful, and, even if this were admitted, it would not follow that the attribution of part authorship to Beaumont was correct.

From the above list, the superiority of Beaumont's genius in "tragedy," that is to say, drama upon the tragic level of seriousness, is apparent, for it includes the three most celebrated plays of this kind in the whole series. And, when we come to examine these plays more closely, we find reason to believe that the principal part in them was decisively taken by the younger writer. The plotting and construction of *Philaster*, *The Maides Tragedy* and *A King and no King*, in spite of obvious faults, show a firmer hand than is visible in any of Fletcher's later work, and it is significant that no source has been found for the plots of any one of these three plays, which, not improbably, are of the authors' own invention. In the essential feature of artistic unity, they suggest the work of the young dramatist who, according to tradition, was consulted by Jonson

---

[1] *The Maides Tragedy*, act II, sc. I.

about his plots, and it seems probable that, in constructive faculty at least, Beaumont was markedly superior to his colleague. Beaumont shows much the same liking for romantic incidents which we find in Fletcher, and sometimes gives a happy solution of an otherwise tragic plot; but he has far more intensity of conception, and in some of his work this is combined with an effective use of tragic irony, such as we do not find in Fletcher's more loosely constructed drama. His characters, too, are more original and striking, and it seems probable that the remarkable creations of Evadne and Arbaces are to be attributed chiefly to Beaumont. Of the more ordinary characters, certain particular types seem to belong especially to him, the love-lorn maiden, for example, as exemplified by Euphrasia in *Philaster* and by Aspatia in *The Maides Tragedy*, and the poetical and romantic young man, as shown in the persons of Philaster and Amintor. Fletcher's heroines, however deep in love, are less poetical, more full of resource and less pure-minded than Beaumont's maidens; while his young men have more of the fashionable gentleman and less of the idealist than these rather sentimental heroes. A peculiar vein of tenderness and delicacy marks some of Beaumont's delineations of lovers in the less exalted sphere, as the Gerrard and Violante of *The Triumph of Love*, and the Ricardo and Viola of *The Coxcombe*. Beaumont, as has been already observed, shows a more distinct affinity than Fletcher with the older Elizabethan school. In pure comedy, Jonson is his master; but, even here, the imitation of Shakespeare is frequent, and still more so in *Philaster*, which has many points of contact with *Hamlet* and with *Cymbeline*, the latter of which was produced, perhaps, in the same year.[1] Fletcher, also, has imitations of Shakespeare; but they are neither so numerous nor so close as those of his partner.

As regards the remaining plays, we have to take account of some other authors, and more especially of Massinger. Massinger is distinguished by a type of verse which has a large

---

[1] See Leonhardt, B., in *Anglia*, vol. VIII, pp. 424 ff.; and Thorndike, A. H., *The Influence of Beaumont and Fletcher on Shakespeare*. The contention of the latter, that *Cymbeline* is an imitation of *Philaster*, and not *vice versa*, is rendered less probable by the fact that there are many undoubted imitations of Shakespeare in *Philaster*, as well as elsewhere in Beaumont and Fletcher.

proportion of double endings (though far fewer than Fletcher's), combined with a free distribution of pauses and a free running-on from line to line; he uses a periodic structure of sentence in serious or poetical passages, and inserts parentheses frequently. He can also be traced by a habit of repeating certain favourite phrases and images, and the combination of these characteristic expressions with the metrical and other indications to which we have referred may generally be regarded as decisive evidence of his authorship. The features imported by Massinger into the work which he shares with Fletcher are a more oratorical style of expression, greater moral earnestness and, in particular, a tendency to throw scenes into such a form that they contain pleading both for and against a given thesis. He is stronger than Fletcher in plotting and construction, and it is observable that, in several of the plays in which these two are fellow workers, Massinger supplies a framework which is filled in by Fletcher, whose strength lies in the management of particular scenes rather than in the conduct of the drama as a whole. This seems to be the case, for example, with *The False One*, *The Beggars Bush* and *The Elder Brother*. On the whole, it may be said that considerable injustice has been done to Massinger by the popular ascription of much of his work to Fletcher: several of the best dramas of the collection owe their merit very largely to Massinger.

Fletcher excelled as a master of immediate stage effect, and none know better how to compensate for the want of higher artistic aims by variety of characters, and by a lively succession of incidents and actions, which leave the spectator no time to reflect upon the effect of the whole. His aim was to keep his audience well entertained; and he was often content to produce a series of effective situations, with no true principle of unity. Langbaine says,

I have either read or been informed that it was generally Mr. Fletcher's practice, after he had finished three acts of a play, to show them to the actors, and after they had agreed upon terms, he huddled up the two last without that proper care which was requisite.

The statement is either true or well invented; and, if true, it would account for the phenomena observed in such plays as

The Custome of the Countrey and *The Pilgrim*. Fletcher's almost regular practice was to take two separate stories, so that the play might not be deficient in persons and incidents, and to work them out side by side, establishing such links between them as he conveniently could, but often leaving them without vital connection. The desire for immediate effect leads to the frequent use of surprises in the development of the plot, and the introduction of incidents for which no due preparation has been made. Hence, also, a too great fondness for violent situations, and for the representation of extreme physical agony, as in *Valentinian* and *A Wife for a Month*. Naturally, stage conventions were utilised by such a dramatist in every possible manner, and a considerable part is played by sudden change of feeling, including violent and irresistible love, and dramatically unjustifiable conversion of character.[1]

Characterisation is naturally weakened by the excess of incident in the plot. As Dryden says, "the manners can never be evident where the surprises of fortune take up all the business of the stage, and where the poet is more in pain to tell you what happened to such a man than what he was." Fletcher's character drawing, in fact, is rather superficial, and his tendency is to follow certain well marked lines, so that types, rather than individuals, are produced. We have, to some extent, a recurrence of the types already presented in the Beaumont plays; the wicked and lustful monarch reappearing in Valentinian, Antigonus and Frederick, the impossibly loyal subject in Aecius and Archas, the blunt soldier in Memnon and Leontius. On the other hand, Fletcher seems especially responsible for the types of superhuman virtue and of incredible vice in women, which appear in his serious drama, Lucina, Ordella and Evanthe, on the one hand, and, on the other, Brunhalt, Lelia and Hippolyta. About all these there is a certain element of exaggeration: Fletcher's imagination is not fully to be trusted to present the simple and natural effects of true modesty and chastity in women, and this is an undeniable blot upon his work in the higher drama. In the characters which properly belong to comedy, he draws from the life and is often highly successful. There is the young man

---

[1] See *John Fletcher* by Hatcher, O. L., pp. 60 ff., where this subject is well worked out in detail.

of wit and gallantry, brilliant and irresponsible, who may or may not be in love, but is entirely free from romantic sensibility: Monsieur Thomas, for example, or Don John, Mirabel or Valentine. These, we feel, are the men whom Fletcher has actually known in living society: their profligacy is rather a matter of fashion than anything else; they are generous and good-hearted, as a rule, and the vice which colours their conversation and behaviour is not of a very deep dye. Then, we have the corresponding young woman, witty and resourceful, well able to take care of herself for the most part, but wanting in the poetical tenderness of a Viola or an Aspatia. There is a certain charm about these girls; but their chastity is too much of the formal order, and, if we are to judge them by their speech, we must condemn them as wanting in delicacy. Nevertheless, Fletcher's Celia and Oriana, Mary and Alinda, are, to some extent, akin to Shakespeare's Beatrice and Rosalind.

The stories which Fletcher uses for his plays are, perhaps, never of his own invention. Occasionally, he draws from historical or quasi-historical sources, as in *Thierry and Theodoret*, *Valentinian*, *Bonduca*, *The False One*, *The Island Princesse* and *The Prophetesse;* but he deals with these as with romance. The only example of a drama in which regard is paid to the truth of history is afforded by *Barnavelt*, which is based upon contemporary events in the Netherlands. He took stories from many various authors, from Bandello (through Painter's *Palace of Pleasure*) from the *Astrée* of Honoré d'Urfé and from d'Audiguier; but the material which suited his genius best was that which he derived directly or indirectly from Spanish sources.[1] To these, he turned comparatively late in his career; but, from the years 1619 onwards, he used them very freely. Among the Spanish stories of which he is known to have made use are *Historia de Aurelio y de Ysabela*, *El Español Gerardo*, no less than three of the *Novelas Exemplares* of Cervantes, and also his romance of *Persiles y Sigismunda*. Besides these, very probably, there were others which have not been distinctly identified. The abundance of incident and the lively style of narration in these stories exactly suited Fletcher's purpose; but, even here, he usually follows his method of

[1] Cf. on this subject the chapter on the influence of Spanish upon English literature in Vol. VIII, *post.*

combining two stories together, so as to increase the number of characters and the bustle of the action. For the most part, it is evident that French or English translations of these Spanish stories were used by Fletcher in the construction of his plots, and it has been questioned whether he was acquainted with the Spanish language. The contemporary Spanish stage might have supplied him with abundant materials, and its methods in comedy were not very unlike his own; but Spanish plays were not very accessible to English readers; and, though the assumption has frequently been made that the Beaumont and Fletcher plays are partly founded upon Spanish dramas, it is to be noted that this has in no instance been actually shown to be the case. A recent attempt to prove that *Loves Cure* is taken from a comedy by Guillén de Castro can hardly be regarded as successful.[1]

Fletcher's rapidity of production, evidently, was very considerable, and a tolerably correct estimate may be formed of it from the work of some of his later years, which, owing to the existence of official records, may be dated with tolerable accuracy. In the four years 1619–22, he seems to have produced at least sixteen plays, six by himself alone and the remainder in combination with Massinger. The total reckoning of about forty plays for the last twelve years of his life, of which fourteen or fifteen were written by himself alone, and the remainder in combination with other authors, gives a result not very different from this, and implies a ceaseless activity in production which would leave little leisure for reflection. He was not a great literary artist, but a highly gifted craftsman, with much fertility of invention and a thorough mastery of the practical requirements of the stage; while, at the same time, his work bears witness to a true vein of poetical feeling, and has an easy grace of style which must attract even those who are most repelled by his want of high ideals. In this connection, it seems opportune to call attention to the exceptional excellence of the songs which appear throughout this collection of dramas. Massinger does not introduce songs into the plays of which he is sole author, and, though Beaumont was certainly a song-writer—there is an excellent song in *The Woman Hater*, for example, and some of those in *The Maides Tragedy* are proba-

[1] Stiefel, A. L., in Herrig's *Archiv*, XCIX, pp. 271 ff.

bly his—yet it is evident that the songs which we find in the plays must be due, for the most part, to the lyrical genius of Fletcher. Altogether, there are upwards of seventy; and, of these, at least twenty are extremely good. Besides being of exquisite quality, the lyrics have a remarkable range of subject and treatment: "Hence all you vain delights," the poet's celebration of melancholy, is followed, in the same play, after the lapse of a few scenes, by the spirited laughing-song "O how my lungs do tickle"; in *Valentinian*, "Care-charming Sleep" stands side by side with the drinking song, "God Lyaeus, ever young." "All ye woods and trees and bowers" in *The Faithfull Shepheardesse*, "Tell me, dearest, what is love" in *The Captaine* and "Beauty clear and fair" in *The Elder Brother* are examples of the more gracefully poetical form of lyric; while a more popular and spirited kind is exemplified in the battle song "Arm, Arm," the convivial lyrics "Sit, soldiers, sit and sing" and "'T is late and cold,"the beggars' songs in *The Beggars Bush*, "Cast our caps and cares away," and the rest, the kitchen song, "Three merry boys," in *The Bloody Brother*, and the spirited ballad "Let the bells ring" of *The Spanish Curate*. It may fairly be said that no dramatist of the age except Shakespeare has given such undeniable proof of lyrical inspiration as Fletcher.

The plays of Beaumont and Fletcher are traditionally classified as tragedies, tragicomedies and comedies, and, in the preface to *The Faithfull Shepheardesse*, Fletcher defines the second of these forms in a characteristically superficial manner, as follows:

A tragicomedy is not so called in respect of mirth and killing, but in respect it wants deaths, which is enough to make it no tragedy, yet brings some near it, which is enough to make it no comedy, which must be a representation of familiar people, with such kind of trouble as no life be questioned.

The happy ending of what Dryden calls "serious plays" was, as we have seen, more in accordance with the taste of the public than the tragic castastrophe, and, like Beaumont and Fletcher, Shakespeare also accommodated himself to the popular demand. Of the whole collection which passes under the names of Beaumont and Fletcher, twelve dramas rank as tragedies, in the strict sense of the term, and about twenty may be called tragicomedies. There would, however, be no advantage in attaching importance to this distinction: the tragedies and tragicomedies belong essentially to the same class—plays in which the romantic interest predominates; while, at the same time, though there may be a difficulty, sometimes, in drawing the line between tragicomedy and comedy, the latter, on the whole, is to be regarded as a distinct genus, and may properly be dealt with separately.

Apart, then, from comedy, the first production was probably *The Faithfull Shepheardesse*, a pastoral drama by Fletcher alone. Though superior in liveliness of dramatic action to the Italian pastoral dramas which served as its models, it was unsuccessful on the stage—a fact attributed by its author to the absence of that peculiar combination of "mirth and killing" intermixed with "Whitsun ales and morris-dances" which the public expected from a "pastoral tragicomedy." In respect of poetical beauty, *The Faithfull Shepheardesse* ranks very high, and Milton paid it the compliment of imitation in *Comus*.[1] The greater part is in rime; but the opening scenes are mainly in blank verse, and it is noticeable that here Fletcher does not display the metrical peculiarities which are a marked feature of his style elsewhere, a fact which, perhaps, should make us cautious in the application of metrical tests to the earliest plays of the series, though in *The Maides Tragedy* Fletcher's characteristics are already quite apparent.

Philaster is said by Dryden to have been the first play which brought Beaumont and Fletcher into notice, and it certainly enjoyed great popularity. Its merits, both dramatic and poetical, are undeniable; but the plot has been justly criticised because of the too ready credence given by Philaster to the charge against his mistress. The character of Euphrasia-Bellario, who follows in the disguise of a page the person to whom she is romantically attached, is, to some extent, a reproduction of Shakespeare's Viola, and close resemblances have been noted between this play and others of Shakespeare; but the use which we have here of surprise as a means of dramatic effect is highly characteristic of the authors. The

---

[1] As to the place of *The Faithfull Shepheardesse* in English pastoral drama, cf. *post*, Chap. XIII.

poetical merit of several passages in *Philaster* is well known, and especially the description of the first finding of Bellario.

The leading place among the dramas of Beaumont and Fletcher has always been held by *The Maides Tragedy*, and the justice of this popular judgment cannot reasonably be questioned. The plot, like those of *Philaster* and *A King and no King*, seems to be of the authors' own invention. The tragic situation, unpleasing as it may be, is admirably developed, and the two principal characters, the brother and sister Melantius and Evadne, are powerfully presented and may fairly claim the merits of truth and consistency. There is a certain weakness, however, in the character of Amintor, whose reverence for the sacred name of king amounts to a disease; and Aspatia, in spite of the pathos of her situation and the poetical attractions with which she is invested, is lacking in reserve and dignity and displays too much extravagance in seeking her own death at the hands of Amintor. Little further fault is to be found with *The Maides Tragedy*, of which the action is developed in a series of scenes of great dramatic effectiveness, culminating in that between Melantius and Evadne at the crisis of the plot. The dramatists exhibit a true knowledge of human nature in showing us how the profligate effrontery of Evadne, against which the pure-minded Amintor is powerless, breaks down when confronted with her brother's ruthless determination. Her sensuous nature is, at first, capable of being influenced only by physical terror, and it is through this motive that she is brought to realise the depth of infamy to which she has fallen. With equal truth, she is represented as readily accepting the idea of blotting out her guilt by a deed of violent revenge, and as imagining that she will pave the way to a reconciliation with Amintor by a deed which merely strikes him with new horror. Some of the minor characters are excellently drawn, and the scene in which Melantius urges Callianax in the very presence of the king to yield up to him the keys of the fort has true comic humour, while, at the same time it is strictly appropriate to the plot and the characters. A good deal of imitation of Shakespeare is again apparent—especially in the celebrated quarrel between Melantius and Amintor, which is partly suggested by that between Brutus and Cassius in *Julius Caesar*.

A King and no King, licensed for the stage in 1611, was

hardly less celebrated than *The Maides Tragedy*, and undoubtedly it displays dramatic power of a very high order. The
praise of this play must be qualified, however, by consideration of one capital fault. The supposed incestuous passion,
with which the plot deals, instead of leading to a tragic catastrophe, is fully condoned on the strength of a merely accidental
discovery. Apart from this, the drama is admirable. In the
vainglorious and passionate character of Arbaces, we have an
original creation of great merit, to which the blunt Mardonius,
with his fearless plain-speaking, serves as an admirable foil;
while Bessus, imitated, to some extent, from Bobadill, is one
of the most amusing specimens of his class. There is a concentrated power in the development of this drama which creates
a strong impression as to the dramatic ability of the authors,
though, for the reason which has been stated, the total result
remains not altogether satisfactory.

Cupid's Revenge was, perhaps, acted in 1612. The plot
has been found fault with as based upon mythology; but this
does not seem to be a valid objection here. Whatever the
machinery may be, we accept the actual results as the natural
punishment of youthful arrogance, the brother and sister who
have planned to put down the worship of love being themselves
involved in ruin through their passion for unworthy objects.
The real weakness of the drama lies in the want of concentration: the death of Hidaspes occurs in the second act, before the
main complication has been fully developed, and the death of
her brother Leucippus at the end of the fifth act is, after all,
accidental and unnecessary. The characters of Leucippus and
of Bacha are well sustained, and the scenes between them are
effectively conducted. In the disguises of Urania and in the
rescue of Leucippus by the citizens, we have a repetition of
devices already used in *Philaster*.

Four Plays in One, of uncertain date, consists of an induction and four "*Triumphs*"—"*of Honour*," "*of Love*," "*of
Death*" and "*of Time*"[1]—the former two, probably, by Beaumont and the latter two by Fletcher. Beaumont's contributions are here distinctly the more interesting and valuable.

The Captaine is an ill constructed drama (as the authors

---

[1] Cf. *ante*, Chap. IV, as to *Five Plays in One* assigned on insufficient grounds
to Thomas Heywood.

seem to be aware), having two sets of characters with little connection between them. It has no merits sufficient to compensate for the odiousness of the character of Lelia, whose conversion is not rendered in the least credible. The play, however, contains two charming songs, "Tell me, dearest, what is love," and "Away delights."

The Honest mans Fortune was played in 1613; but it contains no apparent trace of Beaumont's style. Several authors—probably Tourneur, Massinger and Field—were here concerned with Fletcher, and, between them, they produced a piece of patchwork which is far from satisfactory as a drama, though particular scenes and speeches deserve praise. Fletcher's part, apparently, is confined to the fifth act. To nearly the same date belongs the first production of *King Henry VIII*, in which we find excellent work by Fletcher in combination with that of Shakespeare.[1]

Bonduca, for which Fletcher was mainly responsible, is one of the most effective of the tragic romances. It is founded upon ancient British history; but the materials are very freely handled, the stories of Boadicea and Caractacus being brought into combination. The play presents a spirited succession of camp and battle scenes, made interesting, first, by the figures of Bonduca and her daughters, and then by those of the heroic Caractacus and the brave boy Hengo—the latter an original creation of the dramatist, which strongly engages our sympathies.

Valentinian, by Fletcher alone, is, in some respects, the most typical example of his work in tragedy. The situation is admirably prepared in the first act, and the events are successfully conducted through the scenes of the second to a tragic climax in the third. From this point, however, the author's desire to rouse interest by new and surprising developments gets the better of his feeling for dramatic propriety. A new series of events is introduced, for which we are totally unprepared; and the revolting treachery of Maximus towards his friend, together with the revelation of his selfish designs, turns our sympathy away from the quarter to which it was at first directed, and leaves us finally puzzled and dissatisfied. Aecius, perfectly plainspoken to his sovereign on the subject of

[1] Cf. *ante*, Vol. V, Chap. VIII, p. 219.

his vices, but steadily maintaining the principle of loyalty and discipline, is an excellent character, and by no means deserves the reproach of servility which was cast upon him by Coleridge and has been repeated by other critics. It may be added that this tragedy is exceptionally rich in beautiful lyrics.

The date of *The Bloody Brother, or Rollo, Duke of Normandy* is uncertain; but it was probably produced about the year 1616. It is an effective drama, and was reckoned by Rymer with *Philaster, The Maides Tragedy* and *A King and no King*, as among the most celebrated tragedies of its age. Four authors seem to have been concerned in this play, and it is probable that the remarkable political reflections in the first scene of the fourth act are to be ascribed to Jonson. A small part only is by Fletcher, to whom, however, are due the striking scenes between Rollo and Edith in the third and fifth acts. Of the former of these scenes, Coleridge remarks that it exhibits "probably the grandest working of passion in all Beaumont and Fletcher's dramas"; the latter he criticises severely because of the momentary weakening of Edith's resolve, comparing her with lady Anne in *Richard III*. But it is one thing for a woman to hesitate in the execution of her purpose to kill, because of the apparent repentance of her victim, and quite another for her to yield to flattery and accept as a lover the murderer of her husband. Fletcher, Massinger and a third author, apparently, took part in the tragedy of *Thierry and Theodoret*, which probably belongs to the year 1617. Here, the purity and self-sacrifice of Ordella are well contrasted with the wantonness and cruelty of Brunhalt, and the scene in the fourth act between Thierry and Ordella has been justly admired. "I have always considered this to be the finest scene in Fletcher," is Lamb's remark, followed, nevertheless, by criticisms of the conduct of it, as slow and languid compared with Shakespeare's best.

The Queene of Corinth is a poor play. The sympathy which Merione at first excites is totally destroyed by her subsequent behaviour. *The Loyal Subject*, licensed in the autumn of 1618, exhibits, in the person of its hero Archas, a partial repetition of Aecius. Like many of Fletcher's plays, this is simply a dramatised romance, with no proper complication or resolution. The story is interesting enough; but the disguise of young

Archas serves no such useful purpose as to compensate for its improbability, and the conversion of Boroskie can hardly be called natural.

The Knight of Malta has many of the elements of a fine drama, especially in the first and fifth acts, which are by an unknown author. The character of Oriana is exalted and yet human; while Mountferrat is a genuinely romantic villain. But the device of Miranda in fighting against Oriana's champion, in order to save her credit by voluntary defeat, has no merit except that of surprise.

The plot of *The Mad Lover* is hopelessly absurd, and very deficient in respect of unity; but the courtship of Memnon is certainly amusing, and the conclusion of the play is well managed. There is a poor attempt at a fool, the only character of the kind in Beaumont and Fletcher's plays. *Women pleas'd* is still more faulty in construction. It contains two very distinct plots, with two separate sets of characters, which have little or nothing to do with one another, a practice too often followed in the later plays. There are some interesting scenes, but the drama cannot be said to be of much value as a whole.

The tragedy of *Sir John van Olden Barnavelt*, by Fletcher and Massinger, has special interest as a dramatisation of contemporary history, and is remarkable as an indication of the readiness with which these authors were able to utilise such materials as presented themselves. It is a somewhat hasty piece of work, produced in August, 1619, and dealing with events which had taken place in May of the same year. The trial scene is rhetorically effective; but the character of Barnavelt is not represented in a sufficiently consistent manner, and the necessity of reproducing the actual course of events was not favourable to a strictly dramatic development.

The Custome of the Countrey, by Fletcher and Massinger, founded on the *Persiles y Sigismunda* of Cervantes, is a drama of considerable merit, but unfortunately marred by grossness in some of the scenes. The scene in which Guiomar conceals the supposed slayer of her son is admirably managed, and the contrast of Zenocia and Hippolyta is effective; but the conversion of Hippolyta is one of those sudden turns to which Fletcher too frequently sacrifices consistency of character.

It is doubtful whether Fletcher had any hand in *The Lawes of Candy*, and certainly no scene can be attributed to him as a whole. Massinger probably was the principal author, and the judicial pleading between father and son is quite characteristic of him. *The double Marriage*, by Fletcher and Massinger, is a poor play, with a confused plot and no sufficient reason for the catastrophe. On the other hand, *The False One*, produced by the same authors at about the same time, is a drama of considerable interest, and contains much brilliant rhetoric, especially in the speeches of Caesar in the second act. At the same time, it cannot be said to have a genuinely dramatic structure, and, though the conclusion involves the death of several persons, the play, properly speaking, is not a tragedy.

In the plays which immediately follow, romantic interest decidedly predominates. *The Pilgrim*, usually classed as a comedy, is, in fact, as Coleridge calls it, a "romantic entertainment," and one of considerable merit, though the high promise of the opening scenes is not fully kept. We could very well dispense with the madhouse; but the public of that day evidently found such representations attractive. *The Prophetesse*, *The Island Princesse* and *The Sea Voyage* have little merit as dramas, and such interest as they possess is due partly to the remoteness from ordinary experience of the circumstances and localities represented. In *The Beggars Bush*, on the other hand, though the plot is romantic, the interest of the play depends not on this, but upon the attempt at a realistic representation of vagabond life. In this it has distinct originality, and the authors have gone direct to native English sources. The liveliness and truth to nature of these scenes are sufficient to account for the exceptional popularity of the play.

The Lovers Progress is an interesting drama, originally, perhaps, by Fletcher, but extensively revised and altered by Massinger. The play exhibits love and friendship in an exalted and poetical manner: the speech of Clarange near the beginning of the second act, describing his friendship with Lidius, reads like a personal reminiscence by Fletcher of his own relations with Beaumont. The ghost scene at the inn, which was greatly admired by Scott, has some comic humour, but serves chiefly to show how incapable Fletcher was of dealing with the supernatural. The later appearance of the ghost, which is more impressive, occurs in a scene which, in its present form, is due to Massinger.

The Maid in the Mill, by Fletcher and William Rowley, is an ill constructed play, with some poetry, and some fairly good comic business.[1]

A Wife for a Month, by Fletcher alone, has an ingeniously complicated plot, and is far superior in construction to most of the author's dramatic romances. The rather unpleasant situation is developed with considerable power and skill, and the play contains many poetical passages. The immodest speeches of the "chaste wife" Evanthe, and the easy forgiveness of Frederick and his instruments of villainy, are characteristic of Fletcher.

The vexed question of authorship connected with *The Two Noble Kinsmen* cannot here be discussed. Fletcher's contribution to this fine heroic romance is, on the whole, of secondary importance; but one of his scenes, the last in the third act, is, dramatically, perhaps the most effective in the play.[2] *Loves Pilgrimage* is a romance from Cervantes, apparently rewritten by Shirley with insertions from Jonson's *New Inne*. It has some merit as a story, and the serious scenes are unusually thoughtful. *The Faire Maide of the Inne* was produced after Fletcher's death, and it is doubtful whether he had any hand in it, for his style is not clearly perceptible in any scene. The plot, derived from Spanish sources, is badly put together and extremely improbable. Another example of a drama wrongly ascribed to Beaumont and Fletcher in the seventeenth century is *The Coronation*, which is contained in the folio of 1679, but is known to be by Shirley. On the other hand, *A Very Woman, or The Prince of Tarent*, ascribed to Massinger, is, apparently, in part by Fletcher, to whom we may reasonably ascribe the whole of the third act, including the lively slave-market scene, and a part of the fourth. *The Faithful Friends*, printed for the first time in 1812, has no sufficient claim to be included among Beaumont and Fletcher's works.

The list of comedies begins with *The Woman Hater*, which, apparently, is by a single author, and is now generally attributed

---

[1] As to the distinctness of the shares of Fletcher and Rowley in this play see *ante*, Chap. III.

[2] Compare *ante*, Vol. V, Chap. X.

to Beaumont alone.   It exhibits strongly the influence of Jonson, and, though not a comedy of humours, in the full sense of the term, turns entirely upon the "humorous" eccentricity of the principal character. This feature is still discernible, though much less obvious, in *The Scornful Ladie*, an excellent comedy of its kind, dealing with English domestic manners. This was one of the most popular plays of the series, and exercised a considerable influence on the later comedy, especially by virtue of the character of the steward Savile, and his relations with his masters.   The conversion of Morecraft, which is criticised by Dryden as unnatural, is not really open to this objection.   The usurer has become convinced by experience that what pays best is extravagance, and, therefore, he is following his natural instincts in becoming a prodigal.   The mock heroic style, which is one of Beaumont's characteristics, appears, to some extent, in these comedies, and reaches full development in *The Knight of the Burning Pestle*, a masterpiece in its own kind.   The idea suggested by *Don Quixote* was here ingeniously and brilliantly applied to the purpose of ridiculing the taste of the city in drama—a fact which probably accounts for its being coldly received by the popular audience before which it was first acted.   Its comic merits are, undoubtedly, of a high order, especially in the characteristic figures of the citizen and his wife and in their criticisms of the performance.

In *The Coxcombe*, we have a romantic comedy with two distinct plots. For the Ricardo and Viola story, Beaumont is mainly responsible, and this little romance is treated in a charming manner. The tinker and his trull are represented, probably by Fletcher, with effective realism, and the scenes at the farmhouse are interesting and natural. Side by side with this, we have a comedy of intrigue, taken, perhaps, from the *Curioso Impertinente* of Cervantes. Some of Antonio's tricks recall those of Loveless in *The Scornful Ladie*.

It cannot be said with certainty that Beaumont had a part in any of the remaining comedies, and the genius of Fletcher is decisively dominant from this point onwards, though other writers sometimes worked with him. The faults of Fletcher as a dramatist—looseness of construction and superficiality in character—are less fatal in comedy than in serious drama, while his abundance of lively incident and his brilliant dialogue produce their full effect. Nevertheless, his comedies suffer too frequently from want of vital connection between the various intrigues utilised by the plot, and even the best of them succeed rather by clever stagecraft than by genuinely artistic merit.

Several of these plays may be classed together as exhibiting the Jonsonian principle of "humour," though hardly in the Jonsonian manner. These are, especially, *The Little French Lawyer*, *The Nice Valour* and *The Humorous Lieutenant*. In the first, by Fletcher and Massinger, the character of La Writ, who gives a title to the play, is genuinely comic, but not absolutely necessary to the plot. *The Nice Valour* is a poor play, notwithstanding a confident assertion to the contrary in the epilogue; but it contains several good lyrics, including the song, "Hence all you vain delights." *The Humorous Lieutenant*, by Fletcher alone, takes its name, like *The Little French Lawyer*, from a character which has no very essential connection with the principal plot. The part which concerns the lieutenant is pure farce, lively and amusing enough; while, in the main plot, we have the romance of an unusually attractive pair of lovers, though it must be remarked that their situation is a very improbable one.

This combination, or juxtaposition, of a romantic with a comic plot, which has been noted as a frequent feature of the so-called tragicomedies, is exemplified, also, in *The Spanish Curate*, which consists, in fact, of a romance and a comedy, combined under a title which belongs properly to the comedy. We have here two distinct stories with very small connection between them, though an attempt is made at the conclusion to unite them under a single moral lesson. Roughly speaking, it may be said that the romance is by Massinger and the comedy by Fletcher: each is excellent, but the comedy is the better of the two. The character of the curate and his relations with his parishioners are presented with the greatest comic vigour, and the intrigue of Leandro and Amaranta furnishes a good example of the manner in which Fletcher anticipated the comedy of the Restoration.

The co-operation of two or more dramatists was evidently favourable to the production of this class of drama. But there is to be found, chiefly among the plays which are ascribed

to Fletcher alone, a type of pure comedy which is less liable
to the charge of want of unity. Some of these plays, as *Wit
At severall Weapons*, *Wit Without Money*, *The Womans Prize*
and *The Night-Walker* have London for their locality and
represent, more or less, the manners of contemporary English
life. *Wit At severall Weapons* is a poor play, and the authorship is very uncertain. *Wit Without Money*, by Fletcher alone,
is much better, having, at least, a tolerably well connected plot
and lively dialogue. *The Womans Prize: or, The Tamer Tamed*
is a supposed continuation of the marriage experiences of
Petruchio, the tamer of the shrew. His Katherine being dead,
he has been transplanted to English ground and is united in
marriage to an English wife, who turns the tables upon him
in an exhilarating manner. This comedy is a good example
of Fletcher's more farcical style. *The Night-Walker, or the
Little Theife* has more of London local colour than any of the
rest but this is probably to a great extent due to Shirley, who
worked upon the play after Fletcher's death. It is a lively
comedy, but the plot is a tissue of improbable incidents, with
melodramatic scenes of coffins and graveyards.

Fletcher's best comedies, however, are to be found among
those of which the scenes are laid abroad and the plots taken
from foreign sources, while the manners are those of the society
with which he is familiar. *Monsieur Thomas* can hardly be
called a good play, though it has good scenes. The dilemma
of the travelled young gentleman, who is obliged, at the same
time, to convince his father that he is a rake and his mistress
that he is a reformed character, has comic possibilities which
are not quite effectively worked out. On the other hand, *The
Chances* and *The Wild-Goose Chase* stand in the first rank among
Fletcher's comedies, and in them we see, in full perfection, that
lively and brilliant style of dialogue which gained him the
reputation of understanding the conversation of gentlemen
better than any other dramatist of his time. In *The Chances*,
there is a series of highly improbable incidents, derived from
a novel of Cervantes; but the very name of the comedy suggests the idea of fortuitous complications, and the treatment
is in accordance with this idea. The two young gentlemen,
Don John and Don Frederick, are presented in a very lively

and natural manner, and their landlady is a decidedly happy
creation, for which, however, hints had been given by Cervantes.
The Wild-Goose Chase, again, has good characterisation and a
well managed plot, though the tricks to catch Mirabel are
rather too palpable, and his final yielding not quite natural.
Of this play, the actors who first published it record that,
notwithstanding his innate modesty, the author, when he saw
it performed, could not forbear to join in the general applause.
It is the original of Farquhar's comedy *The Inconstant.* Of
all Fletcher's comedies, *Rule a Wife And have a Wife* is that
which was most popular and kept the stage longest, and it is
certainly a very good specimen of its kind. Its two plots are
reasonably well connected, the characterisation is firm and good
and several of the scenes, especially that in which Leon asserts
himself, are, dramatically, very effective. The underplot is
amusing, but less so than the novel of Cervantes from which it
is taken.

Loves Cure, or The Martial Maid apparently contains little
or nothing which can be ascribed to Fletcher. It is not without
merit, if we concede the very improbable situation upon which
its action depends; but the merit, perhaps, is chiefly due to a
Spanish original, though it seems unlikely that this original
was the comedy of Guillén de Castro which deals with the
same story. *The Noble Gentleman* and *The Elder Brother* were
both produced upon the stage after Fletcher's death. The
former is a rather poor play, and has no apparent traces of his
hand; the latter, one of the best comedies of the series, is by
Fletcher and Massinger. The construction is good and the
characterisation excellent.

It was said by Dryden in *An Essay of Dramatick Poesy* that in
Beaumont and Fletcher's plays the English language perhaps
arrived at its highest perfection; and certainly, for purity of
phrase and vocabulary, for simplicity of expression and for
absence of conceits and violent metaphors, they present an
admirable model both of the more poetical and the more
familiar style of dramatic expression. This merit of style was
recognised by their contemporaries, especially with regard to
Fletcher, as we see from the prologue to *The Chances* and in

compliments such as are addressed to him in the next generation
by Berkenhead.

> No savage metaphors (things rudely great)
> Thou dost display, nor butcher a conceit:
> Thy nerves have beauty which invades and **charms**,
> Looks like a princess harness'd in bright arms.

But the praise must also be shared by Massinger, whose poetical
eloquence contributes much to the grace of style which characterises the later romantic plays mentioned in this chapter,
and who may be said to have taken the place of Beaumont by
Fletcher's side in this respect, though inferior to him in constructive skill and in power of dramatic presentation. It is
probable that the popularity of Beaumont and Fletcher on
the stage in the latter part of the century, together with the
acceptance of their language by Dryden as a standard of pure
English, had more influence than is commonly acknowledged
upon the development of English style during that period in the
direction of classical simplicity.

APPENDIX TO CHAPTER V

List of the plays which have been attributed to Beaumont and
Fletcher, in approximately chronological order, with indications
of the probable authorship of the plays and of the several portions
of them, and also of the chief sources from which their plots are
derived.

*In cases where no source is mentioned, none is certainly known. Where
no date of printing is given, it may be assumed that the play was first printed
in the folio of* 1647.

The Woman Hater, entered in Stationers' register, 20 May, 1607; printed
1607. Beaumont. Plot, partly from Paulus Jovius, *De Romanis Piscibus*,
cap. v.

The Faithfull Shepheardesse, printed before May, 1610. Fletcher. Some
traits suggested by Tasso's *Aminta* and Guarini's *Pastor Fido*.   •

The Knight of the Burning Pestle, perhaps acted at Whitefriars, 1609;
printed 1613. Chiefly Beaumont. General idea suggested by *Don Quixote*,
though this is denied by the publisher.

The Scornful Ladie, acted 1609 or 1610; printed 1616. Beaumont and
Fletcher.

The Coxcombe, first acted probably 1610. Beaumont and Fletcher. For
the story of Antonio, cf. Greene's *Philomela* and *El Curioso Impertinente*
in *Don Quixote*.

Philaster, acted probably 1610 (but the supposed reference in *The Scourge
of Folly* is doubtful); printed 1620. Mainly Beaumont; Fletcher, perhaps
act v, sc. 3, 4 and detached passages elsewhere.

The Maides Tragedy, acted probably 1611; printed 1619. Beaumont,
acts I, II, III, IV, sc. 2, act v, sc. 4; Fletcher, act IV, sc. 1, act v, sc. 1, 2, 3.

A King and no King, licensed 1611; printed 1619. Beaumont, acts I, II,
III, IV, sc. 4, act v, sc. 2, 4; Fletcher, acts IV, sc. 1, 2, 3, act v, sc. 1, 3.

Cupid's Revenge, perhaps acted at court, Jan., 1612; printed 1615. Beaumont and Fletcher. From Sidney's *Arcadia*, bk. II.

Four Plays, or Morall Representations, in One; no indication of date.
Beaumont probably wrote the induction and the first two *Triumphs*, Fletcher
the rest. *The Triumph of Honour*, partly from Chaucer, *of Love*, Boccaccio,
Decameron, day v, nov. 7, *of Death*, cf. *Palace of Pleasure*, bk I, nov. 42, *of
Time*, probably suggested by Lucian's dialogue *Timon*.

The Captaine, acted at court early in 1613. Fletcher and another, perhaps Massinger.

The Maske of the Gentlemen of Grayes-Inne, and the Inner-Temple, performed Feb., 1613; printed probably 1613. Beaumont.

King Henry VIII, acted June, 1613; printed in the Shakespeare folio, 1623. Shakespeare and Fletcher, perhaps revised by Massinger.

The Honest mans Fortune, acted 1613; licensed again, probably with alterations, 1624. Apparently by four authors, divided perhaps as follows: Tourneur, act I; Massinger, act III, sc. I; Field, act IV; Fletcher, act V; the rest doubtful. The very distinctive metrical style of act I is like that of *The Atheist's Tragedie*, the only extant play published with Tourneur's name. The style of Field resembles somewhat that of Beaumont. The same story is found in Heywood's *History of Women*, printed 1624.

Wit At severall Weapons, date unknown. Probably Middleton and Rowley.

Monsieur Thomas (also known as *Father's own Son*), date uncertain; printed 1639. Fletcher. Partly from the *Astrée* of d'Urfé, vol. II, published 1610.

The Tragedie of Valentinian, not later than 1614 (by list of actors). Fletcher. From the *Astrée*, vol. II, bk. XII.

The Tragedie of Bonduca, not later than 1614 (by list of actors). Fletcher and, perhaps, Field (*e.g.* act II, sc. I and act IV, sc. 4). Holinshed; some traits perhaps from *The Valiant Welshman*.

Wit Without Money, soon after Aug., 1614; printed 1639. Fletcher.

The Womans Prize: or, The Tamer Tamed, date unknown. Fletcher. A sequel to Shakespeare's *Taming of the Shrew*.

The Bloody Brother, or Rollo, Duke of Normandy, date uncertain; printed 1639 ("by B. J. F.") and 1640 ("by John Fletcher"). Probably four authors: Massinger, acts I, V, sc. I; Fletcher, act II, sc. 3, act III, sc. I (part), 2, act V, sc. 2; Jonson, act II, sc. I, 2, act IV, sc. I, 2; Field, act III, sc. I (except scene of Rollo and Edith), act IV, sc. 3.

The Queene of Corinth, probably 1617 (allusion to Coryate's *Greeting* (1616), act III, sc. I). Fletcher, Massinger and a third author. Based on a common story, cf. *Gesta Romanorum*, tale 4; not taken from *La Fuerza de la sangre* of Cervantes.

Thierry and Theodoret, probably after April, 1617; printed 1621. Fletcher, act I, sc. I, act II, sc. 2, act IV, sc. I, act V, sc. 2; Massinger, act I, sc. 2, act II, sc. I, act IV, sc. 2; a third author, acts III and V, sc. I. Historical basis; immediate source, perhaps de Serres. The name de Vitry seems to indicate an allusion to the death of marshal d'Ancre, April, 1617.

The Loyal Subject, licensed Nov., 1618. Fletcher. (The plot of Heywood's *Royall King and Loyall Subject*, from Painter, bk. II, nov. 4, has only a slight resemblance to this story.)

The Knight of Malta, 1618 or the beginning of 1619 (by list of actors). Fletcher, acts II, III, sc. I, act IV, sc. 2, 3, 4; Massinger, act III, sc. 2, act IV, sc. I (?); third author, acts I, V. The style of the third author is somewhat like that of Field, but better than his usual work.

The Mad Lover, before March, 1619. Fletcher.

The Humorous Lieutenant, 1619 (by list of actors). Fletcher. Partly from Plutarch, lives of Pelopidas and Demetrius. A somewhat fuller text than that of the folios was printed by Dyce in 1830 from a MS. in which the play is entitled *Demetrius and Enanthe*.

Sir John van Olden Barnavelt, acted 1619; printed 1883. Fletcher and Massinger. Founded on the events of May, 1619.

Women pleas'd, 1619 or 1620 (by list of actors). Fletcher. From the *Historia de Aurelio y de Ysabela*, of Juan de Flores, of which several translations were current, combined with Chaucer's *Wife of Bath's Tale*. For various scenes of the underplot, cf. Boccaccio, *Decameron*, day VII, nov. 6, 8, and day VIII, nov. 8.

The Custome of the Countrey, 1619 or 1620. Fletcher, acts I, III, sc. 1, 2, 3, act. IV, sc. 3, 4, act V, sc. 5 (part); Massinger, acts II, III, sc. 4, 5, act IV, sc. 1, 2, act V, sc. 1, 2, 3, 4, 5 (part). Two principal elements of the plot are from Cervantes, *Trabajos de Persiles y Sigismunda* (Eng. trans. Stationers' register, 22 Feb., 1619), bk. III, chap. 6, and bk. IV, chaps. 6–10, and most of the names are from this romance, but some applied differently.

The Little French Lawyer, 1619 or 1620. Fletcher, acts II, III, sc. 2, 3, acts IV, V, sc. 1 (*a*), 2, 3; Massinger, acts I, III, sc. 1, act V, sc. 1 (*b*). Partly from part II of *Guzman de Alfarache* (vol. 1, Chap. 4), or from a similar story elsewhere.

The Lawes of Candy, about 1620. Probably Massinger and another author (not Fletcher). Partly from Cinthio, *Hecatommithi*, dec. X, nov. 9.

The False One, about 1620. Fletcher, acts II, III, IV; Massinger, acts I, V.

The double Marriage, about 1620. Fletcher, acts II, III, sc. 2, 3, act IV, sc. 3, 4, act V, sc. 1; Massinger, acts I, III, sc. 1, act IV, sc. 1, 2, act V, sc. 2, 3. For the plot, cf. *Gesta Romanorum*, tale 5.

The Pilgrim, acted at court, Christmas, 1621. Fletcher. Perhaps partly from d'Audiguier, *Les diverses fortunes de Pamphile et de Nise* (1614), which, again, is from Lope de Vega's romance *El Peregrino en su patria;* but the resemblance is only in trifling details, and there may be no connection.

The Wild-Goose Chase, acted at court, 1621; printed 1652. Fletcher.

The Island Princesse, acted at court, 1621. Fletcher. From *La Conquista de las Islas Malucas* by Bart. de Argensola, printed 1609; but Fletcher deviates from his source in acts IV and V.

The Beggars Bush, acted at court, 1622, but produced probably some time earlier. Fletcher, act II, sc. 1, 2, acts III, IV; Massinger, acts I, II, sc. 3, act V.

The Prophetesse, licensed 14 May, 1622. Fletcher, acts I, III, V, sc. 3; Massinger, acts II, IV, V, sc. 1, 2. Partly historical: the story of Diocletian and the prophetess is told by Vopiscus.

The Sea Voyage, licensed 22 June, 1622. Authors doubtful: considerable portions of acts I and IV are by Fletcher, but no scene, as we have it, can be attributed wholly to him; it is doubtful whether Massinger had any share: the metre, generally, is very defective.

The Spanish Curate, licensed 24 Oct., 1622. Fletcher, acts II, III, sc. 1, 2, 4, act IV, sc. 3, 5, 6, 7, act V, sc. 2; Massinger, acts I, III, sc. 3, act IV, sc. 1, 2, 4, act V, sc. 1, 3 (Massinger deals with the main plot, and Fletcher with the underplot). From *Gerardo the Unfortunate Spaniard*, a translation, published 1622, of the (prose) romance by Gonzalo de Cespedes y Meneses, entitled *Poema tragico del Español Gerardo*. The situation in the main plot, of Don Henrique, Don Jamie, etc., is from the conclusion of the first part of *Gerardo*, pp. 231 ff. (ed. 1622), but the final development is different: the plot of Leandro, Lopez, etc. follows closely the story told by Leandro in the second part pp. 246–266, omitting the conclusion as supplied by Violante.

The Maid in the Mill, licensed Aug., 1623, as by Fletcher and W. Rowley. Fletcher, acts I, III, sc. 2, 3, act V, sc. 2 (*a*). From *Gerardo*, pp. 394–418, with change of conclusion, and Painter, bk. II, nov. 22.

The Lovers Progress, end of 1623 (by list of actors); the original play was, perhaps, *The Wandering Lovers*, licensed 6 Dec., 1623, as by Fletcher. In its present form it has been revised by Massinger (see prologue), and this being a case of revision and not co-operation, mixed work is to be expected and occurs frequently. Acts IV and V are almost entirely by Massinger. From d'Audiguier, *Histoire tragicomique de nostre temps sous les noms de Lysandre et de Caliste*, 1616.

A Wife for a Month, licensed 27 May, 1624 (the name of Tooley among the actors is probably a mistake for Lowin). Fletcher.

Rule a Wife And have a Wife, licensed 19 Oct., 1624, printed 1640. Fletcher. The underplot is from Cervantes, *El Casamiento engañoso* (*Nov. Exempl.*).

The Two Noble Kinsmen, date uncertain; printed as by Fletcher and Shakespeare, 1634. Fletcher wrote act II, sc. 3, 4, 5, act III, sc. 3, 4, 5, 6, act IV, sc. 1, 2, act V, sc. 2, and parts of other scenes. From Chaucer's *Knight's Tale*.

The Nice Valour, or, The Passionate Mad-man, in its present form not earlier than 1624 (allusions in act V, sc. 3), but the play bears marks of revision, and was, perhaps, originally much earlier. Fletcher and another, perhaps Rowley, but Fletcher's part is much altered.

The Chances, acted 1625 or 1626 (after Fletcher's death, see prologue). Fletcher, but probably touched here and there by another hand, *e.g.* in act I, sc. 1, 9, act II, sc. 4. From Cervantes, *La Señora Cornelia* (*Nov. Exempl.*).

The Elder Brother, acted after Fletcher's death (see prologue), printed 1637. Fletcher, acts II, III, IV; Massinger, acts I, V. Source connected with that of Calderon's later drama, *De una causa dos efectos*.

The Faire Maide of the Inne, licensed 22 Jan., 1626. Massinger and another (not Fletcher). The disowning of Cesario by his mother is probably taken from *La Cour Sainte* of Nicolas Caussin, published in 1624 (not 1632, as stated by Koeppel). The plot of the play does not at all resemble the story of *La ilustre Fregona* of Cervantes.

The Noble Gentleman, licensed 3 Feb., 1626, as by Fletcher. He may have planned the play and written some passages, but no complete scene can be attributed to him.

Loves Cure, or The Martial Maid, date uncertain but not earlier than 1622 in its present form. No scene can be attributed to Fletcher; Massinger probably wrote acts I, IV, V, sc. 1, 2. There is no real ground for the suggestion (by Stiefel, A. L.) that this play is taken from the Spanish comedy by Guillén de Castro, *La fuerza de la costumbre*. The two dramas are founded on the same story, but the treatment is entirely different.

The Night-Walker, or the Little Theife, licensed as corrected by Shirley 11 May, 1633; printed 1640; the original play was, perhaps, as early as 1614. As it stands, the first three acts are by Fletcher, with revision, and the last two by Shirley, who must have rewritten this part of the play.

Loves Pilgrimage, revived 1635, with alterations, perhaps by Shirley, including some matter from Jonson's *New Inne*. Fletcher appears most markedly in act I, sc. 2, acts II and III. From Cervantes *Las dos Doncellas* (*Nov. Exempl.*).

A Very Woman, or The Prince of Tarent, licensed 1634; printed as Massinger's, 1655, and never included among Beaumont and Fletcher's plays. As we have it, it is revised from an earlier drama (see prologue): Fletcher was probably the author of acts III and IV, sc. 1, 3. It is commonly identified with *A Woman's Plot*, acted at court 1621, because of the entry in Stationers' register, 9 Sept., 1653, of "A Very Woman or The Woman's Plot," but this second title has no justification in the play, and is, perhaps, a mistake.

The Coronation, printed in the folio of 1679, is by Shirley. *The Widow*, attributed in the quarto to Jonson, Fletcher and Middleton, is probably, by Middleton.

The Faithful Friends was entered in Stationers' register, 29 June, 1660, as by Beaumont and Fletcher, and first printed in Weber's edition, 1812; but it is not likely that they had any share in it.

The following appear to be lost: *The History of Cardenio*, entered in Stationers' register, 9 Sept., 1653, as by Fletcher and Shakespeare, and, perhaps, the same as the *Cardenes, Cardema* or *Cardano*, which was acted at court, 1613; *The Jeweller of Amsterdam*, entered Stationers' register, 8 April, 1654, as by Fletcher, Field and Massinger, probably produced about 1616; *A Woman's Plot*, acted at court, 1621; *The Devil of Dowgate, or Usury put to Use,* "written by Fletcher," mentioned as a new play in Herbert's official register, 17 Oct., 1623; *A Right Woman*, entered in Stationers' register, 29 June, 1660, as by Beaumont and Fletcher; *Mador, King of Great Britain* attributed to Beaumont, Stationers' register, 29 June, 1660. There two latter attributions must be regarded as very doubtful.

CHAPTER VI

Philip Massinger

EVERY biographer of Philip Massinger must echo the frequently repeated complaint that we know very little about the life of many of the chief dramatists of the times of Elizabeth and the first two Stewart kings. We may consider it an exceptional good fortune that we know at least the chief facts of Massinger's early days—that he was born at Salisbury in 1583, the son of Arthur Massinger, who, in some manner, was intimately connected with the "noble family of the Herberts," to use Philip's own expression, and who was evidently highly esteemed by his employers; that his baptism took place on 24 November, 1583, and that he was entered on 14 May, 1602, at St. Alban hall in the university of Oxford. In 1606, he left the university for unexplained reasons without having taken his degree. From Oxford he came to London, where we lose sight of him for many years as totally as of the great immigrant from Stratford-on-Avon about twenty years before.

One fact, however, stands out clearly—that Massinger's London career was far from prosperous. When we hear of him again, in 1613 or 1614, we find him already immersed in those financial difficulties which remained the heavy burden of his life. He reappears as one of the three signatories of a petition for the loan of five pounds, addressed to that powerful personage to whom many needy dramatists used to look more or less hopefully—the theatrical manager and broker Philip Henslowe. In a few additional words, Massinger pathetically calls him his "true loving friend," and the joint request was granted. There was a similar pleading in 1615.

As in the case of this epistle to Henslowe, most of the first

dramatic ventures of Massinger seem to have been joint productions. The first time we meet his name in print, on the
title-page of an evidently successful drama, we find it coupled
with the name of an older and very popular dramatist. In 1622
was published *The Virgin Martir, a Tragedy*, written by Philip
Massinger and Thomas Dekker. But Dekker, whose poetical
temper was different from Massinger's, was neither his first nor
his most important fellow worker. A good many years before
the composition of *The Virgin Martir*, he must have fallen
under the sway of John Fletcher. It is a curious fact that no
early edition of any one of those dramas which have been recognised as the joint labours of Fletcher and Massinger makes
the slightest reference to the participation of the younger
dramatist; all were printed as by Fletcher alone. Massinger
seems to have been quite content to leave the risk and the glory
to his teacher; so far as we know, he never protested against
the omission of his name on the title-pages of the dramas
printed during his lifetime. However, one of his most enthusiastic benefactors and friends, Sir Aston Cockayne, repeatedly insisted on the fact of Massinger's co-operation with
Fletcher—an assertion which, in the case of a considerable
number of Fletcherian plays, has received support from the philological researches of later times. And that he was buried in
Fletcher's grave, probably by his own wish, may be taken as a
striking proof that no coldness had arisen between Massinger
and the man with whom he had associated in the early years of
his dramatic writing.

We are not able to fix the time when Massinger ventured to
present himself as an independent author to the public of the
metropolis; but we may assume that this did not happen much
before the end of the second decade of the seventeenth century.
For the ensuing period of his life we possess a considerable
number of direct utterances of his own, the authenticity of
which is not to be questioned, but the biographical value of
which is somewhat impaired by their official character and by
the consideration necessarily shown in them for the position
and feelings of the persons addressed. These utterances
consist in the dedications prefixed by Massinger to the ten
dramas published by himself. In these letters, Massinger's
prose appears to the greatest advantage; it is, perhaps, a little

pompous now and then, but it is clear and perfectly free from Euphuistic tricks of style.

Much less pleasing are the glimpses of the poet's private life afforded by these documents. Both the first dedication, preceding *The Duke of Millaine* (1623), and the last, composed for *The Unnaturall Combat* in 1639, about a year before his death, exhibit the poet as much dissatisfied with his vocation as a dramatic writer. He speaks of the misfortunes which cast him on this course and numbers himself among those whose "necessitous fortunes" made them choose poetry as their profession. Complaints about the neglect which his age showed to the "contemned sons of the Muses," and about his own depressed circumstances, protestations that he could never have lived without the help of those kind patrons who endeavoured "to rebuild the ruins of demolished poesy" and declarations of his gratitude and his devotion, are intermingled in these epistles with rarer outbursts of consciousness of his poetical powers, remarks about the intrinsic value of his works and hints that there were some eminent men who "have not thought themselves disparaged, I dare not say honoured, to be celebrated the patrons of my humble studies."

Two of the dedications show that the poet did his best to keep up that connection with the Pembroke family which he regarded as a paternal inheritance. In 1624, he dedicated his tragicomedy *The Bond-Man* to the younger brother of the third earl of Pembroke—Philip Herbert, earl of Montgomery—with respectful allusions to the many happy years his father had spent in the service of that honourable house; and, nine years later, in 1633, he recommended his famous comedy *A New Way to Pay Old Debts* to the favourable acceptance of Montgomery's son-in-law, Robert Dormer, earl of Carnarvon, in very humble and complimentary terms. Besides these dedications, two of his rare non-dramatic poems refer to members of the same family. One of these poems is a poetical supplication of uncertain date, addressed to the "Earl of Pembroke, Lord Chamberlain." The earl's Christian name is missing; but the whole tenor of this petition leads to the conclusion that it was meant to reach the ear of the third earl of Pembroke, the William Herbert frequently mentioned in biographies of Shakespeare, who had been appointed lord chamberlain in 1615. It is to be feared, however, that this most persuasive poetical begging-letter, in which Massinger speaks of his "trod-down poverty," had not the desired effect; for, had the earl proved kind, Massinger would assuredly have shown his gratitude by dedicating one of his later dramas to this powerful nobleman. There is an old tradition that William Herbert had been the protector of young Massinger during the years of his university life, but had withdrawn his helping hand later, for unknown reasons. This rumour is not verified by the epistle in question, the manuscript of which was rediscovered but a few years ago; for it contains no reference to former benefits received by the poet.

The other poem, with the motto *Sero sed serio*, is an elegy on the death of Charles, lord Herbert, third son of Philip Herbert, who, after the death of his brother, in 1630, had become fourth earl of Pembroke. The poet blames himself for having remained silent on the occasion of the wedding of this unfortunate young nobleman, which had taken place at Christmas, 1634, a few weeks only before his early death at Florence in January, 1635; and he evidently tries to compensate for this sin of omission by courtly flattery in a funeral poem, the most undignified of all his compositions and a striking contrast to the above mentioned supplication, in which the poet declares that neither a pension nor a place could induce him "to part with his own candour!" It is stated that this fourth earl of Pembroke granted him an annuity of £30 or £40 with reversion to his widow.

The dedications and poems make us acquainted with numerous members of the nobility to whom Massinger felt himself bound for benefits received, or whom he wished to number among his patrons. About his relations to his literary contemporaries we gain very little information from Massinger himself, and not much more from other sources. One of his shorter poems is addressed to James Smith, an obscure clerical poet, whom he praises as the author of a "neat" poem, calling him, after the fashion of Ben Jonson, his "son." One of the many dramas of James Shirley, entitled *The Grateful Servant* (1630), Massinger ushered in by some commendatory verses, whose well weighed and carefully worded praise leaves a deeper impression than the customary hyperboles of similar compositions. Among the poets who did him a similar service at the publication of his own dramas, we find, together with Shirley, Massinger's other fellow dramatists John Ford, Thomas May, Thomas Goffe and his faithful friend and fervent admirer Sir Aston Cockayne.

Massinger is said to have been married: a Miss Massinger, who died in 1762, claimed a direct descent from him. But all the other circumstances of his life which seems to have had its full share of cares besides ceaseless work, are hidden from us. He died in March, 1640, and was buried on the 18th of that month in the churchyard of St. Saviour's church in Southwark, where John Gower had also found his resting place.

Massinger's dramatic apprenticeship, the period of his collaboration with other dramatists, especially with Fletcher, has, of late, frequently attracted the attention of English scholars. Their investigations have resulted in a great increase of the number of plays for which this co-operation is to be assumed. At the time of the publication of the first collected edition of Beaumont and Fletcher's works, in 1647, Cockayne blamed the editor on account of the injustice towards Fletcher implied in the title, inasmuch as Beaumont had written but few of those dramas. As Massinger's friend, Cockayne availed himself of this opportunity to inform the world of another noteworthy fact about which the editor had been silent: he pointed out that Massinger also had to claim a partnership "in other few," adding that he got this information from "Fletcher's chief bosom friend"—possibly from Massinger himself. Not content with Cockayne's few plays, modern enquirers have traced the hand of Massinger in about twenty pieces of the Fletcherian series. It cannot be denied that the modern method of settling questions of doubtful authorship is sometimes purely subjective, and many discrepancies have, accordingly, to be noted between the conclusions reached by different scholars. But, in Massinger's case, the task was facilitated by a striking peculiarity in the writer. Massinger is afflicted with the itch of iteration to an exceptional degree: his repetitions of the same phrases and similes are countless. Wherever such marks appear in great numbers, Massinger's co-operation may safely be held to be very likely. On the other hand, it is not to be doubted that, in all their joint compositions, the older and more experienced Fletcher was the leading spirit, the chief builder, to whose directions Massinger had to attend. That, no doubt, is the reason why he never himself thought of proclaiming his partnership to the world.[1]

A second, much smaller, group of plays consists of those which, in the old prints, are assigned to Massinger and some other dramatist. The oldest of these pieces seems to be the amusing comedy called *The Old Law*. Though published very late, in 1656, as the work of Massinger, Middleton and William Rowley, the mention of the year 1599 in the dialogue of this piece seems to prove that it was composed several years before the beginning of Massinger's dramatic career. It is just possible that he revised the old play; but, if he did so, he carefully abstained from any material alterations. No trace of his individual style is to be discovered in the existing text.

Not the slightest doubt, on the contrary, can be entertained concerning Massinger's co-operation in two other plays attributed to him and Dekker and Field respectively on the title-pages of the old prints. Both plays were published in the lifetime of the three authors: the coarse, but by no means ineffective legendary drama *The Virgin Martir*, in 1622, as the work of Massinger and Dekker, and, in 1632, the impressive tragedy *The Fatall Dowry*, assigned to him and Nathaniel Field, his old friend, the writer of the letter to Henslowe signed also by Massinger and Daborne. Internal evidence corroborates the statements of the printers. As to the scenes of Massinger and those of Dekker, even a careless reader must be struck by the difference of character between them;[2] but it it is a more delicate task to distinguish between the work of Massinger and that of Field.

Massinger's name alone fronts the ten plays, published within the period 1623 to 1639, for which he wrote his dedications, and four other plays, posthumously printed in 1655 and 1658. One of the three dramas which appeared together in 1655, entitled *A Very Woman, or The Prince of Tarent*, is regarded, but without any certainty, as another joint effort of Fletcher and Massinger.[3] In the course of the nineteenth cen-

---

[1] As to the probable shares of Massinger and Fletcher respectively in the dramas in which they collaborated, see appendix to Chap. v.

[2] Cf. *ante* Chap. II.   [3] Cf. *ante*, Chap. v.

tury, two more plays bearing the unmistakable stamp of Massinger's authorship were discovered. Besides these sixteen plays, on which our study of Massinger's art must be based, we know the titles of twelve more, which seem to be irretrievably lost.

Among Massinger's sixteen genuine dramas, only three tragedies are to be found. All his other plays end without bloodshed, even a drama whose historical foundation might exact the death of the hero—one of the new-found plays, bearing the fanciful title *Believe as you List*, published for the first time in 1849. This drama is mentioned in all discussions of the question whether Massinger frequently gave vent to political opinions in his dramas. Generally speaking, the dramatists of his time shrank from touching on the politics of the day, for excellent reasons: they knew but too well that political dramas might have unpleasant consequences for both actors and writers. George Chapman's two sensational dramas, for instance, treating of the story of the life and sudden fall of an ambitious French politician, Charles, duke of Biron, marshal of France, who had been beheaded in Paris but a few years previously, 31 July, 1602, caused a complaint by the French ambassador, in consequence of which the representations of the plays were stopped and some of the actors sent to prison. The author seems to have escaped scot-free; but, in 1608, at the printing of his plays, he experienced the wrath of the censor, who mutilated his text in so ferocious a manner that, in his dedication, Chapman speaks of "these poor dismembered poems." Another playwright, Thomas Middleton, in 1624, in his allegorical drama *A Game at Chesse* made himself the interpreter of the intense dissatisfaction of the great majority of the English people with the policy of James I, who endeavoured to keep up friendly relations with Spain in opposition to a strong national feeling against any alliance with the arch-enemy. The incensed king threatened the players with heavy fines in case of another misbehaviour; but the poet himself was not to be found, and the king's resentment seems to have been of short duration.[1]

That, notwithstanding those warning examples, Massinger could not resist the temptation of meddling with politics, we

---

[1] For an account of *A Game at Chesse*, cf. Chap. III.

know on good authority. In January, 1631, the master of the revels, Sir Henry Herbert, refused to license one of Massinger's plays, "because it did contain dangerous matter, as the deposing of Sebastian, King of Portugal, by Philip II, and there being a peace sworn betwixt the Kings of England and Spain." From the same "Cato of the stage" we hear, besides, that, in 1638, king Charles himself, perusing a new play by Massinger, entitled *The King and the Subject*, marked one passage for alteration with the words: "This is too insolent, and to be changed." The play itself is lost; but the objectionable verses have been preserved for us by the censor himself. They are taken from an angry speech of Don Pedro, king of Spain, proclaiming despotically the absolute right of the king to raise new taxes. It was then the time of king Charles's exaction of ship-money, stoutly resisted by many of his subjects, and it is hardly to be doubted that the poet when composing, and the king when cancelling, this passage were both thinking, from a very different point of view, of the possible effect this manifestation might have on the audience.

Believe as you List, against which the censor had entered his veto in order to avoid giving offence to the Spanish government, was licensed a few months later, in May, 1631, in a revised shape, the poet having made it acceptable by changing the costume of his *dramatis personae*. Instead of the Portuguese king deposed by Spain, Massinger introduced a fabulous Asiatic king Antiochus, deposed and pitilessly persecuted by Rome. After this change, the censor found nothing smacking of recent political changes in the play; and this proves that he did not think of the possibility of another political interpretation, since suggested by S. R. Gardiner.[1] According to this view, Massinger's play had a very real meaning indeed, being intended to mirror the fate of the unfortunate brother-in-law of Charles I, Frederick V, elector Palatine and titular king of Bohemia, who, at that time, was a landless fugitive persecuted by his powerful enemies, just as Massinger's dethroned Antiochus was by the Romans. Prusias, king of Bithynia, who, against his own inclinations, is forced to give up his guest to

[1] "The Political Element in Massinger," *Contemporary Review*, August, 1876; reprinted in the *Transactions of the New Shakespere Society* for the same year.

his enemies, is said to represent Charles himself, who refrained from actively assisting his brother-in-law; Flaminius, the Roman ambassador, is the Spanish ambassador, intriguing against Frederick at the English court; Philoxenus, the king of Bithynia's counsellor, who made common cause with Rome, is the lord treasurer Weston, who used his influence with the king in the Spanish interest; and, finally, the kind queen of Bithynia, who tried in vain to save the hapless fugitive, is Henrietta Maria, queen of England, who cordially disliked Weston.

Some years after the publication of Gardiner's ingenious hypothesis, the main source of Massinger's plot was discovered in the French historian Pierre Victor Palma Cayet's account of the fate of the Portuguese pretender, known as the false Sebastian.[1] A detailed comparison led to the result that the dramatist found the prototypes of all his chief characters in Cayet's work, with the sole exception of the nameless wife of Prusias. It is quite possible, however, that her introduction was caused by the same need of the dramatist which made him add two amatory incidents to his plot: he wanted some female characters to brighten a political story which offered him only male personages. Gardiner's assumption that the dramatist, when he made his Antiochus a fugitive, must have been thinking of Frederick's wanderings, because there was nothing similar to be found in the Sebastian story, is refuted by an examination of Massinger's source. Cayet gives a detailed account of the wanderings of the Portuguese impostor and tells how, flying before the persecutions of the Spaniards, he came first to Venice in the hope of being acknowledged and protected by the republic, and afterwards to the court of the grand duke of Florence, who, by the pressure of Spain, was finally obliged to deliver the pretender into the hands of his enemies. Also, the surprising fact already alluded to, that, at the end of the English drama, we hear only of the imprisonment, not of the death, of the hero, is explained by the circumstance that Cayet, when penning his account, was not yet aware of the final execution of the pretender.

The decisive influence of the French chronicler on Massinger's plot is not to be questioned; nevertheless, it is possible

[1] Cayet died in 1610.

that the dramatist was reminded by some of the circumstances of the Sebastian story of the sad fate of the German prince and the vacillations of the English king, and that, induced by his personal and political sympathies, he did his best to surround Antiochus and his friends with a poetical nimbus. His fugitive, certainly, is no impostor, but a man of kingly bearing. Gardiner observed that the two Herberts, the brothers William and Philip, were opposed to Weston, trying to counterbalance his influence by means of the queen: and the introduction into Massinger's play of the nameless queen of Bithynia and the part taken by her in its action remain the only substantial arguments in favour of the historians' political interpretation.

That Massinger was sincerely interested in the fate of the quondam elector is proved by certain passages in another play, *The Maid of Honour*, containing veiled but unmistakable allusions to his fate and to James I's tardiness in assisting his son-in-law, a slackness which had been blamed by many of his subjects and which was repeated by Charles. Some further passages, which, possibly, may refer to political personages and events of his days, have been pointed out in several other of Massinger's plays, particularly in the tragicomedy *The Bond-Man*, which seems to convey a severe criticism of the royal favourite, George Villiers, duke of Buckingham, and of the unsatisfactory state of the English fleet. All the utterances of Massinger which are supposed to be of a political character show him in opposition to the faction of the court.

The same intellectual courage which made Massinger utter his political opinions without deference to the sentiments of the influential court party was displayed in his dealings with another power whose favour was of the utmost importance to him: he dared to cross the current of one of the most violent prejudices of the public which filled the metropolitan theatres. The church of Rome was regarded by the mass of the English nation as the most dangerous and implacable enemy of their country, and was hated accordingly; the English members of the Roman church were watched suspiciously, being popularly regarded in the light of spies belonging to that hated outlandish power; all Roman Catholic priests had been banished from London by James I, in 1604. The anti-Romish propaganda had also invaded the stage. Thomas Dekker, in his allegorical play *The Whore of Babylon*, strained all his powers, with the exception of his charming poetical gift, to incense his country-men against Rome and Spain; Barnabe Barnes, in his tragedy *The Devil's Charter*, which was played before the king, afforded Londoners an insight into all the abominations of the Roman curia, and, finally, the delightful spectacle of a vicious and murderous pope in the clutches of the devil; while, in Middle-ton's political play *A Game at Chesse*, Ignatius Loyola, founder of the society of Jesus, is made to speak the prologue and to proclaim his vices and his evil intentions concerning England in the most shameless manner. In view of this inveterate hostility, which formed an integral part of the religious and poli-tical persuasions of most Englishmen, it needed great strength and independence of mind to write and publish a drama like Massinger's *The Renegado*. In this play a priest of the church of Rome acts as the friend and leader of all the characters for whom the sympathy of the audience is engaged; in all their difficulties, they appeal to him with a confidence which is justified by his saving them from destruction. And this benefactor is not only a priest but also a member of that brotherhood whom protestants thought they had especial reasons to fear and to hate—a Jesuit.

We do not know whether Massinger, who had been baptised according to the rite of the Anglican communion, ever publicly conformed to the church of Rome: the supposition that he became a Roman Catholic at Oxford and, in consequence of this step, lost the protection of the earl of Pembroke, is nothing more than a guess. But it cannot be doubted that he repeat-edly showed a marked predilection for the religious observances of the papal church. One of his noblest women, the virgin Camiola, heroine of the fascinating drama *The Maid of Honour*, being afflicted by the discovery of the faithlessness of her lover, resolves to take the veil—a harmonious climax to her devoted life, in adopting which Massinger departed from his well known source, a novel in Painter's *Palace of Pleasure*. The saintly Dorothea, whose martyrdom is the subject of the tragedy *The Virgin Martir*, is, it is true, a daughter of the primitive church, to whose glorification even the anti-Popish Dekker did not object.

To the question whether the remarkable independence Mas-

singer manifested in freely expressing his political and religious
sympathies be also a distinctive quality of his dramatic art, an
affirmative answer cannot be given without some restrictions.
When Massinger entered the theatrical world of London, which
was suffering already from an excess of competition and production, he found established in it a great tradition from whose
influence it was impossible for him to escape. We may well
suppose the sensitive soul of a young poet to have been impressed and overwhelmed by the magnificent multitude of
Shakespeare's heroes and heroines! Not that the younger
dramatists surrounding Fletcher always pronounced the name
of Shakespeare with awe and veneration—we have proofs
enough that the younger generation delighted in parodying
famous passages of his works, and that many of them were
ready to extol Ben Jonson or Fletcher in a more exalted strain
than that in which they praised him—but they could not help
succumbing to the influence of his creations, repeating and
imitating him in thoughts, words, characters and situations in
numberless scenes and passages of their own dramas. And,
in Massinger's plays, we meet with many reminiscences of this
kind, though he carefully avoids anything like plagiarism.
Generally speaking, it cannot be said that he possessed an over-
scrupulous conscience in literary matters. In this respect, he
was no better and no worse than most of his contemporaries,
who remorselessly appropriated the intellectual goods of their
fellows: the general story of his successful comedy *A New Way
to Pay Old Debts*, for instance, he borrowed from a play of the
defunct Middleton, without deeming it necessary to allude to
his model in his dedication. But, in dealing with Shakespeare,
his sentiments seem to have been akin to the feeling tersely
expressed later in the verse: "Within that circle none durst
walk but he."

Not Shakespeare, who, searching the human soul, became
conversant with all the great problems of life—not the dead
master, whose eyes had penetrated to the core of things, became
Massinger's teacher, but the living Fletcher, the creator of
a partly realistic, and partly shadowy, world, who always
aimed at stage effects and applause, and was prepared to risk
probability in order to secure them. Undoubtedly, Massinger
owed much of his own dramatic cunning to this apprenticeship

to Fletcher's cleverness in all the technicalities of the stage—
but this gain could not outweigh the heavy loss in power. In
reading Massinger's plays, we often become aware of the contest between two very different forces, his own serious and
earnest manner, as it were, wrestling with the injunctions of
his master to lay hold of the attention of the audience by any
means, however frivolous.

In view of the protracted joint authorship of the two
dramatists, which must have covered many years, it is difficult
to say whether Massinger transplanted Fletcherian motives
and types into his own plays. It is true that the duchess
Aurelia of Siena, whom he added to the plot of *The Maid of
Honour*, greatly resembles her namesake, the sister of the
emperor Carinus in *The Prophetesse;* that the warlike duke
Lorenzo in *The Bashful Lover*, who is suddenly vanquished by
Matilda's beauty, strongly reminds us of the rough old warrior
Memnon in *The Mad Lover*, adoring on his knees the suddenly
revealed charms of the princess Calis; and that intimate con-
nections are noticeable between Massinger's *Parliament of
Love* and Fletcher's *The Little French Lawyer*—but it is possible
that, in these and some similar cases, we have to assume not a
borrowing of Fletcherian motives, but only a readjustment of
his own contributions. To repeat himself was perfectly ad-
missible according to Massinger's artistic code.

As to his relations with either Shakespeare or Fletcher,
Massinger himself leaves us in the dark. Shakespeare he never
mentions, Fletcher but once, and then only to tell us that
Fletcher never had

> Such reputation and credit won
> But by his honor'd patron, Huntingdon.

Furthermore, the name of Shakespeare's famous rival whom
many younger poets delighted to honour—the name of Ben
Jonson—never appears in Massinger's writings. Perhaps he
was not on the best of terms with that outspoken poet. A
few ironical words by Massinger about the strange self-love
of a writer who professed

> that when The critics laugh,
> he 'll laugh at them agen

have been thought—not without some likelihood—to refer to
the angry old man who tried to console himself for the failure
of one of his last dramas, *The New Inne*, by bitterly inveighing
against hostile critics.   As to the possible influence of Jonson's
dramatic method on the compositions of the younger poet, it
is discoverable, perhaps, in his two domestic dramas *A New
Way* and *The City-Madam*.   The impressive but exaggerated
personifications of the vices of avarice, hypocrisy and pride
presented in these comedies are in the manner of Jonson's
types, which were assiduously imitated by later dramatists.
In Massinger's other plays, the traces of Jonsonian influence are
very slight: the small group of patriotic Romans in *The Roman
Actor* calls to mind a similar chorus in *Sejanus his Fall*, and the
foolish wooer of *The Maid of Honour*, Signior Sylli, may claim
kinship with Sir Amorous La-Foole in *The Silent Woman*, by
virtue of his name and some remarks about the family of the
Syllis.

The most striking feature of Massinger's individual art, undoubtedly, is to be found in his great constructive power.   The
structure of his best plays is admirable in the severity of its
lines and in the wise economy shown in the use of his materials.
In most cases, he was content with working out a single action;
the mixture of plots which many of his brother poets preferred,
and of which Shakespeare's *King Lear* had been the great example, seems to have had no attraction for a dramatist whose
intellect favoured clearness above all other poetical charms.
Some of the dramas of his contemporaries resemble mazes in
whose artfully interwoven paths both writers and spectators
ran the risk of losing themselves—a danger which Richard
Brome, for instance, perceived and tried to avoid by drawing
attention to particularly difficult complications by an explicit
remark of one of his *dramatis personae;* Massinger's best plays
convey the impression of being well built and ample halls, in
which we move with a feeling of perfect security.   That he was a
severe critic of his own labours is proved by the clear progress to
be noted in the construction of his plots in the course of years.
The Unnaturall Combat, which the author calls an old work in
his dedication, and which appears to be a free rendering of the
story of the crimes of the Cenci family, has, no doubt, a central
figure in Malefort, the destroyer of his own children; yet it

contains not one but two separate tragedies. First, the tragedy of young Malefort, the son, who revenges the death of his mother and is himself killed by her murderer, his father; and then, the tragedy of the daughter, hunted to death by the father's incestuous passion. In what probably is his second tragedy, *The Duke of Millaine*, we meet with a striking proof that the dramatist had not yet learned to economise his subject: the fate of his heroine reaches the tragic climax at the end of the fourth act, so that he was obliged to fill the fifth act with a new action, not clearly hinted at before, a brother's revenge for the injury done to his sister. It is true that, in the last tragedy composed by Massinger alone, *The Roman Actor*, Paris, the actor, falls a victim to the jealousy of the emperor also in the fourth act; nevertheless, the poet was entitled to speak of this drama as "the most perfect birth of his Minerva," because the fate of the player was not his chief object: he wished to present the tragedy of the bloodthirsty madness of the Roman Caesars, personified in Domitian, whose ruin is prepared and effected in the fifth act.

Our admiration of Massinger's power of dramatic construction is further heightened, if we come to look at the raw materials at his disposal. Nothing, for instance, could be more interesting than to observe how, in *The Roman Actor*, the process of blending the accounts of historians, of Suetonius and Dio Cassius principally, results in well arranged scenes in which no trace of patchwork is to be discovered. Not less cunningly the plot of *The Renegado* is pieced together out of different works of Cervantes. That Massinger's predilection for a single action is not to be explained by the inability to marshal and, finally, to unite a greater number of figures, is demonstrated by the lively scenes of his *Parliament of Love*, for the intrigues in which he availed himself of motives drawn from Martial d'Auvergne, Shakespeare, Marston and, probably, also from Middleton. It must be confessed, however, that, in this case, the fusion is not flawless, Leonora's senseless cruelty showing that the dramatist's wish to use a striking episode of a Marstonian drama was stronger than his respect for what the laws of psychology allow to be possible.

In obedience to the taste of his time, Massinger twice transplanted the action of his plays from the localities named in his

sources to the favourite country of the Elizabethan dramatists,
Italy, and, in most cases, with entire success. Without knowledge of his authorities, it would be impossible to find out that
the duke of Milan and his wife Marcelia, killed by her husband's
jealousy, have been substituted for Herod, king of the Jews,
and his wife Mariamne; or that the story told in his charming
comedy *The Great Duke of Florence*, with its variation of the
motive of the treacherous friend, is a transformation of an old
legend rooted in the soil of England.

Many of Massinger's independent additions to the stories
in his sources are also well calculated to deepen the impression
left by his works. For a few of his plays, no literary source
has been so far traced; but it would be rash to assert that he
entirely invented any of his plots. A far more striking sign of
a certain weakness in inventive power is his tendency to repeat
himself in his technical artifices and in the means used for eking
out his plots. The necessary revelation of a hidden passion is
frequently attained by the simple stratagem of letting a conversation between lovers be overheard by their enemies. The
passionate attempt of Antoninus to waken the flame of an
earthly love in Dorothea's bosom is overheard by his father and
by the princess in love with the youth (*The Virgin Martir*);
Cleora and Marullo are surprised in prison (*The Bond-Man*);
Donusa and Vitelli, Domitia and Paris are watched by the
Turkish princes and Domitian respectively (*The Renegado* and
The Roman Actor); the rivals of Hortensio listen to his decisive
talk with Matilda (*The Bashful Lover*). Also, in other emer-
gencies, the time-honoured artifice of the listener is freely
resorted to. Another of Massinger's favourite situations is
the introduction of one of his male characters with a book in his
hand, like Hamlet, indulging in some short philosophical speculation. By way of amplifying his plot, he repeatedly brings
in a brother revenging a wrong done to his sister. In the last
act of *The Duke of Millaine*, we are surprised by the statement
that the ultimate scope of Francisco's perfidies was to punish
Sforza as the seducer of his sister Eugenia; Marullo-Pisander
acts the part of a slave in Syracuse only to approach Leosthenes,
the faithless lover of his sister Statilia (*The Bond-Man*);
Vitelli risks his life among the Turks to liberate or to revenge
his sister Paulina, robbed by the Renegado (in the play of that

name). The deserted woman herself repeatedly appears as the servant of the new object of her faithless lover's affection: Statilia serves Cleora (*The Bond-Man*), Madame Beaupré the clever and resolute Bellisant (*The Parliament of Love*).

In view of this inclination of Massinger to repeat himself, we are not surprised to find, also, that many of his *dramatis personae* resemble each other in a pronounced manner; the theory of the typical characters of a dramatist[1] stands confirmed by many of his figures. The most typical of his heroines is the passionate woman who falls violently in love at first sight and runs to the embraces of her beloved without any reserve. This class of women is most characteristically represented by the Turkish princess Donusa, who offers herself to the unsuspicious Vitelli and persists in her wooing until he becomes the victim of her seductive charms, notwithstanding his Christian scruples about her being an infidel. With the same self-abandonment, the empress Domitia makes love to the handsome player Paris. Nor can Aurelia, the duchess of Siena, in *The Maid of Honour*, who, at the first sight of young Bertoldo, forgets all about her princely dignity, and claims him for herself, to his intense surprise and to the great dissatisfaction of her court, be rated higher than her heathen sisters, though she retains at least an outward show of decency. Less objectionable, but not less masterful, appears this form of the passion of love in the character of another duchess, Fiorinda of Urbino, in *The Great Duke of Florence*, who abjectly endeavours to induce the unwilling Sannazaro to take herself and her duchy, though she knows that he loves another, the charming Lidia. Another copy of the same type is the inconstant Almira in *A Very Woman*, who obstinately refuses to listen favourably to the wooing of the prince of Tarent, but, later, when he crosses her way once more in the habit of a slave, is immediately charmed with him to such a degree that she, the daughter of the viceroy of Sicily, does not hesitate to offer a nocturnal meeting to him, a slave. Massinger himself so much affected scenes in which a woman acts the part of the wooer, that he introduced a similar situation in a play where there was no pressing need for it: queen Honoria in *The Picture* seeks to

---

[1] See, on the subject of "typical characters," Schröer, A., *Über Titus Andronicus* (Marburg, 1891), *passim*.

seduce the knight Mathias, only in order to be able to refuse him, and, in this manner, to punish him for having praised the beauty and the chastity of his wife.

A somewhat subtler art of character painting we observe in Massinger's delineation of the nature of those women who are not the powerless victims of a sudden passion. Nevertheless, it cannot be denied that the utterances and the behaviour of his virtuous women often reveal that, in drawing female characters, he could rarely escape from the region of the senses. But, though most of Massinger's women are of the earth, earthy, we must not forget that he was able to create at least two women in another mould: the chaste Camiola and the lovable Lidia. Camiola, the Maid of Honour, deserves this appellation, though, perhaps, the poet impaired the nobleness of her presence and of her actions by two superfluous additions: the violence of her refusal of an unwelcome, boisterous wooer— whose bodily defects she criticises in a strain approaching, though by no means equalling, the invectives which the passion- ate Donusa hurls at the head of the unfortunate basha of Aleppo when he comes to court her—and the cautious contract (taken from the source of the play) by which Bertoldo, to liberate whom Camiola spent a fortune, is placed under an obligation to marry her. Perfectly delightful is Lidia, the youthful heroine of *The Great Duke of Florence*. In her, everything is charming: the simplicity with which she talks of her love for prince Giovanni; her naïve conviction that the fiercest enemy "would let fall his weapon" when looking on the sweetness of her lover; her anxious pleading at the feet of the duke, who is righteously angry with his deceitful nephew, and her trem- bling readiness to sacrifice her own hopes to the happiness of the prince. Nothing could be more winning than the manner of her receiving the fatal letter of her boy lover: she kisses it, she scarcely dares to hurt it by breaking the seal fastened by the beloved hand—even Shakespeare's Julia did not prattle more tenderly when kissing and piecing together the fragments of the letter of her beloved Proteus.

With this exception, a comparative survey of the women of Shakespeare and Massinger is the surest means for convincing us how rapidly the moral character of the English stage had changed since the days of the greater poet. The effrontery of

Donusa and Massinger's other women of the same stamp would suffice to indicate the rise of a taste demanding stronger stimulants; but he went far beyond the loss of dignity and of delicacy of feeling which they exhibit. He created the Syracusan Corsica, the lewd wife of old Creon, who tries to seduce her stepson (*The Bond-Man*); Iolante, who, in the absence of her husband, is ready to accept the first handsome stranger as lover (*The Guardian*)—not to speak of bawds like Calipso in the same play, or the drunken hag Borachia in *A Very Woman*. We are but rarely allowed to forget that Massinger is separated from Shakespeare by Fletcher, whose plays had accustomed the public to the open licence of women.

Massinger's male characters, as a rule, are more interesting than his women. If we except one short scene of the patriotic Cleora, his women think and talk of nothing but the dominating passion of love in its different gradations; while their lovers, though meeting their desires, are yet, at the same time, not rarely made the interpreters of the views of the author. The Venetian Vitelli, whose virtue is too weak to resist the temptations of the infidel Donusa, is, by the admonitions of his ghostly counsellor, the Jesuit Francisco, filled with a repentance which rises to religious ecstasy, so that, in the end, he even aspires to the glory of the death of a martyr, becoming the most eloquent exponent of Massinger's religious feelings. Still more distinctly, we hear the voice of the poet himself in one of the speeches of Paris the Roman actor, in a splendid apology for the stage and its poets and players. Paris, the favourite of the Roman public, is cited before the senate, being accused of satirical attacks on persons of rank and of being a libeller "against the state and Caesar." The gist of the actor's defence is that he and his companions cannot help it, if the conscience of the spectators is shaken by what is done and said on the stage. The energetic flow of this *oratio pro domo*, one of Massinger's rhetorical masterpieces, and its superfluousness from the dramatic point of view—for it stands quite outside the action of the tragedy—show how willingly he availed himself of the opportunity offered by the part of the actor to speak against the detractors of his art in general, and against those "Catos of the stage" of whose persecutions he bitterly complains in one of his rare prologues.

In several plays, the passion of Massinger's heroes takes the form of violent, though groundless, jealousy. The jealous whims of Leosthenes irritate the noble Cleora and, finally, estrange her from him; Mathias doubts the fidelity of his wife; the suspicions of Theodosius, the Emperor of the East, threaten the life of Athenais; Marcelia, the proud wife of Sforza, is murdered by the selfish passion of her husband. A far more imposing figure than these egoists, tormented by their own folly, is the hero of the tragedy *The Fatall Dowry*, the sombre Charolais, who kills his adulterous wife and her gallant, and himself falls a victim to his revenge.

Besides these men who, fighting the battle of life, are not entirely absorbed by the passion of love—for, even in the sketch of the murderous Sforza, much stress is laid by the poet on his warlike qualities and the astuteness of the Italian politician who, standing between the French king and the emperor, knows how to reconcile his loyalty with his advantage—we find among Massinger's lovers, also, the conventional types of the contemporary drama: the devoted lover who lives on the smile of his lady, such as Ladislaus, the humble husband of the proud Honoria, Caldorio and the over-bashful Hortensio, and young libertines like Adorio and Alonzo, whose conversion, usually, is as incredible as it is sudden. Massinger's most attractive boy lover, who really has no other hopes, as yet, than "to stonden in his lady grace," and who utters his feelings with charming freshness, is prince Giovanni, the "north-star" to whom Lidia looks up adoringly.

Guilty women of the stamp of lady Macbeth and the two daughters of king Lear, in whose lives not the passion of love but a stormy, and, if need be, sanguinary, ambition, is the dominant influence, are not to be found in Massinger's dramas; only his men appear capable of conceiving and executing criminal plans. His villains, generally, are monsters of the darkest dye; they resemble each other in being free of any redeeming quality. Even if they act as avengers, they display so much baseness of mind that the wrong suffered by them is forgotten in our indignation at their perfidiousness. Francisco, the treacherous favourite of the duke of Milan, is spurred on by his desire to punish Sforza for having dishonoured his sister, an impulse of which we are informed much too late, long after he has forfeited all our sympathy by the wickedness of the means he uses to gain his end.   First of all, he tries to seduce Sforza's wife, and, as he is foiled in this attempt by the resistance of the duchess, he accuses her of having made love to him, and succeeds in instigating her jealous and credulous husband to kill her.   Finally, after having been bitterly reviled by his sister for cautiously sparing the life of her seducer, he enters the ducal palace in the disguise of a Jewish doctor and covers the lips and hands of the corpse of Marcelia with poisonous paint, so that Sforza is killed by kissing her: from beginning to end he acts the part of a perfidious coward, carefully abstaining from any direct attack on his mighty adversary himself.   A still more despicable villain is Montreville, who, pretending to be the friend of old Malefort, avenges himself on him for injuries borne in silence during many years by dishonouring his innocent daughter Theocrine.   As to the murderous and incestuous Malefort himself, one would feel inclined to regard him as an impossible monster, an isolated creature of the poet's fantasy, did not this very isolation strengthen our belief that Massinger's freely treated model was a historical personage, an Italian villain—that Francesco Cenci who had been killed, by murderers hired by his own daughter, some twenty years before the composition of Massinger's tragedy.   Through the enormity of his crimes, Malefort's dark shape assumes gigantic dimensions, and we are not astonished that the poet himself felt the need of annihilating his monstrous creation, not by mortal agents, but by the direct interference of Heaven itself.

Massinger's imperial malefactor, the bloodthirsty tyrant Domitian, does not stand so entirely beyond the limits of humanity as Malefort.   He becomes vulnerable by his infatuation for the profligate Domitia, and this one human weakness proves fatal to him: he spares her life, forfeited by her adulterous passion for Paris, and when, later, infuriated by her imprecations at the murder of the player, he resolves to kill her, it is too late; Domitia herself heads the crowd of his assassins. By a skilful arrangement of the historical background, the dramatist succeeds in making us believe in the life-likeness of his tyrant as the natural outcome of a cruel age.

These criminals, who are finally struck down by the

nemesis of their evil deeds, are the central figures of tragedies
whose action lies in the far past and in foreign lands. But,
even in those two comedies whose *dramatis personae* are intended
to represent countrymen and contemporaries of the poet, we
meet with two great villains: with the heartless usurer Sir Giles
Overreach in *A New Way to Pay Old Debts*, and with the hypocrite Luke Frugal in *The City-Madam*. Sir Giles Overreach,
who tries to bring his spendthrift nephew, one of the victims
of his extortions, to the gallows, who commands his amiable
daughter to offer herself to the lord to whom he wishes to marry
her, and who boasts of his cruelties towards his debtors, be they
widows or orphans, becomes so tremendous a villain, that, in
order to free humanity of the fiend, the conclusion of the
comedy—as, indeed, the whole conception of this ruthless
character—touches the borders of tragedy. Deluded in all
his ambitious hopes, the infuriated usurer goes mad. In the
case of Luke Frugal, who has not hesitated to cause the betrayal
of the women entrusted to his care—the wife and two daughters
of his brother—the poet contents himself with stripping him of
all his splendour and with exposing him to the contempt of all
around him. In these two domestic comedies, one of the most
glaring defects of Massinger's dramatic world, its frequent
want of truth, strikes us most forcibly. The usurer's bragging
proclamation of his vices and his crimes, which reminds us of
the equally impressive and equally unlikely self-accusation of
Chaucer's pardoner, is quite as incredible as is the obtuseness
of the insidious Luke, when confronted by the gross deception
practised on him. The sober light of day is unfavourable to
Massinger's characters; they stand in need of the romantic
twilight of the past, in order to gain a certain, but too often
limited, likeness to life.

As to Massinger's comical scenes, in which the male element again preponderates, his tragedies indicate an evident
tendency to re-establish the purity of the tragic style. In what
probably was his earliest tragedy, *The Unnaturall Combat*,
a comical character appears in the person of Belgarde, a needy
and ever hungry soldier, who, at a sudden favourable turn of
his fortunes, is overwhelmed by claims of paternity something
like Molière's Monsieur de Pourceaugnac; but his chief scene
is in harmony with the serious tenor of the whole work. Find-

ing himself excluded from a banquet in the governor's palace
on account of his threadbare old suit, he comes to it in the
habit which he had worn for the welfare of his country "in
the heat and fervour of a bloody fight"—in his armour,
eloquently and bitterly blaming the ingratitude of the world
which lets soldiers starve in times of peace. In *The Duke of
Millaine*, the report of the jailor as to the effect of a whipping
on some of his former prisoners is more satirical than comical;
and in *The Roman Actor* the dignity of tragedy is never disturbed by an attempt to raise a laugh. In the comedies, on
the other hand, the usual stock of servants and gulls, of pert
pages and humorous old men is to be found. There appear
Calandrino, the boorish servant, aping the manners of the
court; Gazet, the ambitious servant, who aspires to the office
of an eunuch; and many others. The slaves of Syracuse, who,
in *The Bond-Man*, rebel against their oppressors, are represented as ridiculous and abject creatures, with that curious indifference to the sufferings and rights of the people frequently
to be noted in the drama of the period. Two of Massinger's
comical old men, the voracious and venal judge Greedy in *A
New Way*, and the courtier Cuculo, who, in view of his frequent
hints at his statesmanship, appears to be a weak reproduction
of the Polonius type, are farcical, while the free-spoken Eubulus
and the merry Durazzo sometimes speak very much to the
purpose between their jokes: Eubulus, like Belgarde, in favour
of the neglected soldiers for whom the poet, patriotically
anxious about the defence of his country, puts in a good word
on every occasion; Durazzo, chanting the praise of healthy
country life and of the delights of the chase, especially of
falconry, of which "royal sport" he gives a very pleasing
description.

One cannot help observing with what persistency the satire
with which dramatists frequently combined the fun of their
lighter scenes is by Massinger aimed at the inmates of the
courts of princes. In two of his plays, depraved courtiers, who,
persuaded of the force of their own fascinations, think the
seduction of women an easy task, become the victims of practical jokes and are exposed to general contempt. The exaggerated importance attached to exterior appearance and to
more or less worthless ceremonies, the frequent neglect of

true merit, the ridiculous pride shown by noblemen "of the last edition"—these and many other unpleasant peculiarities of court life are referred to by the poet repeatedly, and with a force of expression which might lead us to think that his bitterness was caused by disagreeable personal experiences.   Other objects of Massinger's satire are the projector and the monopolist, the empiric and the astrologer.   Now and then, he attacks his countrymen in general, dishing up once more the well worn complaints about their fondness for hard drinking and for aping in their dress and manners outlandish, particularly French, fashions; and, once, he even permits a connoisseur of human wares, a slave merchant, the remark that all English people, men and women, are stark mad—remembering, very likely, one of the best known jokes of the grave digger in Hamlet.   Notwithstanding such occasional humorous criticisms, we are made to feel that the poet himself was proud of being an Englishman.   At the end of an uncomplimentary conversation of some Italian servants about the gross feeding and the correspondingly gross understanding of Englishmen stands the telling line: "They can fight and that's their all," and Bertoldo, the faithless lover of *The Maid of Honour*, utters a sincere panegyric on England, "the empress of the European isles," though it is true that we can discover a melancholy inflection in the poet's voice, the eulogy referring not to the present but to a past state of things.   Concerning the political situation of his own days, Massinger shared the dissatisfaction felt by many patriotic contemporaries.

It is noteworthy that Massinger's satirical allusions avoid two themes frequently treated by other dramatists of his time: neither satirical remarks of a literary kind, parodies of passages of the works of older writers, nor violent invectives to the address of the irreconcilable enemies of the stage, the puritans, are to be found in his plays, the nearest approach to such an attack being the statement of the jailor in *The Duke of Millaine*, that a sectary who would not yield to any argument of reason was made a "fine pulpit-man" by a trussing of his haunches. Probably, Massinger, who was himself prone to religious meditation, admired in secret the moral rectitude of the puritans and their energy of purpose; he may even have felt oppressed by the consciousness that he was helping to heighten the animosity

of their adversaries by participating in the scurrility and
viciousness then characteristic of the stage. As it is, his comic
dialogue abounds in coarse innuendos. Massinger's comic characters, advisedly, perorate in blank verse; the quacksalver,
however, and the star-gazer are allowed to announce their
wisdom in prose, possibly because it would have been a difficult
task to versify smoothly the strange, half-Latin terms of their
pseudoscientific *galimatias*.

As to versification and poetic diction, Massinger's mastership is indisputable; his dramas contain many passages in
which the beauty of the style equals the vigour of the thought.
He is a great orator, excelling in speeches in which, after the
fashion of lawyers, speakers have to defend some particular
position and to put their case in the most favourable light.
Belgarde, insisting on the merits of the soldier; Sforza, endeavouring to convince the emperor that he, too, might find
him a faithful and useful ally, notwithstanding his loyalty
towards the French king; Timoleon of Corinth, soundly rating
the Syracusans for having shamefully neglected the means of
defence of their country; Paris, in his apology for the stage;
Lidia, in her pathetic pleading for her lover; Athenais, appealing to the compassion of Pulcheria—these and many other
heroes and heroines of Massinger's are never at a loss for
powerful, convincing or moving words when in critical situations. The mechanical tricks of the Euphuistic style are, for
Massinger, a thing of the past; his use of alliteration is very
discreet, in most cases undoubtedly unconscious, and the insertion of Latin words or quotations, in which the older dramatists
delighted, is a great rarity with him—in these respects, he
strikes us as a far more modern writer than his predecessors and
many of his contemporaries. But, on the other hand, it cannot
be denied that he also has his peculiar blemishes and tricks
of style, and, among them, one which is very obtrusive and for
which he has been frequently censured—a mania for repeating
himself. He possesses a considerable store of set phrases,
metaphors and similes, which he strews around on every occasion without troubling himself to vary and individualise his
expressions. Especially numerous and monotonous are his
classical illustrations: Aeson and Medea, Hippolytus, Diana
and Phaedra, Pasiphaë and her bull, Alcides and his poisoned

shirt, and a great many other figures and objects of classical mythology continually remind us of Massinger's having received a classical education, a fact which is also recalled to us by the frequent translations of famous passages of ancient authors noticeable in his verse.

On the other hand, many of Massinger's similes, however bookish, mirror genuinely English impressions, originally received from the contemplation of the sea, its coasts and the life of sailors. The foam-covered rock, the stream which loses its name in the ocean, the ship, returning or outward bound, the small boat wrecked by the weight of its own sails, and many other maritime incidents, are frequently mentioned. In certain situations, which repeat themselves in his dramas, stereotyped formulas are sure to be used: if a beautiful lady is to be won, Massinger's personages never forget to talk of her "virgin fort"; the charms of his passionate ladies, when they take the wooing upon themselves, are so powerful that even an ascetic hermit would be at a loss how to resist them; Lidia and Camiola, both of them in love with men of a higher social position, talk of their north-star and of the impossibility of the wren's building near the eagle. Too often the tinsel of these colourless phrases reminds us of the haste of the dramatist, sacrificing one of the greatest charms of any poem, its freshness of expression, to the wish to have done with his work.

Massinger's fatal fondness for conventional repetitions, which has been pointed out in the situations, characters, thoughts and words of his plays, apprises us of the limits of his merits as a dramatic artist. Notwithstanding our readiness to admire the firmness of his construction and the splendour of his diction, we are too often offended by the monotony of his characters and by the narrow range of their ideas; and his treatment of them exhibits hardly any process of development. As a playwright, it is true, he seeks to perfect himself in the technical part of his art; as a psychologist, he is too much inclined to remain on the surface, from beginning to end. We feel that the dramatist does not sufficiently identify himself with his creations, that he does not live in them, that they are formed more from the outside than from the inside. In consequence of this coldness of their maker, we do not recognise in his figures living beings of our own flesh and blood; too many of them remain cleverly formed and ably managed theatrical puppets. It is a great pity that the straitened circumstances of his life, which obliged him to work rapidly, prevented him from devoting a greater measure of love and care to the delineation of his characters. That he would have been able to rouse them to an intenser, fuller life, is impressed upon us as we look on the thoroughly lovable Lidia, on the pure presence of Camiola and at some of his secondary characters, as, for instance, the faithful Adorni, whose love for Camiola is deeper than the selfish desire to win her for himself.

As to the reception of Massinger's plays by the public of his own days, we know very little. In his dedications, he repeatedly laments the neglect shown by his contemporaries to poetry in general, mentioning, with bitterness in one instance, his own "despised studies"; and the cutting remark that he presumes his *Roman Actor* will, in consequence of "the severity and height of the subject distaste such as are only affected with jigs and ribaldry," indicates, perhaps, that this tragedy had not been successful on the stage. On the other hand, he alludes to the friendly reception of *The Bond-Man;* and, in the dedication of *The Picture*, one of his most entertaining dramas, he is able to mention the general approbation the play had found at its presentment. Of prologues expressive of his sentiments, we have but few, because, with characteristic, and, in this case, very justifiable, conservatism, he strongly objected to this innovation, not falling in with it before the performance of his tragicomedy *The Emperour of the East*, printed in 1631, the first prologue to which begins with a few angry words about the imperiousness of custom. Nevertheless, we are indebted to his poems of this kind for a few noteworthy biographical details. In the two prologues composed for *The Emperour of the East*, he complains of the censures of those

> who delight
> To misapply whatever he shall write,

and of

> the rage
> And envy of some Catos of the stage

by whom "this poor work" had suffered; while, in the prologue of *The Guardian*, he informs us of the failure of two of his dramatic ventures, which was followed by a silence of two years. We are ignorant of the nature of those two unfortunate plays, because many of Massinger's dramas were never printed and the manuscripts were inadvertently destroyed by Warburton's cook.

The posthumous popular fame of Massinger is chiefly based on his comedy *A New Way to Pay Old Debts*, which has kept the stage till recently, the brilliant part of the bold usurer captivating many famous actors. In a more indirect way, the appreciation of the dramatic power of the tragedy *The Fatall Dowry*, printed as a joint production of Massinger and Field, but, undoubtedly, chiefly Massinger's work, has been proved by the adaptations of later poets: by Nicholas Rowe's tragedy *The Fair Penitent*, composed in 1703, which did more for the preservation of Rowe's name as a dramatist than all his independent plays; and by the recent successful version of Beer-Hofmann, entitled *Der Graf von Charolais*, which revived the memory of Massinger all over Germany. The first traces of his influence on the German stage date back to his lifetime: in 1626, an imitation of his and Dekker's dramatisation of the legend of Dorothea was performed at Dresden, where his attractive *Great Duke of Florence* also appeared on the boards in 1661. Later, Massinger attracted the attention of the poets of the romantic school of Germany as one of the most fascinating of Shakespeare's successors: count Baudissin translated several of his plays, and, within the last decades, German translators have repeatedly had recourse to him.

CHAPTER VII

Tourneur and Webster

THE two dramatists who are to be considered in the present chapter have certain points in common. Both, at their best, display a peculiarly sombre genius. The tragedies of both belong to the same school; and both are utterly unknown to us, except by their writings. In point of date, Tourneur would seem slightly to precede Webster. And, for this reason, as well as for others which are more material, it will be convenient to take him first.

Of Cyril Tourneur's life, we know nothing beyond the dates at which his various plays and poems were published. They are as follows: *The Transformed Metamorphosis*, 1600; *A Funeral Poem* on Sir Francis Vere, 1609; *A Griefe on the Death of Prince Henry*, 1613; and his two dramas, *The Revengers Tragoedie*, 1607 and *The Atheist's Tragedie*, 1611.[1] It should be noted that two of these, the poem on Vere and *The Revengers Tragoedie*, have no name on the title-page, and that nothing more than tradition connects them with the name of Tourneur. There is a tepid reference to the author, "as not to be despised nor too much praised," by an anonymous contemporary; and that is all.

On his poems, it is not necessary to dwell. None of them has any merit; and the most elaborate of them, *The Metamorphosis*, is written in that uncouth jargon which had been brought into fashion by Marston in his satires (1598), and which is assailed by Jonson in *Poetaster*. It is, moreover, an involved allegory, the key to which is lost, but which Churton Collins ingeniously interpreted as a cryptic reference to the fortunes of Essex.

[1] A tragicomedy, *The Nobleman*, acted at court in 1613, is now lost.

We pass at once to the two dramas, for it is by these alone that Tourneur survives. A question has been raised as to the relative priority of their composition. The order of publication makes a presumption in favour of *The Revengers Tragoedie;* but it is a presumption which might easily yield to substantial arguments on the other side. The only argument, however, which has been brought forward is the inferiority, or, as it has been called, the "immaturity," of *The Atheist's Tragedie*. Such an argument is manifestly perilous and, if applied to the works of other writers, would lead to curious results. On the other side must be set the fact that *The Revengers Tragoedie*, though it abounds in striking passages and scenes, is singularly lacking in originality of conception; that it belongs to a type of tragedy which had been in vogue for many years before its appearance; that, in fact, it is a rearrangement of the material already treated by Marston in *Antonios Revenge* (1602).[1] *The Atheist's Tragedie*, on the other hand, though, doubtless, inferior in some respects, is strikingly original in its central conception. And it would seem improbable that, after following his own path with much boldness, the dramatist should, in a later play, have fallen back obediently into the well worn rut. The same conclusion is suggested by the metre, which, in *The Revengers Tragoedie*, is exceptionally regular, while, in *The Atheist's Tragedie*, it is marked by what can only be called an abuse of the light endings which abound in the later plays of Shakespeare. We have other grounds for saying that Tourneur was a zealous student of Shakespeare; and it is surely more natural to suppose that, after the example of his master, he passed from the stricter to the looser system, than from the looser to the stricter. The point is by no means certain. On the whole, however, it would appear likely that the order of publication is, also, the order of composition; in other words, that *The Revengers Tragoedie* was written in or before 1607, and that *The Atheist's Tragedie* falls some time between it and 1611.

Neither play can be said to show much trace of dramatic power. The plots are poor in themselves, and one of them is largely borrowed. The characters are, at best, little more than types; and, in one instance, at any rate, the revenger's mother,

[1] See *ante*, Chap. II.

the type is hardly improved by an incredible conversion. The most original character in the whole gallery is that of D'Amville, the atheist. But even he has a fatal resemblance to the Machiavellian monster who, from the time of Kyd and Marlowe, had been a familiar figure to the Elizabethan playgoer. The other characters are either puppets or incarnate abstractions of the various virtues and vices. The wanton personages of *The Atheist's Tragedie* are frankly caricatures. It is as poet that Tourneur claims our attention: a poet whose imagination is poisoned by the sense of universal vanity and corruption, but who lights up this festering material with flashes of high genius, and who is capable, at rare moments, of rising to visions of true beauty, and even grace: "To have her train borne up, and her soul Trail in the dirt" is an instance of the one; the alleged discovery of Charlemont's body by Borachio, of the other. And, to the former, at any rate, many parallels could be brought. His imagination needed a dramatic matter to kindle it; but, when kindled, it followed its own path and paid little heed to any but the purely formal requirements of the drama. To him, a tragedy was an outlet for the expression of his bitter judgment on man and his essentially gloomy view of human life. To this, all personages, all incidents, are subordinated. Of this, all that is memorable in his dramas is the imaginative symbol. In these points, he presents a certain analogy to Webster, but an analogy which, at the same time, is a faint reflection and a caricature.

The outward life of John Webster is as much a blank to us as that of Tourneur. The years of his birth and death are, alike, unknown to us. It may be conjectured, from the known dates, that he was born in the decade 1570–80; and he must have survived at least until 1624, the year of the production of the *Monuments of Honor*. Further than that we cannot go. It would be unsafe to accept the statement—not made until 1698, and not confirmed by the parish registers—that he was clerk of St Andrew's, Holborn. And the one outward fact with which we are left—a fact recorded on the title-page of the *Monuments of Honor*—is that he was a member of the Merchant Taylors' company. With this, we must rest content.

His literary activity falls, naturally, into three periods: the first, that of collaboration and apprenticeship (1602–7);

the second, that of the two great tragedies (1610 to 1614); the third, that of the tragicomedies and, probably, of *Appius and Virginia*, beginning about 1620, the probable date of *The Devils Law-case*, and ending at a time unknown. It will be well to take each of these periods singly, and then to consider the characteristics of his genius as a whole.

During the first period, Webster produced no independent work. He was engaged in collaboration with other dramatists, particularly Dekker; and, owing to a peculiarity of his genius, his individuality was entirely merged in that of his fellow workers. After joining with Middleton and others in two plays, *Caesar's Fall* and *The Two Harpies*,[1] which have perished, he is found in partnership with Dekker, Heywood and Wentworth Smith over a play entered as *Lady Jane*,[2] and immediately followed by a *Second Part* (27 October) apparently from the hand of Dekker only. It has been universally assumed that these two plays are either wholly or in part identical with that which has come down to us under the title *The Famous History of Sir Thomas Wyat* (published 1607); and there is no reason for questioning this assumption.[3] As to the exact relation of the two parts of *Lady Jane* to the existing *Wyat*, there is considerable doubt. The most plausible conjecture is that of Dyce, who held the published version to be rudely cobbled together, with many omissions, from the two parts as originally composed. And the shapeless build of the drama, together with the entire absence of the "coming in of King Philip" mentioned on the title-page, is in favour of this explanation. The only names occurring on the title-page are those of Dekker and Webster; and it would seem tolerably plain that the former was the predominant partner. He was already an old hand at historical subjects. French history, Scottish, Portuguese and, above all, English, had all, during the last four years, been freely dramatised by him. Moreover, the treatment of character, the peculiarities of versification, the general cast of sentiment—all these have analogies in his unaided work. And there are few things, if any, which remind us of the unaided work of Webster.

---

[1] See Henslowe's diary, 22, 29 May, 1602.
[2] *Ibid.*, 15 October, 1602. [3] Cf. *ante*, Chap. II.

We turn, therefore, to the next recorded work—the contributions of Webster to the second edition of Marston's *The Malcontent* (published 1604).[1] It would seem probable that Webster is responsible for nothing more than the induction to that strange and "bitter" drama. Such is the natural interpretation of the words on the title-page, and in the heading to the induction itself. It is confirmed by the manifest identification of "additions"—and this is the word which has caused much misunderstanding—with "induction" in the opening dialogue (ll. 87–91). And no argument, except such as rests upon a strained construction of the title-page, has hitherto been brought to the contrary. The body of the play, which the induction describes as having been "lost, found" and subsequently "played by the King's Servants," is of earlier date. There are strong reasons, as Stoll points out, for fixing it as early as 1600, though this view is not wholly free from difficulties. But it was not printed until 1604, and that year saw two distinct editions: the first without, the second with, the induction. The second edition also contains the "augmentations," which, it may well be, are rather restorations of the "lost" text, as originally written by Marston. The induction – and it is that alone with which we are concerned—can hardly have been written much before the moment of publication. Its composition would naturally fall between the dates of the first and second editions. And this intrinsic probability is supported by internal evidence. The main object of the piece, seemingly, is to justify the king's company for performing a play in which a rival company, that of the Blackfriars, had certain rights. And that company, in its "decimo-sexto" shape—the "little eyases" of the second quarto of *Hamlet*— was not licensed until January, 1604.[2] Any allusion to it in its earlier form, before it passed into the hands of the "children," would be irrelevant. It may be added that, in the words of Sly, "No, in good faith, for mine ease," there is a manifest quotation from the Osric of the second quarto of *Hamlet* (1604). Altogether, then, we can hardly be wrong in dating the composition of the induction within the year 1604. And, on the evidence of the title-page, we are justified in saying that

[1] Cf. *ante*, Chap. II.

[2] See Collier, *Annals of the Stage*, vol. I, pp. 352–3.

Webster was sole author. That he had much reason to be proud of it, no one will assert. The "additions," as Burbage modestly remarks, "are not greatly needed"; and, save in so far as they serve to introduce a hit against the children of the queen's revels, they do little more than "entertain time and abridge the not received custom of music." The induction was a common device of the Elizabethan stage. It had been employed, for instance, in *The taming of a Shrew* (printed 1594) in *Every Man out of His Humour*, in *Cynthia's Revels* and in *Antonio and Mellida*. And it must be confessed that Webster's effort is both flatter in itself and stands in a looser relation to the play which follows than any of these.

We now pass to what have been called the citizen comedies, *West-Ward Hoe* and *North-Ward Hoe*, both written in partnership with Dekker.[1] Both were printed in 1607; but the former was entered at Stationers' hall as early as March, 1605; the latter not until August, 1607. The first three acts of *West-Ward Hoe* have been thought by some critics to belong to 1603, and their authorship assigned to Webster. But there is no valid reason for passing the hatchet between these acts and the last two. And, as the fourth act (sc. 2) contains an allusion to the fall of Ostend—an allusion which is probably, though not certainly, anticipated in the first act (sc. 1)—and as Ostend did not surrender until the autumn of 1604, it is likely that the composition of the whole falls into the last quarter of 1604, and that it was first acted at the beginning of 1605. In no case can *North-Ward Hoe* be dated earlier than about the middle of 1605, seeing that it is plainly a reply to *East-ward Hoe* (by Jonson, Chapman and Marston), which was almost certainly written, as a retort to *West-Ward Hoe*, in the earlier part of that year. And if, as seems probable, it contains a borrowing from Marston's *Parasitaster, Or The Fawne*,[2] which appears to have been first acted, as well as registered, early in 1606, then the composition of Dekker and Webster's second comedy must be placed in 1606–7. In any case, it is clear that, during the time of partnership, long or short, the intercourse between Webster and Dekker, begun (as we have seen) in 1602, must have been of the most intimate kind. And, once more, it was

---

[1] Cf. *ante*, Chap. II.
[2] See Bullen's *Marston*, vol. II, p. 21; Stoll, p. 16.

the younger and deeper poet who sat at the feet of the elder
and more facile.

The plays in question bring us into the thick of one of those
battles of the dramatists which give much liveliness to the history of the Elizabethan stage.   It may be called an afterswell
of the storm which had raged between Jonson, on the one hand,
and Dekker and Marston, on the other, in 1601–2; the storm of
which *Cynthia's Revels*, *Poetaster* and *Satiro-mastix* are the
abiding record.[1] Times had changed since the first round of the
contest.   Marston was now the partner of his terrible enemy;
and, on both sides, the game was now played with the best
temper, a compliment which could certainly not be paid to
Jonson's share in the earlier encounter.   The main plot of
West-Ward Hoe is a tale of three merry wives who, putting their
husbands on a false scent, jaunt off with three gallants to
spend the night at Brentford, then a familiar trysting-place.
They are pursued by their husbands and run to earth at the inn,
but, thanks to a sudden freak of respectability, are able to
prove their innocence; all ends in good temper and reconciliation.   With this is ingeniously interwoven the story of Mistress Justiniano, who is wooed by a rakish earl and yields to
his entreaties, but, at the critical moment, is seized with scruples
and joins with her husband to work a like repentance on her
lover.   Having thus set his own house in order, Justiniano acts
as managing director to the comedy of the three citizens and
their wives, which forms the staple of the drama.   The reply
of Jonson and his partners in *Eastward Hoe* is notably respectful.
In the main, it is a piece of friendly emulation rather than of
satire.   And the picture of citizen life is among the most pleasing, as well as vivid, which have come down to us.   The theme
is plainly suggested by the citizen and prentice portraits in
which Dekker was past master.   The spirit of Simon Eyre and
Candido is caught with such skill that, a few phrases and other
touches apart, the play might easily have been taken for the
work of Dekker himself.   Yet, in the edifying conversion of
Master Francis Quicksilver, the idle apprentice, and most
engaging of scapegraces, there is, manifestly, a spice of burlesque; and it is hard not to believe that the shaft was aimed
at such scenes as the sudden conversion of Bellafront (1604), or

[1] See *ante*, Chap. II.

of Mistress Justiniano in *West-Ward Hoe* itself. The satire, however, is unexpectedly genial; not comparable to that which had been showered on Dekker and Marston in *Poetaster*, nor even to that which was aimed at king James and his country-men in this very play, and which brought the authors within danger of the law. Equally good-humoured is the satire of the rejoinder. Jonson is let off without a scratch. The banter—for it is nothing more—falls entirely on Chapman. There can be no doubt that the "little hoary poet" of *North-Ward Hoe* is intended for the latter. His *Caesar and Pompey*, his liking for French themes, his "full and heightened style," his pro-fessional vanity—all come in for gentle mockery. But the banter consists in nothing worse than placing the "reverend" and moral poet in impossible situations; in bringing him to the house of a courtesan who falls violently in love with him and in causing him to be seized, if only for a moment, as a fit subject for confinement in Bedlam. And, on the whole, the portrait of Bellamont is the most attractive thing in the whole piece; Chapman himself can hardly have taken it amiss. Apart from such quizzing, the plot of the comedy is uncommonly simple. Mistress Mayberry, the wife of a rich citizen, is persecuted by the attentions of two worthless gallants. After repeated rejections, one of them snatches the ring from her finger and shows it to her husband, as a proof of her infidelity. Guided by Bellamont, Mayberry is soon able to convince him-self of her innocence, and bides his time for an appropriate revenge. He beguiles the two slanderers into a trip to Ware, in the course of which he brings conclusive proof that one of them has corrupted the wife of the other. The injured husband is overwhelmed with confusion, and Mayberry completes his vengeance by entrapping the other rogue into marriage with the lady who has already figured gaily in the satire on Chapman. It can hardly be said that either this comedy, or that which opened the series, is so vivid or so full of sparkle as that of Jonson and his associates. But the merit of *Eastward Hoe* is so extraordinary that a play may well fall short of it and yet be extremely good. And that will be the verdict of most readers both on *West-Ward Hoe* and *North-Ward Hoe*.

It remains to ask whether there is any means of determining the part played by Webster in the composition of these plays.

The two are strictly of a piece. In both—whether we regard construction, situations, characters or phrases—we can trace reminiscences or anticipations of Dekker's acknowledged work[1] and there is little or nothing which can be said to bear the stamp of Webster. Whichever of the partners held the pen, it can hardly be doubted that the inspiration, alike in small things and in great, was Dekker's. If there be any one scene where the reader might be tempted to recognise the hand of Webster, it is that in which the earl, expecting to find his mistress, is confronted by her husband in disguise, while a curtain is drawn aside so as to reveal the apparently lifeless body of the woman he had expected to see at his mercy. But even this scene, as Swinburne and others have pointed out, is, so far as the central situation goes, to be closely paralleled from the *Satiro-mastix* and *The Honest Whore* of Dekker. And, though the disguise of Justiniano and some touches both before and after his entry are well in accordance with what we know of Webster, the style of the whole passage, in the main, is rather that of Dekker; and where so much is his, it is hazardous to assume that anything of moment was contributed by his partner. Of the citizen comedics then, as of *Wyat*, it may be said that the conception is Dekker's and that the execution—whether as regards characters, incidents, or style—is, on the whole, entirely in his spirit. That they contain a good deal of Webster's work, need not be doubted. But such work is executive rather than original, derived rather than creative.

So ends the period of Webster's apprenticeship and collaboration. We now pass to the earlier of the two periods which contain his original and unaided work (1610–18). This is the period of *The White Divel* (afterwards known as *Vittoria Corombona*) and *The Dutchesse Of Malfy*. Some three or four years separate their period from the preceding. For *The White Divel* was printed in 1612; and the repeated borrowings from Rich's *New Description of Ireland*, published in 1610, forbid us to place its composition earlier than that year; it may well have been written in 1611. The exact source of this great tragedy is a problem which still remains unsolved. That it is based on events connected with the life of Paolo Giordano duke of Bracciano, and that these events took place in 1581–5,

[1] Cf. Stoll, pp. 64–79.

that is, within the lifetime of Webster himself, is certain. Beyond that, all is obscure. The case, so far as our present knowledge goes, is as follows. Many versions of the story, contemporary or nearly so, exist in Italian;[1] one, by François de Rosset,[2] is known in French. All these are in substantial agreement with each other; and all differ, in many crucial points, from Webster's. The question at once arises: how are Webster's variations to be accounted for? Had he before him a written account differing from all those which have come down to us? Or had he heard an oral statement substantially agreeing with that given in his play and traceable in the last resort to one who had either travelled in Italy, or come, as visitor, from Italy to the north? Or had he read a version corresponding more or less closely with those accessible to us, and retained nothing more than a confused and indistinct memory of it? Or, finally, having, from written or oral sources, a tolerably accurate knowledge of the true facts, did he deliberately alter them for purposes of dramatic effect?

This is not the place to discuss the question in detail. So much, however, may be said. The first supposition, so far as it relates to any record professing to be historical, may be dismissed as highly improbable. The story, as we have seen, was well known and accurately recorded. The actors in it were among the most marked figures of their times: Francesco, grand duke of Florence, the typical Italian "despot" of his day; Sixtus V, the soul of the League and the Armada, the last of the popes who can fairly be described as great. The heroine of the story was niece by marriage of the latter. The circumstances of her second marriage and her murder had formed the subject of trials—one at Rome, the other at Padua and Venice—familiar to all Italy. It is hardly to be conceived that any chronicler should have departed widely from facts thus generally known. Novels and dramas remain. And it is not impossible that, some day, either a novel or, less probably, a drama may be discovered which criticism will recognise as the source from which Webster drew. None such, however, has hitherto been found; though Tempesti, writing a century and a half later (1754), says that the "story was known all over

---

[1] Cf. Gnoli, D., *Vittoria Accoramboni* (1870), pp. 2–6.
[2] *Histoires tragiques de nostre temps*, in or shortly before 1615.

Europe" and had been told by "hundreds of authors." The only novel at present known is the "tragic history" of de Rosset; and that, with the exception of the assumed names and minute additions of obviously romantic embroidery, is in complete accordance with the chronicles; so that, even if it can be proved to have appeared before *The White Divel* was written, it will in no way account for Webster's departure from the historical facts. Of dramas, previous to Webster's, still less is to be said. Santorio, indeed, a contemporary chronicler (1562–1635) says: *Scio ego apud quosdam actitatum tragœdiæ argumentum, datumque spectantibus haud suppressis personis nominibusque.* But in what language this tragedy was written—whether, as we shall see in the analogous case of *The Dutchesse Of Malfy*, the reference may not even be to *The White Divel* itself—unfortunately does not appear.

The other alternatives are not mutually exclusive. It is perfectly possible that an oral statement, for which either an English traveller or an Italian visitor was ultimately responsible, may have reached Webster and that some, at least, of his inaccuracies may be due to the natural negligence of his informant. Intercourse with Italy had never been broken off. France was a common meeting ground of English and Italian. We know, for instance, that Vittoria's own stepson, Virginio Orsini, the Giovanni of the play, had been sent as envoy to England by his uncle Ferdinand, successor to Francesco, at the close of Elizabeth's reign. We know that the same Virginio was reputed lover to Marie de Medici, and that the attention of English dramatists was at this time keenly directed to the doings of the French court, and not least to the love affairs of the royal house.[1] All this would make it natural enough that rumours, more or less accurate, relating to the Orsini and Medici, should reach the ears of Webster. But, once again, there is no evidence. Some, indeed, of Webster's inaccuracies are almost certainly due to lapse of memory. For instance, he has given the official name of Sixtus V wrongly, and has inverted the parts of Flamineo and Marcello. Neither of these changes can plausibly be set down to deliberate intention.

There remains the final possibility that Webster had read

[1] See the circumstance connected with the performance of *The Conspiracie, And Tragedie of Charles Duke of Byron*, 1608, *ante*, Chap. II.

an account not substantially different from that given by the
chronicles, and that most of his variations are made of set purpose; that is, with a view either to suit his own conception of
what the leading characters in such a tragedy should be, or to
secure a more impressive effect. Among the changes made
with the former object would be reckoned the transformation
of the characters of Vittoria's husband and mother, the one for
ill, the other for good; the strain of hypocrisy, not, however,
very consistently worked out, in the character of Vittoria; the
obvious adaptation of her circumstances to those of her kins-
woman, Bianca Capello (the heroine of Middleton's undated
drama, *Women beware Women*);[1] above all, the change in the
character of Lodovico who, in the play, is moved neither by
avarice, nor by the desire to assert the honour of his family,
but by the fixed resolve to exact vengeance for the murder
of an adored mistress, Isabella. Among the alterations made
for the sake of effect might be counted the appearance of the
"lieger ambassadors" at Vittoria's trial and the election of
Sixtus (the presence of the English envoy is historically impossible), the murders of Marcello and Brachiano, the appearance of Francesco as a direct agent in the latter crime,
the ghastly scene at Brachiano's deathbed and, very possibly,
the transference of the riddling *Manet alta mente repostum*
from Lodovico to Isabella. It would clearly have weakened
the dramatic force of the tragedy to reserve the final act, or
even a closing scene, for the nemesis of Lodovico. And it
may well be for this reason that, in defiance of historical facts,
Webster placed his death within a few moments of his victim's.
That would at once bar out the situation in which the memorable phrase was actually uttered—the formal questioning of
Lodovico by the magistrates of Padua. And Webster, impressed (as he well might be) by the phrase, was, on this assumption, at the pains to introduce it under circumstances entirely
different, but hardly less dramatic.

If this be the true explanation—and many things point that
way—it would follow that Webster's treatment of his subject
is far more original than has sometimes been supposed. If we
may believe him to have worked on a chronicle such as those
embodied in Tempesti's *Vita di Sisto V*, or on a novel resem-

---

[1] See *ante*, Chap. III.

bling that of de Rosset, he has, manifestly, made far more sweeping changes in his "source" than seems to be implied by those who speak of his play as drawn from "an Italian novel." He would, in fact, have breathed a new spirit into the whole train of incidents. The figure of Vittoria, indeed, remains much as we might divine it to have been from the historical records; though the lines are deepened, the colours heightened and harmonised, by the hand of genius. The same applies, though in a less degree, to the defiant figure of Brachiano and the deep dissimulation of Francesco and Monticelso. The last, indeed, is the one case in which the dramatist has fallen short of the model supplied by history. In a drama where he could not be the central figure there was no room for the grand, yet sinister, figure of Sixtus. All else, however, would be the creation of Webster: the tragic resignation of Isabella, the fatuity of Camillo, the pathos of Cornelia, the profoundly interesting and subtle portrait of Lodovico. The crucial change, alike for its own sake and for its bearing on the whole structure of the tragedy, is that in the character and motives of Lodovico. The attribution of his long cherished schemes to outraged love and the thirst for vengeance alters the whole nature of the action. It provides the atmosphere of doom which hangs over the drama from beginning to end, and which is deepened by the scenic effects, the sombre episodes, of which Webster was master without rival.

But, whether the positive changes made by Webster in his unknown authority be large or small, the advance of *The White Divel* on any or all of his previous work is incalculable. To the 'prentice, seeing through the eyes and speaking with the voice of his master, has succeeded the skilled craftsman, with an almost perfect command of his material and instruments, with the keenest eye for the hidden possibilities of his task and the utmost originality in handling it. During the half dozen years or so which followed, Webster was by far the most striking figure, Shakespeare excepted, in the long roll of contemporary dramatists. With the men of his own day, he had not the vogue of Beaumont and Fletcher or the personal authority of Jonson. But modern criticism, with one voice, has pronounced his genius to be of a higher and rarer kind. And, though we can still trace a certain awkwardness in his management of the plot—a defect from which he never shook himself entirely free—his work, in other respects, is singularly self-contained, as well as absolutely original.   There is, perhaps, no poet on record who leaped so suddenly into the full possession of his powers.   It is, of course, true that the influence of other writers can be traced very plainly in this, as in his other, tragedy.   His debt to Shakespeare, has often been pointed out. It appears in many turns of thought and phrase; in the portrait of the boy, Giovanni; in the haunting beauty of Cornelia's dirge; in the consummate art, bold yet unostentatious, with which the figure of the heroine is painted: above all, in that union of imaginative reflection, pure poetry and dramatic genius which brings him nearer than any of his fellow dramatists to the author of *Hamlet*.   In his fusion of the two former of these qualities, again, we cannot fail to recognise his relationship, perhaps his indebtedness, to the greatest lyric poet of the period, Donne.

These, however, are matters which concern the individual genius of the dramatist.   Still more significant is his place in the general development of the Elizabethan drama; and, in particular, his debt to the dramatists of revenge.   Here, he falls into line with that long succession of writers, beginning with Kyd, who took up the tale of Seneca's *Thyestes* and *Agamemnon* and, during more than twenty years, rang the changes upon the theme of vengeance through every key and with every variety of accompaniment.   To explain his position, a slight sketch of the history of this theme, as handled by Elizabethan dramatists, may be attempted.

In the older versions of the theme there are three essential features, all of which, in the last resort, are inherited from Seneca.   These are, that a murder has been committed; that revenge is a duty from which the next of kin cannot escape; and that this duty is enforced by the ghost of the murdered man, which appears at intervals to drive home the demand for blood.   So it is with *The Spanish Tragedie;* so with *Antonios Revenge;* so, allowing for certain modifications, with *The Revenge of Bussy d'Ambois* (published 1613) and *The Second Maiden's Tragedy* (licensed 1611);[1] so, unless all indications are misleading, with the lost *Hamlet* (in or before 1596), which has been attributed, on probable, but not conclusive, grounds, to Kyd; so,

---

[1] As to this play see *Ward*, vol. II, p. 672.

finally, with the *Hamlet* of Shakespeare. The first change in the outward framework of the story—in spirit, it need hardly be said that Shakespeare's masterpiece stands poles asunder from the crudities of Kyd, Marston and the rest—seems to have been made by Chettle, whose *Tragedy of Hoffman* belongs to the same year as *Antonios Revenge*.[1]   The change is twofold. The ghost disappears; and, what is far more significant, the avenger of blood is no longer the hero, but the villain, of the piece.   Both innovations are repeated, with important modifications, in the next play of Marston, *The Malcontent* (1604, or earlier), to which, indeed, it is quite possible that the credit of them may belong rather than to *Hoffman*.   The modifications are as follows.   The murderer of the original version is replaced by a usurper who drives the rightful prince into exile.   This, necessarily, involves the disappearance of the ghost.   And revenge, though retained, is retained in a form so softened that the avenger contents himself with melting one of his enemies to repentance and dismissing the other with magnanimous contempt.

It was at this point that Tourneur took up the tale.   Reverting to murder as the starting-point of his action, he entirely dispenses with the ghost and, in the very moment of victory, the cup of triumph is dashed from the lips of his "revenger." It is clear that he felt the theme of vengeance to be an outworn convention.   It is equally clear that he surrendered it with extreme reluctance.   The whole fabric of the piece is based on the assumption that revenge is a binding duty.   And, when the tables are turned, when the performance of the duty is visited at the last moment with condign punishment, it is inevitable that the reader should feel himself defrauded.   Never had a play so lame and impotent a conclusion as this.   And, for that reason, if for no other, it is a relief to turn from *The Revengers Tragoedie* to *The Atheist's Tragedie*.   Here, at any rate, the central thought is consistently maintained from beginning to end.   Here, at any rate, the dramatist flies without faltering to his mark.   The innovation, which he had been blindly feeling after in *The Revengers Tragoedie*, is here boldly carried out.   Vengeance is thrust down from the rank of duties; forgiveness is exalted in its stead.   If the ghost of the murdered

---

[1] See Henslowe's diary, 7 July, 29 December, 1602.

man is restored to something of his former rights, it is to cry
not for revenge, but for mercy; to reiterate, with a fervour
more moral than dramatic, that "vengeance is the Lord's."
The dramatic weakness of the change is obvious enough. But
it is significant as marking the final stage of the tragedies of
revenge.

The White Divel, in all probability, was produced during the
very year in which *The Atheist's Tragedie* was published. At
first sight it might be taken for a reversion to the earlier type of
this class of drama. Revenge for innocent blood is once more
the main theme of the dramatist. It is presented, however,
no longer as a duty, but as a passion; and with the cry of "wild
justice" is mingled the baser note of wounded pride. Our
sympathies, again, so far from being with the avengers, are cast,
rather, on the side of their victim. The result of such changes
is to reduce the motive of vengeance to a secondary place. It
supplies not the core of the building, but its scaffolding, or little
more. The vital interest belongs not to the story—this, in
truth, might have been told more clearly—but to the characters
who sustain it, and the passions which are let loose in its course.
One more proof is thus furnished, if proof were needed, that the
theme of revenge was now losing its fascination; that the
dramatist, even when he professed to work on it, was now
driven by an overmastering instinct to degrade it from its
original supremacy.

The same tendency appears still more clearly in *The
Dutchesse Of Malfy*. Here, again, revenge is the nominal
theme. It is not, however, revenge for murder, but for an
outrage on the insensate pride of family; and it is reinforced
by the yet more sordid motive of avarice—a motive which had
been carefully excluded from the earlier play. The sympathies
of the spectator, which, in *The White Divel*, are somewhat
divided, are, here, solely and absolutely, with the victim. And,
as if to mark the change in the most glaring manner possible,
the whole of the last act is devoted to the nemesis which falls
upon the avengers. The dramatic interest suffers; but the
intention of the dramatist is proved beyond all possibility of
mistake. The upshot of all this is that the motive of vengeance, already weakened in the earlier drama, fades almost
out of recognition in the latter; and that, with *The Dutchesse*

Of Malfy, revenge—except in survivals so obvious as the last act of *Women beware Women*—may be said to disappear from among the dominant themes of Elizabethan tragedy.

With all its great qualities, the first tragedy of Webster is not without traces of immaturity. The crudeness of incident which he had inherited from his forerunners, is not entirely purged away; the plot is wanting in clearness; even the portraiture of the heroine bears some marks of vacillation. Most, if not all, of these weaknesses are absent from *The Dutchesse Of Malfy*. The plot of this play is perfectly simple; the characters, if we except that of Bosola, are drawn with an unfaltering hand; in unity of tone, the play surpasses all others of the period, save those of Shakespeare. As to the sources of this tragedy, and its date, there is little room for discussion. The story is certainly taken, with many refinements, from Painter's *Palace of Pleasure*, as that, in its turn, drew upon the *Histoires Tragiques* of Belleforest, and this upon Bandello. Crawford has proved that Sidney's *Arcadia* not only exercised a deep influence upon the thought and language of the play, but that it also furnished the hint, and more than the hint, of its most highly wrought situation: that in which the duchess is persecuted with every variety of physical and mental torture. It is also more than probable that the echo song, which Webster had in mind (act v, sc. 3), and which he turns to purposes of the highest imaginative effect, is that of the *Arcadia* (book ii) rather than any other. The play of Lope de Vega,[1] which may have been written about the same time, has little in common with Webster's, and can hardly have been known to him. The date of *The Dutchesse Of Malfy*, again, can now be determined within very narrow limits. It was not printed until 1623. But, as the part of Antonio is known to have been created by Ostler, the first performance cannot have been later than 1614, the year of that actor's death. It is true that the opening dialogue apparently refers to the execution of Concini, maréchal d'Ancre, which took place in April, 1617, and speedily became known, through translations of official documents, in this country. There is, however, no difficulty in supposing that this passage was added by Webster some time between that event and the date of publication. Indeed, if,

---

[1] *El Mayordomo de la Duquesa de Amalfi.*

as is practically certain, the play described by Busino, chaplain to the Venetian embassy, in February, 1618, is *The Dutchesse Of Malfy*—the amours of a Cardinal, his solemn exchange of a churchman's for a soldier's garb and his "poisoning" of his sister are specifically mentioned and, in spite of the slight inaccuracy, can hardly refer to any incidents except those of our play—it may well be that the addition was made for a revival of the play at the beginning of that year. In any case it is now certain that *The Dutchesse Of Malfy* was composed within two or three years of *The White Divel*.[1]

The later play is a marked advance upon the earlier. The old motives, as we have seen, are retained, but represented in a softer, a more human, form; and the effect on the imagination is entirely different. The interest is shifted from the avenger to the deed which provokes their malice. The real theme of the drama is not revenge, but the graciousness of a noble and loving woman, and the unflinching firmness with which, in the face of nameless tortures, she possesses her soul, undismayed by all until a brutal deception convinces her that the bodies of her murdered child and husband lie before her. The constancy of the victim, the remorse which it wakens even in the base nature of her tormentor, are painted with the fewest possible strokes, and each is charged to the utmost with imaginative effect. After this, it must be admitted, the interest flags; the fate of Antonio, the miserable end of the persecutors and their accomplice, are in the nature of an anti-climax. Had the play ended with the fourth act, the tragic impression would have been yet deeper and more harmonious than it is. Yet it is easy to see how Webster was drawn into this by-path. During this period—in that which followed it is strangely different—he was filled with notions of nemesis and poetic justice. Hence, the necessity for bringing the two brothers and Bosola to condign punishment. He was also possessed with a gloomy conviction, perhaps partly inherited from Marston, of the corruption of man, and particularly of such men as haunted courts. In the loves of Julia and the cardinal, he found a text for this sermon too tempting to be passed by. Finally, he was strangely attracted towards subtle intricacies of character; and, in the portrait of Bosola, he strove to probe

---

[1] See Wallace, C. W., letters to *The Times*, 2 and 4 October, 1909.

them to their depth. The general result of all this is to deepen the gloom of the atmosphere still further, but, at the same time to blunt the edge of the tragic effect. The true tragedy is with the duchess. When she is gone, what are Bosola and Julia, what are Ferdinand and the cardinal, but hateful superfluities? Even Antonio, beautiful as is the poetry which Webster weaves around him, suffers eclipse when the sun, which gave him light and warmth, is quenched.

From the tragedies we pass to the closing period of Webster's activity (1618? to his death). The plays which would seem to belong to this period are five: *The Guise* (mentioned in the dedication to *The Devils Law-case*), and *A Late Murther of the Sonne upon the Mother* (in partnership with Ford, 1624) both, unfortunately, lost; *The Devils Law-case*, published in 1623; *Appius and Virginia*, in 1654; and *A Cure for a Cuckold*, in 1661. None of the three which survive approaches the level of the two tragedies. All, however, contain occasional flashes of the genius which created *The White Divel* and *The Dutchesse Of Malfy*, though rather of its poetic, than its dramatic, quality. Save in *Appius*, which owes much to the Roman tragedies of Shakespeare, Webster is now working under quite other, and less inspiring, influences. With him, as with other dramatists of the period, the star of Fletcher is in the ascendant.

Appius and Virginia stands apart from the other plays, and may conveniently be taken first. Its date cannot be fixed by either external or internal evidence; a play of the name, however, is mentioned in a list of dramas appropriated to the Lord Chamberlain's company (1639), and it may be Webster's. For his materials, Webster seems to have used Painter's *Palace of Pleasure*, Livy and, possibly, Dionysius of Halicarnassus. Of his own invention, apparently, are the plot of Appius for reducing Virginius to poverty, the quarrel between Virginius and Icilius, the production of Virginia's body by the latter for the purpose of nerving Virginius to vengeance; above all, the introduction of the clown Corbulo and the pretentious advocate, the latter being a familiar butt of the ridicule of Webster. The drama has a certain massive simplicity, which is probably due to the influence of Shakespeare; and the humorous element has been thought, perhaps rightly, to point in the same direction. But the general effect is disap-

pointing. The subject has always proved itself intractable
upon the stage. And not even the pure poetry and pathos
of the father's farewell to his daughter can avail to put our
sympathies entirely on his side.

The two remaining plays have proved strangely baffling to
the critics; and that, no less in regard to source and date than to
intrinsic value. *The Devils Law-case*, as it stands, cannot have
been written before the latter part of 1620; or there is a clear
allusion[1] to an unhappy affray, in August, 1619, with the Dutch
in the East Indies (not Amboina), news of which can hardly
have reached England till the autumn of the following year.
There is a suspicious resemblance in the central incident, the
lying self-slander of Leonora, to incidents in Fletcher's *Spanish
Curate* and *The Faire Maide of the Inne*. The latter, however,
was not licensed for acting until January, 1626; and it contains
an explicit reference to the massacre of Amboina, which did not
become known in England till May, 1624. It can hardly, therefore, have served as material for Webster in or before 1623.
The Spanish Curate, licensed October, 1622, is a more likely
source, or *Gerardo*, itself the source of Fletcher's play, which
was translated into English in that year.[2] It has been urged,
though this seems less probable, that Webster may have taken
the hint from a like incident in *Lust's Dominion*, which,
probably, dates back to 1600. Other sources of Webster's
incidents are Goulart's *Histoires Admirables* (2nd ed. 1606),
which had already been used by him in *The Dutchesse Of Malfy*,
and which suggested the cure by stabbing in this play; perhaps,
also, the trials for sorcery conducted in France 1610–11. An
account of these, by Michaelis, had been translated into
English in 1613—the highly protestant introduction may well
have appealed to Webster—and they seem to be alluded to
more than once in this play (especially at the end of act IV,
where the reference to France is quite irrelevant) and may
even have suggested its title. It is not impossible that the
very name of Romelio may be an adaptation of Romillon,
who took a leading part in these grim investigations. But,
whatever the exact sources of this puzzling drama, its whole
spirit betrays the influence of Fletcher. This appears in the

[1] Act IV, sc. 2.
[2] Cf. *ante*, Appendix to Chap. v.

romantic cast of the incidents, in the irresponsibility of the characters, and in the nonchalant charity of the author towards the insufferable baseness of Romelio. Fletcher's influence, however, is conspicuously absent from the rhythm, unless the marked increase of fluency, as compared with the two tragedies, may be attributed to this source. On the whole, however, there is more substance, and more elevation of spirit, in Webster's tragicomedy than in most of Fletcher's. As a drama, in spite of obvious blemishes, the former deserves more praise than it has commonly received. And there are touches of poetry, as well as of metrical effect, which worthily recall *The Dutchesse Of Malfy*.

A Cure for a Cuckold is assigned by its original editor to the joint workmanship of Webster and William Rowley. Webster's authorship, though it has sometimes been questioned, is attested by the style, as well as by not a few echoes of phrasing. If the underplot, which gives title to the play, is from his hand, we might be tempted to see in it a return to the inspiration of Dekker. Yet if any share belongs to Rowley, it can hardly be other than these scenes. And the question is too speculative to be profitably discussed. As to the influence of Fletcher on the main theme, there can be no manner of doubt; and it is yet more marked than in *The Devils Law-case*. The action is yet more full of startling and romantic incident; the shiftings of mood and purpose are still more sudden; the stress thrown on scenic effect, at the expense of character, is still stronger. That the plot is modelled on anything to be found in Fletcher, cannot be asserted. *The Little French Lawyer*[1] is the only play which, in this respect, offers any analogy; and the analogy is not very close. On the other hand there is the strongest resemblance between the plot of Webster's play and that of Massinger's *The Parliament of Love* (licensed November, 1624). The central incident of both is a duel imposed on a man, without reason, by his mistress—an incident, the germ of which is to be found in *The Dutch Courtezan* of Webster's early partner, Marston.[2] And, considering Webster's docility, it is hard to resist the conclusion that the debt, probably, was on his side. Nor is there anything against this supposition save the opinion, which, after all, has no evidence to support it, that Webster

---

[1] Cf. *ante*, Chap. v.   [2] Cf. *ante*, Chap. ii.

died in 1625 (August–September) and that he worked too slowly to have produced a play in the interval. The point, however, is not of first importance. For the influence of Massinger, at any rate in his earlier work, bore entirely in the same direction as that of Fletcher; and the younger poet may fairly be called the disciple of the elder. Thus, the last play of Webster carries on the tradition of that which had gone before it. Alike in plot and in general spirit, it belongs, directly or indirectly, to the school of Fletcher, and reflects his influence. The seriousness of the two tragedies has completely vanished; and it is ill replaced by the honest highwayman, the seafight, the groundless jealousies and the no less groundless returns to reason, which form the staple of *A Cure for a Cuckold*. In the graver part of the play, there is only one scene, that on the sands of Calais, where the genius of Webster can be said worthily to assert itself. And the comic scenes, which are more likely to be the work of Rowley, are far better sustained than the main plot with which they are interwoven. Fletcher, with all his brightness and poetic feeling has much to answer for; and nowhere was his influence less happily put forth than upon the essentially serious genius of Webster.

Of *The Thracian Wonder*, published in 1661 by the same editor (Kirkman) as *A Cure for a Cuckold*, there is no need to speak. No one, except that editor, has ever supposed that Webster can have had a hand in it. A word will suffice as to *Monuments of Honor*, a city pageant, or *A Monumental Column*, an elegy on the death of prince Henry (1613), the only poem of length by Webster which has come down to us. It contains a few fine lines, more than one of which were subsequently transferred to his dramas—an apologue conceived in the same vein as that of *The Dutchesse Of Malfy*, and a few turns of thought and phrase which recall the author's spiritual affinity with Donne.

It remains only to ask: what is the secret of Webster's genius? What are the qualities which give the distinctive seal to his imaginative creations? For the answer to this question we need hardly go beyond the two tragedies. His later works offer reflections, more or less faint, more or less intermittent, of the qualities we associate with his genius. But the authentic image, the clear-cut features, the colour and the harmony, are here alone.

First, then, within somewhat narrow limits, Webster shows a profound knowledge of human character and a keen sense of the tragic issues of human life. Vittoria and the duchess are among the great creations of the Elizabethan drama. Setting Shakespeare aside, there is no character of that drama which surpasses them in vividness; only two or three which approach them. Nor, in the duchess, at any rate, is there any marked quality to lay hold of. It is by atmosphere and temperament, by her sweet womanliness and unstudied dignity, that she becomes known to us. And these are just the things which are most impalpable, which only the highest genius can bring home to the imagination. No less important, perhaps even more so, is the sense of tragic issues. And, here again, Webster comes nearer to Shakespeare than any other of the Elizabethans, with the possible exception of Ford. Shakespeare found the deepest tragedy in the resistance of inborn heroism to all assaults from without; in the triumph of the inner self, when all outward happiness is dashed in pieces. So it is in *Hamlet*, *King Lear* and *Othello*. And something of the same effect is attained in *The White Divel* and *The Dutchesse Of Malfy*. It is attained, also, in Ford's *The Broken Heart*.

Webster, however, is not only a great tragic dramatist. He is also a great poet. And the same sombre cast of thought which made him the one appears also in the other. His imagination loves to linger round thoughts and symbols, of mortality, to take shape in "strange images of death." The grim horrors of *The Dutchesse Of Malfy* will at once recur to the memory; the yew tree of Vittoria spreads its gloom over the whole drama. Yet nothing is more remarkable than the thrift with which Webster uses this perilous material. His reserve presents the strongest contrast with the wild waste of the other dramatists of blood. Everything in the two tragedies is subordinated to imaginative ends; everything is presented with the self-restraint of the artist. Nowhere is the essentially poetic genius of the dramatist more manifest than here; nowhere does his kinship with all that is best in the other arts, particularly that of the painter, appear more plainly. The latter point has hardly received due attention. Yet no reader can fail to notice the eagerness with which this poet provides a pictorial setting for the action of his drama; the pains he takes to imprint upon the eye the countenance, gestures and bearing of the characters in his most significant scenes. The opening scene of *The Dutchesse Of Malfy* is devoted largely to this purpose. The same appears in the trial scene of *The White Divel*. And other instances, mainly from *The Dutchesse Of Malfy*, will readily suggest themselves. It is doubtful whether this quality is so persistently marked in any other dramatist, with the single exception of Marston. And no one will claim that the pictures of Marston approach those of Webster in imaginative genius. Allied with this, perhaps, is his love of connecting a whole train of thought with a tangible image, of embodying his reflections on life in symbols which, at the first moment, may seem insignificant or repulsive, but which acquire a curious fascination from the surroundings in which he places them. It was this that made him, like Donne or Sir Thomas Browne, a lover of strange learning or forgotten fragments of erudition, and led him, like Burton, to ransack the dust heaps of antiquarian research. The instinct is typical of his age; but no man put it to uses more imaginative. With this peculiar cast of imagination, the style of Webster is in marvellous accord: compressed and pregnant; full, at once, both of grace and of severity; capable of sudden flashes—"Cover her face; mine eyes dazzle; she died young"—capable, also, of a sustained musical cadence, as in Cornelia's dirge, or the wonderful lyric of Leonora.

CHAPTER VIII

Ford and Shirley

ONE of the most significant facts in connection with the two poets who close the list of the major dramatists of the great period is that their work was produced in the years following the publication of the first collected edition of the plays of Shakespeare. Previous playwrights had studied and imitated their predecessors; but, for the most part, such study had been carried on in the theatre. Gradually, the drama had been winning acknowledgment of its right to be regarded as literature, and the appearance of the first folio of Shakespeare, in 1623, may fairly be taken as marking the achievement of victory. The result of this new attitude was twofold: first, the works of the master and his contemporaries could now be brooded over and assimilated in the study, and, secondly, the younger playwrights wrote with a view to being read as well as heard and seen. Evidences of the coming of the change are, or course, to be found before this date, certainly as early as the Jonson folio of 1616; but Ford and Shirley stand out as belonging exclusively to this "literary" stage. Ford is never tired of insisting that he was a gentleman of letters, not a theatrical hack; and Shirley wrote at least one closet drama. In dealing with their works, then, we are discussing not merely the last phase of Elizabethan theatrical activity, but, also, the first chapter of what may be called, in a special sense, modern dramatic literature.

John Ford was a native of Ilsington in Devonshire, where he was baptised on 17 April, 1586. On his father's side, he belonged to an old landed family, and, on his mother's, he was related to lord chief justice Popham. He may have studied at Oxford, since there is a record of the matriculation of a John Ford at Exeter college in 1601; but his university career must,

in any case, have been short, as he became a member of the
Middle Temple in the November of the following year.   Further information about his career is confined to what can be
gathered from the dedications of his works, and from the
exchange of commendatory verses of the conventional sort.
After the publication of his last play, in 1639, he disappears from
view.   He seems to have been a man of a somewhat melancholy temperament, independent in his attitude towards the
public taste, and capable of espousing unpopular causes.

An instance of this last named quality appears in his first
publication, *Fame's Memorial* (1606), an elegy on the death of
Charles Blount, earl of Devonshire, second husband of the
famous Penelope Devereux.   No reason is known why Ford
should have chosen to publish a eulogy of a man who had died
out of favour at court; but the fact is noteworthy as hinting
an interest in a story which, as we shall see, may not improbably
have suggested to him part of the plot of one of his most
famous plays.   The poem itself is long and tiresome, smooth in
versification, abstract in diction, often obscure and affected in
style.

His romantic tendencies were further displayed in the same
year in his *Honor Triumphant; or the Peeres Challenge*.   In
the prose part of this pamphlet Ford supplies a highflown defence of four "positions" which four young nobles had undertaken to support in a tournament in honour of the visit to
England of king Christian IV of Denmark.   The positions
were that knights in ladies' service have no free will; that beauty
is the maintainer of valour; that fair lady was never false;
that perfect lovers are only wise.   The triteness of the matter,
the prevailing hyperbole and the lingering traces of Euphuism
that mark the style, would hardly call for mention here, were
it not that, in the very theses which Ford is half seriously up-
holding we find a significant connection with the motives underlying some of his most important mature work.   What we must
note is that Ford, at the age of twenty, is writing prose and
verse highly romantic in spirit, and involving a tolerant, if not
an admiring, attitude towards conduct entirely at variance
with conventional standards.   *The Monarches Meeting*, appended to this pamphlet, is an early instance of the stanza of
Gray's *Elegy*.

Ford's non-dramatic work closes with *A Line of Life* (1620), a didactic tract on conduct, apparently influenced by Bacon's *Essays*, but lacking their pithiness and epigrammatic vigour. It may be significant of Ford's personal attitude towards religion that this serious lay sermon is purely pagan in inspiration and in spirit.

Omitting consideration of works no longer extant, we find Ford's earliest attempts at dramatic writing made in collaboration with Dekker. *The Witch of Edmonton* is based on the story of Elizabeth Sawyer, who was executed for witchcraft in 1621, and it was probably written soon after that date. The respective shares of Dekker and Ford in this production are still unsettled, perhaps William Rowley, too, had a share in it;[1] but the directness of the moral lesson conveyed, the witch plot with its comedy and its realism in the treatment of humble life and the picture of the yeoman's household, are as characteristic of Dekker as they are unlike anything certainly Ford's. On the other hand, Frank, whose weakness and crime bring about the main tragedy, finds his defence in laying the blame on Fate in the fashion of Ford's other sinners; and in the scenes where this character is prominent, possibly the larger part of Ford's share is to be found. The play is a domestic tragedy of great impressiveness, its chief flaw being the failure of the attempt to join the two plots.

The Sun's-Darling: A Moral Masque (acted 1624, but not published till 1656) is generally believed to have been originally written by Dekker and revised, with additions, by Ford.[2]

The first independent drama printed by Ford was *The Lover's Melancholy*, acted in 1628 and published in the following year. This somewhat slow-moving romance turns on the melancholy of a prince grieving over the disappearance of his sweetheart. The girl, whose loss has also deprived her father of his senses and delayed the marriage of her sister, is present throughout in the disguise of a man, and the love she inspires in the princess is, in turn, the obstacle that prevents her cousin from winning that lady. The discovery of the lost girl's identity, which might as well have occurred in the first act, solves all the entanglements and permits a happy ending; but this discovery is delayed in order to enable Ford to occupy his

---

[1] Cf. *ante*, Chap. ii.   [2] See *ibid*.

scenes with a psychological analysis of the "lover's melancholy." This analysis is strongly influenced by Burton's
Anatomy of Melancholy, from which are directly taken the
materials for the *Masque of Melancholy* in the third act. The
account of the finding of the disguised girl is reminiscent of
Philaster, and is made the occasion for the telling of the story
of the nightingale's death from Strada's *Prolusiones*. The
main plot has recently been traced by Stuart Pratt Sherman
to Daniel's *Hymens' Triumph*, and reminiscences of *Hamlet*,
Lear and other Shakespearean plays are obvious. In spite of
all these borrowings, and of the fact that many of the characters belong to well recognised stage types, the play afforded the
contemporary observer abundant evidence of the advent of a
new dramatist. The delicacy shown in the treatment of
emotion, the sweetness of the verse and the happiness of the
phrasing pointed to a poet who only needed discipline in stagecraft to achieve distinction.

Ford acquired this technical skill with wonderful rapidity, if
we are correct in supposing *The Broken Heart* (printed in 1633)
to have been his next play. The plot of this tragedy shows much
originality, and it is conducted through many intricacies to a
highly effective catastrophe. The princess Calantha loves and
is loved by Ithocles, a brilliant young warrior, who had forced
his sister Penthea, in spite of her love for Orgilus, into a marriage with the jealous Bassanes. Penthea remains faithful
to her husband to the despair of her lover, and Orgilus repulsed, turns to seek revenge. Penthea goes mad and dies,
and, beside her dead body, Orgilus causes to be placed a chair
in which he induces Ithocles to sit, and which closes on him and
holds him helpless while Orgilus stabs him to death. In the
last act, news is brought to Calantha in the midst of revels at
court of the death of her father, then of those of Penthea and of
Ithocles; but she dances on to the end. Orgilus is condemned,
and, in the final scene, Calantha, before the altar, puts a
wedding ring on the finger of the dead Ithocles, hands over
her newly inherited crown to the prince of Argos and dies of
a broken heart. The last two scenes, if somewhat deliberately
theatrical, are among the most beautiful and memorable in the
drama of the period. No source has been found for the story
of Calantha, though suggestions from Sidney's *Arcadia* seem to

have been used throughout. In the prologue, it is implied that the plot has a foundation in fact, and Sherman has ingeniously argued that, in the situation of Penthea, the dramatist consciously treated the story of that Stella whom Ford had long before sought to justify in *Fame's Memorial*. Burton's influence is again discernible in the treatment of the jealousy of Bassanes; but, on the whole, this play is much less imitative than its predecessor. Since something will have to be said on the subject of Ford's dubious morality, it is only just to point out that, in this play, Penthea reaches a lofty standard in her perception of the essential unchastity of a loveless marriage. Yet, as we shall see, her conviction is not unconnected with the theory that undermines the morality of the later plays —the dogma of the supremacy and inevitableness of passion.

The influence of Sidney and Shakespeare persists in the next tragedy, *Loves Sacrifice* (printed 1633). Illicit passion is here the dominant theme. The duke of Pavy has married the beautiful but humbly born Bianca, who is loved by his favourite Fernando. The duchess's virtuous resistance to Fernando's suit leads him to change his passion to friendship, and his strength is soon tested by the weakening of Bianca, who comes at night to his chamber and offers herself to him, purposing to kill herself afterwards. They swear mutual but chaste love. Meantime, the duke's sister Fiormonda, whose love Fernando has repulsed, and the villainous secretary d'Avolos, excite the duke's jealousy and arrange to make him spectator of a love scene between Fernando and the duchess in her bedchamber. The duke breaks in and accuses Bianca. She acquits Fernando of guilt, confesses to having tempted him and brazenly tells her husband that she preferred Fernando as the better man. The duke, enraged, kills her, and then seeks Fernando, who, in turn, acquits Bianca and blames himself. The duke believes, and, at the funeral, eulogises Bianca as a model of chastity when, from the tomb, Fernando enters defiant and drinks poison. The duke stabs himself; and Roseilli, the now accepted suitor of Fiormonda, becomes duke, condemns d'Avolos and divorces his own bride. The purely physical view of chastity which is characteristic of much of the Jacobean drama is nowhere exhibited so extravagantly as here. Ford clearly sympathises with the lovers throughout, and, in the duke's admiring attitude at the close, carries his theory to a climax that would be revolting if it were not patently absurd. In the main plot, the chief literary influences are from *Othello* and *Macbeth* and Middleton's *Women Beware Women*, the story itself being derived, according to Sherman, from Gascoigne's *Ferdinando Jeronimi*. The sub-plot of Ferentes is based on the story of Pamphilus in Sidney's *Arcadia*, the wretched farce being Ford's own.

Tis Pitty Shees a Whore (printed 1633) is the tragedy most frequently cited in evidence of Ford's "decadent" tendencies. The main plot turns on the love of a sister and brother. The sister accepts a husband to conceal her sin, and, when discovery is inevitable, the brother kills her and rushes into the presence of the father with his sister's heart on a dagger. In the general catastrophe that follows, father, husband and brother all die. This simple plot is combined with no fewer than three sub-plots, two of which are woven into it with great skill. The third sub-plot, that of Bergetto, is, in the beginning, farcical; but the foolish hero of it meets his death through a mistake that gives a thrill of horrified pity. The dialogue is rich in passages of great beauty, and the characterisation, especially in the differentiation of the two lovers and their attitude towards the crime, is managed with subtlety. No objection lies against the introduction of the fact of incest, but the dramatist's attitude is sympathetic, and he apparently assents to the fatalism with which the brother excuses his passion. Both the strength and the defects of Ford are here fully revealed; and nowhere else do the tenderness and poetry of his verse, the delicacy of his psychology and the impressiveness of his handling of a dramatic situation, lend their aid to an assault at once so insidious and so daring upon the foundations of accepted morality. The plot, so far as is known, is original, such parallels as have been noted being too remote to be regarded as direct sources.

The air clears in *Perkin Warbeck* (printed 1634), a notable return to the chronicle history, which had scarcely been cultivated for a generation. The play is based on Bacon's *History of Henry VII* and Thomas Gainsford's *True and Wonderful History of Perkin Warbeck* (1618), and, in his substantial adherence to history, the dramatist follows the tradition of this dramatic type. He obviously found his model in the histories

of Shakespeare; and the slightly archaic flavour of the whole
work is increased by the use of blank verse somewhat more
formal and regular than Ford is accustomed to write. The plot,
however, is simpler than in the Shakespearean histories, there
is less richness of episode and the play falls short chiefly in a
certain lack of intensity. The hero derives dignity from the
carefully preserved assumption that he believed in his own
claims, and Huntly and his daughter Katherine, whom Warbeck marries, are admirable figures. In Dalyell, Katherine's
rejected suitor, Ford had the opportunity, of which he might
have been expected to make more, of creating a telling romantic
figure. The comedy is confined to the low-born followers of
Warbeck, who are kept well in character, and who, if only
mildly amusing, have none of the vulgarity of the comic figures
in Ford's earlier plays. On the whole, it is unmistakably a
workmanlike performance.

The comedy of *The Fancies, Chast and Noble* (printed 1638)
is a somewhat careless performance. Octavio, marquis of
Siena, through the instrumentality of his nephew and Livio, a
courtier, induces Livio's sister Castamela to join "the Fancies," three young girls kept in seclusion by the supposedly
impotent marquis. It appears later that the girls are Octavio's
nieces, and that the marquis's relations and intentions are
honourable. But the hoax, which is played not only on the
court but also on the audience, prolongs a more than doubtful
situation. So imperfectly are the motives of the action indicated that it almost seems as if the dramatist had clearly
worked out neither his plot nor his conception of the main
characters, until his play was half written. Livio, the most
interesting man in the piece, is guilty of a puzzling change of
attitude; and Castamela's repulse of the suggestions, first of
the marquis and, later, of her brother, which occasions the
finest scenes in the drama, is weakened by the fundamental
unreality of the situation. The underplot deals with the
relations to her brother and husbands of Flavia, who has been
bought by a great lord from her first husband. Out of this
unpromising material, some effective situations are developed;
but here, too, Ford seems to have been at the beginning uncertain as to the kind of character to give to the heroine. The
prologue states that the plot is original, a claim that by no

means disposes of Sherman's attempt to trace a strong line of influence from Jonson's *Volpone*.

The list of Ford's extant plays closes with the romantic comedy, *The Ladies Triall* (acted 1638). The main plot of this play is very simple. Auria, a noble Genoese driven by poverty to the wars, leaves his young wife under the eye of his friend Aurelio. Adurni, a gallant lord, attempts her virtue and is repulsed; but Aurelio's suspicions are aroused, and, on Auria's return, Aurelio kindles the husband's jealousy. Through the frankness of Adurni, the heroine is cleared, and all ends well. Both husband and wife are nobly drawn, and the suspicious but faithful friend is clearly conceived. The scene in which the wife defends herself is full of dignity and beauty; and the discontented lover, Malfato, late in the play rises in language and conduct to heights that Ford seems not to have contemplated at the outset. This is another of the indications which occur, especially in the later plays, of a certain carelessness and languor in the management of both action and character. It is further exemplified in the sub-plot of Levidolche, where the absurdity of the stage convention of disguise is carried to a high pitch in the failure of Benatzi's nearest relatives to recognise him in ragged clothes. A second sub-plot, that of Amoretta and her mock-suitors, shows the influence of Jonson. The main plot seems to be original, and certainly calls for no great inventive power. Benatzi shows indebtedness to Ancient Pistol.

Several of Ford's productions have perished. Four of these, *An Ill Beginning has a Good End* (1613), *The London Merchant*, *The Royal Combat* and *Beauty in a Trance*, though entered in the Stationers' register, were not printed, and the manuscripts are said to have been among those destroyed by Warburton's cook. In the last of these, as in the masque entitled *The Fairy Knight* and in *The Bristowe Merchant* (both licensed 1624), Ford collaborated with Dekker, and, in *A Late Murther of the Sonne upon the Mother* (licensed 1624), with Webster. These bring the total of the plays in which Ford had a share to sixteen; and it must be remembered in summing up his achievement and his characteristics that we must base our judgment upon little more than half of his work.

It is customary to instance Ford as typical of the decadence of the Elizabethan drama, and it therefore becomes important for a view of that drama as a whole, as well as for an estimate of Ford individually, to enquire what the term means and whether it can be justified. Applied to Ford, it has reference both to his subjects and to his manner of treatment. Of his three tragedies, two are, almost in the modern sense, "problem plays," in which the chief characters are faced by the dilemma of having to choose between love and loyalty to legal ties; the third deals with incest. Here, already, we have themes all but unused by Shakespeare and his predecessors, and the mere fact of a dramatist's absorption in such subjects might be regarded as a symptom of change. But Beaumont and Fletcher, to name no others, many years before had touched these themes, and Ford is generally regarded as marking a more advanced stage than they. The difference becomes more striking when method of treatment is considered. Not only is the difficulty of the tempted soul treated sympathetically by Ford, but the question is almost left open and the burden of guilt is shifted to the shoulders of Fate. In this, there is a clear departure from the assumption by the earlier dramatists of the validity of accepted morality, and there is brought into these tragedies an atmosphere of moral instability. Another evidence of change may be found in the violence and sensationalism of Ford's catastrophes. Fernando, crawling from the tomb to drink his poison and die over the corpse of the woman his love had ruined; Giovanni, rushing into the presence of his father with the heart of his sister-mistress on a dagger; Calantha, with the theatrically contrived setting for her own death—all point to the exhaustion of more natural appeals to the emotions, to a desperate attempt to whip up excitement at all costs. Finally, in his attempts at comedy, Ford sinks to a lower level than any dramatist of his class, and his farce lacks the justification of much of the coarse buffoonery of his predecessors. It is not realistic; it is not the expression of high spirits; it is a perfunctory attempt to season tragedy and romance with an admixture of rubbish, without humour and without joy.

Of the first and most fundamental of these defects, some explanation may be found in Ford himself. We have noted his youthful defence of such romantic propositions as that "knights

in ladies' service have no free will." This and similar ideas
are frequent enough in the romantic pastoralism of Sidney,
Spenser and their contemporaries. But in these writers such
theories of the supremacy and divine origin of love were presented in an Arcadian setting, under purely ideal conditions,
and, on the whole, were kept clear of practical life. The young
Ford was steeped in this romantic idealism, and we have seen
him applying it to actual persons in his apology for Stella
and Charles Blount. But the mature Ford was a dramatist
who had learned his craft from Shakespeare, Jonson, Middleton,
Massinger and the rest; and, when we find this lawless idealism
given form with all the skill in characterisation, dialogue and
action inherited from the masters of realism, it ceases to be a
harmless dream and becomes, instead, a fountain of anarchy.
But it does not lose all its beauty. The depth of Ford's insight
into the human heart torn by conflicting passions, the intensity
of his sympathy, his mastery of a beautiful and tender diction
and of a blank verse of great sweetness, along with such
technical powers as have already been noted, suffice to give
him a distinguished position among writers of tragedy.

James Shirley was born in London in September, 1596, and
entered Merchant Taylors' school on 4 October, 1608, where he
seems to have shown himself an apt scholar. From school, he
went, in 1612, to St. John's college, Oxford, then under the
presidency of Laud. It is recorded by Wood in *Athenae
Oxonienses*, our chief source of information concerning Shirley's
life, that Laud, who liked and appreciated Shirley, objected
to his taking orders on account of his having a large mole on
his left cheek. The length of Shirley's stay in Oxford is unknown; but it was probably short, for he is known to have
transferred himself to Catharine hall, Cambridge, whence he
took his degrees. Having taken orders, about 1619, he obtained a living at St. Albans in Hertfordshire; but, as he was
shortly afterwards converted to the church of Rome, he re-
signed his charge and became a master in the grammar school of
St. Albans, in 1623. In February, 1625, his first play was licensed, and it was probably soon after this that he gave up
teaching for playwriting, coming to London and residing in
Gray's inn. His dramatic labours brought him a considerable

income, and drew the favourable notice of the court, especially of queen Henrietta Maria; but it does not appear that this resulted in any substantial advantage to the poet. His standing in the fashionable world may be inferred from the terms of the dedications of his plays to various noble personages, and, with more assurance, from the fact that he was chosen to write the great masque, *The Triumph of Peace*, which the four inns of court presented to the king and queen in 1634. In 1635, John Ogilby opened a theatre in Dublin, and it was probably he who induced Shirley to visit Ireland. The dates of this visit are a matter of inference; but it seems likely that Shirley first crossed in 1636, and returned to England for a short time in the next year, but did not permanently take up his residence in London again till 1640. While in Ireland, he produced *The Royall Master*, *The Doubtfull Heir*, *The Constant Maid* and *St. Patrick for Ireland*. *The Gentleman of Venice* and *The Polititian* may, also, belong to this period. His dramatic activity continued uninterrupted until 1642, when the closing of the theatres left him with *The Court Secret* on his hands, finished, but not acted. On the outbreak of the civil war, Shirley left his wife and children in London and followed his patron, the earl (later marquis and duke) of Newcastle, to the field; "for that count," says Wood, "had engaged him so much by his generous liberality towards him, that he thought he could not do a worthier act, than to serve him, and so consequently his prince." Wood also reports that Shirley assisted the duke in the composition of certain plays, but this collaboration has not been held to have increased the reputation of Shirley. After the defeat at Marston moor in 1644, Newcastle fled to the continent, and, later, Shirley came back to London, where he attempted to earn money by the publication of earlier writings as well as by new compositions. He was helped by the patronage of the wealthy scholar, Thomas Stanley, but soon returned to his former profession of schoolmaster, which sustained him for the rest of his days. With the reopening of the theatres, he did not resume the writing of plays, though several of his earlier works were revived. He injured his reputation (more, probably, than he benefited his purse) by assisting Ogilby in his translations of Homer and Vergil, using a classical knowledge which he had put to better employment in the writing of Latin grammars. The end is best told in the words of Wood:

> At length . . . he with his second wife Frances were driven by the dismal conflagration that happened in London an. 1666, from their habitation near to Fleet Street, into the parish of S. Giles's in The Fields in Middlesex, where being in a manner overcome with affrightments, disconsolations, and other miseries, occasion'd by that fire and their losses, they both died within the compass of a natural day: whereupon their bodies were buried in one grave in the yard belonging to the said church of S. Giles's, on the 29th of Octob. in sixteen hundred sixty and six.

From the uniformly friendly tone of Shirley's references to his contemporaries and fellow dramatists, and of theirs to him, we infer that he was a man of amiable character; and his more personal writings indicate his modesty. But, beyond these characteristics, there is little in the record to help to a picture of the man.

In 1646, Shirley collected and published a number of his non-dramatic poems. A manuscript in the Bodleian library[1] supplies variant versions of a large number of these, and a few additional pieces. For the most part, these poems are amorous and personal, and show, to a much greater extent than his dramas, evidences of that discipleship to Ben Jonson which he was ever ready to acknowledge. Many of them appeared originally as songs in the dramas, or as prologues and epilogues; others as epithalamiums, epitaphs and elegies. Though conventional in manner and matter, they are often graceful and ingenious. One song rises far above the rest, and is one of the great lyrics not merely of Shirley's age, but of English literature. "The glories of our blood and state," the funeral chant which closes *The Contention of Ajax and Ulysses*, would have been sufficient to ensure a place for Shirley in our anthologies, even had all memory of his dramas been lost. *Narcissus, or The Self-lover* is almost certainly a republication of *Echo, or The Infortunate Lovers*, which Shirley had issued in 1618. This is an example, not without beauty, of the elaborate re-telling of Ovidian tales which many Elizabethan poets attempted. Shirley's immediate model seems to have been the *Venus and Adonis* of Shakespeare.

[1] Rawlinson. Poet. 88.

To the closing of the theatres, which checked the production of Shirley's dramas, we are indebted for the preservation of an exceptionally large proportion of them; for the enforced cessation of acting during the puritan domination led to the printing of many plays that might otherwise have perished in manuscript. Out of some forty dramatic pieces recorded as Shirley's, not more than three have been lost. Of the remainder, seven are tragedies, twenty-four are comedies, three are masques and three belong to none of the recognised dramatic types of the time. The tragedies, though comparatively few, contain Shirley's most memorable work. They begin with *The Maides Revenge* (1626), based on a story of the jealousy of sisters from Reynolds's *God's Revenge against Murder*. The characters are mostly familiar types re-drawn with fair skill. The comic element reaches a climax in an amusing farcical scene in the study of a quack, who is seen treating a succession of patients. Five years passed before Shirley again attempted tragedy; and, when *The Traytor* appeared, in 1631, he showed that he had mastered the technique of stagecraft. The plot of this really great drama is a free treatment of the story of Lorenzino de' Medici, who, as the Lorenzo of the play, is represented as a villain of consummate agility and daring; prompted solely by unscrupulous ambition, he plays with amazing skill upon the licentious nature of his brother the duke and upon Sciarrha's fiery sense of family honour. Although the way in which Cosmo yields his betrothed to his friend Pisano fails to convince, the plot, as a whole, is admirably contrived and well knit, and, in general effectiveness, ranks with such a play as Beaumont and Fletcher's *Maides Tragedy*, to which, probably, it is indebted. Shirley's favourite device of concentrating the comic element in one elaborate scene is well exemplified here in the mock trial of Depazzi by his page. Few plays of the period convey so vivid a picture of the Italy of the renascence on the side of ambition and intrigue.

In the same year, Shirley produced *Loves Crueltie*, in which he achieves a rare intensity in the depicting of unlawful passion. The initial motive which launches the heroine on her downward career is as natural as it is original. Clarissa's husband has a friend, Hippolito, who refuses to meet her, lest her beauty should tempt him to disloyalty to his friend. Piqued by curiosity, she visits Hippolito at his dwelling, and, without disclosing her identity, involves him in the intrigue that finally brings disaster on the whole group. In spite of the disgusting talk of the old rake Bovaldo, the moral effect of the play is sound and impressive to a high degree. One leading situation is to be found in the *novelle* of Margaret of Navarre and of Cinthio; the rest may be of Shirley's invention.

The Dukes Mistris (1636) would be better classified as a tragicomedy, since the four main characters are happily reunited at the close, and only the two villains die. But the tone of the drama is serious throughout, except for the comic underplot, which turns on the assumed preference of the hero's friend Horatio for ugly women. The distinction of the play lies in the lofty character of the two heroines, the neglected duchess, to whom the wandering affections of the duke finally return, and Ardelia, who resists successfully the solicitations of the duke and, finally, is married to her betrothed. In the killing of the villain Valerio, behind the arras, there is an evident reminiscence of the death of Polonius.

The Polititian, also, might be called a tragicomedy, since the plot ends happily for most of the persons who claim our sympathy, and the tragic element is hardly greater than that in *Cymbeline*, which, in the figure of the villainous step-mother, it somewhat resembles. The story is said by Langbaine to resemble one in the first book of the countess of Montgomery's *Urania;* but the question of priority needs further examination. Though not printed till 1655, this play may have been produced in the Dublin period (1636–40). Like *The Gentleman of Venice* (licensed 1639), the date of the production of which is, also, subject to some uncertainty, it has prefixed to it interesting "small characters" of the persons, summarising their chief qualities. The plot is laid in Norway, and moves in an atmosphere which, at times, recalls *King Lear* and *Hamlet*.

In *The Cardinall* (1641), Shirley believed that he reached his highest achievement, and, but for *The Traytor*, which surpasses it in construction, we should be obliged to agree. Its quality is indicated when we say that, though strongly reminiscent of Webster's *Dutchesse Of Malfy*, it is not altogether unworthy of its great model. A peculiar change takes place in the fifth act, in which the cardinal, hitherto somewhat in the

background and scheming on behalf of a favourite nephew,
comes forward as a villain of the deepest dye, seeking in rape
and murder the satisfaction of his own lust and revenge.
Another unexpected turn is given at the close by the discovery
that the dying confession of the cardinal, which the convention
of the tragedy of blood leads us to accept as genuine, is a mere
trick contrived to poison the duchess with a pretended anti-
dote.   But the excess of ingenuity, and the double catastrophe,
do not prevent us from understanding the claim that we have
a tragedy greater than any produced in England between its
own date and the nineteenth century.   In the intensity of its
interest, the vitality of its characters, the splendour of its poetry
and the impressive fusion of the great tragic motives of ambition, love and revenge, it brings to a fitting close the tremendous
file of Elizabethan tragedy.

The comedy of Shirley falls into two main classes, the
comedy of manners and romantic comedy, the latter sometimes
described in the early editions as tragicomedy.   The scenes of
the comedies of manners are, with one exception and that only
nominal, laid in London or its immediate neighbourhood, and
the time is contemporary.   One or two are satirical in purpose,
others are dramas of situation or intrigue; but all serve to lay
before us a lively picture of city life in the time of Charles I.
Though noblemen appear occasionally among the *dramatis
personae*, the scenes are not laid at court, and the society
represented is that of the man about town and the well-to-do
citizen.   This group of plays, ten in all, begins with Shirley's
first dramatic attempt, *Love Tricks: or, The Schoole of Comple-
ment* (1625).   This somewhat dilettante and imitative production contains much topical satire, and it is redeemed from
insignificance by the detached comedy scene which gives the
play its sub-title, and which, in an amusing manner, parodies
the affectations of polite address by the device of a school where
they are taught for a fee to all comers.   *The Wedding* (1626)
shows a great advance in construction, and the serious plot is
skilfully conducted to an effective *dénouement*.   It turns upon the
interruption of a wedding by a charge against the purity of the
bride; and the interval before the lady's character is cleared
serves to test the qualities of the chief persons more deeply than
is usual in this kind of comedy.   The farcical underplot, here

again, provides a highly comic scene in the duel between a fat man and a lean one, both arrant cowards. *The Wittie Faire One* (1628) is bright in dialogue and ingenious in construction, with somewhat conventional characterisation. But the modern reader finds it hard to accept an ending as happy in which a girl of character and spirit accepts as husband a rake who has been frightened into respectability by the preposterous device of all his friends behaving as if he were dead. The principal comic scene is provided by a foolish knight receiving lessons in geography from his tutor. *Changes: Or, Love in a Maze* (1632) is admirably named, since the plot is so contrived that the three pairs of lovers attach and detach their affections as often as possible in the course of five acts. The farce consists in dressing up a page as a rich widow, who is wooed by the foolish knight, Sir Gervase Simple. An amusing piece of satirical literary criticism is introduced in the scene where Caperwit, the poetaster, discusses the function of adjectives in verse. The value of *Hide Parke* (1632) is almost altogether in the minutely realistic study of fashionable life, especially of horse racing in the park. The underplot lacks emphasis, the interest is scattering and the characterisation is sketchy. *The Ball* (1632), again, is highly topical, being evidently designed to dissipate slanderous reports that had been circulated concerning the newly originated subscription balls, and, perhaps, also to give the actors opportunity for personating "divers . . . lords and others of the court," as the master of the revels complained they did. Romantic interest is entirely subordinated to the exposing of a variety of typical humbugs and fraudulent adventurers. On the title-page of the original edition, Chapman is named as Shirley's collaborator; but, in spite of a strong suggestion of the older method of Jonson in the handling of the types, it is clear that, in the play as we have it, Chapman's share is negligible.[1] Though in execution a lively picture of contemporary manners, *The Gamester* (1633,) in its main intrigue, is strongly reminiscent of the *novella*. It was made, says Sir Henry Herbert, "out of a plot of the king's, given him by mee," but Langbaine found the story both in the *Ducento Novelle* of Malespini[2] and in Margaret of Navarre's *Heptameron*.[3] Though coarser in tone and incident than is usual with Shirley,

---

[1] Cf. *ante*, Chap. II.   [2] Part II, nov. 96.   [3] Day I, nov. 8.

the comedy is worked out with great ability, and the sordid improbability of the Hazard-Wilding plot is, in part, atoned for by
the fine romantic spirit of the underplot of Leonore and Violante. The making and unmaking of the younger Barnacle as
a "roarer" supplies some good farcical scenes. The conduct
and influence of the chaste wife, Bellamia, raise *The Example*
(1634) to a much loftier level than the preceding play. The
difficult feat of rendering a would-be adulterer's conversion
plausible is skilfully accomplished here, though why he should
insist, later, on fighting with the husband is not made very
clear. Here, again, Shirley shows himself critical of current
literary style; and, in the character of Sir Solitary Plot returns
again to the method of the comedy of humours. *The Lady of
Pleasure* (1635) is frequently regarded as Shirley's best performance in its kind. The main plot, which turns on the
curing a wife of her desire for a life of fashionable folly, is
thoroughly sound and well carried out. The minor plot of the
young widow Celestina gives occasion for some fine speeches,
but is less convincing in itself. The satire against rakish men
about town is scathing enough; but, like many satirists, Shirley
proves unable to touch pitch without defiling himself. In *The
Constant Maid*, a play of the Dublin period, the author displays
no new or striking characteristics. It is a conventional comedy
of artificial misunderstandings, supported by an equally conventional underplot and a masque.

The most numerous group of Shirley's plays is that of
romantic comedy. The scenes of these fourteen dramas are
laid in the Mediterranean countries, usually Italy, and the
action, in almost every case, takes place at court. The list of
dramatis personae is headed by a king or duke, and most of the
characters are courtiers. The nature of the incident is often
appropriate to the nominal scene; but the kind of social intercourse pictured, to a large extent, is that of the court of Charles
I. The main plot is usually serious, and, much oftener than in
the comedy of manners, comes within sight of tragedy, thus
accounting for the name "tragicomedy," by which they are
sometimes described in early editions. There is more stress
on character, too, than in the lighter comedies, and the plot
is apt to work up to a more exciting climax and to make more
use of suspense.

The distinction between these two types of comedy was much less clearly recognised by Shirley at the beginning of his career than later. Thus, the first two comedies of manners have several characteristics of the romantic comedy, and, on the other hand, *The Brothers* (1626), though laid in Madrid and touching depths of feeling not usually reached in light comedy, is not a court comedy, and, in the story of Jacinta and her lovers, deals with material quite appropriate to the group we have just been discussing. The main theme is the foiling of the tyrannical father who seeks a wealthy alliance for his daughter; and this familiar type is nowhere more unmercifully ridiculed. But the more serious secondary theme which gives the name to the play, the enforced rivalry of two brothers for the approval and fortune of their father, is saved from tragedy only by the resuscitation of the parent who had pretended death in order to test his elder son. In *The Gratefull Servant* (1629), the type of romantic comedy is thoroughly established The tone of the main plot is raised to an uncommon height by the disinterested Foscari, who is willing to be supposed dead rather than hinder the marriage of his betrothed lady to the duke. This kind of generosity, which occurs not unfrequently in Shirley, forms a link between him and Thomas Heywood, and has the effect of giving the reader an amiable impression of the author rather than of convincing him of the probability of the story. In the disguised heroine Leonora, and, in the self-important steward Jacomo, one is forcibly reminded of *Twelfth Night*. The conversion of the unfaithful husband Lodwick, in the underplot, is very dubiously managed.

If, as seems probable, Fleay is right in identifying the next play, *The Bird in a Cage* (printed 1633) with *The Beauties*, licensed in 1633, the number of Shirley's lost plays is reduced to two. A sarcastic attack on Prynne, then in prison, forms the dedication, and may have suggested the re-naming of the play. The comedy contains some novel spectacular elements, such as the birdcage in which the hero gets himself smuggled into the castle where the princess is confined, and the play of Danaë, appropriately acted by the ladies-in-waiting to amuse their mistress. The scene at the close, where the lovers stand together against the wrath of the outwitted duke, is not without nobility. *The Young Admirall* (1633) won the special approbation of the master of the revels as being in the "beneficial and cleanly way of poetry." It is, indeed, exceptionally free from coarseness, and, in every respect, an excellent piece of stagecraft. The interest of plot is very high, the motives adequate and varied, the characters clearly conceived and originally presented and the speeches often highly poetical. It turns on a series of problems, such as love against patriotism, and conjugal love against filial love. Amusing farce is provided by a trick played on Pazzarello, a coward who is persuaded that a witch has made him invulnerable. The source of the play is stated by Stiefel to be Lope de Vega's *Don Lope de Cardona;* and the same scholar has found, in Tirso de Molina's *El Castigo del Penseque* (printed in 1634) a Spanish original for *The Opportunitie* (licensed in the same year). This amusing play turns upon the matrimonial opportunities lost by a travelling adventurer who arrives in Urbino and is mistaken by everyone for the absent son of a prominent courtier. Shirley departs from his source in the last act by depriving the hero of both the ladies he had wooed, whereas the Spanish author makes him lose the duchess but marries him to one of her ladies. The point of the plot of *The Coronation* (1635) lies in the successive discovery of two brothers of a reigning queen, whose crown thus shifts from head to head, producing a succession of effective situations, in which lies the chief merit of the play. It contains a masque, but no low comedy. This piece was included in the second folio of Beaumont and Fletcher's works, but no considerable part of the play is to be ascribed to any hand but Shirley's. The main interest of *The Royall Master*, performed first in Dublin and printed in 1638, lies not in a somewhat conventional, if skilful, central intrigue, but in the secondary figure of the young girl Domitilla, who imagines that the king is in love with her, and is cured of her infatuation by her royal master, who pretends to seek her love basely. This situation is taken from the *Decameron;*[1] the main plot is stated by Stiefel to be Spanish in origin.[2] Another Dublin play, licensed in 1640, is *The Doubtfull Heir*. The interest here, as in *The Coronation*, lies in the surprises of the action, the fortunes of Ferdinand, the lost heir of Murcia,

[1] Day x, nov. 7.
[2] For modern analogues, see *Ward*, vol. iii, p. 116, note 1.

undergoing a series of most violent changes; while the charm of the piece is in the constancy of the hero and his betrothed, which gave the play its original name *Rosania, or Love's Victory*. There are two plots of almost equal importance in *The Gentleman of Venice* (1639). In one, an interesting contrast of character is elaborated between the duke's son, supposed to be the gardener's, and the gardener's son, supposed to be the duke's. In the other, a plot of an uncommonly painful nature is handled with delicacy. *The Arcadia*, printed in 1640, but, perhaps, performed some years before, is a frank dramatisation of the main incidents of Sidney's romance, with much elaboration of the farcical elements. *The Humorous Courtier* (printed 1640), also of uncertain date of production, has an ingenious plot, but is spoiled by the gratuitous coarseness of the scenes dealing with Orseolo, the pretended misogynist but actual libertine, who gives the play its name. The main plot turns on the testing of her courtiers by the duchess of Mantua, who, secretly betrothed to the duke of Parma, gives out that she means to marry at home and enjoys the spectacle of her lords covering themselves with ridicule in their efforts to gain her hand. *The Imposture* (1640) was considered by Shirley to be in the first rank of his compositions. It is, indeed, cleverly manipulated, and the interest is well maintained through a highly complicated plot. But the devices are lacking in both novelty and probability. An ambitious favourite, seeking to secure the daughter of the duke of Mantua for himself, substitutes for her his own discarded mistress when the son of the duke of Ferrara comes wooing. The low comedy is supplied by a young coward Bertholdi, who seeks to ingratiate himself with the gallants by offering to each in turn the hand of his widowed mother, a lady of wit and independence. *The Sisters* (1642) was the last play by Shirley performed before the theatres were closed. It is a lively and amusing treatment of the theme of the proud and the humble sister. After the former has been fooled by a captain of bandits masquerading first as a fortune teller and then as a prince, she is discovered to be the child of a peasant, and the estates and the real prince go to her modest rival. The farce is frankly absurd, but, on the stage, must have been highly amusing. The dedication has an interesting picture of the condition of poets in England just before the war began, and the prologue contains eulogies of Shakespeare, Fletcher and Jonson. *The Court Secret*, the latest of Shirley's regular dramas, was not acted till after the Restoration. It deals with the familiar theme, already several times employed by him, of the hidden heir, and surpasses other works on the subject only in the extreme intricacy of the plot. Mendoza, the father of the supposititious prince is handled with some freshness and humour, being rendered miserable by the possession of "the court secret," but without the courage to reveal it. The real and the false princes are treated with a delicacy of comparison that distinguishes them clearly from the similarly situated but broadly contrasted pair in *The Gentleman of Venice*.

A number of miscellaneous pieces remain to be mentioned. The most curious of these is the extraordinary hodge-podge written for the Dublin theatre, and called *St. Patrick for Ireland* (printed 1640). The main plot, derived from the life of the saint, may be regarded as something between a chronicle history and a miracle-play; the love story is tragicomedy; the figure of Rodamant is farcical. The device by which a lover gets access to a virtuous girl in the guise of a god is as old as Josephus and was already familiar on the English stage. A bracelet making the wearer invisible is used both in the serious and in the low comedy parts. Though the piece contains scenes and speeches that might find appropriate enough place in regular dramas, the effect of the whole is grotesque; and even the noble figure of St. Patrick suffers in dignity from its patchwork background.

Interesting in a different way is the allegorical drama, *Honoria and Mammon* (pub. 1659), an elaboration of a morality, *A Contention for Honour and Riches*, which Shirley had printed in 1633. The purpose of the "Moral," as he calls it, is the exalting of the scholar as against the courtier and the soldier, and the exposing of the deceitfulness of riches. In its form, there is much conventional dramatic material; but, on the allegorical side, it is a more interesting production. The characters, which, in the earlier form, are largely abstractions, become, in the revision, types; and this change makes them much more effective for the pictures of contemporary life in which lies the main value of the piece.

The Tragedie of Chabot Admirall of France (licensed 1635) is ascribed on the title-page of the quarto to Chapman and Shirley. Chapman was dead before the play was acted, and Shirley may have given it some revision; but, in all essentials, it is evident that it is the work of the older poet.[1]   Like most of Chapman's tragedies, it is founded on French history; it is full of his weighty diction and serious thought; and it is much less well adapted to the popular stage than we should expect had Shirley had any considerable share in it.

Besides the masques introduced into nine or ten of his plays, Shirley has left three separate productions of this class: *The Triumph of Peace* (1633), *The Triumph of Beauty* (printed 1646) and *Cupid and Death* (1653).   The first of these has already been referred to as the great entertainment presented by the inns of court to the king and queen.   Except in scale and splendour, it does not differ notably from most other productions of its kind, and to-day it is memorable chiefly as a document in social, rather than in literary, history.   *The Triumph of Beauty* deals with the judgment of Paris, and it is introduced by an extensive and obvious imitation of the rehearsals of "Pyramus and Thisbe" by Bottom and his friends in *A Midsummer Night's Dream.*   *Cupid and Death*, on the familiar fable of the exchange of the weapons of the two deities and its disastrous results, was written for performance before the Portuguese ambassador.

The Contention of Ajax and Ulysses for the Armor of Achilles (printed 1659), though often described as a masque, is, in reality, nothing of the sort.   It is a short dramatic piece, based on Ovid's *Metamorphoses*, intended for private production.   It contains nothing spectacular and no dancing.   Some of the speeches are eloquent, though both the main characters suffer from the obvious comparison with Shakespeare's *Troilus and Cressida*.   The piece is now remembered for the great lyric already mentioned, with which it closes.

Of the originality of Shirley's plots, it is at present somewhat hazardous to speak.   In the foregoing pages, we have been able to indicate sources for only about one-fourth of his plays, and it has been customary to credit him with a greater share of inventiveness than most of his fellow dramatists.   But

[1] Cf. *ante*, Chap. II.

Stiefel, who proved the Spanish origin of the plot of *The Opportunitie*, named another for *The Young Admirall*, and stated that *The Wedding*, *The Humorous Courtier*, *The Example* and *The Royall Master* are, also, from Spanish sources. If this can be made good, it is clear that it is too soon to pronounce on the question of invention in this sense. But, from those plays whose sources are known, we can draw inferences as to his skill in treating a source; and our evidence is sufficient to justify us in crediting to him a high degree of ability in making over a story for stage purposes, in leading the interest up to a well prepared climax and in arranging effective situations. This last power had, indeed, distinguished most of his predecessors in the seventeenth century, but he does not so often as, say, Beaumont and Fletcher, sacrifice the unity of impression of the whole play, or the consistency of character, for the sake of single sensational scenes.

In characterisation as in theme, he had both the advantages and disadvantages of the situation described at the beginning of the present chapter. Fifty years of drama lay behind him of which to follow or avoid the example. Could we read half a dozen of the best plays of Shirley without any knowledge of his predecessors, we should, doubtless rank him much higher in the literature of the world than we do; but he is usually read, as he wrote, at the end of the series, and we are thus obliged to recognise constant echoes, reminiscences and imitations of the giants who went before. It was, perhaps, hardly possible for any writer of his date to avoid the familiar types and situations which had been often employed. A dramatist of the time of Charles I had to walk through a field honeycombed with pits, and it was futile to seek to follow a straight course and avoid them all. If frequent conventionality in these matters implies decadence, then Shirley was undoubtedly decadent.

The moral standards of Shirley were not those of Ford, Shirley has his share of grossness, both in incident and dialogue, but this grossness is neither more frequent than in his predecessors, nor is it by any means habitual. Of Ford's moral agnosticism there is no trace in Shirley. In some of his plays, the moral is almost obtrusive; in none of them is the general drift immoral. Nor is he notable for the violence or sensationalism of his catastrophes. The slaughter which closes *The*

Traytor, Loves Crueltie and *The Cardinall* is no more wholesale than that at the end of *Hamlet* or *King Lear*, and in intention at least, it is like Shakespeare's, the necessary outcome of character and previous action, not, like Ford's, an ingenious horror concocted for a final thrill. In comic power, he stands high above Ford. Without being primarily a comic artist, Shirley yet displays much genuine comic power, both in conceiving amusing situations, and in creating comic characters. In versification too, Shirley seems to belong to an earlier and sounder school than Ford. His metre is singularly correct, and easily read; Ford uses much licence and not infrequently gives us lines hard to scan. Both men were capable of great sweetness of melody, and both adorned their finer speeches with a wealth of flowery imagery, not always dramatically appropriate, but frequently of great beauty and imaginative suggestiveness.

Yet, with all Shirley's greater soundness, greater versatility, surer versification and admirable craftsmanship, one feels that there are certain heights and depths achieved by Ford which the younger man never reached. When we turn to the most wonderful things in Ford, we find a tenderness, a poignancy and an insight that Shirley cannot match. Shirley is the more balanced mind, the better workman; Ford, the rarer genius. The best things in both give them assurance of their place in the ranks of the greater dramatists of their age, and, if so, then of any age. And these facts must be carefully considered before, together or apart, they are set down as examples of their art's decline.

CHAPTER IX

Lesser Jacobean and Caroline Dramatists

THE Elizabethan drama, undoubtedly, followed a natural law of development. It culminated in tragedy in the first decade of the seventeenth century, because men and women reveal themselves most fully and finally in the furnace of affliction; and, therefore, the dramatist who desires to express the truth of human nature arrives, sooner or later, at tragedy as his most penetrating and powerful method. After the height has been reached a necessary rest and suspension of effort ensue, and of such a nature was the Jacobean and Caroline age of the drama. But a second cause was at work to increase this exhaustion and to hasten the decadence of an art that had lost its freshness. The tension of feeling as to things political and religious, which led, at last, to the civil war, was unfavourable to all artistic effort, but was especially hurtful to the drama. It took possession of the minds of all but the most frivolous. Theatre-goers ceased to be drawn from all ranks, as they were in Elizabeth's days and began to form a special class composed of careless courtiers and the dregs of the town populace. Such a class required only lesser dramatists to supply its wants; and, as we approach the date of the closing of the theatres (1642), the greater lights go out one by one till only a crowd of little men are left, writing a drama which has neither form nor spirit remaining in it.

The accident of the survival of Henslowe's diary helped us to group together in some kind of natural order the more active of the lesser Elizabethan dramatists. We have no document of this sort to aid us in the case of the Jacobean and Caroline writers; but we are confronted by a remarkable personality whose relations with the dramatists and poets of his age were as honourable and unselfish as Henslowe's were mercenary and mean. A young dramatist, writing to Henslowe for a loan, signs himself, in Elizabethan fashion, "your loving son." It was a slight extension of this usage which made Jonson the literary father of a large family of "sons," all proud to be sealed of the tribe of Ben. His position as the leader of literary and dramatic taste and the centre of literary society in London was a new thing in English life, and his influence was so commanding and complete that most of the lesser dramatists stood in some sort of relation to him, either of attraction or repulsion: they were either friends or foes. It may also be conjectured that Jonson's art lent itself to imitation by lesser men more readily than Shakespeare's. Shakespeare's apparent artlessness covered a far more subtle method and mystery than did Jonson's strict canons of conformity to definite theories of dramatic composition. Secondly, Jonson's theory of "humours" simplified human nature and enabled the lesser dramatist, in setting about the composition of a comedy, to choose his basic humour, and get to work on inimitable humanity with some confidence. And, thirdly, while Jonson's massive common sense and satiric intensity are, in bulk, colossal, they can be readily imitated by lesser men who manufacture smaller pieces of the same stuff. Jonson's most remarkable plays were quarries from which contemporary writers chose what suited them, diligently working it into some sort of artistic shape. For these reasons Jonson occupies an exceptional relation towards the literature of the Jacobean age, and may be regarded as a centre round which the lesser dramatists are grouped. He fails us only when we deal with romantic tragicomedy, in which species Fletcher and Massinger are the dominating influences. But the lesser writers of romantic drama are so weak that we shall have no space for detailed examination of their work.

We propose to begin our survey with John Day, adding a list of smaller men, whose comedy is either Elizabethan in general character, or Elizabethan with the additional influence of Middleton's hard, bright realism. We shall next consider the work of two men who came personally under Jonson's tuition and have a special right to be entitled his "sons"—Nathaniel Field and Richard Brome. Field's work, like John Day's, has distinction and originality. Brome was a careful and strenuous craftsman, pursuing his vocation steadily till the stage was silenced. Field was the foremost actor of his day, and Brome was intimately acquainted with stage life. Together, they cover the Jacobean and Caroline age till 1642. Both of them continue the Elizabethan impulse, and Brome may justly claim to be noted, with Shirley, as having worthily maintained the Elizabethan tradition till the end. Brome has left fifteen plays, none of which is without its interest, and, on the whole, he is the most considerable writer who will come before us. Two other men, although they have no claim, like Field and Brome, to a place among those who continue the Elizabethan dramatic impulse, nevertheless are distinguished by a wit and genius raising them above the crowd of lesser men who show that the Elizabethan impulse is dead. These are Thomas Randolph and Sir John Suckling. When we have dealt with their work, there remain to us only dramatists whose plays are either meritorious and dull, or extravagant and dull. We shall make an effort to discover among these the precursors of the next age, and, accordingly, the last name on our list will be that of Sir William D'Avenant.

As a member of the group of robust collaborators who wrote assiduously for Henslowe during the last year of Elizabeth's reign, John Day failed to produce distinctive work. It was, perhaps, by writing for the children of the revels that he struck into his own vein and produced three plays, which, because they stand apart in style and manner from the main stream of dramatic work, attract an attention hardly due to their actual merits as literature. And they have a second claim upon the student. Day's pleasant little masterpiece, *The Parliament of Bees*, which is not a play, is directly related to his plays; and we can see in his plays those qualities at work which make *The Parliament of Bees* charming. *The Ile of Guls* was produced in the spring of 1605. The plot is taken from Sidney's *Arcadia*. Duke Basilius has left his kingdom under his brother and retired with his queen and two daughters to a "desert isle," sending a general challenge "to all the youthful blood of Africa" to

> Woo, win, entice, or any way defeat
> Me of my charge, my daughters of their hearts.

The successful suitors—both of them, apparently—

> Shall with their loves wear my imperial crown.

But, before the play begins, there is a prose induction containing the conversation of three gentlemen, who interrupt the
prologue, supposing him to be the boy who should provide
them with stools. They ask whether the play has any connection with the recent *West-Ward Hoe* [1] and suppose that there
is some political libel in it since the title, *Isle of Guls*,
is obviously suggested by Nashe's *Isle of Dogs*.[2] To the dis-
appointment of the first gentleman, the prologue protests
fervently against these suppositions. He desires "to hear vice
anatomized and abuse let blood in the master vein"; he asks
of the play, "Is there any great man's life charactered in 't?
. . . And there be not wormwood water and copperas in 't,
I 'll not like it." The second gentleman cares for none of these
things; his tastes are simpler; "Is there any good bawdry
in 't, jests of an ell deep and a fathom broad?" He wants
scenes "that will make a man's spirits stand on their tip toes and
die his blood in a deep scarlet, like your Ovid's Ars Amandi."
When the prologue objects that chaste ears would never endure
it, he retorts, "What should chaste ears do at a play?" But
the third gentleman cares for neither railing nor bawdry; he
requires "a stately penned history" . . . "high-written"—
"mere fustian," his friend calls it, "full of tear-cut thunder-
claps."

Upon these three kinds, says the dramatist, the popular
audience insists—"all these we must have and all in one play
or 't is already condemned to the hell of eternal disgrace." The
induction shows that Day intended to produce a new style if he
could; it shows, also, that he was very much afraid of failing;
he has none of Ben Jonson's sturdy scorn of popular taste;
when the prologue is finally allowed to speak, we get only a
faint-hearted defiance of "Opinion's voice," whose tyranny is

> The misery that waits upon the pen
> Of the best writers.

It is not surprising, therefore, that Day fails to emancipate
himself from the evils he deprecates. In the matter of bawdry

---

[1] Cf. *ante*, Chap. VII.   [2] Cf. *ante*, Vol. V, Chap. VI.

especially, he yields to the base demands of "opinion."   He is
not more coarse than others and he makes no attempt to dye
our blood in a deep scarlet; but he takes his story and his
characters from Sir Philip Sidney's *Arcadia* and besmirches
the sweet and noble romance of his original with the indecencies
of the work-a-day Elizabethan drama.   It may be urged that
Shakespeare does the same thing, even in *As You Like It*.
But Shakespeare creates such a soul of purity in his heroines
that their most outrageous jests and words fail to hurt them.
Day puts no soul at all into his women; his characters have
almost no personality.   Although he protests that he will not
be a satirist, it is his railer, Dametas, who comes nearest in
his play to being a live man, and the duke and his queen are
vulgarised as well as the heroines.   We are frequently reminded of Shakespeare's earlier comedies in reading Day.
In *The Ile of Guls*, we catch echoes from *A Midsummer Night's
Dream*.   But this similarity almost forces us to compare
Day's duke and duchess with Shakespeare's Theseus and
Hippolyta.   What would have become of the romance and
charm of Shakespeare's play if Theseus—and, with him,
Hippolyta—had been involved in a clumsy intrigue, depriving
the king and hero of all grace and dignity?   The two pairs of
lovers are equally uninteresting.   It is enough to say that Day
in no way differentiates them; and we are unable to care much
about what happens to either couple.   All these things interfere with our appreciation of Day's art in providing us with a
pretty tangle, neatly and deftly untied at the end.   Such an
art there is in *The Ile of Guls*, and it is a new thing in the
Elizabethan drama as Day uses it.   It points forward to
Restoration comedy, and has some kinship with the comedy of
Molière.

And it is not only in his plot that Day shows clear conception
of a comedy different from the Shakespearean romantic comedy
and from the Jonsonian comedy of humours—both of them
full of life and humanity; in his dialogue there is a new note—
a new convention of epigram and repartee—which, together
with neatness of plot, marks the typical Restoration comedy.
In *The Ile of Guls*, the plot by which all the characters are
collected together at the end of the play blindfolded, as it were,
to find themselves plain gulls when the bandage is taken off, is

cleverly and neatly elaborated; but, in the course of the play, we also have a continued effort to present a dialogue duly arranged and ordered, in which the wit has a scheme and keeps the rules. The most notable instance is the famous tennis match scene in the second act. Bullen says truly: "Outside of Shakespeare's early comedies it would be difficult to find among the dramatists of the time such another *tour de force* of sprightly repartee"; but, although Shakespeare's early work, probably, was the chief influence in producing Day's type of comedy, there is a noticeable contrast between the two kinds. The copiousness and exuberance of all the punning and repartee of *Love's Labour's Lost* produce an effect the exact opposite of Day's balanced and considered epigrams. Shakespeare gives his characters full play in the scenes of quip and repartee; Day holds his in. His art has not enough vigour and flow in it; Shakespeare's has too much. Shakespeare, again, is eager to break loose from the fetters of rime for the larger scope and movement of blank verse; Day, on the contrary, desires to get back to rime; he has not breath enough for Elizabethan blank verse. Shakespeare's fountain gushes and leaps, with much danger to artificial restraints of all sorts; Day's rivulet, on the contrary, flows obediently whither it is led, and often trickles nearly dry. Elizabethan extravagance and overstrain are foreign to his art, which is Attic, or even Doric, in its simplicity and orderliness. It is not, therefore, to be wondered at that Day never does himself justice in his plays; he is too much hampered and confused by the alien conditions in which his genius has to work. In *The Ile of Guls*, it is only the induction which is quite easy and lucid. The tennis scene, perhaps because the terms used are no longer familiar, is hard to follow, and the verse effects are too complicated. We see what the artist means, but his execution is not perfect. A scene in *Law-Trickes*, where the countess discourses to her maids as they sew, is his nearest approach to dramatic effectiveness in his own style. This play, probably, was written in 1606, and *Humour out of Breath* in 1607. The three plays present, quite recognisably, a new dramatic type, but they do not coherently and adequately realise it.

The title *Humour out of Breath* is actually quoted from *The Comedy of Errors*, and the influence of Shakespeare's early comedies is very evident in all three plays; but the neatness and compactness of Day's prose style in his dialogue is more akin to the manner of another master—John Lyly. Lyly does not exhibit in his comedies the copiousness and exuberance which characterise Shakespeare's first work. Lyly's plays, even more than Day's, lack flesh and blood, and belong to a world of moonshine and shadow. But, within their limits, they have a true charm of fancy, and their style escapes the pedantry and tediousness of the writer's prose work, and is as deft and crisp as Day at his best. To complete the parallel, we may note that Lyly (supposing him to be their author[1]) gives us a handful of beautiful lyrics, remarkable as belonging not to the true Elizabethan type, but, rather, to the later style of Herrick. Day's best lyric work in *The Parliament of Bees* is, in the same way, post-Elizabethan. It must be compared with Browne's *Pastorals* or Milton's *L'Allegro*.

Day describes *The Parliament of Bees* as "an allegorical description of the actions of good and bad men in these our days." But he composed it from scenes contributed to two plays which have reached us under the titles *The Noble Souldier* and *The Wonder of A Kingdome*. Dekker, in co-operation with Samuel Rowley, was mainly responsible for these plays. Between their style and Day's, there could be no real accord, and only enough of Day is left to make it clear that *The Parliament of Bees* was not, as we might suppose, completely fresh work constituting a new departure in the art of the writer. Scenes contributed to more than one play were the groundwork upon which Day composed his dainty and graceful series of "Colloquies" or "Characters." The fact throws a true light on Day's dramatic work; but the drama was not his natural vein. What would be interesting to know is how he came to write *The Parliament of Bees*. In the excellent prose tract, *Peregrinatio Scholastica*, written, apparently, before *The Parliament*, he speaks of himself as "becalmed in a fog of necessity," that is to say, he writes because he needs money, which he hopes to get not only from the printer, but, also, from the patron to whom he dedicates his book. He says, also, that he is lying at anchor "before the Islands, Meliora Speramus." Fleay's tempting suggestion is that Day means holy orders by this, and by the

---

[1] On this question, cf. *ante*, Vol. V, Chap. VI, p. 140.

"shrine of Latria," towards which, in the allegory, the "sometimes student of Gunvill and Caius Colledge in Cambridge"
is travelling. If this were so, it would be necessary for the old
playwright, until he was duly ordained, to make money by
some more edifying form of literature than plays. He, therefore, wrote *Peregrinatio* and, after that, used certain scenes from
old plays to make his unique *Parliament of Bees*. There is
extant a manuscript copy of *The Bees* earlier than the quarto
of 1641, and the changes are not all of them merely in style;
the poem is made definitely graver in revision. The delightful
first title disappears as too flippant—"An olde Manuscript
conteyning the Parliament of Bees, found In a Hollow Tree
In a garden at Hibla, in a strandge Languadge, And now
faithfully Translated into Easie English Verse by John Daye,
Cantabrig." The poem, it should be noted, is not a masque
in the ordinary and technical sense. It rather resembles a
series of pastoral eclogues. The successive scenes have no con-
tinuity, except such as is supplied by the idea of making all the
characters bees. Day conceives his poem as a series of satires;
but he charges his bees to

> Carry an humble wing
> Buzz boldly what I bid, but do not sting
> Any particular.

It is only the usuring bee whom we can identify:

> Most of the timber that his state repairs
> He hews out o' the bones of foundred players:
> They feed on poets' brains, he eats their breath.

This can be none other than Philip Henslowe.

We gather, from both *Peregrinatio* and *The Parliament*,
that Day was not seeking orders from any unworthy motives.
The prose of the tract is more fluent than that of the
plays. The style of the poem, too, has, more fully than that
of the plays, Day's special gift—"a sense of delicate music in
the fall and arrangement of quite common words."[1] In spite
of the "fog of necessity" around him, the writer is at peace
with himself and the world. A note of peevishness and
bitterness which occasionally obtruded itself in his earlier work

[1] *Nero and other plays*, p. 208.

has disappeared, and the poet's music in his last poem is serene, spontaneous and sweet.   John Day died before the quarto of *The Parliament* was printed, probably in the autumn of 1640.

A belated Elizabethan of considerable interest whose extant work was printed in the early years of king James was Robert Armin, reported to have been trained by Tarlton and called his "son."   He followed William Kemp as player of Dogberry about 1599, continued in Shakespeare's company for some years and has a place in the list of players in the 1623 folio.   His single play, printed 1609, is entitled *The History of the two Maids of More-clacke; With the life and simple maner of John in the Hospitall*.   On the title-page, there is a cut of Armin in the character of John in the hospital.   In his words to the "friendly peruser," Armin calls the play "a Historical discourse," and says that he would have "againe inacted" John, if he had been able.   His age, presumably, prevented him, for he seems to have been born about 1564 and was dead by 1612.   He adds, "you shall find verse, as well blancke, as crancke, yet in the prose let it pass for currant."   The blank verse of the play is in so disordered a state that it has been compared with the mutilated 1603 quarto of *Hamlet*.   The phenomena suggest the solution that Armin was not responsible for the verse, but supplied the prose of the old-fashioned fool's part of John, in which, earlier, he had made a hit.   He was no more the author of the serious part of the play, than William Kemp was of the whole of *A Knack to Know a Knave*.   But the play is interesting, in spite of its corrupt condition.   There are in it indications that, in some form or other, it dates back to Elizabeth's reign; but, also, echoes from Shakespeare's tragedies—from *Macbeth*, for instance—which date, apparently, from about 1608.   Humil's doubt of his mother's honour reminds us of Hamlet, and the play is worth careful study for its bearing on the *Hamlet* problem.   The plot is absurdly complicated and full of incident, and, in this respect, we are reminded of Chettle's *Tragedy of Hoffman*.   The play has genuine dramatic power, forcible eloquence and fine poetry, all of which we should be inclined to ascribe to Dekker or Chettle, if another author than Armin himself must be looked for.   There are, however, some resemblances between Armin's other works and our play.

In 1605, he published *Foole upon Foole, or, Sixe Sortes of Sottes*, a prose tract, amplified, in 1608, into *A nest of Ninnies*,[1] in the dedication of which "To the most true and rightly compleat in all good gifts and graces the generous Gentlemen of Oxenford, Cambridge, and the Innes of Court" he declares "I have seene the stars at midnight in your societies." This, apparently, gave offence to some of the graver spirits among the old player's hosts, and his next and last tract, dated 1609, contains a kind of apology for it. This tract, *The Italian Taylor and his Boy*, a verse translation from the Italian, is written with considerable dexterity, and raises our opinion of Armin's gifts and scholarship. It is curious that we should have nothing from his pen earlier than 1605, although Nashe and Harvey, in 1593, speak of him as a common pamphleteer and "son" of Elderton.

Middleton's influence on comedy is apparent in the two surviving plays of the lawyer Edward Sharpham—*The Fleire*, acted probably early in 1606, and *Cupid's Whirligig*, produced about a year later. Both plays were frequently reprinted, from 1607 onwards. They owed their popularity to their wit and rapidity of action, but can hardly claim to be more than farces; there is in them the shadow of Middleton's art, and more than the substance of his grossness. Much better than these is Lodowick Barry's single play *Ram-Alley or Merrie-Trickes*, acted perhaps as early as 1609 and extant in several quartos. Ram alley was a particularly disreputable lane, leading from Fleet street to the Temple and of the coarseness promised by the title of the play we find, as it proceeds, a full supply. But this realistic indecency is relieved by some breath of life and character. Many echoes from Shakespeare's plays are introduced, both by way of parody and of imitation. There is much of the London of the period—both of the place and its manners—in this comedy; and it not only shows force in its presentation of life and character, but is also marked by a vigour in its blank verse, which, in one or two places almost reaches distinction. The prologue says that, if the play succeeds, the writer will attempt something more serious, which even puritans will accept as satisfactory. Barry, no

[1] Cf. *ante*, Vol. IV, p. 602.

doubt, overrated the complaisance of puritans; but he was right in feeling that he had in him the power to produce work of a higher rank altogether than his Ram alley obscenities. It is disappointing that this one play and his name are all that we know of him.

Two other single plays, *Greene's Tu Quoque* and *The Hog hath lost his Pearl*, we may mention at this point, because they belong rather to the early comedy of Haughton than the later Jonsonian comedy. They are less touched by Middleton's influence than *Ram-Alley*. The clever acting of Thomas Greene made *Greene's Tu Quoque or The Cittie Gallant* very popular about 1611. It was printed in 1614 as "written by Jo. Cooke, Gent.," and Thomas Heywood contributes a preface stating that both the author and the actor Greene are dead. It is one of the pleasantest and liveliest among the productions of the lesser dramatists. The blank verse is not so good as Barry's; but Cooke's art and his capacity for working out a comic idea are above the ordinary, and his prose is excellent. The master, Staines, changes places with his man, Bubble, and coaches him to take his place in the fashionable world. There is an excellent scene in which the affectations of the Italianate Englishman are taken off, probably aimed at Coryate. The women in the play remind us of the girls of Porter and Haughton; they are, perhaps, more refined—the sisters of university students rather than of tradesmen—but they are very naturally and pleasantly drawn. A scene in which Joyce, anxious to hide the state of her heart, confounds and bewilders her lover, first by her silence and then by her speech, recalls the vigorous domestic comedy of Porter.[1] It is curious that we should know nothing whatever of "Jo. Cooke," and that, like Barry, he should have just one play to his credit. *The Hog hath lost his Pearl* is, again, the single play of a writer whose name—Robert Tailor—is all that is known about him. Tailor's literary capacity is below that of either Barry or Cooke. To a play of low comedy, he tacks on a romantic plot of a painful character[2] which only a master of dramatic art could make endurable. Tailor manages the prose of his comedy much better

---

[1] See *ante*, Vol. V, Chap. XIII.

[2] Otway's *Orphan* deals with the same plot.

than the verse of his moral romance; the main interest of the play, however, is not in its style or story but in the circumstances of its production. Sir Henry Wotton, in a letter dated 1612,[1] tells us that "some sixteen apprentices," having secretly learnt their parts, "took up the White Fryers for their theatre," and invited their friends to see them perform *The Hog hath lost his Pearl.* The sheriffs intervened before the end of the performance and carried off six or seven of the apprentices to prison. He adds that it was supposed that Sir John Swinnerton was meant by the hog, and the late lord treasurer by the pearl. The prologue of the printed play alludes to this incident, but says that

> our swine,
> Is not as divers critics did define,
> Grunting at state affairs or invecting
> Much at our city vices;

if the play pleaseś, "we 'll say 't is fortunate, like Pericles." Like the two plays mentioned before it, Tailor's is full of interest for the student of Jacobean London.

We come now to the main stream of Jacobean dramatic work, in which the influence of Jonson, both personal and by his art, is all-pervasive.

Among the extant plays of the reign of king James, two by Nathaniel Field are of such merit as to suggest that the writer, probably, would have risen above the ranks of the lesser dramatists, had he persevered in the prosecution of his art. He was born in 1587, a few months before his father's death. That father was the famous preacher John Field, whose rousing discourse upon the collapse of a gallery in Paris garden in 1583 has come down to us.[2] It contains interesting details about the catastrophe and a violent attack upon theatrical performances, with valuable information about London players and their theatres. Nat's elder brother, Theophilus, was educated at Cambridge and rose to be bishop of Hereford; and it is singular, therefore, that Nat Field's name should be found first among the six "principal comedians" of the band of

---

[1] *The Life and Letters of Sir Henry Wotton*, ed. Smith, L. P., vol. II, p. 13.
[2] Cf., as to this incident, *post*, Chap. XIV.

lads called the children of the queen's revels, who acted in Jonson's *Cynthia's Revels* in 1600. These boys were the "young eyases" discussed by Hamlet. For a time, as has been seen,[1] they rivalled men players in public favour; and Field, as he grew older, maintained his position and may claim to have succeeded Burbage as the leading actor on the English stage. Jonson, no doubt, owed a debt to Field for his clever acting in *Cynthia's Revels* and *Poetaster*, and the debt is repaid by the mention of Field, in 1614, in *Bartholomew Fayre*— "Which is your Burbadge now? . . . Your best actor, your Field?" Field joined the King's company before he finally retired from the stage, and, in the 1623 folio of Shakespeare's plays, he is seventeenth in the list there given of twenty-six players. Jonson told Drummond[2] that "Nat Field was his scholar." An interesting proof of Jonson's regard for Field is afforded by the insertion of an extra sheet[3] of commendatory verses addressed by Field to Jonson in some copies of the 1607 quarto of *Volpone*. Field's verses are amateurish—he speaks justly of his "weak flame"—but they show a great awe of Jonson, whom "to dare commend were damnable presumption." The lines should be compared with the much more mature address "to his worthy and beloved friend Master Ben Jonson on his Catiline."[4] Field had been educated by Mulcaster at the Merchant Taylors' school, but "taken" by N. Giles as one of the company of the children of the revels. Giles was accused of kidnapping boys against their parents' wishes, and we may conjecture that Field would not have been annexed, had his strenuous father been alive to protect him.

Field's first play, *A Woman is a Weather-cocke*, was produced in 1610. In the first scene, Scudmore is discovered reading a vehement letter from Bellafront, the lady he loves. To him, thus occupied, enters his friend Nevill on his way to a

---

[1] Cf. *ante*, Chap. II, and *post*, Chap. XI.

[2] They read Horace and Martial together; see *Notes of Ben Jonson's Conversations with Drummond*, ed. Laing, D., p. 11.

[3] It is contained in the British Museum copy, C 12, c. 17, which was presented by Jonson to John Florio with an inscription in Ben's autograph to "his loving father and friend, the aid of his Muses." See Percy Simpson in *Notes and Queries*, Ser. VIII, vol. VIII, p. 301.

[4] But in this age where jigs and dances move
How few there are that this pure work approve

wedding. The lover very prettily takes his friend into his confidence, enlarges like a Romeo on his mistress,

> Whose face brought concord and an end of jars,

and passionately proclaims,

> She is the food, the sleep, the air I live by.

He ends with the lady's name; whereupon his friend blurts out in amazement, "But that's the wedding I was going to." This dramatic scene is put before us with a force and vividness remarkable in so young a writer. In itself, it is an excellent beginning; but the Jonsonian "humours" of the next scene jar a little. They are not in the same key as the romantic passionate opening of the play. But Field's wit is considerable and is not a mere copy of Jonson. His manner has a sprightliness and good-humour, and an occasional naturalness, which are his own, and differentiate his comic style quite definitely from Jonson's.

The second act is constructed on the same plan as the first. It begins with a semi-romantic scene and ends with "humour." When captain Pouts, who has been rejected by Katharine, publicly insults her at the door of the church in which she has just been married to Strange, she urges her new husband to vindicate her honour; and, perhaps, no better example could be given of Field's capacity as a writer of strong, direct, blank verse than her invective:

> Thou wert ordained,
> And in thy cradle marked to call me wife,
> And in that title made as my defence,
> Yet sufferedst him to go away with life,
> Wounding my honour dead before thy face!
> Redeem it on his head, and his own way,
> Even by the sword, his long profession,
> And set it clear amongst the tongues of men,
> That all eyes may discern it slandered,
> Or thou shalt ne'er enjoy me as a wife.

The verse is in the manner of Shakespeare in the *Henry V* period, although with less music and very little imaginative decoration, and the excellence of its directness and spontaneity is due, no doubt, to Field's training as an actor. His use of language, too, is free, like Shakespeare's—to be understood by the audience though not always approved by the grammarian. In the passage quoted, "his long profession," with the meaning, "for so long a time his profession," has a Shakespearean sound, as, also, has the rather enigmatic, but still forcible, "made" of the third line. Strange's speech, a little later, about the law's inequalities, again, is forcible, eloquent blank verse. But the second part of the plot overloads the play as a whole. Field, as a scholar of Jonson desires to show his dexterity as a plotter; but, like all young writers of promise, and like all immature dramatists, he gives his audience too much, and cannot endure to limit his own scope.

In this play, which is full both of matter and of varied promise of dramatic ability, Ben Jonson is obviously the master most consciously copied. The "humours" are in Jonson's manner, as are the complicated plottings. The compression of the action into exactly one day is in accordance with Ben's teaching. It might be contended that a certain intensity in the serious scenes copies the splendid passion of Volpone, which is the high-water mark of Jonson's art. This, however, would be a mistake. The serious scenes of the play are essentially romantic and idealistic, suggesting *Romeo and Juliet* rather than *The Alchemist*. But Romeo has been brought up as a player and has appeared upon the public stage from his childhood, and Ben Jonson has been his schoolmaster. He has, therefore, lost all exterior softness and sentiment, and, at first reading, a certain hardness and bravado in his manner deceive the student. Field's second play, *Amends for Ladies*, followed hard upon the first, and was intended to atone for the many hard things said against women in the first play. There are three heroines, the lady Honour, the lady Perfect and the lady Bright, who, as maid, wife and widow, vindicate respectively, the claims of their sex to constancy and virtue. It will be seen, therefore, that, again, the scheme of the play is too full of incident; there are three plays in one. The second play, on the whole, is a more hasty piece of work than the first; it has the drawbacks of an after-thought; but there is a distinct maturity and strengthening to be noted in its style. Field's natural bent is, more obviously than before, to draw ideal heroes, headstrong and indomitable. He does not yet show much power of characterisation; his heroes and heroines are all repetitions of one type. We remember that one of his great parts was Bussy D'Ambois, and that Chapman addresses some lines "to his loved son Nat Field." The comic scenes of the second play are less original and less amusing than those of the first. There is something perfunctory about "the merry prankes of Moll Cut-purse, Or, the humour of roaring." And, again, all that part of the play which uses the plot of "The Curious Impertinent" in *Don Quixote*, in which a husband, in order to prove his wife's virtue, eggs on his friend to tempt her, is intolerable to modern feeling. Field's audacity and directness of treatment make him, when his subject is unpleasant, unusually outrageous, even for the Jacobean stage. Yet he cherishes an ideal of incorruptible and unassailable virtue which was rare in the drama of the period.

Besides writing these two comedies, Field collaborated both with Fletcher and Massinger. Of these collaborations, we need mention only *The Fatall Dowry*, produced about 1619, shortly before Field retired from the stage.[1] It has been common to refer to Field the lighter parts of plays in which he collaborated; but what we have noted in his work will make it highly probable that Field, quite as much as Massinger, was responsible for the romantic side of the play and especially for the uncompromising honesty of Romont. In this respect, Chapman was his master; and, from Chapman and Jonson equally, he learnt to remind his reader that "a play is not so idle a thing as thou art, but a mirror of men's lives and actions." And yet this profession irked him; "thou know'st where to hear of me for a year or two and no more," he says, in the address to the reader which we have quoted. He married about 1619 and became a publisher, dying in 1633. In 1616, he addressed a letter to Sutton, the preacher at St. Mary Overy, who, like Field's own father, was a great denouncer of the stage. Field very loyally defends his profession; but his letter is very remarkable for its religious earnestness, which, in itself, is enough to explain his retirement.

Richard Brome,[2] like Field was in a special sense educated

Cf. *ante*, Chap. VI.   [2] Pronounced "Broom."

by Jonson, and it will be convenient to consider his work after Field's.

The stagekeeper who opens the induction to *Bartholomew Fayre*, having occasion to pronounce the play "a very conceited, scurvy one," looks behind the arras "lest the poet hear me or his man, Master Brome." This was in 1614. Prefixed to Brome's *Northern Lasse*, and dated, therefore, not later than 1632, we have Jonson's characteristic sonnet "to my old faithful servant and by his continued virtue my loving friend . . . Mr. Richard Brome." In the first line, "I had you for a servant, once, Dick Brome," we almost hear Jonson speak. He goes on to say that Brome has sedulously worked at his profession:

> You learned it well, and for it served your time,
> A prenticeship.

Fleay regards this apprenticeship as extending over the whole of the seven years 1623 to 1629. In 1623, we first hear of Brome as an author. *A Fault in Friendship* was licensed in that year, "written by Brome and young Jonson." Unfortunately, the play has not survived; but we may allow ourselves to suppose that the servant and the son pursued their dramatic studies together, under the father's august and austere supervision. We know nothing of Brome's parents; but a sonnet of some literary merit by a brother Stephen is printed among the poems prefixed to *The Northern Lasse*. We must beware, therefore, of assuming that Brome was of very lowly rank and uneducated till Jonson took him in hand. This notion is suggested by the low life in Brome's plays, as well as by a humility towards public and private patrons in Brome's prologues and epilogues, which, sometimes, is almost servile. But the sonnet must not be ignored; and, when we find Jonson, in a well known epigram,[1] expecting his "man" to read "a piece of Virgil, Tacitus, Livy, or of some better book" to his guests at supper, we conjecture that the servant was not so much a valet as a secretary and amanuensis, whose duties, from the first, in connection with Jonson's dramatic and literary work, required a grammar school education. The same inference is suggested by the easy use of Latin in the sketch of the amusing pedant Sarpego

[1] Epigram ci.

in *The City Witt*. Jonson is copied unblushingly. Sarpego's speech, "Diogenes Laertius on a certain time demanded of Cornelius Tacitus, an areopagite of Syracusa, what was the most commodious and expeditest method to kill the itch," is modelled on Clove's in *Every Man out of His Humour*: "Aristotle in his daemonologia approves Scaliger for the best navigator in his time, and in his hypercritics he reports him to be Heautontimorumenos!"[1] But there is very little of this misuse of long words and classical names in the part; Sarpego redeems his promise, "His grace will see that we can speak true Latin and construe *Ludovicus Vives*"; and his Latin has a sprightliness and comicality hardly to be attained by a writer whose studies began after his school days were over. But, if Brome's education was not much inferior to Field's, the contrast between the personal characters of Jonson's two "sons" is all the more striking. Field has more than a touch of Jonson's arrogance, and inherits some of his strength of style. Brome's meekness verges on servility. The note of self-depreciation continually recurs:

> A little wit, less learning, no poetry
> This playmaker dares boast.

He is always reverent and loyal to Jonson; but his attitude of deference to his audience, and his modest estimate of his own powers as a writer, make quite clear his unlikeness to his master. For all his sedulous imitation of Jonson's style and methods, Brome has little of his master's soul in him. He can only be Jonson on a small scale; but Jonson on a small scale is not Jonson. Brome's sketches of London life are varied, minute, careful, spirited, and yet they displease; they cannot be read continuously without weariness, and are extremely coarse. Some critics have been pleased to decide that Brome describes life from the groom's point of view, and have ascribed his coarseness to his want of education and humble origin. The truer explanation is that he uses Jonson's manner without Jonson's full-blooded, massive humanity, without his satiric intensity, without his intellectual power; so that the Jonsonian

[1] This parallel is noted in Faust's dissertation, *Richard Brome*, Halle, 1887, p. 52.

scenes in Brome, his numerous efforts to describe the humours of London life, repel or tire the reader.

Fifteen of Brome's plays have come down to us. Four of these were published in quarto in Brome's lifetime; five were printed together, in 1653, shortly after his death; five more in 1659; and one other, in quarto, in 1657. The plays have been conveniently classed under the headings of comedies of manners, romantic comedies and romantic dramas of intrigue. These divisions exhibit Brome's debt to Jonson, for the first class is much the largest, including nine plays.[1] But these nine plays are not purely Jonsonian. *The Northern Lasse* is the earliest of the extant plays. It was printed in 1632 and, again, in 1635 and in 1663. It was the most popular of Brome's plays and definitely made his reputation as a writer. It is full of humours, which fill up the scenes of an ingenious plot; but its popularity was mainly due to the romantic note struck in the character of the northern lass herself. The modern reader finds it hard to detect the charm of Constance; she is very thinly and imperfectly drawn, and her "northern" speech is clumsy; but she pleased John Ford and Thomas Dekker. It would appear that the seventeenth century found in her some faint anticipation of the charm of the Scottish heroines of *The Waverley Novels*. Brome did not get this romantic note from Jonson, and the six romantic plays suggest to us that it was more natural to him than Jonson's hard, intellectual satire, and that he would have done better work if he had used it oftener. But the nine plays of Jonsonian humour and plot have certain merits. Brome always does his best. He works without enthusiasm, but steadily and conscientiously, and, as pieces of stagecraft, the plays are never contemptible. As a picture of the London of the period, they are full of interest and value. If their outlook were broader, if they depicted not only the vices and follies of life, but, also, its virtues and amenities, they would be read with eagerness, but it is not fair to blame Brome only for this defect. It is the weakness of the satiric method of Jonson that it tends continually to describe only what it can scourge, so that its world gets uglier

---

[1] *The Northern Lasse, The Antipodes, The Sparagus Garden, Covent Garden Weeded, The New Academy or The Exchange, The Damoiselle, The Court Beggar, The Madd Couple well matcht, The City Witt.*

and uglier. Brome's temperament fitted him for a kindlier
type of comedy, and there are many indications in his plays
that he would have produced better work under a gentler
master than Jonson. Jonson's satire is often mitigated by the
introduction of a purely comic idea, which is not vicious or
even eccentric, but merely whimsical, such as Morose's hatred
of noise. Brome shows a special aptitude in copying his
master in this respect, and his touch is lighter. Jonson is
sometimes over-ingenious and his workmanship heavy-handed.
The Antipodes is Brome's best effort in this kind.

Among the less interesting of the comedies of manners
which may be regarded as fairly representative of Brome's
usual work, *The Sparagus Garden*, acted 1635, takes its title
from the custom of going to eat asparagus in a garden where it
was grown. Such places were haunts of disreputable people of
both sexes, and the "humours" of the garden are coarse though
sketched with much vivacity and some wit. They bulk so
largely in the play that it is justly classed as a comedy of
manners. The scenes in which Timothy Hoyden, a yeoman's
son from the country, is shown the way to become a fine gentleman, are excellent comedy; they are whimsical as well as witty,
and written with a genuine gaiety. When Brome's humours
have this gaiety and lightness of touch, we are reminded of
another master than Jonson; we are conscious of something
of the spirit of Dekker. Among the commendatory verses
prefixed to *The Northern Lasse* are some characteristic lines
"To my Sonne Broom and his Lasse," by Thomas Dekker.
How much friendship these words imply we have no means
of discovering; but Brome is more truly a "son" of Dekker
than of Jonson. His best and happiest work is in the vein of
Dekker. But the scenes of our play are not all in the asparagus
garden. The first two suggest a quiet domestic drama which
might turn to tragedy or comedy, but would not harmonise
properly with the garden humours. Two young men decide to
attempt the reconcilement of two angry old men by proposing a
match between the son of one of them and the adopted daughter
of the other. The first scene describes the attempt and its
failure. In the second scene, the two friends try to console
the son for their failure and resolve to help him. Brome's
verse rises to an almost passionate height, as Gilbert insists that

> Love is wit itself,
> And through a thousand lets will find a way
> To his desired end.

Both these scenes describe common life simply and naturally, and with a touch of idealism not very common in Brome, who recants his usual creed when he confesses:

> Poets they are the life and death of things.

The play is a mine of allusions and references to the life of old London. From this point of view, Brome will always be worth reading.

The brightest and pleasantest of Brome's comedies of manners is *The City Witt, or The Woman wears the Breeches*. It is the best, just because it most successfully keeps in one key. Fleay contends that it is the earliest of the extant dramas, and says: "Dekker's influence is more clearly visible in it than in the other plays." He means that the gaiety and lightness of touch which we have noted as Dekker's rather than Jonson's are very noticeable in the play. But the prologue, composed by Brome for a revival of the play, states that it "past with good applause in former times"; adding that

> It was written when
> It bore just judgment and the seal of Ben.

We must suppose, therefore, that Dekker's influence was subordinate to Jonson's, and that Brome himself was unconscious of the force of the former. Its strength was due to its suitability to Brome's temperament. The lines prefixed to *The Northern Lasse* were the last we have from Dekker's pen; he probably, died before the end of 1632.

In his plots, Brome is apt to be over-ingenious, so that the action of his plays is either obscure or too episodical. It is the merit of *The City Witt* that its episodes are all held together by one central idea which is clear and simple, so that the play is well-knit and easily keeps the attention of the spectator to the end. A young citizen, Mr. Crasy, by his kindness and easy-going disposition, has involved himself in many difficulties, and discovers that his fair-weather friends all fall away when he asks for their help. He disappears, therefore, and returns disguised, with the object of bringing his false friends to book for their meanness. The play is a lively and laughable protest against worship of rank and money, and has in it a true breath of that unworldly spirit which is conspicuous in Dekker's best plays. The protest is all the more effective as coming from the tradesman's level. In that age, the development of trade brought with it new temptations. Dishonest speculation and the making of fortunes by all sorts of trickery were becoming common. At the same time, the new devices by which bankruptcy was made profitable were scorned by old-fashioned tradesmen. Crasy declares

> I must take nimble hold upon occasion
> Or lie for ever in the bankrupt ditch
> Where no man lends a hand to draw one out.
> I will leap over it or fall bravely in 't,
> Scorning the bridge of baseness, composition,
> Which doth infect a city like the plague,
> And teach men knavery that were never born to 't.

His troubles are largely due to the odious malice of his mother-in-law, Mistress Pyannet Sneakup, who illustrates the evil effect upon tradesmen's wives of the degenerate times. Her son-in-law asks gently, "May not an honest man—," when he is taken up by the irate lady—

Honest man! Who the devil wished thee to be an honest man? Here 's my worshipful husband, Mr. Sneakup, that from a grasier is come to be a Justice of Peace: and, what, as an honest man? He grew to be able to give nine hundred pound with my daughter; and what, by honesty? Mr. Sneakup and I are come up to live i' th City, and here we have lyen these three years; and, what? for honesty? Honesty! What should the City do with honesty, when 't is enough to undoe a whole Corporation? Why are your wares gumm'd; your shops dark; your prices writ in strange characters? what, for honesty?

This "woman of an eternal tongue, this creature of an ever-lasting noise" is the most considerable character in the piece; but Sarpego is equally good in another direction. We have already touched upon him. His sudden scraps of Latin are very comical—"*O Dii! Quem video? Nonne Mr. Sneakup?*"— any one wonders how far they were followed by the audience. Some of his paraphrases are very happy—"*Tempora mutantur;*

the town 's ours again"; "*Lupus in fabula;* the devil 's in the
woman's tongue"; "*Sic transit gloria mundi;* the learned is
coney-caught." The briskness and bustle of the play are
maintained to the end, and, if it were not for the absence of
Mrs. Tryman from the list of *dramatis personae*, the *dénouement*
would be a complete surprise. Crasy's honesty, his "unsuspicious freeness" and "most easy goodness" flavour the play
and convince us that Brome, with all his grossness, was
unsophisticated.

By way of proving this point more fully and carrying further
the comparison of Brome with Dekker, we may next consider
Brome's masterpiece, *A Joviall Crew, Or, The Merry Beggars.*
It was the latest play written by Brome, being produced in 1641
and continuing on the stage till it came to be the very last play
acted before parliament closed the theatres in 1642—"it had
the luck to tumble last of all in the Epidemicall ruin of the
Scene!" In his prologue, Brome notes that his title promises
mirth,

> Which were a new
> And forc'd thing in these sad and tragic days;

but, since he finds that plays are now liked which tediously and
tearfully relate lovers' distresses, up to the point at which

> some impossibility
> Concludes all strife and makes a comedy,

he, therefore, composes a kind of parody on this popular style,
in which he hopes the sadness will not make any woman weep.
This interesting account of the genesis of the play would
hardly have been surmised by the critic without the author's
help. The finest thing in the play, and, indeed, in all Brome's
writings, is the description of the steward Springlove's annual
hunger for the green grass and the careless content of the
wandering beggar.

> You kept a swallow in a cage that while.
> I cannot, Sir, endure another summer
> In that restraint with life: 't was then my torment
> But now my death.

We have to wait till the days of George Borrow and R. L.
Stevenson for a repetition of Brome's conception of the joy and

glory of vagabondage. The sketch of the beggars' content is combined with a very natural picture of the kind and compassionate master and squire. There is a touch of religious feeling in the picture of Oldrents's kindness of heart, and his compassion for the poor and unfortunate; the only drawback to the charm of the play is the occasional coarseness of the realism in the description of the jovial crew of beggars. The first act of this play is work of high and rare merit. Brome's English is admirably plain, unaffected and direct; his blank verse is unadorned, but clear and natural, and he reaps the reward of his simplicity. To the student of decadent romanticism, this play has the perfection of a cup of cold water in a dry and thirsty land.

A Joviall Crew is classed among Brome's romantic dramas of intrigue;[1] and two plays, *The Queen and Concubine* and *The Queenes Exchange*, have been reckoned as pure romantic dramas. This division, of course, is merely intended to meet the requirement of convenience. Of the six romantic plays, the last two mentioned and *The Love-sick Court* best illustrate Brome's ideas of romance and poetry, and thus call for some notice. Brome's modest conception of himself as a playwright and not an author or poet—his disinclination to indulge in imaginative effort—stamps him as out of sympathy with the fashionable taste for lengthy imaginative sentiment. He had a real sense of artistic form, and recoiled not only from the sentimentality, but from the incoherence, both in plan and metre, of the later Caroline drama. We have already quoted his account of the composition of *A Joviall Crew*. In the prologue to *The Antipodes*, he complains that "opinion" cares only for plays that

carry state,
In scene magnificent and language high,
And cloathes worth all the rest, except the action.

The taste of the journeyman playwright, on this head, was certainly far sounder than that of the king and his court. Yet Brome did essay romantic drama, and with very interesting results. *The Love-sick Court* was, probably, the earliest of the batch; *The Queenes Exchange* dates from about 1632, and *The*

---

[1] With three others, *The Love-sick Court, The Novella* and *The English Moor.*

Queen and Concubine from after 1635. In these plays we see Brome manfully striving to write as a poet and to achieve a good romantic play. In the first two, he is often at a loss; his art fails him, and only fumbling work is produced; but *The Queen and Concubine* marks a very definite advance, and shows that Brome might have produced excellent romantic work if his public had asked for it. Shakespeare, rather than Fletcher, is the master from whom Brome takes his suggestions, and the good queen Eulalia, whose trials and virtues are touchingly described, is a blend of the patient Grissill of Dekker and queen Katharine in *Henry VIII*. There are two fine songs in the play; one of them—"What if a day, or a month, or a year"—possessing the true Elizabethan charm of Campion or Dekker. The shining merit of Brome in these plays, for all their feeble workmanship, is his capacity for the unsophisticated and direct expression of emotion. We escape from inflated sentiment and return to a simplicity of moral feeling which belongs to the earlier days of the drama. Brome's humility was described above as almost servile; and the suggestion was made that his unaffected modesty is reflected in the restraint and the natural-ness of his art. Like Day, Brome proves his manliness when he falls on evil days. He wrote his dedication of *A Joviall Crew*, when it was printed in 1652, a few months before his death, "in these anti-ingenious Times," when the theatres had been closed for ten years. "Since the Times conspire to make us all Beggars," he says, "let us make ourselves merry." That is what his "play drives at." He does not flinch in his extremity: "I am poor and proud," he tells us; "you know, Sir, I am old and cannot cringe." This is his last word.

Among Jonson's most eager admirers was Thomas Ran-dolph; but he was not, like Field and Brome, a pupil of the old poet. He was a king's scholar of Westminster school, who became a fellow of Trinity college, Cambridge. At the end of 1629, a year of plague broke up the schools at Cambridge, and Randolph made Jonson's acquaintance during his stay in London; he was probably adopted as a "son" before he returned to Cambridge. He had written by this time his two earliest "shews"—*Aristippus* and *The Conceited Pedler*, which were printed in 1630. These lively sketches recall that early type of dramatic performance, the clown's jig, in which a famous comedian, such as Tarlton, poured forth an improvisation of his own, which was a mixture of prose, verse and antics. But it is Randolph's command of racy English, his high spirits and his exuberant wit that suggest this comparison. His pieces belong to that large body of "college drama" which is described in another chapter.[1] *Aristippus, or, The Joviall Philosopher* is a dispute on the rival merits of ale and sack. All the technical terms of Aristotle's logic are crowded into a hilarious laudation of sack and a decrying of malt liquor, which never flags. Randolph's classical and scholastical learning supplies matter for a cataract of ingenious puns and word play, and, therefore, his transference of Aristotelian metaphysic into English farce is to be contrasted with, rather than compared to, Robert Browning's profuse employment of the details of Attic drama in his *Aristophanes' Apology*. Both poets, while crammed with learning, have no pedantry in their nature. The marvellous agility of some of the riming in *Aristippus* is another point of contact with Browning's poetry.

In March, 1632, king Charles visited Cambridge, and the Trinity men acted before him *The Jealous Lovers*, written for the occasion. It is Randolph's only failure. Its dramatic character is so bad that the ability of the writing cannot redeem it. After the king's visit, Randolph left Cambridge for London, "called thence to keep the flock of Corydon." In *An Eglogue to Mr. Johnson*,[2] he describes how he had relished his Aristotelian studies—"those deep and learned layes" which "the shepherd of Stagira used to sing"; but now he has to keep "another's flock," and not he but "the Master shears the sheep." Fleay's interpretation of this passage is that Randolph was manager of prince Charles's men acting at Salisbury court in 1632 and 1633. At Salisbury court theatre, Fleay thinks. *The Muses Looking-Glasse* was presented towards the end of 1632. (It was not printed till 1638, when the writer was dead.) This theory accords very well with the character of Randolph's masterpiece, and explains the genesis of this new and distinct type of dramatic art. It is just such a work as the writer of *Aristippus* might be expected to produce if he were called upon to expand his short "shew" into some-

[1] See *post*, Chap. XII, where more is said about *The Jealous Lovers*.
[2] *I. e.* Ben Jonson.

thing that could compete in length, interest and dignity with
the plays of a better class. Randolph's creative capacity
had been stimulated to this effort by close contact with the
drama of the London stage; but the Aristotelian student is still
in evidence. The main part of the piece consists of a series
of fifteen scenes, in which the vices of Aristotle's *Ethics* appear
in couples or singly and, in accordance with the theory of
comedy put forward in the first act of the piece, hold up a
mirror in which spectators may note their own defects; this is
how comedies "laugh" people "into wit and virtue." These
scenes, therefore, are planned like the "colloquies" of Day's
Parliament of Bees; but the contrast is great between Day's
delicate rimes and Randolph's masculine and emphatic blank
verse, which only occasionally uses the heroic couplet. Kolax,
the flatterer, remains on all the time because "Any vice yields
work for flattery." In these strongly written scenes, the influence of Jonson's satiric plays is very obvious. In act I,
there is an excellent scene in which Comedy, Tragedy, Mime
and Satire dispute together and expound their functions according to classic theory. Before the vices come in, we have a
masque,

a rude dance,
Presented by the seven deadly sins.

In act v, after Mediocrity, the mother of virtues, has ex-
pounded in a hundred lines Aristotle's doctrine of the mean,
she presents a masque of her daughters, "wherein all the Vertues dance together." The invention of all this is both copious
and happy. The author describes his work as containing

No plot at all, but a meer Olla Podrida,
A medley of ill plac'd and worse penned Humours,

borrowed from the man

to whom he owes
All the poor skill he has, great Aristotle.

Randolph is pleasantly unconscious that the creative and artistic faculty is too often, as in Jonson's case, smothered, rather
than nourished, by theory, however sound. But we have still
to mention the most delightful feature of the play. The
"moralising" scenes are presented before Bird, a feather-man,

and Mistress Flowerdew, "wife to a Haberdasher of Small Wares." These worthies bring feathers and pins and looking-glasses to sell to the players; but they belong to "the Sanctified Fraternity of Black-Fryers": that is to say, they are puritans. This device is not new. Beaumont used it admirably in *The Knight of the Burning Pestle*. But Randolph employs it to lighten the didactic tendency of his main scenes; moreover, his two puritans are to be converted to the theory of comedy put forward in the play; they are, therefore, described with more good humour, with more restraint and naturalness, than is usual in Elizabethan comedy. When the virtues are to be presented, Bird hopes there are no "cardinal vertues"—

> I hate a vertue
> That will be made a Cardinal,

—he adds that even "Bishop vertues are unwarrantable," and, generally,

> Vertues in Orders are unsanctified.

He is disturbed when the virtues dance:

> O vile, absurd, Maypole-Maid-Marian Vertue!

Yet, as the play goes on, Mistress Flowerdew begins to relent:

> I have picked
> Out of the garden of this play a good
> And wholesome salad of instruction.

And, finally, both are mollified. Bird says

> I 'll teach devotion now a milder temper,

while Mistress Flowerdew admits,

> I might have gone to hell the narrow way.

We have called *The Muses Looking-Glasse* Randolph's master-piece, though this title might be claimed for his fine pastoral *Amyntas*. But the later production has to compete with even finer work by Jonson and Fletcher, while the former is unique of its kind. Randolph died in 1635, at the age of twenty-nine; and he is to be counted among those poets whose achievement, considerable as it is, is an earnest only of what his matured powers might have given us.

It remains to attempt a hurried survey of the lesser drama·tists of the end of the age, who were writing from the later years of James until the closing of the theatres. They exhibit very clearly the exhaustion of the great dramatic impulse which begins with Marlowe and ends with Shirley and Brome. A tasteless and featureless mediocrity or a pretentious extravagance are the characteristics of work which was ceasing to conform to type and losing all sense of true dramatic form. On a first casual inspection, the more meritorious of these plays seem better written and more judiciously planned than much of the Elizabethan work which has survived; but a closer study reveals the essential insipidity of the later work, due, in the first place, to exhaustion of the dramatic impulse, and, in the second, to the deterioration of the audiences and the practical cessation of a demand for good plays.

Thomas May, the historian of the Long parliament, whose character Clarendon and Marvell[1] unite in decrying, began his literary career with two comedies, *The Heir* and *The Old Couple*, written about 1620. *The Heir* is a Fletcherian tragicomedy; *The Old Couple*, which Fleay thinks the earlier of the pair, a play of Jonsonian intrigue and manners. After producing these plays, May turned to the work by which he is best known—his translations of the *Georgics* and of Lucan's *Pharsalia*. Jonson wrote lines "to my chosen friend the learned translator of Lucan, Thomas May, Esq.," and May was a contributor to *Jonsonus Virbius*. Jonson's influence and that of the classics would seem to have turned May to classical drama, and he produced three tragedies, of which the first, *Antigone, the Theban Princess* is dedicated to Endymion Porter, and may have been written before 1626. Fleay has suggested that May is the author of the anonymous *Nero*, printed 1624. We are to suppose that the fire and energy of this fine play were the result of May's first study of Tacitus, perhaps before he had been too much obsessed by Jonson's influence and method. But May's study of Tacitus would seem to have been later than 1624. His *Cleopatra* is dated 1626, and *Julia Agrippina* 1628. May's imagination is pedestrian; his style is regular and painstaking. *Nero* is the work of a scholar whose imagination is fiery and strong, and who contrives to crowd into his play a great deal

---

[1] "Most servile wit and mercenary pen."

of the excitement, the incident and the underlying unity of the
Roman historian's picture of the tyrant.   May's first two plays
are meritorious; there is care and correctness in the blank verse,
and much careful invention in the plot and the conception of
the characters; but his classical plays are no better and no
worse than his continuation of *Pharsalia*.   They are pale reflections of Jonson's work in *Sejanus* and *Catiline*.   May is
nothing more than a "son" of Ben, who copied his adoptive
father's least inspired work.

Meritorious, like May's, was the work of Robert Davenport, whose activity begins in 1624.   Three of his plays survive,
two comedies and a tragedy.   The tragedy is a careful re-
writing of Munday and Chettle's *Death of Robert, Earle of
Huntington*.[1]   Chettle's drama is stripped of its crudities and
banalities; so far as may be, the horrible is replaced by the
pathetic, and a considerable adornment of poetic diction and
imagery is added.   The versification, of course, is brought up to
date and irregularities disappear.   The old play has a deeper
significance than that which it expresses: we read it with im-
patience; but we remember it with interest, because of its
suggestion of horror and gloom.   Davenport, on the other
hand, we read with respect for his industry, and we forget him
at once.   It is a plausible conjecture that his comedies were
remodellings of older material; so that all his work looks backward.   But *The City-Night-Cap* and *A New Tricke to Cheat
the Divell* are, both of them, interesting and able comedies, like
the two plays of May which we have just considered.   The
former dates from 1624.   As this play takes its main story
from "The Curious Impertinent" in *Don Quixote*, there can
be nothing surprising in the fact that, in some respects, it is
unpleasant; indeed, its comic part is intolerable; but, on the
romantic side, it has merit.   It contains echoes of *Measure for
Measure*, of *Cymbeline* and of *A Winter's Tale;* it is high-minded,
with some grace of diction and force of eloquence, but dramatically unreasonable and wrong.   The other play is slighter and
more humorous, and, on the whole, more agreeable.   Two
of Davenport's friends were players; of his circumstances
nothing is known.

Thomas Nabbes seems to have belonged to the same social

[1] Cf. *ante*, Vol. V, Chap. XIII.

level as Davenport, and, like him, to have produced his tragedy, *Hannibal and Scipio*, by revising an older play; he was a friend of Richard Brome. His *Microcosmus* is a morality play which he calls a masque. His best work is to be found in his three comedies, *Covent-Garden*, 1632, *Totenham-Court*, 1633, and *The Bride*, 1638. Nabbes breaks away from the prevailing coarse type of comedy, intended to hit the taste of the man about town, and takes pains and pleasure in representing people of virtuous life and conversation. With just a little more distinction and force, both in his writing and in his characterisation, Nabbes would have risen above the ranks of third-rate dramatists. *The Bride* is a comedy of considerable effectiveness, distinguished among the plays of its time by the goodness and purity to be found in its men and women. His heroes and heroines are amiable and sincere; somewhat colourless when compared with stronger dramatic work; but without the two diseases of the time, the convention of coarseness, and the convention of fantastic sentiment.

Two writers who were among the "sons" of Ben and of great repute in their day need not detain us long. William Cartwright was the son of an innkeeper at Cirencester. He was educated at Westminster and Christ Church, Oxford, and rose to be the most noted man in his university as a strenuous scholar, an admired dramatist and a "seraphical" preacher. His first play, probably, was his comedy *The Ordinary*, produced about 1635. This was followed by three tragicomedies, *The Lady Errant*, *The Royall Slave* and *The Siedge or Love's Convert*. After taking holy orders in 1638, he did not write any more plays. He died in 1643. His plays, therefore, were probably composed hurriedly. They are essentially the work of a man of parts, who writes for reputation without any true respect either for his art or for himself. His comedy is a flashy and vulgar imitation of Jonsonian "humours," as tedious as it is coarse. His tragicomedies belong to the school of enervated romance which pleased king Charles and was suited to the French tastes of the queen. *The Royall Slave* was presented before the king and queen at Oxford on 30 August, 1636, by the students of Christ Church, and, again, six months later, at Hampton court, by the king's players. The students are said to have acted best. Very probably, professionals found it difficult to adapt themselves to the extravagant sentiment and preciosity of Cartwright's style. Jonson's saying, "my son Cartwright writes all like a man," suggests a directness of style and truth of inspiration which are not found in Cartwright's plays.

Jasper Mayne, dramatist, translator and archdeacon, was a Devonshire man, educated at Westminster school and Christ Church, Oxford. Like his friend Cartwright, he was an admired preacher. He produced a tragicomedy, *The Amorous Warre*, and a comedy, *The Citye Match*, which was acted at Whitehall by the king's command in 1639. It is a much better comedy than Cartwright's, with plenty of life and movement in it, and, although it has no moral elevation, it is without Cartwright's obscenity. Mayne's[1] most useful contribution to the literature of his country was his translation of Lucian.

The tragicomedies of Cartwright and Mayne belong to the group of romantic plays specially characteristic of the closing years of the drama, written to please the court and the current liking for inflated sentiment and fantastic emotion. But, before we deal summarily with these plays, a figure of some consequence calls for a less perfunctory consideration.

In 1642, the year of the closing of the theatres, Sir John Suckling poisoned himself in Paris. All his plays are not worth his handful of incomparable lyrics; but they have some salt of genius in them which entitles them to a place of their own among the work of lesser dramatists. *Aglaura*, a tragedy of court intrigue, of which the scene is supposed to be Persia, was acted in the winter of 1637, when its literary qualities received less attention than the novelty and magnificence of the scenery used and the dresses presented by the author to the actors. King Charles is said to have requested an alternative final act with a happy ending, which Suckling afterwards wrote. Flecknoe saw the play when it was revived at the Restoration, and his criticism, that it was "full of flowers, but rather stuck than growing there," applies to all Suckling's dramatic work. He has imagination, fancy and wit, but these faculties are not usually employed upon his plot and his characters. The famous lyric, "Why so pale and wan, fond lover?" occurs in the fourth act of *Aglaura*. *The Goblins* was

[1] Both Cartwright and Mayne contributed to *Jonsonus Virbius*.

probably written next; it was acted in 1638, and is Suckling's best play. His goblins are thieves who masquerade as devils, and their pranks are mixed up with the feuds of two noble families and a double love story. The so-called goblins administer justice in the style of Robin Hood and his men in older plays. Suckling's restless temperament expresses itself in the impossible rapidity and abruptness of the action; but the sprightliness of the play is undeniable and its mixture of song and witty dialogues caught Sheridan's attention, and, undoubtedly, influenced his style. His lyric "Here 's to the maiden" is suggested by a catch in *The Goblins*. Although *The Goblins* is Suckling's most satisfactory performance, the tragedy *Brennoralt* is a work of more promise and a more striking evidence of his poetic capacity. It did not appear till 1646; but it had been printed in a shorter form in 1640 as *The Discontented Colonell*. The interest of *Brennoralt* lies mainly in our seeming to detect in the hero something of the inner self of the author, and to find that self better and sounder than the shallow prodigal who caught the public eye. The gloomy colonel, in spite of his strict loyalty, is clearly aware of defects in his king. The rebel Lithuanians are meant for Scots, of about the year 1639. The rebels having been informed that the king cannot be unjust to them "where there 's so little to be had," their leader Almerine replies, "Where there is least, there 's liberty." Suckling's style perceptibly strengthens in the play. The fine things are less obviously stuck in. Sententious force, by which his political experience receives apt expression, is added to genuine poetic vigour. Brennoralt is left alive, his rival and both the heroines being dead. The false Caroline ideal of tragicomedy prevents the solution of suicide demanded by the tone of the play. But the melancholy, disillusioned character of Brennoralt, who points forward to Byron, rather than backward to Marston, may help to explain Suckling's own suicide, which seems very inconsistent with the rest of his career. The versification is spasmodic and formless. A blank verse line, here and there, suggests to us what the metre is supposed to be, and, occasionally, such a line as "Oh! it is wisdom and great thrift to die!" proves that Suckling had it in him to write blank verse. In all his plays he has a trick of appropriating Shakespearean

phrases and lines, and, in *The Goblins*, the courtship of Orsabrin
and Reginella is copied unblushingly from the courtship scenes
in *The Tempest*. Although Shakespeare's work is weakened,
Suckling's courtship scenes are the prettiest scenes in his play,
and his hero Orsabrin is a brave spirit of true heroic strain.

A friend and companion in arms of Suckling, who died
before him in 1639, was Shackerley Marmion, author of the
considerable poem *Cupid and Psyche*. He produced three
comedies before his poem, not, as we should expect, in the
romantic vein, but all of them rather thin imitations of Jonson.
The Antiquary is the best of these. Veterano, from whose
pursuits the play is named, is an original conception; but the
author fails to give him life, lacking the capacity to use the
opportunity with which he has provided himself.

In conclusion, we may rapidly enumerate among later
writers of the Jacobean age those dramatists who are important
only because they initiated the type of play which, in its full
development in the Restoration period, came to be known as
the "heroic drama." In this connection, the insipid and
tedious tragicomedies of Lodowick Carlell have importance.
Carlell is said to have come from the stock which afterwards
produced Thomas Carlyle. He was a Scot, born in 1602, who
came to court to make his fortune and rose to the position of
keeper of the forest at Richmond. Of his plays, which began
in 1629, four tragicomedies remain, two of which are in two
parts. They are taken from contemporary romances, Spanish
or French. French romance, as written by D'Urfé and Mlle.
de Scudéry, was characterised by a refinement of sentiment
which cut it off from real life and made it vapid and extravagant. In our own drama, the romance of Fletcher shows a
tendency to exaggeration; the dramatic thrill ceases to represent reality; it begins to have a note of hysteria, and to enjoy
its own deliciousness; emotion is dwelt upon, sentiment is
refined, till love, honour and friendship are taken altogether
out of the world of reality. Queen Henrietta Maria's French
tastes and upbringing added the example of French romance
to tendencies already prevailing in England, and rendered the
influence of the court upon the drama merely enervating.
Fleay says that Carlell's plays "show what rubbish was
palatable to Charles and Henrietta." The peculiar extrava-

gance of romantic sentiment which these plays exhibit goes along with a looseness and incoherence of blank verse very accurately described by the same critic as "a riot of hybrid iambic." Dryden's use of rime was almost needed to bring back some form into this chaos. The plays of Henry Glapthorne are noticeable from this point of view. His three comedies, at their worst, sink as low as Cartwright and, at their best, touch the level of Mayne or Nabbes; but his more serious work, consisting of *The Ladies Priviledge*, *Argalus and Parthenia* and *Albertus Wallenstein*, approaches more nearly to literature than any of the parallel efforts of Carlell, Mayne, Cartwright, or Thomas Killigrew. The first of these plays, which ends as a comedy, belongs to the type of tragicomedy in which extravagant sentiment insists upon submitting itself to absurd tasks in the effort to prove its heroism. The second is a pastoral, also conforming to the tragicomedy type; and the third is history treated on the same lines. The plays, therefore, illustrate the enervating and disintegrating effect of heroic sentiment on all the chief forms of English drama. But it is William D'Avenant whose work best enables us to observe the transition to the heroic drama of Dryden. His first two plays were tragedies in Fletcher's grimmest style, dated 1626 and 1627, and these were followed by two able comedies which enjoyed considerable popularity. After 1630, illness incapacitated him for several years; and, when he resumes work as a dramatist, his style has altered, and four plays, *Love and Honour*, 1634, *The Platonick Lovers*, 1635, *The Fair Favourite*, 1638, and *The Unfortunate Lover*, 1638, show him under French influences and as the leading exponent of the cult of platonic love, of which queen Henrietta herself was the patron. *The Platonick Lovers* is a budget of speeches and disputations on this unreal and undramatic theme; it is curious to the student of manners, but futile as literature. D'Avenant lived to revive the theatre shortly before the Restoration, and to contribute to its literature after that date. He will, therefore, receive some further notice in a later volume.

CHAPTER X

The Elizabethan Theatre

WHEN Elizabeth came to the throne, she found attached to the court not only musicians and minstrels, but eight players of interludes. This body had been a permanent part of the court establishment for some reigns; and, in the new theatrical activity of Elizabeth's reign, it was supplanted by other bodies, but not dissolved. It accompanied her occasionally on her progresses, and only gradually died out. Companies of such players had long been attached to the households of men of wealth and position, whose "livery" or badge they wore on their sleeves. A statement in Heywood's *Apology for Actors* (1612) may be taken to mean that some kind of royal licence was considered necessary or advisable by these companies, so far back as the reign of Henry VIII.

In many cases, these companies supported themselves by playing before the public in various parts of the country. The practice seems to have been for players, on coming to a town, first to attend the mayor, to inform him whose servants they were and to receive his licence for public playing. If the mayor liked the company or wished to honour their master, he would pay them a sum (which the entrance money charged to the public would supplement[1]) to give a first performance before the corporation, to which the public were admitted. Several cases are on record where players received a fee, though they were forbidden by the town's by-laws or otherwise to give a performance. Travelling players appeared frequently, also, at private houses, at weddings and on other festival occasions; and, occasionally, even in churches. At Exeter,

[1] Murray, John Tucker, "English Dramatic Companies in the towns outside of London, 1550–1600," *Modern Philology*, vol. II, p. 539.

Yarmouth and Worcester, there seem to have been regular playhouses; at other times, the actors played at the guildhall, or in an innyard. Such incidents as the remonstrance issued by the privy council to the lord president of the north in 1556, touching the seditious plays acted by "certain lewd persons naming themselves to be the servants of Sir Frances Lake," suggest that some, at least, of the companies attached to great houses had received no recognition or licence from the crown; while "common players of interludes," orders for whose regulation or arrest were occasionally issued, did not belong, either in fact or in name, to any nobleman's establishment. In addition to companies bearing the names of patrons, there were still in existence a large number of wandering troupes of jugglers and players, descendants of the old minstrels, who owned no kind of patronage. Certain municipal corporations had their band of players; and, in Cornwall and elsewhere, local associations of amateurs still met to perform town or village plays and pageants which the reformation had shorn of their old glory. The competition of travelling companies was, perhaps, as important an element in the decadence of these local bodies as was the hostility of the puritans.

A few months after her accession, Elizabeth issued a proclamation providing that no interlude should be played without being notified beforehand and licensed by the mayor or chief officer of a town, or, in the country, by lieutenants or two local justices of the peace. And, in 1572, the question of these unattached companies was finally settled by a law providing that common players in interludes not belonging to a baron or honourable personage of greater degree, or not having a licence from two justices of the peace, should be deemed rogues and vagabonds. This, practically, is the close of the history—so far as their influence on the progress of the drama is concerned —of any theatrical bodies except those definitely under patronage. The early part of Elizabeth's reign saw not only the triumph of the professional actor over the amateur, but the supplanting of the old player of interludes by the better equipped companies then newly formed by nobles anxious to please their sovereign.

In the city of London, jurisdiction over public theatricals rested, under the proclamation of 1559, in the mayor and corporation, steady foes of the drama. The decay of the feudal system under the Tudors had increased the importance not only of the immediate neighbourhood of the court, but of the capital; and London was now the centre of theatrical activity. Elizabeth's own love of the play tended to the same result; and the privy council, on the whole, supported her in defending the acted drama against the attacks of the city government. The difference between court and city was the cause of many disputes and much uncertainty, as is shown at length in a later chapter[1] of this volume, where it is also related how an unforeseen result of the city's opposition was the enormous stimulus given to theatrical art by the building of playhouses outside the common council's jurisdiction but within easy reach of the citizens of London.

The quarrel[2] was due to other causes besides the religious difference, and the inevitable conflict between the feudal privilege from which companies drew their origin, on the one hand, and, on the other, the rights of the corporation, which meant the growing importance of the middle class. A very reasonable objection was advanced against the overcrowding of narrow streets by people riding or, later, driving to the playhouses, and by the concourse of loafers and beggars; furthermore, apprentices and others were tempted to play truant and occasional tumults or crimes resulted from the massing of numbers of people in holiday mood. A theatrical performance, like the performance of a miracle-play in earlier times, meant a procession through the streets with drums and trumpets. It would not be fair, however, to ascribe to plays alone all the disturbances which are on record. Such incidents as those which took place outside the Theater in 1584, when "one Browne, a serving man in a blew coat, a shifting fellowe," attacked an apprentice with a sword, were due rather to the fact that the neighbourhood of this house was the "ordinary place for all maisterles men and vagabond persons . . . to meet together and to recreate themselfes."[3] The gravest cause

---

[1] See *post*, Chap. XIV.

[2] For an interesting suggestion as to the influence of the Blackfriars playhouse in and after the year 1597, see Wallace, C. W., *Children of the Chapel*, chap. XII.

[3] *Remembrancia*, vol. II, p. 103.

for the corporation's objection to plays—a cause which the privy council readily supported them in avoiding—was, however, the recurrence of the plague, to the grievous and prolonged visitations of which full reference is made in the chapter discussing the conflicts between puritanism and the stage.[1] But, in the reigns of Elizabeth, James I and Charles I, every year was a plague year, and, besides 1582–3, 1585, 1586, 1593, 1603, 1613, 1625 and 1636 were very bad plague years.   It was important to check the spread of infection by preventing the gathering of crowds, and plays were forbidden whenever it seemed desirable.   Early in the reign of James I, all performances were prohibited when the number of deaths a week reached 30; and, in or about 1619, 40 was fixed as the limiting number.[2]   This frequently entailed the closing of places of public performance during the whole of the summer and autumn, when companies sometimes "broke," sometimes went on tour in England and sometimes travelled abroad.   The history of these travels is well worth study, but lies outside the scope of this work.[3]

In the conflict between the drama and the corporation, the weight of Elizabeth herself was thrown entirely on the side of the drama.   The list of performances at court shows that, while masques were frequently performed by amateurs at the beginning of her reign, their place was almost entirely taken later by the performances of professional actors whom her patronage helped to bring to efficiency.   The stock excuse offered by the privy council for contravention of the prohibitive regulations of the city authorities is that players must be allowed full opportunities of practising their art in order that they may exercise it fitly before the queen, during the Christmas holidays or at Shrovetide—the great seasons of performances at court.   In 1583, the queen, at the suggestion of Walsingham, and probably as a countermove to a decision of the common council, had her own company selected from the best actors of the day; and every attempt was made to regard public

---

[1] See *post*, Chap. XIV.

[2] Greg's *Henslowe's Diary*, vol. II, p. 145.

[3] See Cohn, A., *Shakespeare in Germany* and "The English Comedians in Germany," by Harris, C., in *Publications of the Modern Language Association of America*, N. S. vol. XV, No. 3, and cf. the opening passages of Chap. XII, Vol. V, *ante*.

performances as mere rehearsals for those at court. It is easily possible to make too much of the pretext, which, doubtless, was convenient at the time. The chance of a play being awarded a place among the few to be performed at court would scarcely have sufficed to encourage playwrights to produce work of the quantity or the character left by Elizabethan dramatists. Occasional state performances, rewarded with a small fee, could not be prize enough to keep large numbers of men working hard at acting, and at nothing else, all the year round; and players grew well-to-do and respectable, not because they played now and then at court, but because court favour enabled them to meet the ardent desire for theatrical performances which had been largely thwarted in previous troubled reigns, but which, when it could be indulged, to a great extent supplanted the love of athletic or acrobatic exhibitions that had had to suffice for earlier times. Such exhibitions still survived; but the drama either swept them into its own net, or tried to make their separate existence dependent on its pleasure as regards time and place of performance. The patronage of the queen and the eagerness of nobles to supply her with a favourite amusement provided the opportunity, rather than constituted the cause, of the people's new interest in the play. It is true that the royal favour first enabled the stage to stand alone, both as an art and as a business; but, after 1591, the queen's own company having by that time lost its prestige, royal patronage as an active force dwindled until the accession of James I; and, if the honour of playing at court was still eagerly sought, it was largely for the sake of the immunity from molestation by the city which the privy council usually extended to the companies selected. Nevertheless, the hope of playing before the queen seldom debarred a company from producing a satirical or seditious play which would attract the public.

The opposition between the city government and the privy council was, indirectly, a benefit to the art of the theatre, in that it led at once to control and to encouragement. The somewhat complicated history of the various moves on both sides shows the common council determined, with varying success, to keep players out of the city, the privy council determined to check sedition and, while fostering dramatic art, to limit the number of playhouses and companies, and each party inclined to oppose, or to neglect, the recommendations of the other. The position of players was uncertain and sometimes dangerous, as is proved by their petitions and remonstrances, and by the occasional imprisonment of offending companies. In such circumstances, only the strongest could survive with dignity or comfort. The tendency was always towards consolidation, though the experiment of the Queen's company, formed in 1583, was not to prove successful for long. The path of the Chamberlain's and the Admiral's companies was smooth and profitable on the whole, and the steady influence of royal favour supported them.

That influence became all important on the accession of James I. The position of the favoured companies, thenceforth, was assured by the issue of licences which brought them directly under royal patronage and by the statute of March, 1604, which abolished private patronage by forbidding nobles to license men to go wandering abroad. All public theatricals remained directly under royal patronage during the reigns of James I and Charles I, until the ordinance of the lords and commons of September, 1642, brought them to an end.

Playwrights and players were further subject to the control of the master of the revels. Originally instituted, as it seems, by Henry VII, for the management of the finances and the material of performances at court, the office grew constantly in power. It became the duty of the master of the revels to summon the companies before him and, after seeing them perform, to select such actors and such plays as he approved and order such changes to be made in the plays as, in his opinion, should render them suitable for performance before the sovereign. At least so early as 1574, we find him empowered to examine every play that was to be played in any part of England. No play might be played or printed without his licence, and he had the power to alter, to forbid and even (as the action of Sir Henry Herbert, master of the revels under Charles I, would seem to show) to destroy, any play he found objectionable. He was entitled to charge a fee for every play he examined, and for every play which he licensed for printing, besides a fee which rose from 5s. a week in 1592 to £3 a month in 1602, for licensing each playhouse;[1] and, later in the period, we find the two leading companies paying him, first the results of two performances, and then a fixed sum in every year. Sedition, no doubt, was the offence he principally attempted to check; but profanity and immorality were also the objects of his attention.

Besides the companies of players under royal or noble patronage there were, on Elizabeth's accession, two other classes of dramatic company, both composed of boys or youths. These were the "children" of St. Paul's and of the chapel royal, and the boys of the public schools, Eton and Westminster and Merchant Taylors'.[2]

The most important of the companies of men was that which was originally formed by Robert Dudley, earl of Leicester, and which, in 1574, was the first to receive the royal licence. The numbers of the company mentioned in the document are five: James Burbage, John Perkyn, John Laneham, William Johnson and Robert Wilson; but two or more boys and some minor actors must, also, be supposed to have been attached to the company. When the first playhouse, the Theater, was built in 1576, it was occupied by Leicester's company, who remained there, probably, until in 1583, its place was taken by the new Queen's company, into which Burbage, Laneham and Wilson were drafted. In 1585, Leicester took his company abroad with him; in 1587, they were touring in England and acted at Stratford-on-Avon. Of those who believe that Shakespeare became a member of this company, some hold that he joined it during, or shortly after, this visit to his native town. In 1588, Leicester died, and, not long afterwards, the leading actors of the company that had gone abroad are found as members of the company of Ferdinando Stanley, lord Strange. The new company, which, through some kind of amalgamation with the remains of the Admiral's men, during these years included Edward Alleyn himself, played first at the Cross Keys inn in Gracechurch street, and later, in February, 1592, at Philip Henslowe's playhouse, the Rose in Southwark.[3] On 3 March, 1592, they produced a new play entered by Henslowe in his

---

[1] Greg's *Henslowe's Diary*, vol. II, pp. 114–118.

[2] Of these boys' companies a separate account is given in the next chapter (XI) of the present volume.

[3] Greg's *Henslowe's Diary*, vol. II, pp. 45, 73.

diary as "harey the vj," which is believed by many to have been Shakespeare's *King Henry VI, Part I*. If so, the conditions of the time imply that Shakespeare, by that date, was a member of the company. In April, 1594, lord Strange, who had become earl of Derby in September, 1593, died, and the company passed under the protection of Henry Carey, lord Hunsdon, then lord chamberlain, to be thenceforth known as the Chamberlain's servants. In the June of 1594, they played a short time with the Admiral's men at the playhouse at Newington Butts; but, in the same month, the Admiral's men, with Alleyn at their head, resumed an independent existence. In March, 1595, we have the first documentary evidence that Shakespeare was a member of the company: the treasurer's accounts show that "Wil. Kempe," "Wil. Shakespeare" and "Rich. Burbage" received payment for two comedies played at court on 26 and 28 December, 1594. In 1595 or 1596, the company was at the Theater. The first lord Hunsdon died in July, 1596, and the company descended to his son George Carey, second lord, who, in March, 1597, himself became lord chamberlain. In July, 1597, the Theater was shut up and the company possibly played at the Curtain, before moving, in 1599, into the most famous of all Elizabethan playhouses, the newly erected Globe on the Surrey bank. In this playhouse, Shakespeare was a shareholder, and at this playhouse and by this company all Shakespeare's plays written after that date were produced. In May, 1603, the company received a patent, as the King's men, a title which they retained till the suppression in 1642. Thenceforward, they were members of the royal household, holding the rank, as the Queen's company had before them, of grooms of the chambers, and being entitled, every two years, to four yards of scarlet cloth for a cloak, and a quarter of a yard of crimson velvet for a cape. Their licence permitted them to play at their usual house, the Globe, and within the liberties and freedom of any other city, university, town or borough whatsoever. In 1608,[1] the Blackfriars playhouse was occupied by this company, who, thenceforth, continued to use both houses till all the playhouses were closed by the ordinance of 1642. The company's career was un-

[1] Wallace, *op. cit.* pp 44–45.

eventful in the sense that it was seldom in trouble; though, in 1601, it was under suspicion of implication in the Essex conspiracy; in 1615, it was summoned before the privy council, in the persons of Burbage and Heminge, then its leaders, for playing in Lent; and, in 1624, Middleton's *Game at Chesse*, which attacked the Spaniards, caused the players, at the instance of Gondomar, the Spanish ambassador, to be inhibited for a fortnight.   Many lists of actors are extant to show the composition of the company, and among its principal members at various times were Shakespeare, Richard Burbage, Augustine Phillipps, John Heminge and Henry Condell (afterwards the editors of the first folio Shakespeare), Slye, Pope, William Kemp and John Lowin.   Richard Burbage died in March, 1619; Shakespeare retired in 1610; Condell in 1619; Pope died in 1604, and Slye in 1608.   Concerning the parts played by the principal actors, information is scanty.   Shakespeare is known to have acted in Ben Jonson's *Every Man in His Humour* (tradition assigns him the part of old Nowell) and *Sejanus;* Rowe, making enquiries about his acting early in the eighteenth century, "could never meet with any further account of him this way than" (what he heard, possibly, from Betterton) "that the top of his performance was the ghost in his own Hamlet"; Oldys records that "one of Shakespeare's younger brothers" had seen him play Adam in *As You Like It;* and, in 1610, John Davies of Hereford states that Shakespeare "plaid some kingly parts in sport," which is open to the interpretation that he acted the parts of kings on the stage.   Of Richard Burbage, as an actor, more is known.   His name appears as early as 1592.   There is good evidence that he was the original Richard III, Hamlet, Othello and Lear in Shakespeare's plays, and it is probable that he also played Romeo.   It is supposed, with reason, that he was the creator of all the leading parts in the plays which Shakespeare wrote for the company; and there is evidence that he played, also, the leading parts in all the most successful of Beaumont and Fletcher's plays produced in his lifetime, as well as in the plays of Ben Jonson produced by his company.   In fact, he was the leading man, especially in tragedy, of the company—a position in which Taylor succeeded him.   Malone had read in "some tract, of which I have forgot to preserve the title" that Heminge was the original Falstaff, a part which is soon found in the hands of Lowin; and Condell is supposed by Collier to have played Bobadill.

The Queen's company, as we have seen, was formed in 1583 at the suggestion of Sir Francis Walsingham. Its members were selected by the master of the revels, then Edmund Tilney, from the best companies of the day, including Leicester's and the earl of Warwick's, and it was licensed by the privy council. It played frequently at court between 1584 and 1591, and its public house was, probably, the Theater; but in, or about the end of, 1592, it had left London, and it is not heard of after Easter, 1594. The original members included James Burbage, John Laneham, Robert Wilson and Richard Tarlton from Leicester's company, and Laurence and John Dutton from Warwick's. James Burbage, originally a joiner by trade, had been the chief of Leicester's company. Of Laneham, as an actor, nothing is known, and Wilson is more famous as a playwright.[1] Tarlton is a famous figure in the theatrical history of the time. A clown, who took to the stage, as it appears, comparatively late in life, he achieved a popularity that long outlasted his death. His extemporal riming and his "jiggs" were the delight of the groundlings, and he left some volumes of verse and jests, besides the play of *The Seven Deadly Sins*, the "platt" or scheme of which survives in manuscript at Dulwich.[2] Among the authors whose plays this company acted were the university wits, Greene, Lodge and Peele; and, possibly, Marlowe's *Jew of Malta* was in their *répertoire*.

A company under the patronage of Charles second lord Howard of Effingham is found acting at court between 1576 and 1578, and probably continued to exist until 1585. Soon after Howard's appointment as lord high admiral, a company appears as the Admiral's, playing at court and evidently, also, at some innyard. The partial dispersal of this company and its loose combination with that of lord Strange have already been mentioned. In October, 1592, Edward Alleyn, who is first heard of in January, 1583, as a member of the earl of

---

[1] That is, supposing him to be the R. W. who wrote *The Three Ladies of London*, and *The Three Lords and Three Ladies of London*. On Wilson, see *Ward*, vol. I, p. 140, and *Fleay's English Drama*, vol. II, *s. v.* Wilson, Robert, senior.

[2] As to Tarlton, cf. *ante*, Vol. V, Chap. XIII, and Vol. IV, p. 411 and bibl.

Worcester's company, and joined, in or about 1589,[1] that of
the Admiral, married Joan Woodward, step-daughter of Philip
Henslowe, who, in the previous spring, had put in order[2] his
playhouse, the Rose in Southwark. By 1594, the Admiral's
men had severed their connection with Strange's (then the
Chamberlain's) company, and started independently at the
Rose with Alleyn as their leading actor. Barabas, in Marlowe's
Jew of Malta, Tamburlaine and Dr. Faustus were among the
parts he created and it is probable, also, that Orlando Furioso
in Greene's play of that name was in his *réperto're*. By 1592,
Nashe is found comparing him with Roscius and Aesop to their
disadvantage; Ben Jonson has left a tribute to him as one
"who gave so many Poets life." In 1597, he "left playing":
whether for good or only temporarily is not certain. There is
no direct evidence that he ever acted again, and his only recorded public appearance in a similar capacity is his delivery
of an address to James I at his reception by the city on 15
March. 1604. In 1597, Howard was created earl of Notting-
ham, and his company is sometimes called by that name.
Though deprived of its leading actor, it continued, with the
usual interruptions, to perform at the Rose, until the building
of the Fortune by Henslowe and Alleyn in 1600. This remained the company's house, except for a few years in its
latest period. Early in the new reign, the company was
transferred to the patronage of prince Henry, James's eldest
son; after prince Henry's death in 1612, it was taken up, for
a time at any rate, by Frederick V, elector palatine, who
married James's daughter Elizabeth in February, 1613, and
was known as the Palsgrave's company; and, in 1632, prince
Charles, afterwards Charles II, became its youthful patron.
It was for this company that Marlowe wrote *The Jew of
Malta* and *Dr. Faustus;* and Lodge, Greene, Ben Jonson,
Dekker, Chapman, Drayton and Middleton, were, at one
time or another, in its employ as authors.

Besides the three of whose history a slight sketch is here
given, there were, of course, many other companies of players.
In spite of the privy council's restraining supervision and the
enmity of the city, there were seldom less than four or five

---

[1] Greg's *Henslowe's Diary*, vol. II, p. 83.
[2] Greg, *op. cit.* vol. II, pp. 40–48.

companies, besides usually two companies of boys, acting in and about London at the same time. The amount of competition, therefore, though not excessive as in the present day, was sufficient to maintain a healthy rivalry, which may be contrasted in its results with the evils that followed upon the establishment of two, and only two, "patent" houses after the Restoration.

When Elizabeth came to the throne, the usual places of public theatrical performance in London were certain innyards. An account written in 1628 enumerates five of these yards, where plays were publicly performed: one in Gracechurch street (the Bell), one in Bishopsgate street (the Bull), one on Ludgate Hill (the Bell Savage), one in Whitefriars and one "nigh Paul's." Plays were also performed at an inn in Blackfriars, and at the Cross Keys in Gracechurch street. The exact arrangement or appliances of a play in an innyard it is now impossible to establish. Whether the platform stage stood in the centre of the yard or against one end is not known; or whether a price was charged for admission, or whether the performers depended for reward on the goodwill of the audience. The galleries which surrounded the yard on three sides were, obviously, good positions for spectators, and we may imagine a crowd standing round the stage, on three, or even on all four, sides of it, in the "yard," a name which was applied also to the ground level of the playhouses proper when these came to be built. A statement made by Flecknoe, in his *Short Discourse of the English Stage* (1664), that some remains of these theatres were, at that day, to be seen at the Cross Keys and the Bull, would imply, if it is to be trusted, that some kind of permanent structure was erected; but the evidence is too slight and too late in date to be made a foundation for conjecture.

The opposition to playing in the city led to the erection, in 1576, of the first Elizabethan playhouse, the Theater. It was built by James Burbage, formerly a joiner by trade, and a member of the earl of Leicester's company. Just outside the city walls on the north lay Finsbury fields, an open holiday ground where archery, fencing, sword-play and other sports were practised, and where the trained bands drilled. At the

edge of these fields, on land that had but recently belonged
to the priory of Holywell, and close to the road leading from
Bishopsgate to Shoreditch church (the site is now in the triangular pa ch between Curtain road, Holywell lane and Great
Eastern street) James Burbage put up his playhouse. It was
outside the city, but on the edge of a neighbourhood inhabited
by noblemen and "strangers born" (*i.e.* both foreigners and
English people not of London birth and citizenship), and easily
accessible from Bishopsgate, or through Cripplegate or Moor-
gate and across the fields. Burbage acquired the land by
lease from Giles Allen for 21 years from 13 April, 1576, and
borrowed 1000 marks ($£666.\ 13s.\ 4d.$) from his father-in-law,
Brayne, with which to build his playhouse.

The word "theater" had been in use before for the platform
on which shows were given, and Burbage probably named his
playhouse the Theater on that account. In shape, as we know
from several indications, as well as from the account left by
de Witt, a Dutchman who visited London, probab'y about two
years before its demolition, the Theater was an amphitheatre.
Much has been written on the various influences which may
have combined to cause the adoption of this shape. The
Roman amphitheatres at Dorchester, Banbury and Shrews-
bury, which were still in use for sports or dramatic exhibitions;
the Cornish "rounds," where the *guirimir* or miracle-plays
were acted; the arrangement of stage and scaffold at a London
performance of miracle or morality; even the disposition of the
churches during a religious play—all these have been called
in; while, for the internal arrangement of the building, the
innyard is supposed to be largely responsible. It seems hardly
necessary to go so far afield to account for what was the natural
and simple plan. It must be remembered that already, on the
south of the Thames, there were "rings," "scaffolded about,"
in existence within which bears or bulls were baited, and fencing
or sword-play matches took place. For a spectacle which can
be watched equally well from any point, the circle is the formation into which spectators naturally gather; and, just as
naturally, there is one point of the circle that is left free for the
convenience of ingress and egress by the performers to and
from the ring. When James Burbage built his playhouse on the
edge of Finsbury fields, a common meeting ground for sports,

the drama, though it was rapidly absorbing these sports, had not taken their place, and the Theater was not confined to dramatic performances. To make his playhouse round, with the platform stage occupying a large part of the ground-space, but touching at one point the edge of the circle, was only to do what all constructors of amphitheatres had done before—the easiest thing. The erection of a room or building in which the actors could dress, and from which they could make their entrances, would naturally follow. The stage was a movable platform on trestles. When some sport for which it was not wanted was to take place, it was taken to pieces and packed away; and Burbage's innovation, reduced to its fundamental principle, was merely the building of a high wall all round his ring, so that his spectators should be compelled to pay for admission. The innyard, doubtless, was responsible for the galleries round the inside of that wooden wall, which increased the housing accommodation and gave a measure of privacy to those who desired it. Neither to indoor performances at court, nor to those which may be supposed to have taken place in the courtyards of noblemen's houses, can any debt be traced in the plan of the Theater.

The lease from Giles Allen to Burbage contained a clause by which, if the lessee, within ten years of the date of the lease, spent £200 in buildings, he should be entitled to an extension of the term to 1607 and to take down the buildings he might erect. In 1585, a new lease was prepared, but not executed. Early in 1597, negotiations began again for an extension of the lease, and it appears that Allen consented to execute it, on condition that the yearly rent was raised by £10, and that the Theater should be used as a playhouse for five more years only. James Burbage died in 1597, and was succeeded in the property by his sons Richard and Cuthbert. The lease expired, and the Theater was closed. The company probably moved to the Curtain; and, in the winter of 1598–99, availing themselves of the clause in the lease, the Burbages forestalled Allen by pulling the Theater down, to erect it on the other side of the river as the Globe.

The history of the Curtain is obscure. There is evidence that the Theater was the first playhouse to be built; but the Curtain is mentioned very shortly afterwards, and its opening may be dated in 1577. It stood near Finsbury fields, not far to the south of the Theater, within the precinct of the same priory of Holywell, and took its name from Curtain close, a meadow once in the possession of the priory on which, later, was built a house called Curtain house. The name survives in Curtain road, Shoreditch. Who built it and what it cost are points yet to be discovered; but that, like the Theater, it was round in shape and built of wood are suppositions that can hardly be controverted, even if reliance be not placed on the argument that Shakespeare's *King Henry V* (the prologue of which refers to "this wooden O") was acted here in the summer of 1599. It would be unsafe to deduce from the word "cockpit" in the same passage that the Curtain was unusually small. Its history was uneventful. On the closing of the Theater, the Chamberlain's company seems to have removed there, and they kept it open during the early days of the Globe. When leave was sought to open the Fortune in Cripplegate, it was granted by the privy council on the understanding that the Curtain was to be closed; nevertheless, it remained open, and, after the accession of James I, became the home of queen Anne's (lately the earl of Worcester's) company. It is mentioned as in use in 1623, and as standing in 1627.

Little is known of the playhouse at Newington Butts. The direct evidence consists of, first, an entry in the privy council register for 1586, stating that the council had desired the lord mayor to prohibit plays in the city, and had taken the like order for the prohibiting of plays at the Theater "and th' other places about Newington"; secondly, an undated warrant from the privy council, now referred to August, 1592,[1] rescinding an order which had restrained lord Strange's servants from playing at the Rose, and had enjoined them to play three days (? a week) at Newington Butts; thirdly, an entry in the accounts of Philip Henslowe, the theatrical manager, at the head of a list of receipts from performances: "In the name of God Amen begininge at Newington my Lord Admeralle men and my Lorde Chamberlen men, As ffolowethe 1594"; and, last, an enumeration by Howes, in his continuation of Stow's *Annals* (1631), of the London playhouses built within the last sixty years,

---

[1] Greg's *Henslowe's Diary*, vol. II, pp. 45 and 52–53. For the text, see *eund., Henslowe Papers*, p. 43.

which concludes with: "besides one in former time at Newington Buts." Indirect evidence has been drawn from analogy.[1]
The warrant of the privy council above mentioned implies
that the house had then been standing for some years. Nothing further is known of its history.

Philip Henslowe, by trade a dyer, and an acute man of
business interested in undertakings of various kinds, leased an
estate in the Clink liberty, Southwark, in 1585, and, in 1587,
was contemplating the building upon it of a playhouse, of
which, if it was built at all, we hear nothing till some years
later. In his diary or book of accounts, which is one of the
chief authorities for the dramatic history of the period, he is
found in February, 1592, sharing the receipts of lord Strange's
men—nothing being said of the playhouse at which they were
acting. Another entry (in a book which must be admitted
to be one of the most confused account-books ever kept, besides having suffered from neglect and unscrupulous treatment)
is a statement of the money he spent "a bowte my playe
howsse" (the Rose) "in the yeare of o^{r} lord 1592." Nothing
is said in the account about repairs, and it bears all the marks
of a building account; while Henslowe's want of regularity in
following the Marian or the popular system of dating by the
year—or, indeed, any system at all—makes the confusion still
greater. It seems pretty certain, however, that 1592 here
means 1592; that the account is not for building, but for extensive repairs amounting almost to rebuilding; and that the work
was completed in the early part of the year, in time for lord
Strange's men to occupy the house in February. This implies
that the playhouse contemplated in 1587 had been built and,
therefore, used.[2] In June, 1594, the Rose on the Bankside in
Southwark was the playhouse of the Admiral's company,
with Edward Alleyn at its head. Alleyn "left playing" in
1597; and, in 1598, the Chamberlain's company moved across
the water from the Curtain, and built the Globe. The prosperity of the Rose began to decline, perhaps through unequal
competition. By 1600, it had fallen into a bad state of repair,

[1] By Ordish, p. 144.

[2] The account of the Newington Butts house and the Rose given above
follows that of Greg, *Henslowe's Diary*, vol. II, pp. 43–48 and 73. For another view, which must be held to be superseded, see Ordish, pp. 149–155.

and its situation was considered inconvenient in winter. When the Admiral's company moved to the Fortune, in 1600, other companies occasionally occupied the Rose till 1603. After the accession of James I, it was used sometimes for sports. The Rose was built mainly of timber, lath and plaster, though entries in Henslowe's accounts for bricks and bricklaying seem to imply a brick foundation for the wooden walls. The stage was painted; there was a tirehouse, or actors' dressing-room, behind it, with a room over it, and a flagstaff.

Though the Blackfriars was the next playhouse to be built, it is more convenient to consider first the most important of Elizabethan playhouses, the Globe. The reason why the Chamberlain's men left the Curtain for the other side of the river is not clear. There may have been some decline in the attractiveness of Finsbury fields as a holiday ground; or the common council may have protested with effect against the usual procession through the city. Bankside was certainly a popular resort, and Southwark the district where pleasure-seekers went to see bull-baiting and bear-baiting, to the public gardens and to the stews. Unable to come to terms with the landlord of the Theater, Richard and Cuthbert Burbage, as we have seen, pulled down their old playhouse and used the materials in building the Globe, which stood, as is commonly supposed, to the south-west of Paris garden and to the south of what was then Maiden lane and is now the east-to-west part of Park street, on ground at present occupied by a brewery.[1] This was the house, from its opening till 1642, of the Chamberlain's and King's company; here Richard Burbage acted, and here Shakespeare's greatest plays were produced. Our knowledge of the appearance and construction of the Globe is chiefly derived from the contract for the building of the Fortune, which was to be made like it, specifically in certain details, as well as generally, with certain minor exceptions. The contract will be quoted in connection with the Fortune theatre. Shops, stews and playhouses all had signs at that time, and the earliest Globe was so called from its sign of Atlas bearing the globe on his shoulders. It appears in a drawing of 1610 as a round

[1] On the situation of the Globe, however, see Wallace, C. W., in *The Times* of 2 October, 1909, p. 9, col. 4, and subsequent correspondence in *The Times* and *The Athenæum*.

structure, rising above a larger round substructure of some considerable height, which, it has been suggested, enclosed a passage leading from the entrance door (or doors) to various entrances to the "yard." Structure and substructure were, almost certainly, of wood, resting on a foundation of bricks and cement. Its interior arrangements will be discussed later. On Tuesday, 29 June, 1613, a new play on the history of Henry VIII called *All is True* was being performed, and, when the king entered the masque at cardinal Wolsey's, certain "chambers" were shot off. "Some of the paper or other stuff," is Sir Henry Wotton's account, "wherewith one of them was stopped, did light on the thatch" (on the roof over the galleries). The house was burned to the ground within less than an hour. "Yet nothing did perish but wood and straw, and a few forsaken cloaks." Another contemporary statement says that the escape of the audience was marvellous, "having but two narrow doors to get out." Whether these two include the door by which the players entered the tiringhouse, or whether they were both for the use of the audience, cannot now be determined. The usual practice appears to have been to have one entrance door only to the body of the house. A contemporary ballad advises "stage-strutters" to give up their dissipations and spend their money on tiles for the roof. This advice, or the latter part of it, seems to have been taken when the playhouse was rebuilt in the following year, more handsomely than before, its "thatched hide" being then a thing of the past. The cost of the new playhouse was £1400, and it was the "fayrest that was in England." Its shape on rebuilding was octagonal outside, and, apparently, inside also.

It has been supposed that, after the King's company began to act at the Blackfriars, the Globe became their summer playhouse, the Blackfriars being used in winter. Further evidence is needed before this question can be determined, though we have seen that the situation of the Rose was considered inconvenient in winter; the Globe is found in use in February.

In February, 1596, James Burbage, already in difficulties with the landlord of the Theater, bought of the executor of Sir Thomas Cawarden, late master of the revels, for £600, the freehold of a complicated collection of rooms, great and small, stairs, cellars and yards (including "seven great upper rooms"

all on one floor, formerly one great and entire room), which lay
in Blackfriars, near the Pipe office, adjoining the house of Sir
George Cary.   The buildings, which had been in the occupation
of Cawarden, were in the old precinct of the "Blackfriars
preachers," or Dominican monks, and had formed part of their
monastic dwelling.   Blackfriars, in those days, was a popular
resort, not, like Finsbury fields, for the people, but for nobles
and gentry, who went there to play tennis; there were also
a few aristocratic houses on a small portion of the site of
the monastery.   In making up his mind to establish a playhouse, in defiance of the law, within the city walls, Burbage
must have counted for support less on the people than on
the nobility; and, to some extent, the proceeding is an
argument in favour of the view that royal and aristocratic
support was the chief encouragement of the drama.   These
seven rooms Burbage turned into an indoor or "private"
playhouse, spending on it a larger sum than had hitherto been
spent on any playhouse in London, and constructing a building which recent discoveries have shown to be much larger than
was commonly supposed.[1]   The term "private" does not imply
that the public were excluded; the corporation, in an order for
the suppression of the Blackfriars in 1619, refer to it explicitly
as a "publique playhowse."   Burbage's intention, however,
was, doubtless, to construct a playhouse which should attract
aristocratic patrons by greater seclusion and comfort, the auditorium being completely roofed over, and, perhaps (though this
is thorny ground), by a stage which might reproduce to some
extent the scenic completeness attained in the indoor performances at court.   In November, 1596, the inhabitants petitioned against the establishment of a playhouse in their midst,
but ineffectually.   In July, 1597, letters patent were issued to
Nathaniel Giles, master of the chapel children, to impress boys
for the Queen's service; and, about this time, the chapel
children are found occupying Burbage's new playhouse.   In
1600, Richard Burbage leased the Blackfriars to one Henry
Evans for 21 years at a yearly rent of £40, and Evans continued the children's performances.   Later, came trouble over
Evans's too drastic exercise of the powers granted to Giles

[1] See, in *The Times*, 11 September, 1906, p. 6, cols. 1 and 2, "Old Blackfriars Theatre," by Wallace, C. W., and *eund.*, *Children of the Chapel*, chap. 1.

under the patent; the playhouse ceased to pay; the lease was assigned; the chapel children, who, after James's accession, had been reconstituted as the children of queen Anne's revels, lost the royal patronage after their performance of *Eastward Hoe* in 1605, and were again obnoxious in their production of *Biron*.   In August, 1608, Richard Burbage took back the lease to Evans, and, a little later, the King's company began to use the house themselves.   In January, 1619, the corporation tried to close the Blackfriars, but the privy council stepped in and confirmed its use; and the King's company continued to play there without interruption till 1642.

The move of the Chamberlain's men to Bankside left the north bank of the Thames without any strong theatrical attraction, and Henslowe and Alleyn endeavoured (not without strenuous but ineffectual opposition from local and municipal authorities) to cater for the population of that part of the town by building the Fortune playhouse off Golding (now Golden) lane in the parish of St. Giles without Cripplegate.   The extant contract for the building, made by Henslowe and Alleyn with Peter Street, carpenter, is so interesting, in the light it throws on the material and structure of the Globe and the Fortune, and, indirectly, of Elizabethan playhouses in general, that part of it deserves quoting *verbatim*.

The frame of the saide howse to be sett square and to conteine ffowerscore foote of lawfull assize everye waie square w^{th}outt and fiftie five foote of like assize square everye waie w^{th}in wth a good suer and stronge foundacōn of pyles brick lyme and sand bothe w^{th}out & w^{th}in to be wroughte one foote of assize att the leiste above the grounde And the saide fframe to conteine Three Stories in heighth The first or lower Storie to Conteine Twelve foote of lawfull assize in heighth The second Storie Eleaven foote of lawfull assize in heigth And the Third or upper Storie to conteine Nyne foote of lawfull assize in height all which Stories shall conteine Twelve foote and a halfe of lawfull assize in breadth througheoute besides a Juttey forwardes in either of the saide Twoe upper Stories of Terne ynches of lawfull assize with ffower convenient divisions for gentlemens roomes and other sufficient and convenient divisions for Twoe pennie roomes wth necessarie Seates to be placed and sett Aswell in those roomes as througheoute all the rest of the galleries of the saide howse and wth suchelike steares Conveyances & divisions

w^{th}oute & w^{h}in as are made & Contryved in and to the late erected Plaiehowse On the Banck in the saide pishe of Ste Savio's Called the Globe W^{th} a Stadge and Tyreinge howse to be made erected & settup w^{th}in the saide fframe wth a shadowe or cover over the saide Stadge. . . . And wch Stadge shall conteine in length ffortie and Three foote of lawfull assize and in breadth to extende to the middle of the yarde of the saide howse The same Stadge to be paled in belowe wth good stronge and sufficyent newe oken bourdes And likewise the lower Storie of the saide fframe w^{th}inside, and the same lower storie to be alsoe laide over and fenced wth stronge yron pykes And the saide Stadge to be in all other proporcōns Contryved and fashioned like unto the Stadge of the saide Plaie howse Called the Globe W^{th} convenient windowes and lightes glazed to the saide Tyreinge howse And the saide fframe Stadge and Stearecases to be covered wth Tyle and to have a sufficient gutter of lead to Carrie & convey the water frome the Coveringe of the saide Stadge to fall backwardes And also all the saide fframe and the Stairecases thereof to be sufficyently enclosed w^{th}oute wth lathe lyme & haire and the gentlemens roomes and Twoe pennie roomes to be seeled wth lathe lyme & haire and all the fflowers of the saide Galleries Stories and Stadge to be bourded wth good & sufficyent newe deale bourdes of the whole thicknes wheare need shalbe and the saide howse and other thinges beforemencōed to be made & doen To be in all other Contrivitions Conveyances fashions thinge and thinges effected finished and doen accordinge to the manner and fashion of the saide howse Called the Globe Saveinge only that all the princypall and maine postes of the saide fframe and Stadge forwarde shalbe square and wroughte palasterwise wth carved proporcōns Called Satiers to be placed & sett on the Topp of every of the same postes.[1]

The contract is dated 8 January, 1599/1600, and the work, which was to cost £440, was to be finished by 25 July. The actual cost worked out at £520, and the playhouse appears to have been opened in November or December, 1600, by the Admiral's men, who occupied it throughout the remainder of the period. It is noticeable that the outside was square. The Fortune was burned down in 1621, and all the wardrobe and playbooks were destroyed; it was rebuilt, some two years later, round in shape and of brick. It appears, in its later years, to have become a popular house, rather despised by the more refined.

---

[1] Transcribed from Greg, *Henslowe Papers*, pp. 5 and 6.

The Rose fell out of use in 1603, and the importance of the Blackfriars and the Fortune robbed Bankside of much of the patronage of playgoers.   When the Globe was burned in 1613, it seems to have been feared that the King's men would move back to the north of the river; and a petition was addressed to the king by the company of Watermen, praying that the players might not be allowed to have a playhouse in London or Middlesex within five miles of the city—which petition was not granted.

In 1589, Francis Langley, who held a small office at court, purchased the manor of Paris garden.   In November, 1594, we find the lord mayor protesting against his intention to build a playhouse on his property.   The project was not dismissed; but it is not certain when the Swan playhouse was built.   It may have been open in 1596.   The Swan was used for plays, at any rate until 1620, and was still standing, though in a dilapidated state, in 1632.   Dramatically, its history is unimportant; but the house has acquired notoriety from the fact that a contemporary drawing, or copy of a drawing, of its interior—the earliest view known of the interior of a playhouse—is in existence.   Probably in or about the summer of 1596, John de Witt, a Dutchman, visited London.   (It may be noted here that much of our information concerning the London playhouses of the day comes from foreigners, to whom they were objects of great interest and surprise.)   The drawing in question was discovered in the library at Utrecht, in the commonplace book of another Dutchman, Arend von Buchell, accompanied by a descriptive passage headed *Ex observationibus Londinensibus Johannis De Witt*.   The passage, with the drawing, may have been copied from a now lost letter or journal written by de Witt. The drawing, a rough sketch, must be used, therefore, with caution; but so many of its details correspond with the details of the Swan found in the contract for the building of the Hope, which was to be like it in many respects, that it may be taken as giving a rough idea of the general plan of an Elizabethan public playhouse.[1]   The drawing is made from a point which,

[1] All reproductions of this drawing (*e.g.* in Ordish, *Early London Theatres*, p. 265) having beneath them the words *Ex observationibus Londinensibus Johannis De Witt*, taken from the manuscript, are made, not from the original, but from the engraving published by Gaedertz in his *Zur Kenntnis*

roughly speaking, would correspond to the position of a man sitting in the middle of the front row of the upper circle of a large modern theatre, or the gallery of a small one.

The main features of the playhouse are clear enough. It is a tall, round (or, possibly, oval)[1] structure some fifty feet high,[2] with three roofed galleries, divided into "rooms," or boxes, running right round it and interrupted only by the tirehouse behind the stage. The yard is open to the sky; there are no seats in it, and the audience can stand close to the stage on three sides, finding it probably between waist-high and shoulder-high. The description accompanying the drawing states that the building would hold *tres mille homines in sedilibus*—three thousand persons in the *sedilia* or galleries. Calculations have been made[3] to prove that, if de Witt is rightly reported and meant what he said, and if the number of rows in the three galleries be taken to be eleven, a house two thirds of the size of the present Drury Lane theatre would be required to afford sitting accommodation for that number of spectators, if every seat in the entire circle was full; while the open yard would give standing room to a great many more. The number 3000, moreover, is not so surprising as appears at first sight; and that the Swan theatre should provide room for $1\frac{1}{2}$ per cent. of the total population of London and Westminster does not seem fantastic, when it is remembered that, according to John Taylor, three or four thousand persons daily crossed the river to Bankside in the days when the Globe, Rose and Swan were all open as playhouses, and bear-baiting, also, was in progress. A difficulty is caused by de Witt's statement that the Swan was built of flint-stones heaped together and supported by wooden columns, painted so like marble as to deceive the shrewdest eye.

---

der altenglischen Bühne, Bremen, 1888. For a full-sized reproduction direct from the original, see Wheatley, *On a contemporary drawing of the Interior of the Swan Theatre*, N. S. S. 1888; and for a reproduction on a reduced scale, *The Quarterly Review*, April, 1908, facing p. 450. The engraving is fairly accurate; but the lines indicating the part of the circumference of the playhouse furthest from the tirehouse have been omitted, to make room for the misplaced words mentioned above.

[1] That is, round, or oval, inside. In Vischer, *View of London*, 1610, it appears twelve-sided. See, also, the 1627 map of the manor of old Paris garden in Furnivall's *Harrison's England*, vol. II, facing p. i.

[2] For a calculation of the measurements, see Wheatley, *u.s.*

[3] In Wheatley, *u.s.* But see Greg, *Henslowe's Diary*, vol. II, p. 134, note 1.

In no extant specification, not even that of the Hope, is there any mention of stone, and another foreigner, who visited London two years later, expressly states that all the playhouses on Bankside were of wood—sometimes, as we know from other sources,[1] plastered over. Various suggestions have been made for getting round de Witt's statement. It is simpler to believe him correct and to suppose that, in this feature (as, perhaps, in another to be dealt with later) the Swan was exceptional.

The extant contract with the builder[1] shows that the Hope on Bankside, which had been a bear-house, was newly built as a playhouse by Henslowe and Jacob Meade in 1613. Possibly, the burning of the Globe in that year induced Henslowe to try for the Bankside public once more. The house was occupied by the lady Elizabeth's and the Prince's companies, and Ben Jonson's *Bartholomew Fayre*, which was acted there in 1614, informs us that it was a dirty and evil-smelling place. In 1616 apparently, it fell out of use as a playhouse. As the contract states, it was of the same size as the Swan and the roof over the galleries was tiled, not thatched. Vischer's *View of London* (1616) shows it octagonal outside; but Hollar (1647) makes it round. It was of wood, with a brick foundation.

Three other playhouses belonging to this period must be mentioned. The Red Bull stood at the upper end of St. John street, Clerkenwell, and seems to have been opened about 1599. In 1633, Prynne's *Histrio-Mastix* mentions it as recently rebuilt and enlarged. It was occupied early in James I's reign by the Queen's company, and remained in use, till 1642, by this and other companies. Between 1642 and 1660, several attempts were made to act there; it was opened at the restoration by Rhodes, formerly prompter at the Blackfriars; Samuel Pepys saw a play wretchedly performed to a poor house there, in 1661; and, by 1663, it was abandoned.

The Cockpit was a "private" playhouse in Drury Lane, and seems to have been erected on the site of a cockpit in or about 1615. It was opened by the lady Elizabeth's company, which, in 1625, passed to queen Henrietta; and it remained in use till 1642. After 1660, it was occupied by the Duke's company

---

[1] *E. g.*, the contract for the Fortune: *ante*, pp. 290–1.
[2] Printed in Greg, *Henslowe Papers*, pp. 19 f.

under Sir William D'Avenant, till they moved to the new theatre in Portugal row, Lincoln's Inn fields in 1662. Its second
name, the Phoenix, probably came into use when it had been
restored after the sacking of it by the 'prentices in 1617.

The Salisbury court or Whitefriars playhouse was built in
1629 near the hall of the old Whitefriars monastery, which had
previously, at any rate since 1610, been used for plays. It was
occupied first by the children of the King's revels, and then by
the Queen's. It was a "private" playhouse, and was in use for
a brief time after the restoration.

The capital difference between the pre-rebellion public stage
and the modern stage lies in the fact that the former was a
platform stage, while the latter is a picture stage. The modern
audience sees the drama as a moving picture in a frame, or as in
a room with one wall, and only one, knocked out. The Elizabethan audience surrounded the stage on three sides, partly
encroaching even on the fourth; they saw the drama as a scene
enacted in their midst and—in the case of the groundlings,
the spectators standing in the yard—very close to them. It is
practically impossible for performers on the stage to compose
groups that shall show an equally artistic shape on three sides
at once, and the use of daylight prevented many of the visual
effects that have been practised since the time of Garrick.
The eye was appealed to less forcibly than the ear. The drama
was rhetorical, and the actor more of a rhetorician than he
is to-day, since the audience looked to his enunciation of the
poet's words for much of the pleasure that the picture stage
supplies through the eye. "Spectacular" plays, such as
England's Joy, produced at the Swan in 1603, were not unknown; spectacle was aimed at and enjoyed; but word, voice
and action were the chief elements in the drama. And authors,
being free from the modern playwright's necessity to lead up to
a "situation," a stage picture, on which the curtain may fall
sharply at the close of each act, made the play, rather than
each division of it, the artistic whole.

The stage begins with the bare platform on trestles, which
could be taken away when the space was needed for sports that
did not require it. Later, the space between the platform and
the ground is found concealed with boarding, and a low rail runs

round the edge of the stage. The rudest performance, whether
in innyard or "ring," supposes some place where actors can
dress and wait concealed, and whence they may have access to
the platform when their turn comes. This gives opportunity
for a background—a matter, however, of small importance in a
stage open on three sides—and also develops into the tirehouse.
Questions as to the nature and use of this background and as to
the development of the tirehouse into a somewhat elaborate
structure lie at the root of all the difficulties in the restoration of
an idea of the Elizabethan stage.

It is impossible not to turn back with curiosity to the drawing of the Swan theatre, the earliest extant view of the stage of
the period. The platform it shows is supported near the front
on two rough, solid beams, concealed by no "paling." Halfway, or rather more than halfway, towards the back, two very
solid turned pillars, resting on heavy square bases and with
capitals above, stand on the stage, at a distance from each other
of nearly its whole breadth, and support the front edge of a
pentroof, which seems to project over the stage to a much
smaller distance than the position of the pillars would indicate.
This discrepancy is but one of many difficulties raised by the
drawing. Behind the pillars, under the pentroof and right
at the back of the stage, rises a wall with two large arched
doors, each about halfway between the centre of the back wall
and its outer extremity. On the wall, between the doors, the
draughtsman has written *mimorum aedes*, indicating that this
is the "actors' house." At some distance above the tops of
the doors, the wall is broken by a gallery, in which sit what
may be musicians, or actors taking part in the play, but what
certainly seem to be spectators; and, above the gallery again,
the wall rises to the point where the upper edge of the pentroof
starts. Above the level of the pentroof, there appears another
story, of equal or nearly equal width with the wall of the tirehouse. There are two windows in it, facing the auditorium,
and, in a little doorway open in the side, on the (spectator's)
right, a man, either holding a flag or blowing a trumpet, stands
on the upper edge of the pentroof (which must be supposed to
turn the corner of the building on both sides). The roof of
this upper story, apparently, is thatched, and from the summit
on the (spectator's) right flies the flag bearing the sign of the

house, a swan. Near the front of the stage, an actor in woman's dress is sitting on a bench; behind the bench stands another, also in woman's dress; while, from the corner on the (spectator's) left, an actor, bearing a long spear or staff, is striding along the front of the stage towards the centre. There are no hangings of any kind visible in any part of the drawing.

Some features in the drawing may be recognised from other descriptions as correct—the existence of the tirehouse, the turret, the waving flag showing that it is a play day, the blowing of the trumpet showing that the play is about to begin (though the draughtsman has shown the house as empty). Further examination raises a number of difficulties.

In the first place, this stage is not movable; or, if it can be removed, those two heavy pillars supporting the small pent-roof must rest, not on the visible bases on the stage, but on the ground below. If the stage is moved, the pillars will be in the way of any exhibition that is taking place, and it is difficult to imagine that these pretentious bases are shams. We are forced to conclude that the stage of the Swan was not movable. Again, how far are these pillars intended to be from the back wall of the stage, the front wall of the tirehouse? The drawing shows them at the very east a third of the way down the stage; yet the perspective is so faulty that the pentroof seems to project at the most a few feet forward from the wall. Granted that the pillars are right and the pentroof wrong, the latter still does not correspond at all closely with the "heavens" or roof, which, in the Hope, as we know from the contract, was to extend all over the stage, and which is known to have existed in other playhouses of the period. The matter is trifling at first sight, but is of importance because, mainly on the position of the pillars in this drawing, a whole theory of the production of plays has been formed.[1] To clear the ground, it may be said at once that there is no occurrence before 1640 of anything which can fairly be considered evidence of a front curtain on a public stage (though, doubtless, it was in use at court and university performances), and that the theory of the common use of a front curtain is no longer tenable. On

[1] Chiefly by Brodmeier, C., *Die Shakespeare-Bühne nach den alten Bühnen-anweisungen*, Weimar, 1904. It has been exhaustively criticised by Reynolds, G. F., *Some principles of Elizabethan staging*, Chicago, 1905.

the other hand, there is ample evidence that, somewhere on the stage, there were hangings of silk, or wool, or "painted cloth," sometimes, apparently, when tragedies were acted, of black. Of hangings painted in perspective to represent the scene of the play, there is no mention in a public or private playhouse, though they were in use at court and university performances. We hear of actors peeping through before the play begins, and of an impatient audience throwing things at the hangings. Stage directions printed in the playbooks, though rendered an untrustworthy guide by the impossibility of telling whether they were drawn up by the author or manager, or by the printer or some other unauthorised person, and whether they applied to performance at court, in a public playhouse, a private playhouse, or a provincial hall or innyard, seem to show that the public stage of the day required at least three divisions: namely, the front part of the stage; a back part, commonly used for interiors, which could be disclosed by the drawing of curtains, and which, when disclosed, could, of course, absorb the front part and occupy the entire stage; and, thirdly, a place above to serve for upper chambers, balconies like Juliet's, galleries, towers and so forth. Arguing from this and from the position of the pillars in the drawing of the stage of the Swan, the theory referred to supposes a regular course of "alternation" throughout an entire play, much like that which was followed by each act of an old-fashioned melodrama, in which the front scene was used while the back scene was being "set," the author's duty, in the days of Elizabeth as in our own, being to contrive a scene of some sort, which the plot might or might not require, to fill up the time needed by the "tire-men" or sceneshifters. Accordingly, the theory mentioned supposes a curtain or "traverse" hung between the pillars shown in the drawing of the Swan, that is, at about one third, or half, of the depth[1] of the stage which should conceal from spectators the preparations for the next scene going on behind it.

The attempt to work out this "alternation" theory by dividing the extant plays of the period into front and back

---

[1] Some confusion might be avoided if the word "depth" were consistently used for the measurement from the front of the stage to the back, and "width" for that from side to side.

scenes has not been successful.[1] A further difficulty arises
from the fact that not all the spectators were in front of the
stage. A traverse between the pillars would not conceal what
was going on behind it from people on either side of the stage.
To block out their view, further traverses at right angles to
that between the pillars would be necessary. The result,
inevitably, would be to conceal not only the back scene from
them, but a great deal of the front scene, too, on which action
would be in progress. An even greater difficulty attends the
suggestion that, since there are notable instances where it
would be absurd for actors to enter the front scene by the only
available entrance, that is, through the traverse, there must
have been hangings all along both sides of the stage so that
actors might enter from the sides. It is to be noted, too, that
this theory supposes the upper stage or balcony to be concealed
by the traverse. This would mean that all scenes in which the
balcony was occupied must be back scenes, which is not easy
to establish, and makes it impossible that the audience should
ever have used the balcony; while three extant illustrations of
the stage—the title-pages to Richards's *Messallina* (1640) and
Alabaster's *Roxana* (1632), and the picture of a "droll" on
the stage of the Red Bull which forms the frontispiece to Kirkman's *The Wits* (1673)—distinctly show the traverse hanging
from below the balcony, while the first and the last show a
separate curtain for the balcony itself.

This theory seems to lose sight of the simple origin of the
stage—a temporary platform erected in the midst of a crowd
and surrounded by spectators regarding it from nearly all the
four sides—and to err from over-anxiety to credit an Elizabethan audience with a susceptibility to the incongruous. The
very naïve tradition of the miracles and early moralities, in
which two or more scenes, sometimes representing localities
hundreds of miles apart, were on the stage simultaneously,
had not died out; and the audience may be fairly supposed to

[1] See Reynolds, *op. cit.*, and Wegener, R., *Die Bühneneinrichtung des
Shakespeareschen Theaters*, Halle, 1907. For the practical defects of Brodmeier's proposed reconstruction, see Archer, W., in *The Quarterly Review*,
no. 415, April, 1908. The "Elizabethan" stage reconstructed at Harvard
in 1904 was planned on the alternation theory. For an illustration and
description, see "Hamlet on an Elizabethan Stage," by Baker, G. P., *Shakesp.
Jahrbuch*, vol. XLI (1905), pp. 296 ff.

have been no more offended by the conventions of dramatic space than is a modern audience by those of dramatic time, which allow an imaginary half-hour to pass in an actual five minutes. In his *Apologie for Poetrie* (written about 1580–1) Sidney writes:

> For where the stage should alwaies represent but one place, . . . there is . . . many places, inartificially imagined. But if it be so in *Gorboduck*, how much more in al the rest, where you shal have *Asia* of the one side, and *Affrick* of the other, and so many other under-kingdoms, that the Player, when he commeth in, must ever begin with telling where he is, or els the tale wil not be conceived?

His words are borne out by numerous cases in extant plays, where two or more places are imagined to be on the stage at the same time; and it scarcely needs the evidence of ascertainable instances to prove that an Elizabethan audience would not have the least objection to seeing properties (such as the bench in the drawing of the Swan) brought on the stage without concealment and left there after they had served their turn, though it is extremely likely that susceptibility to the incongruous grew, as time went on, under the influence of Jonson and the classical playwrights. In spite of this, it is abundantly clear that there was a back stage, which could be revealed by drawing a curtain.

The fact is significant that, just as the Hope, though planned on the lines of the Swan, was to be built of wood, not flint, so, in the contract with the builder, it is directly stated that he "shall also builde the Heavens *all over* the saide stage to be borne or carryed *without any postes or supporters to be fixed or sett uppon the saide stage.*" It is possible, therefore, that the pillars of the Swan were as the drawing shows them, and that the pentroof covered half or nearly half the stage; but that the plan was found inconvenient, was confined to the Swan and was discarded by Henslowe when he built the Hope. In that case, the Swan may have had the front and back scenes divided by the lofty traverse, and have used them as suggested by the theory summarised above; but it is at least unfortunate that the draughtsman should have hit on a playhouse the arrangement of which was unique and discredited.

The construction may well have been different in different houses; and there are several ways in which the necessary back stage may be reconstructed and the requirements of stage directions fulfilled, without imposing a strict "alternation theory" or incurring the difficulties referred to above. According to one scheme,[1] the pillars supporting the "heavens" (if pillars there be) play no part in the division of the stage. The stage proper runs right back to the wall of the tirehouse. The gallery either does not project, or projects only very slightly, in front of that wall. From the level of its floor, hangings fall to the stage, occupying, not the whole width of the stage, but most, or the whole, of that part of it which lies between the two doors, the doors being left uncovered. For this purpose, it is necessary to suppose the doors further apart than they are in the drawing of the Swan. These hangings, when drawn back, reveal the lower chamber of the tirehouse in use as part of the stage, possibly with a floor raised slightly above the stage level. Here, the strolling players in *Hamlet* would perform, and here, Henry VIII would sit in his closet. The room would be big enough to hold a fair number of people; in the Fortune, for instance, an inner chamber 20 feet wide would still leave $11\frac{1}{2}$ feet on either side for the doors. And the scene could always overflow on the stage proper. And since a third entrance is frequently mentioned and almost always necessary, a door in the back of this chamber must also be supposed, large enough to admit of "properties" such as beds, banqueting tables and so forth being brought through it. The stage proper is thus entirely free of hangings, except those in front of the chamber under the tirehouse; and the fact that this chamber must have been low and dark seems of less importance when it is remembered that plays were acted in unencumbered daylight. There were hangings, also, in front of the balcony above. The theory is not without its difficulties, the chief of which are that many of the audience must have been unable, from their position in the house, to see into the inner chamber, and that, when there were actors or spectators in the balcony, they, too, would have been unable to see

---

[1] This account follows, in the main, that suggested by Chambers, E. K., "The Stage of the Globe," in the *Stratford-on-Avon Shakespeare*, vol. x, pp. 351 f.

into it.[1] This view, to some extent, is borne out by the title-pages of *Messallina* and *Roxana* mentioned above; but, as neither of these shows the whole width of the stage, no certain conclusions can be drawn from them. Another scheme makes the gallery project some feet from the wall of the tirehouse, with the traverse hanging from its floor and concealing all the doors when it is drawn. There is, thus, a kind of corridor stage behind the stage proper; but, once more, any actors or spectators there may be in the gallery will be unable to see what is taking place on the back stage, and it is also necessary to imagine that every scene in which doors are mentioned must have been a scene in which the back stage was used. To obviate these difficulties, a suggestion has recently been put forward[2] that the two side doors were not flat in the wall of the tirehouse but set in walls slanting towards it, while the traverse before the corridor hangs further up the stage (*i.e.* nearer the back wall) and, when drawn, conceals only the third, central door. The same suggestion curves the gallery forward at each side, at an angle corresponding with that of the walls containing the side doors, so that its occupants might see the back stage, and even provides semicircular projections, or bays, in order to make quite sure.[3]

The space beneath the stage was sometimes "paled in" by boarding, which, though not shown in the drawing of the Swan, must have been a common feature, because many instances occur of actors (especially when playing ghosts) appearing and disappearing through trapdoors, and of dead bodies being thrown down through them. We read of flames and even of a "brave arbour" appearing from below. If the stage was strewn with rushes, as it seems to have been, the use of the trap must, sometimes, have been difficult; and, in any plays where the

[1] Wegener's suggestion (*op. cit.*), that there was a kind of *ekkyklema* on which deathbeds and the like could be wheeled over the back stage and brought forward, does not seem to be supported by sufficient evidence, though such a contrivance would certainly have been useful.

[2] By Archer, *u.s.* See, in particular, the reproduction of a model by an architect, Walter H. Godfrey, of a stage according to the specification of the Fortune, illustrating Archer's article. The model itself was on view in the *Exposition théâtrale*, Paris, 1908.

[3] One objection to this arrangement is that it would make the drawing of the traverse (which we know the gallery to have had) a very complicated affair.

trapdoor was needed, the "matting" on the stage, which Sir Henry Wotton mentions, apparently as an unusual thing, in his account of the burning of the Globe in 1613, must have been out of the question. There was also, in some playhouses at all events, an appliance by which players could be let down from above, as if descending from heaven, though it appears to have been more difficult to draw them up again. Whether the appliance worked from the balcony or the "heavens" is not ascertained.

Painted scenery on the public stage there was none, though the mention in an inventory of the Admiral's men's properties, compiled by Henslowe in 1598, of "the clothe of the Sone and Mone," certainly seems to imply some attempt of this nature, and though the figures of men and animals frequently appeared in the woven or painted hangings. But there is abundant evidence that the properties were many and elaborate. Houses, beds, rocks, ramparts, wells, property horses, and even structures serving as shops, are mentioned as being brought on the stage, and there is strong evidence for the solid representation of woods and separate trees.[1] Though there was no attempt at creating a picture, considerable care and expense were incurred in the provision of properties. Yet these attempts at realism, for which an Elizabethan audience, according to its lights, had as keen a desire as a modern audience, long went hand in hand with the simplest devices. The names of the places were fastened over the doors, especially in cases where the stage represented two scenes at once; and where the presence of spectators on the stage reduced the space, the properties for which there was not room were sometimes indicated by nuncupative cards, a practice which prevailed, at this time, also in France. Such cards, however, must be distinguished from the "title-boards," which, in private theatres, were fastened up, or held up by the speaker of the prologue, to give the title of the play.

Performances at private playhouses[2] may be taken to have approximated to those at universities, inns of court and royal residences, in aiming at the taste of more refined audiences than

---

[1] On properties, see Reynolds, *op. cit.*, and his article, "Trees on the stage of Shakespeare" in *Modern Philology*, vol. v, p. 153.

[2] On this question, see Wallace, *op. cit.*

did the public playhouse—though too much stress should not be laid on the supposition. Noblemen, ambassadors and other great people went to the public playhouses; but, while it is on record that Elizabeth went to the Blackfriars, she is not known to have ever visited the Globe. Private playhouses were completely roofed over, and, though performances took place there in the afternoons as in public playhouses, they were, occasionally at all events, performed in artificial light, the windows being covered over. Instead of the "yard" filled with "understanding" spectators or "groundlings," there was a pit, with seats.

The evidence shows that a performance at court was very different from a performance in a public or private playhouse. It was for this honour, ostensibly, that the company worked all the year, and, when the master of the revels had selected, after competition, the companies and the plays they should perform, the author was often called upon to revise his play; and the performance ended with prayers for the queen. Elizabeth's accounts show an annual outlay for airing and furbishing up the court stock of costumes and appliances, besides considerable expense for wires, lights, properties and mechanical contrivances.[1] The old *domus* of the miracles survive in the "painted houses" of the players at court; and there can be little question that painted scenery was not unknown.[2] Under James I, great advances were achieved by the arts of stage decoration and production through the masques written by Ben Jonson and mounted by Inigo Jones; but the public stage was little affected, if at all. Not until the return of D'Avenant and other adherents of Charles I and II from France and Italy, to be followed by Betterton's mission to Paris—not until the drama became more nearly dependent on court favour than it had been made even by the exclusive royal patronage of companies on the accession of James I, did the public stage make a corresponding advance; and then it drew its inspiration from other sources. The main appeal to the eye in public playhouses before the rebellion was made by the

---

[1] All the evidence has been collected by Feuillerat, A., *Documents relating to the Office of the Revels*.

[2] For distinct evidence of scene shifting in a university performance, see Nichols: *Progresses of King James I*, vol. i, p. 538.

costumes of actors. Now and then, as in miracles, a rudimentary attempt at dramatic propriety in costume was made. For the most part, players wore the ordinary dress of the day, some, even of the male characters, appearing in wigs, and some —especially, it would seem, in cases of disguise and of minor players acting more than one part—having their faces concealed by masks. Makeshift and errors of taste were not unknown even in London playhouses; but Henslowe's extant accounts show that the costumes were splendid and costly— velvet, gold lace, copper lace and other rich materials being freely used. The speaker of the prologue appeared in a black cloak.

The creation of an atmosphere for the play (which is the aim that modern stage production is endeavouring, often in strangely inartistic fashion, to achieve by scenery) was left to the descriptive words of the poet, the voice of the actor and the imagination of the audience. The audience of those days must certainly be supposed to have been more susceptible to the message to the ear, and less to deficiencies in the message to the eye, than that of our own time; but, while taking into account the larger part played by the Elizabethan drama in intellectual life, we must be careful not to credit the spectators with a much greater earnestness in the playhouse. Abundant evidence proves that—what with the throng of groundlings in the yard, intent mainly on the fighting and the broader humour; what with the gallants making their way through the tirehouse and lying or sitting on stools on the stage,[1] smoking the pipes which their pages filled for them, and intent on displaying themselves rather than on listening to the play; what with the women of the town and their admirers in the galleries; what with here and there a Bobadill or Tucca ready to brawl at any moment—the Elizabethan audience, whether in a public or in a private playhouse, was not the rapt body of enthusiasts which later times have been tempted to imagine it. It included, however, Walsinghams and Southamptons, refined and intellectual admirers of the drama, and their numbers must have exceeded those of the Sidneys who scoffed and of the Northbrookes who railed. It is impossible to reconstruct past

---

[1] On this subject, see Wallace, *op. cit.* chap. XI.

acting; but it is safe to conclude that the players whose duty it was to embody the creations of Shakespeare, Marlowe, Beaumont and Fletcher, to the satisfaction of the best intellects of the reigns of Elizabeth and James, with practically no scenic illusion to aid them, must have cultivated to a high degree the arts both of declamation and of expressing character. The improvement in the drama consequent on the coming of university wits probably called forth a corresponding improvement in the actor's art, and there is some evidence that a decline in acting followed or accompanied the decline of the drama in the seventeenth century. That declamation was often attended by its besetting sin of rant is recorded in Hamlet's advice to the players (*Hamlet*, act III, sc. 2) as well as in various passages of other contemporary writers, which imply that the actors of the Fortune (in its later days), the Red Bull and the Cockpit were great offenders in this respect, and that the evil grew during the latter half of the period. The player's response, however: "I hope we have reform'd that indifferently with us, Sir," coupled with the admonition of Hamlet, is pretty good evidence that, at the Globe, declamation was not allowed to degenerate. As to the quality of the character acting, the elegy on Richard Burbage shows how vivid this was at its best; though, of course, it is impossible to tell how deeply, even under Shakespeare's guidance, Burbage penetrated into the significance of the characters he played. The evidence of Flecknoe, who, in his *Short Discourse of the English Stage* (1664) praises Burbage for a "delightful Proteus" that maintained his character throughout, "even in the tyring-house," must represent a tradition and an ideal rather than the statement of an eyewitness. That the female characters were all played in the playhouses by boys, youths, or young men, generally implies, to modern minds, incongruity and poor acting; but the popularity of boys' companies goes to show that boys when thoroughly trained, can do better than we give them credit for to-day.[1] The spectacle, at any rate, must have been pleasanter than that of women playing male parts, and "squeaking Cleopatra" may have boyed her greatness with better artistic effect than some actresses have achieved.

---

[1] See Wallace, *op. cit.* chaps. IV and IX; and cf. Raleigh, W., *Shakespeare* (1907), pp. 119–120.

Much of the inequality in the plays of Shakespeare, as well as of their popularity during his lifetime, can be explained by the consideration that he wrote for a mixed audience, and succeeded in pleasing all.[1] The appeal of his plays to the best intellects of the time needs no showing. For the more intelligent of the common spectators, in whose lives the drama filled the place now occupied by the lending library, the press and, to some extent, the pulpit, there was not only the strong story but the expression of comment and criticism on many aspects of life and on facts of the varied world, some of them only remotely connected with the actual plot. For lovers of sport and action, there were exhibitions of swordplay, wrestling and so forth, which the drama had woven into its own texture, besides battles, murders, and other incidents which, as St. Évremond noticed a century later, the English public liked to see on the stage. For all amateurs of wit, there were exhibitions or contests in punning and jesting—another form of entertainment which the drama, to a great extent, absorbed into itself—ranging from the keen wordplay and literary parody to the gross joke or hint for the groundlings. That Shakespeare would willingly have dispensed with the latter, we know from the passage in *Hamlet* referred to above. The "gag" of the clown must have been the more annoying because it was the common practice to conclude a performance, and sometimes to interrupt it, with a "jig," performed by Tarlton, Kemp, Armin, or some other "fool"—an indispensable member of every company —answering to the "laughable farce" which followed the tragedy until days within the memory of living men. To the possible attractions of the playhouse must be added music, played both during and between the acts. That at Blackfriars was especially esteemed, as was, naturally, that of the children's companies, and public theatres attempted to emulate their success in this matter. Where the "noise," or orchestra sat, is not certain; it was not till after the Restoration that it was placed between the stage and the audience, and, in the period under notice, it probably occupied in some playhouses the space marked *orchestra* in the drawing of the Swan, perhaps on both sides of the stage. The occurrence of songs in plays is well

[1] On this question, see Bridges, R., in the *Stratford-on-Avon Shakespeare*, vol. x, and contrast Bradley, A. C., in *Oxford Lectures on Poetry*, pp. 361 ff.

known; and we read that in the country, at any rate, the music was more popular than the play itself.

Another fact to be noticed is the intimate connection between author and company. It was not only actor-authors, like Shakespeare and Nathan Field, who attached themselves to one company and wrote their plays for it during life or a term of years. The tradition that Hamlet was made "fat" because Burbage was fat, and the still less trustworthy tradition that Iago was written for a comedian, with opportunities introduced into the part for making the audience laugh, do not go so far to prove the effect of this practice on Shakespeare's work as does the consideration that any sensible playwright writing for a certain company will take care that the parts are adapted to its members. Authors often worked very fast, plays being written sometimes in the short space of a fortnight; and they looked for very little reward. The Admiral's company seems to have ordered and produced more new plays than the Chamberlain's and King's company,[1] whose plays, possibly, could bear more frequent repetition; and they only paid sums varying from £5 to £8 for a play until 1602, though as much as £25 seems to have been obtainable later in the period under notice. The author seems to have received a fee for altering his play for production at court; but, though the company received a regular fee of £6. 13s. 4d., with a present of £3. 6s. 8d. for each play performed at court in London, and double those sums when the performance entailed a journey to Hampton court or Windsor, the author cannot be proved to have had a share of this reward. He was present, no doubt, when the company assembled at an inn to read and consider his new play over refreshments paid for by the company, and he had a right to free admission to the playhouse— a privilege which Ben Jonson used to abuse by sitting in the gallery and making wry faces at the actors' delivery of his lines. The author received a fee for altering his play for a revival, 5s. for a prologue and epilogue and, sometimes, a *bonus* at the first performance; and there is good evidence that,

---

[1] So Fleay, *Stage*, p. 117, says that he has "not been able to trace . . . more than four new plays produced by them [the Chamberlain's company] in any one year." Greg, *Henslowe's Diary*, vol. II, p. 112, n. 1, suggests that the preservation of Henslowe's and the loss of the King's company's papers may partly account for the disproportion.

in certain cases, if not regularly, the author had a "benefit," as later times would have phrased it, on the second or third day of performance. If his play was published, he could gain 40s. by dedicating it to a patron.

The play was bought by the company, though there are scattered cases in which individual persons exercised the rights of ownership; the manuscripts formed part of the stock owned in shares by the company, who could sell the play, if they wished, to another company, but, naturally, disliked printing it, lest a rival company should produce it unlawfully. For the same reason, the author was not encouraged to print his play; the company purchased the copyright, and it was considered sharp practice for the author to sell it also to a bookseller. Many plays crept into print in a mangled form through some surreptitious sale by a member of the company, or through stenographers, who attended the playhouse to take down what they could of a successful play.

The bulk of the profits on a play went, not to the author or authors, but to the company. Finance was mainly conducted on the share system. One share or more might be purchased, or might be allotted instead of salary; and, in the second half of the period, shares were clearly regarded as property that could be sold or devised by will. The proceeds of each performance, after certain deductions had been made, were divided among the members of the company according to their holdings of shares. In the case of Henslowe's company, at the Hope, those deductions, at one time, in 1614, included the money received for admission to the galleries and through the tiringhouse, half of the sum going to Henslowe and Meade as owners of the theatre, and the other half to Henslowe on account of advances made by him for the stock of costumes, which was also the company's property. Henslowe has been generally accused of harshness and injustice in his dealings with the companies under his control. Pawnbroker and money-lender, he acted, doubtless, to some extent, on the principle put into his mouth by his players in their *Articles of Grievance and Oppression* of 1615: "should these fellowes Come out of my debt, I should have noe rule with them." Excessive value placed upon clothes and other property which he purchased for them, bonds for repayment and the not infrequent "breaking," or disbanding, of companies which protested, kept his actors in a state of subjection. The case may have been different with the Chamberlain's and King's company; but we are ignorant of its internal arrangements during nearly the whole period. The recent discovery[1] of documents setting forth the company's financial arrangements during the years 1598 to 1615 is entitled to rank among the most important contributions to what is known in this field. In 1599, a lease of the site of the Globe was granted for 31 years, one half of the interest in the property to the brothers Burbage, who paid one half the whole annual rent of £14. 10s. 0d., the other half to Shakespeare, Heminge, Phillipps, Pope and Kemp, who paid the other half of the rent in equal shares, i.e. £1. 9s. 0d. each. In 1610, Shakespeare and the four other holders of tenths admitted Condell to an interest, their shares thus becoming twelfths; and, in 1612, these twelfths were further divided into fourteenths by the admission of William Osteler. This arrangement lasted till 1630, each share, it appears, being assigned on the death of its owner to the Burbages or the survivor of them, to be reassigned to some new actor. In the Blackfriars, Richard Burbage held one seventh share, leaving one seventh each to Shakespeare, Heminge, Cuthbert Burbage, Condell, Slye and Thomas Evans, each of the seven paying an annual rental of £5. 14s. 4d.—a total of £40. 0s. 4d. This arrangement also lasted till 1630. In the documents in the suit brought by Thomasin Osteler against her father Heminge, the purchase value of one seventh of the Blackfriars is estimated at £300, and the purchase value of one-fourteenth of the Globe at the same sum; and a year's profits on each are estimated—no doubt somewhat in excess, for purposes of the suit—at £300. In return for this, each actor-sharer not only paid his share of the cost of building and keeping up the playhouse and of the incidental expenses—wardrobe, servants and so forth—but gave his services as actor; and the later passing of the shares by sale or demise into the hands of persons other than actors led to dispute and litigation. The almost equally

---

[1] Made by Wallace, C. W., and communicated by him to *The Times* of 2 and 4 October, 1909, p. 9. This discovery, with others recently made by the same investigator, will be dealt with at length in *Shakespeare, The Globe and the Blackfriars*, a work now being prepared by him for publication.

important discovery by Halliwell-Phillipps of papers concerning a dispute of this nature among sharers in the Globe and Blackfriars playhouses in 1635 has thrown a light on the later finances of those houses. The company was then divided into three classes: housekeepers, sharers and hired men and boys. The housekeepers' shares in the Globe were sixteen in number, and, at the date of the dispute, they were held as follows: three and a half by Cuthbert Burbage, son of James and brother of Richard, three and a half by the widow of Richard Burbage, now Mrs. Robinson, two by the widow of Henry Condell, three by the actor John Shankes and two each by the actors Taylor and Lowin. There were thus, among the housekeepers, three actors holding seven shares, all of which they had purchased, and the remaining nine shares were owned by "neither actors, nor his Majesties servants," but the heirs or legatees of actors. The Blackfriars was divided into eight shares, three being in the hands of Cuthbert Burbage and the widows of Richard Burbage and Condell, the remaining five in the hands of Shankes, who held two, and Taylor, Lowin and Underwood (another actor), who had one each. The housekeepers had to pay the rent of the two houses (which they put down at £100 yearly, while their opponents reckon it as £65, less a sum of between £20 and £30 for a sub-let portion of the premises), and to keep them in repair; they received one half of all the money taken except at the outer doors, that is to say, half of all the fees for galleries, "rooms" and admission through the tirehouse, for which a fee was charged, and for stools on the stage, which had to be hired. The shareholders, i.e. actors who were not housekeepers, had, in earlier years, received money taken at the outer doors only; by 1635, they divided exactly with the housekeepers the fees for galleries, and so forth, and have to deduct out of their earnings about £3 a day for wages to hired men and boys, music, lights and the like, and also sums spent for costumes and for purchase of plays. Considerable though their profits seem to have been, certain shareholders felt that too much money went into the hands of the housekeepers and that the existing distribution among the actor-housekeepers was unfair, and their petition to the lord chamberlain for a compulsory sale to themselves of certain shares was, apparently, granted.

The price of shares, doubtless, varied with the company, the circumstances and the date. In 1593, Francis Henslowe appears to have paid only £15 for a share in the Queen's company on the eve of a provincial tour, and, two years later, the same actor paid £9 for a half share in another company. The values of shares in the Globe and the Blackfriars in 1615 have been mentioned above. In 1633, Shankes paid £350 for one housekeepers' share in the Blackfriars for a term of five years, and two housekeepers' shares in the Globe for a term of one year. The pleadings in the dispute referred to state that actors who were not housekeepers received £180 each in the year 1634, while the housekeepers' shares appear to have brought in something over £100 each share. A writer in 1643 speaks of housekeepers sharing as much as 30s. a performance. The sums are not surprising when we remember that, to the price of admission (which varied between one penny at a public playhouse to six at a private) paid to the single "gatherer" at the entrance door, were added the extra fees, amounting sometimes to 2s. 6d., demanded by the extra "gatherers" within, for the use of the various parts of the galleries. Hired men were engaged by contract either by the company or the manager, and received a weekly salary, varying from 5s. to 8s. Boys were bought as apprentices by individual players, for sums varying from £2 to something like £15, their masters, presumably, also maintaining them; and, in some cases, boys appear to have been bought and maintained by the company. Strict regulations were made for the behaviour of all members of the company, shareholders and hired men alike, and fines were exacted for lateness, drunkenness, absence from rehearsal and other offences.

A man who was at once a sharing actor and a playwright, like Shakespeare, clearly had it in his power to make fairly large sums of money;[1] and Alleyn, who had other sources of income, was in an even more fortunate position. No surprise need be felt at Shakespeare's purchase of New iPlace, or at Alleyn's heavy outlay on property at Dulwich and his renowned benevolence. The fortunate and respectable actor—even though he held no office under the crown like Alleyn's—was

[1] Wallace, u.s., calculates Shakespeare's yearly profits from the Globe as never exceeding £300, and a similar amount from the Blackfriars.

received into good society and was befriended and admired by the best intellects of his time; he lived a comfortable and secure existence, and, perhaps, indulged in the purchase of a coat of arms. Henry Condell was a sidesman of the parish of St. Mary's, Aldermanbury, in 1606: his respectability is unimpeachable. But the besetting sins of the player—luxury, extravagance and intemperate living—for which Hazlitt found generous excuses in later years, seem to have existed then as ever. We read much of the player's love of fine clothes and display. And there can be no doubt that the frequent interruptions caused by the plague, the deterrent action of such managers as Henslowe and the notorious uncertainty of theatrical affairs, resulted in much poverty and distress among lesser actors and lesser companies. Those on tour, especially, suffered hardships, being forced to pawn their wardrobe, to "pad the hoof" instead of riding from town to town and to beg, instead of play, for their keep. The extremes of the profession were as far apart then as now; but the age of Elizabeth and James undoubtedly raised it as a whole into respect as well as popularity; and the outspoken envy of those—by no means all of puritanical bent—who railed at the pride and display of actors was the natural result of the advance which the period witnessed. During the reign of Charles, the greater prevalence of the plague, the shadow of coming troubles and the deterioration of the drama itself caused something of a decline, and the rebellion brought all to a close.

CHAPTER XI

The Children of the Chapel Royal and their Masters

THE Chapel Royal and its relations to the history of drama in England form an extremely puzzling and interesting subject of enquiry. The origin of the chapel is lost in unrecorded antiquity, the date of its earliest histrionic efforts is uncertain and the records of its later activity are woefully incomplete. But it entered the histrionic field early; it was, if we may trust the extant records, a pioneer in the production of some important kinds of plays; some of its authors seem to have set fashions in dramatic composition; and Shakespeare himself honoured its rivalry with one of the few clear notices of things contemporary that we have from his pen.

Of the membership and organisation of the chapel in the earliest times, we have not any systematic account; but, under Edward IV, according to *Liber Niger Domus Regis*, it consisted of a dean, twenty-four chaplains, two yeomen, eight children, a master of song and a master of the grammar school. Later, a sub-dean was added, the number of boys was increased to twelve, and there were various increases in the number of chaplains, or gentlemen of the chapel, to say nothing of the long list of probationers awaiting vacancies among the gentlemen; but these changes affected the size and not the functions of the institution. It has always been an organisation primarily for the celebration of divine service in the royal household, and its functions in its earliest years, as during the last three centuries, were, perhaps, limited strictly to this primary purpose.

But under the Tudor sovereigns, if not earlier, notable unofficial additions were made to its functions. Both the gentlemen and the children took part, frequently if not regularly, in the pageants, masques and plays produced at Christmas and on other festal occasions.   During the reigns of Henry VII and Henry VIII, the gentlemen seem to have figured in pageants and plays nearly as often as the children; but their histrionic career seems to have ceased early, perhaps because even then such frivolous performances seemed inappropriate to gentlemen "endowed," as *Liber Niger* specifies, "with virtues morolle and specikative, as of the musicke, shewinge in descante, eloquent in readinge, suffytyente in organes playinge."   It is very probable, indeed, that the histrionic activity of the gentlemen began with morality plays and pageants presenting moral allegories, and ceased soon after the drama and other amusements of the court took a more secular turn. The histrionic career of the children—possibly because they were children—continued longer.   In 1569, to be sure, they were attacked in a pamphlet entitled *The Children of the Chapel Stript and Whipt:*

Even in her majesties chappel do these pretty upstart youthes profane the Lordes Day by the lascivious writhing of their tender limbs, and gorgeous decking of their apparell, in feigning bawdie fables gathered from the idolatrous heathen poets;

but it was not until the following century that the children ceased to act.   It is with the children, therefore, rather than the gentlemen, that we are here concerned.

The earliest record relating to the children and their master[1]

---

[1] In his introduction to *The Old Cheque Book of the Chapel Royal*, Rimbault says: "The earliest facts on record relating to the 'King's Chapel' are contained in the *Liber Niger Domus Regis*, a manuscript of the time of Edward IV"; and this statement has been taken by later writers to mean that we have no earlier notice of the organisation.   There exists, however, in the Patent Rolls, a long series of earlier notices, beginning with the mention of "Thomas de Lynton, Dean of the Chapel of the King's Household," 20 August, 1380.   Among the most important of these are: the notice of John Boor as dean in 1389; the acquittance (10 March, 1403) "to Richard Kyngeston, late dean of the King's Chapel within the household, who received divers jewels, vestments, . . . for the same from John Boor, late Dean of the Chapel of Richard II by indenture, and has delivered them to Richard Prentys, now dean . . ."; various licences to Prentys in 1406 and 1412; and the commission, 20 November, 1433, to distribute among the clerks who had been in the chapel of Henry V the sum of £200, bequeathed to them in his will.

that has been found is the commission (12 July, 1440)

to the king's clerk, Master John Croucher, dean of the Chapel within the king's household, to take throughout England such and so many boys as he or his deputies shall see to be fit and able to serve God and the King in the said Royal Chapel.

We have here no mention of anyone specially delegated for the training and supervision of the boys, and it is possible, though unlikely, that there was no such officer, and that there had been no children in the chapel choir before this time, or, at least, no special official recognition of them.   These suppositions, however, may be thought to derive a certain support from the next two entries: 4 November, 1444, a

grant to John Plummer, one of the clerks of the King's Chapel, for the exhibition of eight boys of the Chapel and for his reward, of 40 marks yearly, from Michaelmas last, so long as he have the keeping of the said boys or others in their place, from the ulnage of woollen cloth for sale and from a moiety of the forfeiture thereof in the town and suburbs of Bristol;

24 February, 1445, a

grant, during good behaviour, to the king's serjeant John Plummer, one of the clerks of the Chapel, for his daily labours in the teaching and rule of the king's boys of the Chapel, of the said teaching, rule and governance.

This grant was surrendered 30 May, 1446, for another of the same tenor. In any event, the first master of the children was not, as is commonly supposed, Henry Abyndon, for he was certainly preceded by John Plummer.

From 1465, the series of masters can be made out with tolerable completeness and certainty. On 2 July, 1465, there was a

grant to the king's servitor Henry Abyndon of 40 marks yearly from Michaelmas last from the issues of the county of Wilts for the provision of clothing and other necessary apparel of the boys of the Chapel of the king's household and for their instruction and governance, so long as he shall have the said provision, instruction and governance;

and this grant was renewed 14 February, 1471. It is not yet ascertained when Henry Abyndon (or Abingdon) ceased to be master; but, on 6 February, 1479, a

grant was made to Gilbert Banaster of 40 marks yearly from the petty custom in the port of London and ports and places adjacent for the maintenance, instruction and governance of the boys of the Chapel of the household from Michaelmas last, on which day he undertook these, so long as he shall have the same.

When Banaster's successor was appointed does not appear; but this successor was almost certainly not William Cornish, as is commonly supposed. Cornish, as we shall see, was the successor of William Newark.[1] Newark was granted a corrody from the priory of St. Mary, Thetford, at some date prior to 23 November, 1480; nevertheless, in the document of this date he is not called master of the children but "one of the gentlemen of the King's Chapel," and in the grant (6 April, 485) of a yearly rent of £20 from the king's manor of Bletchingley, county Surrey, he is spoken of only as "the King's servant." It is, however, clear that he was the predecessor of Cornish as master of the children. On 23 May, 1509, he was appointed "gentleman of the Chapel in the royal household and master of the boys of the Chapel, during pleasure." As this was scarcely more than a month after the king's accession, and as he was already a gentleman of the chapel in 1480, the appointment, doubtless, was only a renewal of one made in the preceding reign. On 12 November, 1509, he is mentioned as lately deceased; but the appointment of his successor seems, for some reason, to have been delayed for several years, for among the "Fees and Annuities Paid by the King in 1516" occurs a record of £26. 13s. 4d. to "W. Cornyshe, Master of the Children of the Chapel, *Vice* W. Newark, during pleasure," and it seems improbable that Newark would have been mentioned if any master had come between him and Cornish, or if Cornish had held the appointment since Newark's death.[2]

---

[1] It is, of course, very unlikely that Cornish preceded Newark, was replaced by him and then succeeded him. That Cornish was master in 1493 seems to be one of Collier's unjustified inferences.

[2] Of Clement Adams, who is said (*Babees Boke*, p. lxxvi) to have been master of the children in 1516, no such record can be found. John Melyonek and Philip Van Wilder are also sometimes given as masters, in 1484 and 1550 respectively; but they were merely commissioned to take up singers for the chapel.

Cornish is mentioned as late deceased on 7 November, 1524, and he seems to have been succeeded, though not immediately, by William Crane, who had long been one of the gentlemen of the chapel. Crane's appointment as master of the children is dated 12 May, 1526. His immediate successor was Richard Bower. The official appointment was made 31 October, 1545, but it was to date from 30 June, 1545, "since which time he has by the king's command exercised the office." Whether Crane was then dead or not, is not certain. In the "Augmentations," a William Crane, apparently the person here in question, is recorded as receiving his annuity on 8 May and 16 October, 1545, and there is a later record of payment of an annuity out of St. Edmondesburye to a William Crane in 1546. It seems, however, probable that there were two William Cranes, whose names appear in the records of these years, as there seems also to have been a Richard Bowyer (*alias* Styrley, or Strylly, or Strelley) who has sometimes been confused with Richard Bower, gentleman of the chapel and master of the children. According to the entry in *The Old Cheque Book of the Chapel Royal*, Bower died 26 July, 1563; but Stow gives 1561 as the year, and this seems supported by the fact that, on 4 December, 1561, a commission to take up children for the chapel was issued to Richard Edwards, who is expressly called master of the children. Edwards, perhaps the most famous of the masters, did not long enjoy his office, as he died 31 October, 1566. He was succeeded by William Hunnis (erroneously called Thomas and John in contemporary documents), who served until his death, 6 June, 1597. With Nathaniel Giles, who was appointed master three days later, our interest in the masters of the children ceases, for he was the last under whom the boys were permitted to act. Not only did the boys who acted cease, at the accession of James, to be called children of the chapel and become children of the queen's revels; but, when in 1626, Giles was commissioned to take up boys for the king's chapel, it was expressly provided

that none of the said Choristers or Children of the Chappell, soe to be taken by force of this commission, shal be used or imployed as Comedians, or Stage Players, . . . for that it is not fitt or desent that such as should sing the praises of God Almighty should be trained or imployed in such lascivious and prophane exercises.

The importance of the children of the chapel in dramatic history is due, in part, to their histrionic success and, in part, to the success of some of their masters, and other authors who wrote for them, in dramatic composition. Of the work of the earlier masters, we, of course, know very little. Gilbert Banaster is commonly credited with dramatic composition on the basis of Warton's remark that he "wrote in English verse the *Miracle of saint Thomas*, in the year 1467"; but a *miracle* is not necessarily a miracle-play. William Cornish seems, however, from the entries in the "Household Book of Henry VIII," to have composed some of the plays produced by the boys under his direction. If the "story of Troylous and Pandor," performed by him and the children before the king at Eltham, Christmas 1515, was written by him, he may be regarded as the earliest known dramatiser of romantic fiction. Ward suggests that this may have been merely a pageant; but there is no evidence that it was customary to use similar stories as the subjects of pageants, though, undoubtedly, as the list of costumes and the number of actors—fifteen—indicate, this play was highly spectacular. But pageants usually bore such titles as "the Golldyn Arber in the Arche yerd of Plesyer" (13 February, 1511), "Dangerus Fortrees" (9 March, 1511), or "the Pavyllyon un [on] the Plas Parlos" (6 January, 1515), and the "accounts" usually contain elaborate descriptions of the pageant features. Moreover, it should be remembered that, not long after this, plays on similar subjects were not uncommon, though, unfortunately, only one of them has been preserved to us. It seems, therefore, only fair to ascribe more importance to this record than has usually been done, and to regard Cornish as a pioneer in the production, if not in the composition, of romantic drama. The interlude called "the triumpe of Love and Bewte," "wryten and presentyd by Mayster Cornyshe and oothers of the Chappell . . . and the chyldern of the sayd Chappell," Christmas 1514, was of a more conventional character, and can hardly have been more than an allegorical pageant, with words and music. It should, perhaps, be mentioned that Cornish had the devising of the pageants on Sunday night at the Field of the Cloth of Gold.

Whether William Crane was an author is unknown. He was certainly a man of much business; in 1523, letters of protection were granted him as gentleman of the king's household, *alias* gentleman of the chapel, *alias* comptroller of the petty custom of the port of London, *alias*, of London, draper; and, at various times, he was granted permission to import woad and wine and to export double beer, and he was appointed to furnish five of the king's ships. He seems to have been a favourite of the king, and received many grants in addition to his salary and allowances.

Richard Bower's claim to rank as a dramatic author depends, so far as we know, upon his identification with the "R. B." who wrote *Apius and Virginia*.[1] This, though by no means certain, seems highly probable. We have no earlier copy of the play than that printed in 1575; but it was entered in the Stationers' register in 1567/8, and seems, from the allusion to the sweating sickness, to have been written not later than 1551, the last year, according to Creighton, of the occurrence of this epidemic in England. Whether written by Bower or not, the play obviously belongs to a group of plays which show certain similarities in motives and technique. The group includes, besides this play, Edwards's *Damon and Pithias* (and, probably, also his lost *Palamon and Arcyte*), Fulwell's *Like wil to like*, Pikeryng's *Horestes*, Wapull's *The Tyde taryeth no Man*, Preston's *Cambises*, the anonymous *Common Conditions*, and *Syr Clyomon and Syr Clamydes* and, perhaps, some others. One has only to read these plays in succession to be struck with their mutual resemblances. Most notable, perhaps, are the large amount of attention given in them to "stage business" and the provision of action; the use, in several of them, of unrelated comic scenes for the same purpose; the similarity of the rustic characters which appear in most of them; the use, in most of them, of a Vice who "plays with both hands," inciting to evil or folly and then aiding in its punishment; the curious warnings to the audience to beware of "Cosin Cutpurse"; and the no less curious allusions to the "trump of fame." These characteristics are less marked

---

[1] As to this play, cf. *ante*, Vol. V, Chap. IV, pp. 71–72.

in the work of Edwards than in the other plays; but this may be due to his greater independence and originality. The group would seem to have originated with *Apius and Virginia*. If this be the case, we may attribute the existence of the group to the prestige of the children of the chapel and their masters.

In regard to one of these plays, a word may be permitted, although it does not strictly belong to this chapter. We know from the title-page of *Cambises*,[1] that it was written by Thomas Preston, and it is universally assumed that this was the Thomas Preston who gained the favour of Elizabeth on her visit to Cambridge in 1564. Commentators on *A Midsummer Night's Dream* have not only recognised that Shakespeare ridiculed this play, but have also seen in the lamentations of Flute over Bottom's loss of sixpence a day for life an allusion to the pension given by the queen to Preston on her memorable visit. The fact need not be insisted upon that sixpence a day is a different thing from the £20 a year granted to Preston,[2] but it seems not amiss to point out that Preston's two Latin orations were the prime basis of the queen's pension and choice of him as her scholar. Nor does it seem very probable that the distinguished scholar, who was fellow of King's college in 1556, B.A. in 1557, M.A. in 1561 (and incorporated M.A. at Oxford in 1566), and proctor of his college in 1565, who was, directed by the authorities in 1572 to study civil law and, four years later, to proceed to the degree of LL.D., and who became master of Trinity hall in 1584, should have published, in 1569 and 1570, *Cambises* and the two ballads entitled:

> A geleflower gentle or swete mary golde
> Where in the frutes of terannye you may beholde

and

> A Lamentation from Rome how the Pope doth bewayle
> The Rebelles in England cannot prevayle.

Surely the Preston of Cambridge would not have published these things; or, if he had, neither he nor his publishers would have failed to print his academic titles.

[1] As to *Cambises*, see *ante*, Vol. V, Chap. IV, pp. 71–72.

[2] It is, perhaps, more to the point to observe that 6*d*. a day was exactly the wages of the yeoman of the queen's revels, while the master received only £10 a year.

So much is known of Richard Edwards and William Hunnis that only the briefest notice of them can be given in the space available here.[1] It may suffice to say that Edwards was a university man (as Richard Bower may also have been) and Hunnis obtained, in some way, the equivalent of a university training. Both were celebrated by contemporary writers as authors of dramatic and of non-dramatic works, the fame of Edwards lasting till 1598, though his death occurred in 1566. Non-dramatic writings from the pens of both have been preserved; of their dramatic compositions, we have only Edwards's *Damon and Pithias*, though chance has preserved for us a very detailed account of his other known play, *Palamon and Arcyte*, produced at Oxford in 1566.[2] Mrs. Stopes has suggested that Hunnis was the author of the *Tragedie of the King of Scots*, produced by the children in 1567, the first recorded performance after his succession to the mastership, and of several others of the plays produced under his supervision. Among these were *Narcissus*, 1571, the *History of Loyaltie and Bewtie*, 1579, the *History of Alucius*, 1579, and a satirical *Comedie or Morrall devised on A game of the Cardes*, 1582. Probable as the suggestion is, we have no means of verifying it. But the accounts of Edwards's *Palamon* and Hunnis's *Narcissus* indicate that, as stage managers, they carried on the traditions of the group of plays discussed above. The two passages are so interesting in themselves and so important in their bearing upon the history of the stage that they may be quoted briefly:

In the said play [*Palamon and Arcyte*] was acted a cry of hounds in the Quadrant, upon the train of a fox in the hunting of Theseus, with which the young scholars, who stood in the windows, were so much taken (supposing it was real), that they cried out, "Now, now!—there, there!—he's caught, he's caught!" All which the Queen merrily beholding, said, "O, excellent! these boys, in very troth, are ready to leap out of the windows, to follow the hounds."

[1] Good accounts of Edwards have long been accessible, and Mrs. C. C. Stopes has published two notable articles on Hunnis. (See bibliography.)

[2] As to *Damon and Pithias*, cf. *ante*, Vol. V, chap. IV, and, as to this play and *Palamon and Arcyte*, Chap. XII of the present volume. The university drama *Narcissus* mentioned in the same chapter is, of course, a different play from that mentioned in the text.

This part, it seems, being repeated before certain courtiers, in the lodgings of Mr. Robert Marbeck, one of the Canons of Christ Church, by the players in their gowns (for they were all Scholars that acted) before the Queen came to Oxford, was by them so well liked, that they said it far surpassed *Damon and Pithias*, than which they thought nothing could be better. Likewise some said, that if the author did any more before his death, he would run mad: but this comedy was the last he made; for he died a few months after. In the acting of the said play, there was a good part performed by the lady Amelia, who, for gathering her flowers prettily in a garden then represented, and singing sweetly in the time of March, received eight angels for a gracious reward by her Majesty's command. By whom that part was acted I know not, unless by Peter Carew, the pretty boy before mentioned.

A scene in *Narcissus* may have been suggested by this play, as the *History of Loyaltie and Bewtie* may, possibly, have been suggested by Cornish's *Triumpe of Love and Bewte*, of 1515. The revels accounts for 1571—2 contain the following:

John Tryce for mony to him due for Leashes, & Doghookes, with staves, & other necessaries: by him provyded for the hunters that made the crye after the fox (let loose in the Coorte) with theier howndes, hornes, and hallowing, in the playe of narcisses. which crye was made, of purpose even as the woordes then in utteraunce, & the parte then played, did Requier . . . John Izarde for mony to him due for his device in counterfeting Thunder & Lightning in the playe of Narcisses.

For reasons which will soon appear, it seems improbable that Nathaniel Giles, the last of the masters with whom we are concerned, composed any plays for production by the children. But the *répertoire* of the boys was probably not confined, even in the early years of their histrionic career, to the plays written by their masters. Unfortunately, the early records are too scanty and too indefinite to permit of very positive statements on this point. As early, however, as 1584, two of the most distinguished authors of the time had written for them. John Lyly's *Campaspe* and *Sapho and Phao* were played before the queen by the children of the chapel in conjunction with the children of Paul's before this date, and another play by the same author, *Love's Metamorphosis*, originally written for the children of Paul's was transferred to the chapel boys at some date before its publication in 1601. One of the most interesting of the plays of George Peele, and, in the opinion of some critics, his best play, *The Araygnement of Paris*, also bears upon the title-page of the first edition (1584) the statement that it had been "presented before the Queenes Majestie by the Children of her Chappell." Fleay, indeed, assigns the presentation of it to 5 February, 1581, and the same writer gives 1581 as the date for *Campaspe* and 1582 as the date for *Sapho and Phao*. These dates seem probable; but we are not here concerned with their accuracy, as the essential fact is that both Lyly and Peele wrote for the children of the chapel. That Greene wrote anything for them is unlikely, but the *Tragedie of Dido Queene of Carthage*, by Marlowe and Nashe, is stated on the title-page to have been played by them, and it is highly probable that it was they who played Nashe's *Pleasant Comedie, called Summers last will and Testament* at Croydon in September, 1592. The play alluded to here as having been presented by the same company in the preceding summer was, according to one of Fleay's conjectures, Marlowe and Nashe's *Dido;* according to another, the anonymous *Warres of Cyrus*, published in 1600; we have no means of knowing whether it was either.

To one unfamiliar with the stage history of the time these records might seem inadequate evidence for the brilliant and influential histrionic career ascribed to the children of the chapel. But those who know how scanty the records are will recognise that no other company in these early years presents greater claims to having exercised a real leadership in the drama. The children of Paul's were, indeed, at one time served by Lyly as dramatist;[1] but he began with the children of the chapel, who seem, in fact, to have been pioneers in many important features of both dramatic and histrionic development.

---

[1] That Lyly ever occupied the official position of vice-master (*i.e.* assistant master) of Paul's, seems a solemn inference from a jesting satire. Harvey says he "played the Vicemaster of Poules and the Foolemaster of the Theater." Was there, then, a Foolemaster of the Theater? That neither epithet need be taken seriously is indicated by the additional "sometime the fiddlesticke of Oxford, now the very bable of London." So far as we know, there was no such officer as vice-master of Paul's. "Vice," in "Vicemaster," is, doubtless, the counterpart of "Foole," in "Foolemaster."

That there were other companies of boys—notably those of Paul's and those of Windsor, those of Westminster school and those of Merchant Taylors'—and that many companies of men players performed at court and in public, does not detract from their primacy in these early years.

The opinion expressed above that Nathaniel Giles, who, as will be seen, became master in 1597, wrote nothing for the chapel boys is a mere conjecture, but is supported by two facts: first, that not long after he became master he seems to have allowed other men to use his commission to procure boys for the chapel to provide a company of professional child actors; and that, from this time onward, the actual choir boys of the chapel do not seem to have taken any part in the presentation of plays at court or in public. Since the professional company was supplied with plays by professional dramatists, and the boys under the immediate personal care of Giles did not produce plays, it is very improbable that he wrote any.

On 9 June, 1597, Nathaniel Giles, bachelor of music and master of the children of St. George's chapel, Windsor, became master of the children of the Chapel Royal, in succession to William Hunnis. By a privy seal of 3 July, he was authorised to take up boys for the service of the chapel. No essentially new provision appears in this commission. Giles is authorised to take up "suche and so many children as he or his sufficient Deputie shall thinke meete," and to provide "sufficient lodging for him and the sayd Children, when they for our service shall remove to any place or places"; but the former clause is repeated from earlier commissions, and the latter would never have seemed anything more than a more explicit expression of a similar clause in previous commissions but for the events which ensued. At some unknown date after the issue of this commission, James Robinson and Henry Evans joined with Giles in exploiting the commission. They took up more boys than were needed for the chapel choir, lodged them in Blackfriars and established a regular theatrical company of the children of the chapel.

The highest interest attaches to this professional company of boy actors, but it is at present impossible to determine exactly when their career began. The Blackfriars property was purchased from Sir William More on 4 February, 1596, by James

Burbage, apparently because of its suitability for a playhouse. In November of the same year, the inhabitants of Blackfriars petitioned the privy council against Burbage, declaring that he "is now altering it and meaneth very shortly to convert and turne the same into a common playhouse." How effective this petition was in hindering or delaying the projected playhouse we have no means of knowing.[1] Burbage died early in the following year, and the next unmistakable evidence we have in regard to the Blackfriars playhouse is that, on 2 September, 1600, Richard Burbage, son of James, leased it for twenty-one years to one Henry Evans; but it is certain that, before this date, it had been used as a playhouse by the children of the chapel, and that Evans was already interested in the company. In testimony given in a lawsuit in 1612, Richard Burbage says:

true yt is that this defendant, consideringe with himselfe that, except the said Evans could erect and keepe a companye of Playinge boyes and others to playe playes and interludes in the said Playhouse *in such sort as before tyme had bene there used*, etc.;

and Evans speaks of the playhouse as "then or late in the tenure or occupacion of this defendant" (*i.e.* Evans himself). It is commonly held that the children of the chapel were playing there as early as the end of 1598, and this is probably true.

The evidence we have seems to indicate that Giles was only passively interested in the project, and that someone else— perhaps Henry Evans—first saw the great possibilities which lay in procuring, under the liberal terms of Giles's commission, a company of boy actors and exploiting them in the private playhouse of the Blackfriars. After about a year and a half of experience, we may suppose, Evans decided to take a long lease of the property, and this was effected on 2 September, 1600. It was not very long, however, before he got into trouble about taking up boys. On an ill-fated Saturday, 13 December, 1600, James Robinson, acting as deputy for Giles and as agent for Evans, seized Thomas Clifton, a thirteen-year-old boy, as he was on his way to school. Unfortunately, the boy's father, Henry Clifton, esquire, of Toft Trees, Norfolk, not only secured the

---

[1] The order for the suppression of the Blackfriars playhouse, dated 21 January, 1619, states, however, that "their honors then (*i.e*, in 1596) forbad the use of the said house for playes."

aid of Sir John Fortescue, one of the privy council, to have his son released, but, about a year later, brought the matter before the court of Star chamber. A decree was rendered censuring Evans for taking up gentlemen's sons and ordering the severance of his connection with the company and playhouse. In anticipation, perhaps, of these proceedings, Evans, in October, 1601, transferred all his property to his son-in-law, Alexander Hawkins. After the decree was rendered, Evans, acting through Hawkins, further entered into an agreement with Edward Kirkham, William Rastall and Thomas Kendall, allowing them to share in the management and profits of the playhouse. This is not the place to recite the quarrels between these shareholders; it may suffice to record that the success of the children was very great, that the profits of the undertaking are said to have been very large and that the company continued, with some vicissitudes, to act as the children of the chapel until, at the accession of James, they were re-named the children of the queen's revels, and, finally, were replaced by the company of men to which Shakespeare belonged.

During these years, this professional troupe of boys was served by some of the foremost dramatists of their time. Among the earliest was, doubtless, Chapman, who, perhaps, joined them in 1598, when he left the employ of Henslowe. He appears to have written for them his *May-Day*, his *Sir Gyles Goosecappe*, his *Gentleman Usher* and the extant version of *Al Fooles*. Another even more notable writer for their stage was Ben Jonson, from whom they received not only *The Case is Altered*, but, also, *Cynthia's Revels*, *Poetaster* and, perhaps, *A Tale of a Tub*. There is also some reason to believe that some of Marston's plays were written for them. Unfortunately, much of the stage history of the time is purely conjectural, but it seems practically certain that their vogue had become so great by 1601-2 as to draw from Shakespeare the airily satirical lines in *Hamlet* concerning the "eyrie of children, little eyases, that cry out on the top of question and are most tyrannically clapped for it."

The names of some of these boy actors of this later period are known, some from Henry Clifton's bill of complaint and some from the lists in Ben Jonson's plays. One of them,

Salathiel Pavy, as is well known, died early, and was celebrated by Johnson in a graceful, if somewhat "conceited," epitaph, full of the highest praise for his abilities as an actor. Others became renowned as members of the king's company in later years.

As to the ages of the boys, it is difficult to speak with certainty. Young Clifton was thirteen years old when "taken up," and William Hunnis found it necessary, in earlier times (1583), "to kepe bothe a man servant to attend upon them and lykewyse a woman servant to wash and kepe them cleane." In the case of the boys of the choir, it was customary, from early times, for the sovereign to provide for their education at one of the universities so soon as their "breasts (*i.e.* voices) changed"; but, no doubt, when their principal function was acting they were held longer as children of the chapel, and Philip Gawdy writes in 1601: "'T is sayde my Lady of Leoven hath marryed one of the playing boyes of the chappell."

The success of the companies of choir boys in both early and later times was, doubtless, due, in no small degree, to the songs scattered through their plays and the instrumental music before the play began and between the acts. Other companies, of course, had incidental songs, but, apparently, not so many of them, and instrumental music seems not to have been given in the public theatres. That it was a prominent feature of the performances given by the boys, notwithstanding Clifton's declaration that his son and other boys taken up by Robinson Evans and Giles were "childeren noe way able or fitt for singing, nor by anie of the sayd confederates endevoured to be taught to sing," we know from passages in several contemporary plays, as well as from the explicit statements of the duke of Stettin who visited Blackfriars on 18 September, 1602.

The special interest felt by queen Elizabeth in the chapel boys at Blackfriars may have been due, in part, at least, to their music. At any rate, there cannot be any doubt of her interest in them. According to a letter from Sir Dudley Carleton to John Chamberlain, she attended the play at Blackfriars on Tuesday, 29 December, 1601. The duke of Stettin speaks, indeed, as if the queen had established the theatre and provided the rich costumes of the plays, but the evidence in the suit of Kirkham *vs.* Evans *et als* (1612) indicates that the managers, Evans, Kirkham and their fellows, bore all expenses and took all profits. Kirkham was, indeed, yeoman of the revels, and had charge of the costumes and properties provided for the revels at court, but, though he may have been able to borrow from the revels garments for the use of his company, he could not have bought them without special authorisation. There is no evidence that the queen had any active part in the establishment or maintenance of the children of Blackfriars, though, of course, the company could not have been established or maintained without her tacit consent. She was fond of the drama and of music. On 8 April, 1600, the privy council addressed a letter to the Middlesex justices expressing the queen's pleasure in the performances of Edward Alleyn and his company, and her desire that he should he allowed to erect the Fortune theatre.

Hasty as this survey of the long and brilliant career of the children of the chapel has, necessarily, been, it can hardly fail to have suggested their very great importance in the history of the drama and the stage. They were pioneers in more than one interesting movement, they produced plays by some of the foremost dramatists of their time, they were prominent in the curious, not to say ludicrous, "war of the theatres," and they were finally put down because of the vigorous political satire spoken through their mouths.

CHAPTER XII

University Plays

Tudor and Early Stewart Periods

I T has been pointed out earlier in this work that, while the
humanist movement at Oxford and Cambridge in the sixteenth century did not result in any important contributions to classical scholarship, it was remarkable for the
production of a large number of Latin plays.[1] In the previous
volume,[2] the rise of the renascence academic drama on the
continent was briefly traced, and its influence on early Tudor
comedy, especially school plays, illustrated. But, in England,
school plays had a comparatively limited vogue. It was at
the universities that the humanist drama, written and acted
by scholars, found its real home. Originating in didactic tendencies, and encouraged, as has been shown, by the framers
of college statutes,[3] its aims, at first, were educational rather
than literary or recreative. But, amidst the medley of plastic
influences in English university life, it was inevitable that
drama at Oxford and Cambridge should not remain purely
academic, in the narrower pedagogic sense. The gradually
increasing proportion of plays in the vernacular produced on
college stages, the ceremonial visits of kings and queens and
other royal personages to "shows" at the two seats of learning,
the attractions, for the scholar playwrights and their audiences,
of controversies, whether local and personal or of national
significance—these were among the factors which speedily
enlarged the bounds of university drama, and developed within
it that variety of types which the following pages will attempt

[1] See Vol. III, p. 482.
[2] See Vol. V, Chap. v, p. 113.
[3] See *ibid.*, p. 116.

to sketch. But, to the last, it remained conscious, at least intermittently, of its distinctive origin and mission. Though influencing the popular stage, and being influenced by it in turn, yet, in the main, it followed an independent and diverging track, and it has both merits and limitations which are peculiarly its own.

Mummery and impersonation in their more primitive forms can be traced back at the universities to the later fourteenth century. Though Warton's reference to "the fragment of an ancient accompt-roll of the dissolved college of Michael-House in Cambridge" (it was merged in Trinity college) containing expenditure, under 1386, on a *comedia*, cannot now be verified, it may reasonably be taken as authentic. The statutes of New college, Oxford (1400) and of King's college, Cambridge (1443) expressly provide for the celebration of the favourite medieval ceremony of "the boy bishop" on the feast of the Innocents and of St. Nicholas's day respectively. In the King's college account-books there is an entry of expenses incurred *circa ludos* on Christmas day, 1582, and of a payment *lusoribus in aula collegii*, on the following day. Similar entries of expenditure on Christmas *ludi* or "disgysynges" are found in 1489, 1496, and later.[1] The account-books of Magdalen college, Oxford, show that provision was made for "the bishop" on St. Nicholas's day frequently between 1482 and 1530, as well as for scriptural *ludi* on the chief church festivals, and miscellaneous interludes and entertainments. The register of Merton college, Oxford, records the election of another mock dignitary, *Rex Fabarum* or king of beans, who was chosen on or about the eve of St. Edmund (19 November). In the first entry, in 1485, the election is said to be *per antiquam consuetudinem*, and the names of successive "kings" are given annually till 1539, when the ceremony seems to have fallen into disuse.[2]

It was while such medieval plays and ceremonies retained a flickering vitality that humanist drama at the universities began. At Oxford, the mention in the Magdalen accounts

---

[1] See *Plays performed in Cambridge Colleges before* 1585 by Smith, G. C. Moore, in *Fasciculus Joanni Willis Clark dicatus*, p. 267.

[2] The register is in MS. but the present writer has been given facilities for consulting it.

for the first time of a *comedia* in 1535, and, again, in 1539, and of a *tragedia* in 1540, probably indicates the transition to neo-classic types. According to Anthony à Wood, the Magdalen comedy of 1535 was *Piscator or The Fisher Caught*, by John Hoker, a fellow of the society. In 1536, the *Plutus* of Aristophanes was acted in Greek at St. John's college, Cambridge. The production in 1546 of the Athenian playwright's Εἰρήνη or *Pax*, by John Dee the astrologer, at Trinity college, Cambridge, of which he was a fellow, seems, also, to have been in the original tongue. But these precedents were not followed, and there appears to be no record of a classical tragedy being acted in Greek on the Tudor university stage.[1]

Seneca, not Sophocles, was the pattern of the English humanist when he essayed to write tragedy.[2] It is thus typical of the blending of old and new influences that the earliest extant university plays should be on scriptural subjects, and should be cast in approximately Senecan mould. Their author was Nicholas Grimald, born in 1519, and a member, successively, of Christ's college, Cambridge, and of Brasenose, Merton and Christ Church, Oxford. [3]

The first of these plays, *Christus Redivivus*, printed at Cologne in 1543, was written and acted at Brasenose, as Grimald relates in a dedicatory epistle, soon after his migration to Oxford in 1540. It combines a Senecan treatment of the Gospel story of the resurrection, in which Mary Magdalene plays the most effective part, with a comic underplot centring in the four Roman soldiers who guard the sepulchre, and who are cleverly discriminated types of the military braggart. Grimald's second tragedy, *Archipropheta*, printed at Cologne in 1548, was written in 1547, on his election to the newly constituted society of Christ Church. It dealt with the career of John the Baptist, which Buchanan had already dramatised in his *Baptistes*, acted at Bordeaux a few years previously.[4]

---

[1] John Cristopherson, according to Warton, exhibited in 1546 at Trinity college, of which he was afterwards master, a *Jephtha* of his own composition in Greek and in Latin. The MS. of the Greek play is in the library of Trinity college.

[2] Smith, G. C. Moore, *u.s.*, pp. 269–270, mentions performances at Cambridge of *Troas*, 1551/2 and 1560/1, *Oedipus* and *Hecuba*, 1559/60, and *Medea*, 1560/1 and 1563. These were almost certainly Seneca's plays (*Troas= Troades*).

[3] On Grimald's English poems, see Vol. III of the present work, pp. 201–203

[4] See Vol. III of the present work, pp. 181, 182.

But, in spirit and in style, the two plays are remarkably different from each other. The Scottish humanist follows the strict Senecan model, and makes the Baptist the mouthpiece of his own political and religious opinions. In Grimald's work, John plays a comparatively passive part. The interest centres in the voluptuous passion of Herod and his unlawful wife Herodias, which is portrayed with a lyrical intensity and opulence of phrase unmatched in Tudor drama till the time of Marlowe. Equally foreign to the scriptural theme and to the Senecan convention is the comic note struck by Herod's fool, Gelasimus.

These two Latin tragedies of Grimald, if they were known to Roger Ascham, did not earn from him in *The Scholemaster* the commendation of being "able to abyde the free touch of Aristotles preceptes and Euripides examples" which he reserved for Buchanan's *Jephthes* and the *Absalom* of Thomas Watson of St. John's, Cambridge. Watson, owing to scruples on a minor metrical point, never published the play; but it is probably that preserved in the Stowe MSS. 957, which is a tragedy of the strict Senecan type. The story of the revolt in the royal house of Israel lent itself as naturally to Senecan machinery as did legendary dynastic feuds of early British kings, and Chusi's relation to David, in act IV, of the overthrow of Absalom's ill-armed troops and of his hapless end, is a vivid piece of narrative.

Religious drama of an entirely different type made its appearance on the Cambridge stage when, during the Lent of 1545, Kirchmayer's *Pammachius* was acted at Christ's college. Though it was condensed for the occasion, no excisions could disguise its savage anti-papal satire. It was inevitable that the orthodox chancellor of the university, Gardiner, bishop of Winchester, should write letters of remonstrance to the vice-chancellor, and order him to hold an enquiry concerning the performance. Dissatisfied with the report, Gardiner laid the matter before the privy council, which instructed the vice-chancellor to reprove the offenders, but took no further disciplinary measures. The members of Christ's college probably avoided controversial dramas in future; but entries in the college accounts testify to great dramatic activity in the immediately following years. The leading spirit in these entertainments was William Stevenson, who entered Christ's in 1546, graduated B.A. in 1550, M.A. in 1553 and B.D. in 1560, and was twice elected a fellow of the college. A play by him is mentioned in the accounts for 1550–1, and, again, in those for 1551–2; and, in the following year, he is reimbursed 18*d.* for expenses on his "plaies." There is another entry of a play by him in 1553–4, and a final one in 1559–60, during the second tenure of his fellowship. Hence, it has been plausibly conjectured that Stevenson is the author of *Gammer Gurtons Nedle*, "played on stage, not longe ago in Christes Colledge in Cambridge. Made by Mr. S. Mr of Art."[1]

The first edition of this comedy was not published till 1575, but its printer Colwell had obtained, in 1562/3, a licence to issue *Dyccon of Bedlam*. As "Diccon the Bedlem" is the leading figure in "Mr. S.'s" play, the licence probably refers to it, and there are bibliographical grounds for the conjecture that the work was printed long before it was put on sale. A reference to arrest "in the kings name" in act v suggests that the comedy was written before the death of Edward VI in July, 1553. If Stevenson were its author, it would thus appear to have been composed between 1550 and 1553, and, if the title-page is to be trusted, revived later, probably in 1559–60. However this may be, *Gammer Gurtons Nedle* is of enduring interest as the earliest university play in English which has come down to us. At first sight, it shows little trace of scholarly influences. The "fourteener" in which it is mainly written is a rough and tumble metre; and the dialogue, often coarse in strain, is, as a rule, in that south-western dialect which became the conventional form of rustic speech on the Elizabethan stage. The plot turns on the complications produced in a small village society by the loss of the gammer's needle, and the characters are typically English, including Diccon, who combines the *rôles* of a Vice and a vagrant Tom of Bedlam. But, on closer examination, the effect of classical models is seen. The comedy is divided into acts and scenes, and the plot has a real organic unity. The parts played by the

---

[1] The traditional ascription of the play to John Still rests merely upon a conjecture of Isaac Reed in 1782, and may be dismissed. But it is remarkable that John Bridges, dean of Salisbury, a member of Pembroke college, is spoken of in two of the Martin Marprelate tracts, 1588, as the reputed author of the comedy.

different personages in the village community, from "Master Baily" and the curate downward, are neatly discriminated. The triumph of pastoral convention had not yet blurred for English humanists the outlines of genuine English country life.

The golden period of academic drama may be dated from the visits paid by queen Elizabeth to the two universities early in her reign. The visit to Cambridge began on 5 August, 1564, and, in a letter from Grindal, bishop of London, written about three weeks before, the university authorities were admonished to

put themselves in all readiness to please her Majestie, to welcome her with all manner of scholastical exercises, viz. with Sermons, both in English and Latin; Disputations in all Kinds of Faculties; and playing of Comedies and Tragedies; Oratios and Verses, both in Latin and Greek.

Under the direction of Roger Kelke, "who was by the Vice-Chancellor and Heads of Colleges specially appointed to set forth and teach such plays as could be exhibited before her Grace," a varied dramatic programme was provided. It began with a performance of the *Aulularia* of Plautus[1] on the evening of Sunday, 6 August, in King's college chapel. A "great stage containing the breadth of the Church from the one side to the other" was erected for the performance at the queen's own cost and so keen was her interest that she remained till the final *plaudite*, without betraying the slightest weariness, though some of her suite grew impatient, owing to their ignorance of Latin or their desire for sleep.

On the following evening, a tragedy called *Dido*, written by Edward Halliwell, fellow of King's college, was performed. It was in hexameter verse, and drawn, for the most part, from the *Aeneid*. Like the earlier school drama on the same subject, acted before Wolsey in 1532,[2] it is not extant; but the contemporary narrative of Nicholas Robinson describes it as *novum opus sed venustum et elegans*, though considered too long by some carping spectators.

---

[1] Plautus appears to have been the favourite classical dramatist at Cambridge in the sixteenth century. Smith, G. C. Moore, *u.s.* pp. 269–271, records sixteen performances of his plays between 1549 and 1583; four performances of comedies by Terence are noted during the same period.

[2] See *ante*, Vol. V, Chap. v., p. 114.

A still more regrettable loss is that of the next evening's play, *Ezechias*, an English Biblical drama by Nicholas Udall.[1] As Udall was an Oxford man, and had been dead for about seven years, the production of a play by him on this occasion is somewhat remarkable, and was probably due to his long connection with court entertainments. Though the work is not extant, the accounts of the performance by Hartwell and Robinson show that it dealt with Hezekiah's destruction of the idols of the grove and the brazen serpent, the resentment of the populace, the mission of Rabshakeh at the head of the Assyrian host and the mysterious destruction of the invaders in a single night. As in the case of miracle-plays, lighter episodes were evidently mingled with Biblical incidents. *Mirum vero quantum hic facetiarum, quantum leporis in re tam seria ac sancta, et veritatis tamen certa serie nunquam interrupta.*

Great "preparations and charges" had been "employed and spent about" another play, *Ajax Flagellifer*, a Latin version of the Sophoclean tragedy, which was to be given on 9 August, the eve of the queen's departure. But she was so much wearied by her exertions that the performance had to be abandoned.[2] Before her departure on the following morning, Elizabeth gave a present in money and other marks of her favour to Thomas Preston, fellow of King's, afterwards author of *Cambises, king of Persia*, who had pleased her by his acting in *Dido* and his skill in disputation.

This visit of the queen to Cambridge had its counterpart two years later in one to Oxford, which began on Saturday, 31 August, 1566, and lasted till Friday, 6 September. She arrived from Woodstock, and had to undergo so formidable a succession of welcoming orations from the university and civic authorities on her way to Christ Church that she was unable to be present the following evening at the first play performed in her honour in the college hall. On a stage specially prepared at the queen's own cost, with "stately lights of wax, variously wrought," *Marcus Germinus*, a comedy in Latin prose, was performed. It was the joint composition of several Christ Church scholars, and was produced with the help of Richard

---

[1] On Udall's other plays, see *ante*, Vol. V, Chap. v. pp. 116–119.
[2] See *post*, p. 357, as to the performance of an *Ajax Flagellifer*, doubtless the same play, before James I.

Edwards. From the analysis of the plot given by Bereblock, it appears that it dealt with a conspiracy against Germinus, a native of Campania, in the reign of Alexander Severus, by jealous rivals who think that they have compassed his ruin, but whose designs are foiled by the evidence of honest freedmen.

On the following night, 2 September, the first part of *Palamon and Arcyte*, an English play by Richard Edwards, was acted in the queen's presence.[1] The report of the magnificence of the decorations, and the eagerness to see Elizabeth, drew such a vast crowd of spectators (*infinita ac innumerabilis hominum multitudo*) that part of the wall of the staircase leading to the hall collapsed, killing three persons and wounding others. The catastrophe, however, did not interfere with the performance or with the queen's enjoyment of it. From the analysis of the plot given by Bereblock, it is evident that it was exactly on the lines of Chaucer's *Knight's Tale*. The first part ended with Theseus's discovery of the two rivals for Emily's love fighting in the wood, and his determination that the matter should be decided by a tournament. The second part, acted on 4 September, dealt with the tournament, the victory of Arcite, his sudden death and the betrothal of Palamon and Emily. The loss of the play, which anticipated by about half a century the treatment of the same theme in *The Two Noble Kinsmen*, is a matter of great regret. Not only was the queen delighted with it, but a party of courtiers who had seen a rehearsal of it "said it far surpassed *Damon and Pithias* than which they thought nothing could be better."

The series of plays performed before the queen during this visit terminated with a Latin tragedy, *Progne*, by James Calfhill canon of Christ Church. The plot was drawn from the sixth book of Ovid's *Metamorphoses*, and dealt, doubtless on Senecan lines, with the gruesome tale of the revenge of Progne, wife of king Tereus, upon her husband for the wrongs done to herself and her sister Philomela. It is not surprising that such a work "did not take half so well as the much admired play of *Palamon and Arcyte*."

But the relative merit of the pieces performed during these two royal visits to the universities is of less import than the

---

[1] On Edwards's previous career as a dramatist see *ante*, Vol. V, Chaps. IV and V.

remarkable variety of their subjects and their style. A play of Plautus, a tragedy on Dido in Vergilian hexameters, an English verse play on Hezekiah, a Latin version of the *Ajax* of Sophocles, a neo-Latin prose comedy, an adaptation of *The Knight's Tale*, a tragedy in the Senecan manner on an Ovidian theme—here is a microcosm of the motley literary elements which, combined with features of more popular origin, went to the shaping of the Elizabethan drama. It was into academic societies in which such varied stage productions formed part of the regular ritual of social and intellectual life that, within the next two decades, Marlowe, Peele, Greene and Nashe were to enter, and it was thence that they were to carry away lessons destined to exercise a momentous influence on the future of the London theatre.

To the immediately following years, no extant university play can be assigned with certainty. But, from the register of Merton college, Oxford, we learn that performances, both in English and in Latin, were given in the warden's house or in the college hall. On 3 January, 1566/7, *Wylie Beguylie*,[1] an English comedy, was performed by the scholars, *merito laudandi recte agendo;* and this was followed, about a month later, by the *Eunuchus* of Terence. In the January of the following year, the Merton scholars revived Edwards's *Damon and Pithias*, and, a few days later, acted the *Menaechmi* of Plautus.

Byrsa Basilica by J. Rickets, a play of unique character suggested by the foundation of the Royal Exchange in 1570, appears, from the epilogue, to be of university origin, though it deals in fantastic fashion with the career of Sir Thomas Gresham, and with various aspects of London commercial life, in bizarre combination with the figures and machinery of southern comedy.[2] The political and dynastic, instead of the economic, aspect of the national annals furnished material for another,

---

[1] The loss of this early Oxford play in the vernacular is particularly unfortunate, as we cannot tell whether it bore any relation to the later *Wily Beguiled* (printed 1606), which was almost certainly a Cambridge play (cf. Ward, vol. II, pp. 612–3). *Wily Beguiled*, however, was influenced so directly by *The Spanish Tragedie*, *The Merchant of Venice* and *Romeo and Juliet* that it is doubtful whether it can be connected with the Merton comedy of 1567.

[2] Gresham's civic career, with an admixture of episodes from the general history of the period, afterwards furnished materials for the popular stage in Part II, of Thomas Heywood's *If You know not me, You know no bodie* (1606).

and better-known, play, which attained unusual popularity and which is of special interest as illustrating the Senecan treatment of a theme which afterwards became the basis of a Shakespearean chronicle history play. This work, preserved in a number of manuscripts, is *Richardus Tertius*, by Thomas Legge, master of Caius college, Cambridge, and twice vice-chancellor. It was acted at St. John's college in the spring of 1580, and in two of the manuscripts the list of performers is given. It ranges over the long period from the death of Edward IV to the battle of Bosworth field, and, hence, is in tripartite form, consisting of three *actiones* performed on successive evenings. It thus departs from the strict Senecan model in its comprehensive sweep and in its disregard of the unities of time and place. It also dispenses with the moralising chorus. Otherwise, it is a typical Senecan tragedy, in metre and language, in motives and situations and in the general conception of a royal tyrant akin to Nero in *Octavia* and to Atreus in *Thyestes*. It has the characteristic faults of the school to which it belongs—monotony and an excess of wire-drawn declamation—but Legge had genuine skill in technique and expression, and taught the lesson that structural design and rhetorical embellishment are essentials in a historical play. Greene, who took his B.A. at St. John's in 1578, was still in residence at Cambridge when the play was produced, and Marlowe entered the university in the following year. There can be little doubt that Legge's drama was known to them, and that, at least indirectly, it also influenced Shakespeare in *Richard III*. The Senecan series of reverses of fortune in Shakespeare's play, the passages of semi-lyrical declamation, the dialogues in στιχομυθία, the peculiarly sombre colouring of the work and the two wooing scenes, which have no source in Holinshed but are anticipated in Legge's tragedy, all point strongly to this conclusion.

Not long after the production of *Richardus Tertius*, a number of Senecan plays dealing with more remote and exotic historical subjects were performed. *Solymannidae*, an anonymous tragedy, was acted, at one of the universities, in March, 1581/2. It treats of the murder of Mustapha, son of Sultan Solyman II, at the instigation of his ambitious step-mother Rhode, who wishes the throne for her own son Selymus. Another Senecan tragedy on an oriental historical theme *Tomumbeius*, by George Salterne of Bristol, deals with the tragic fate of Tuman-bey, who became sultan of Egypt in 1516. Its dedication to Elizabeth proves that it was written during her reign; but, otherwise, its date and place of performance are unknown. Even more uncertain is the *provenance* of the pseudo-historical Senecan tragedy *Perfidus Hetruscus*, the plot of which has points of contact with *Hamlet*. On the death of Sorastanus, duke of Tuscany, his brother Pandolphus seeks to gain the throne by conspiring against his nephews Columbus and Lampranus. His chief agent, at first, is a Jesuit Grimalfi (an indication that the author was a strong protestant), who, however, is slain by the ghost of Sorastanus. Through the further machinations of Pandolphus, Columbus is banished by Lampranus; but the ghost of Sorastanus appears to him in exile, and bids him return to kill his uncle. He obeys the command and fights a duel with Pandolphus, who sends for a poisoned cup of wine. The traitor himself drinks by mistake from the poisoned cup, but recovers, and afterwards strangles Columbus, and poisons Lampranus during his sleep. He succeeds to the vacant dukedom, but dies after donning the crown which he himself had poisoned. Preserved in a single manuscript, and never printed, this play has not attracted the attention to which its plot entitles it. It is of greater interest than the much better known *Roxana*, by William Alabaster, of Trinity college, Cambridge, acted about 1592. This is a close version, with most of the names altered, and with no indication of its source, of an Italian play, *La Dalida*, by Luigi Groto, published in 1567. Alabaster lays the scene in Bactria; and the plot, which centres round Roxana, a princess of the imaginary royal house, exceeds even the usual measure of horrors in a Senecan tragedy. Doubtless, this characteristic (in consequence of which "a gentlewoman fell distracted" at the performance), together with the elegant Latinity of the play, gained for it the popularity of which an echo remains in Dr. Johnson's laudatory allusion to it in his *Life of Milton*.

The Senecan school of university dramatists produced its most important figure in William Gager, who is included in Meres's list (1598) of the chief dramatists of the day, though, strange to say, among writers of comedy. Born between 1555 and 1560, he entered Christ Church, Oxford, in 1574, graduated in 1577 and became a doctor of civil law in 1589. During his long residence, he took the lead in writing plays for performance by members of his college. With the exception of his single comedy, *Rivales*, no longer extant, they were Latin tragedies on classical subjects. The first of these, *Meleager*, was produced in 1581, and revived, three years later, in the presence of the earl of Leicester, chancellor of the university, and Sir Philip Sidney. The author of *An Apologie for Poetrie*, as he watched the performance, must have rejoiced that there had arisen a dramatist who carried out to the letter his critical precepts, preserving the unities in the strictest fashion, and taking care not to match "hornpipes and funerals."

In 1583, before another visitor of distinction, Albertus Lasco, prince palatine of Poland, two other plays by Gager were acted, the comedy *Rivales* already mentioned, and "a verie statelie tragedie," *Dido*, in the preparation of which George Peele took part. For this tragedy, which was produced with "strange, marvellous, and abundant" scenic effects, Gager, like Halliwell at Cambridge twenty years before, drew the chief situations and much of the dialogue (though cast into Senecan form) from the *Aeneid*. Another of the Christ Church dramatist's tragedies, *Oedipus*, of uncertain date, is only partly extant in manuscript. But the last and finest of his classical plays, *Ulysses Redux*, was printed a few months after its production in February, 1591/2, when *Rivales* also was revived. *Ulysses Redux*, though Senecan in form, is far from being a lifeless piece of classical imitation. Drawing its subject from the later books of the *Odyssey*, it is not unworthy of its source. The incidents are skilfully grouped, and many of the scenes, including the fight between Irus and Ulysses, and the efforts of the suitors to bend the bow, are full of dramatic vigour. The conjugal effection of Penelope for her lord is provided with an affective foil in the passion of the handmaid Melantho for Eurymachus—an un-Homeric episode which Gager develops in the spirit of romantic drama.

But of greater permanent value than Gager's tragedies is his masterly defence of academic plays and players contained in a letter to John Rainolds of Queen's college, afterwards president of Corpus, a puritan antagonist of the drama. Of both sides of the correspondence an account is given in a later chapter of this volume.[1] The arguments with which Gager meets Rainolds's objections to the impersonation of women by men in feminine attire, and to Sunday performances, are full of interesting references to contemporary college life, and he sets forth eloquently the aims and ideals of academic playwrights and actors.

We doe it to recreate owre-selves, owre house, and the better parte of the Universitye, with some learned Poeme or other; to practyse owre owne style eyther in prose or verse; to be well acquantyed with Seneca or Plautus . . . to trye their voyces and confirme their memoryes, to frame their speeche; to conforme them to convenient action; to trye what mettell is in everye one, and of what disposition they are.[2]

But Seneca and Plautus were not the only exemplars with whom university dramatists were "well acquainted." From about 1580 onwards, their productions in the sphere of comedy, even when written in Latin, had, usually, an Italian, and not a classical, source. To this period belongs *Victoria*, by Abraham Fraunce of St. John's, Cambridge, a metrical Latin version of Luigi Pasqualigo's prose comedy *Il Fedele*, published in 1575. This is a typical product of the southern stage, with a complicated intrigue between rivals for the favours of a married lady, with impersonations and disguisings and with the stock figures of a braggart and an enamoured pedant. Fraunce's version, except for the addition of an episode taken from *The Decameron*, and the revision of portions of the later acts, is very close. It thus contrasts with the free English adaptation of *Il Fedele* by Anthony Munday, *Fedele and Fortunio*, wherein the braggart, who is called captain Crackstone, becomes the chief figure in the comedy.[3]

A more ingenious and skilful adaptation from the Italian than *Victoria*, though from *The Decameron* and not from a play, is the anonymous *Hymenaeus*, acted at St. John's, Cam-

---

[1] See *post*, Chap. XIV.

[2] For a full account of Gager's letter, by the present writer, see *The Fortnightly Review*, August, 1907.

[3] See *ante*, Vol. V, Chap. XIII, and bibl. Vol. V, pp. 520-521 for an account of Munday's play.

bridge, probably in March, 1578/9. The list of actors, which included Fraunce, is virtually identical with that which took part in *Richardus Tertius*, except that the latter has a considerably larger cast. Boccaccio tells of the remarkable experiences of a gallant called Ruggieri, who makes love to the beautiful young wife of an aged doctor of Salerno, and who swallows a sleeping draught by mistake. In *Hymenaeus*, the young wife is the daughter of an elderly father, with three suitors—a doctor, a drunken German, and a young Venetian whom she favours. It is the Venetian who drinks the potion prepared by his rival, the doctor, for the heroine's father, and who, in consequence, goes through a series of adventures which nearly ends on the gallows, before he succeeds in winning his mistress's hand. To the same group of Latin comedies in Italian style, though no immediate source of them has been hitherto traced, belong several St. John's college plays of somewhat later date. These include the pastoral *Silvanus* (January, 1597), with resemblances of situation to the Silvius-Phoebe-Rosalind love-complication in *As You Like It*, and with a Latinised echo, in the closing song, of the August roundelay in *The Shepheards Calender;* and *Machiavellus* (December, 1597), in which the bearer of the title *rôle*, and a Jew, Jacuppus, carry on a contest with a remarkable series of disguises, plots and counterplots, for the hand of the heroine, till her betrothed, who is supposed to have been killed in the wars, returns just in time to claim her once more as his own. Two comedies which can be traced to their Italian sources are *Leander* (1598 and 1602) and *Labyrinthus* (1602), performed at Trinity college, Cambridge, and written by Walter Hawkesworth, fellow of the college, who acted the chief part in both plays. Their popularity is evidenced by the number of manuscripts in which they are still extant; but they were merely Latin adaptations of *La Fantesca* and *La Cintia* respectively, both by G. B. della Porta, the Neapolitan playwright. Of all these Cambridge versions of Italian comedies, the most important is the anonymous *Laelia*, acted at Queens' college in 1590, and revived in 1598. It is founded on *Gl' Ingannati* (1531), and its action is similar to that of the main plot of *Twelfth Night*. The source of Shakespeare's play has always been doubtful, though Rich's *Apolonius and Silla* and Emanuel Ford's *Parismus* have features in common with it. Nor is it safe, as has been attempted by W. H. Furness and F. E. Schelling, to identify *Laelia* as the direct original of *Twelfth Night*, though it is just possible that it may have been. In any case, the university play and the Shakespearean comedy present an instructive contrast of methods, the advantage not being all on one side. *Laelia* lacks the lyric beauty, the delicate, imaginative charm of *Twelfth Night*, without hint of its superbly humorous underplot; its characters are of the conventional southern type, including the stock figures of a pedant and a nurse. But the plot of *Laelia* is a very deft piece of stagecraft; and, by representing Flaminius (Orsino) as having loved Laelia (Viola), before he transferred his affections to Isabella (Olivia), it makes more plausible the final union of hearts between hero and heroine.

The plays dealt with hitherto in this chapter are academic in the sense that they were written and acted by university men within college walls, and that, whether English[1] or Latin, they were influenced, almost without exception, by the classical or Italian models which were of paramount authority in learned societies of the renascence period. We now have to deal with a group of comedies which are academic in a more special and intimate sense; which deal with the studies and the experiences of scholars young and old, with the notable figures of contemporary university life, with the immemorial feud of town and gown.

Of these plays, chiefly connected with Cambridge, probably the earliest extant, as it is one of the most diverting, is *Pedantius*, a Trinity college comedy. Though not published till 1631, it probably dates from the winter of 1580 or spring of 1581. Nashe, in *Strange Newes*, ascribes it to "M. Winkfield," *i.e.* Anthony Wingfield, fellow of Trinity, who, in March, 1581, was a successful rival of Gabriel Harvey for the office of public orator. Nashe, who matriculated at St. John's, in October, 1582, cannot well have been mistaken, though claims have

---

[1] It is curious that the Cambridge authorities, when asked to "prepare A Comedie in Englishe" to be acted at court by students before the queen at Christmas, 1592, wrote to Burghley, "Englishe Comedies, for that wee never used any, wee presentlie have none." See "Dram. Records from Lansdowne MSS." in *Malone Society Collections*, vol. 1, part 2, p. 199.

been made[1] on behalf of Edward Forcet or Forsett, fellow of Trinity, who is named as author in a Caius college manuscript of the play.

Pedantius is an admirable combination of Plautine machinery and types with the conditions of English university life in the later sixteenth century. The lovesick pedant of southern comedy is here transformed into a Cambridge humanist, who is the unsuccessful rival of a freedman for the hand of a slave girl Lydia, and whose rhetorical flights avail him nothing except to stave off payment of his tailor's bills. But the pedant is not merely modernised, he is individualised into a caricature of Gabriel Harvey. This is vouched for by Nashe in *Have with you to Saffron Walden*, where he declares that, in "the concise and firking finicaldo fine schoolmaster," Harvey "was full drawn and delineated from the soule of the foote to the crowne of his head." Internal evidence confirms the identification. Not only is Pedantius, as was Harvey, according to the view of his enemies, a fop and a sycophant, but phrases from the Cambridge rhetorician's works occur repeatedly in the play, and his *Musarum Lachrymae* is directly named. As satellite and contrast to the main figure appears another contemporary academic type, the solemnly argumentative, logic-chopping philosopher Dromodotus.

The university stage, in this burlesque of Harvey, may claim the dubious honour of having first made use of the drama in England for purposes of personal attack. And, according to Nashe, there were other plays, now lost, ridiculing members of the Harvey family. *Tarrarantantara turba tumultuosa Trigonum, Tri-Harveyorum, Tri-harmonia*, a show at Clare hall, was directed against the three brothers, Gabriel, Gilbert and Dick, while *Duns Furens: Dickey Harvey in a Frensie*, at Peterhouse, so exasperated its butt, "the little minnow," that he broke the college windows during the performance and was set in the stocks "till the Shew was ended, and a great part of the night after." Doubtless, personal satire, in some form, was a feature of *Terminus et non terminus*, acted at St. John's in or soon after 1586, and written by Nashe and another member of the college. For, according to Harvey (*Trimming*

[1] See G. C. Moore Smith's introduction to his edition of the play in Bang's *Materialien*.

of Thomas Nashe), the latter was expelled for his share in it; why Nashe, who appears to have played the part of "Varlet of Clubs" in the show, was more leniently dealt with, does not appear.

For attacks on academic personages like the Harveys, Latin was the suitable instrument; but, when college playwrights took a hand in the chronic feud between university and town, as represented by the civic authorities, they naturally fell back upon the vernacular. A remarkable episode in this connection is chronicled by Fuller in his *History of the University of Cambridge*, under date 1597-8.

> The young scholars . . . having gotten a discovery of some town privacies from Miles Goldsborough (one of their own corporation) composed a merry (but abusive) comedy (which they called *Club-Law*) in English, as calculated for the capacities of such whom they intended spectators thereof. Clare-Hall was the place wherein it was acted, and the mayor, with his brethren and their wives were invited to behold it, or rather themselves abused therein. A convenient place was assigned to the townsfolk (riveted in with scholars on all sides) where they might see and be seen. Here they did behold themselves in their own best clothes (which the scholars had borrowed) . . . lively personated, their habits, gestures, language, lieger-jests, and expressions.

So incensed were the civic dignitaries at the insult, that they complained to the privy council, which, however, made little of the matter, merely sending some "slight and private check to the principal actors."

Fuller's narrative is scarcely to be accepted as authentic in all its details,[1] and it is noticeable that no mention of the incident is found in the register of the privy council. But the play to which he alludes, and which was thought to be no longer extant, has recently been rediscovered in manuscript in the library of St. John's college, Cambridge, by G. C. Moore Smith. The manuscript is imperfect, lacking the title and

---

[1] In his introduction to *Club Law*, Smith, G. C. Moore, argued that the date of the production was 1599-1600, and that the mayor of Cambridge, satirised as Niphle, was John Yaxley. Since then, he has found confirmation of his conjecture in a Jesus college MS., ascribed to Fuller himself, which mentions the production in 1599-1600 at Clare hall of "Club Law *fabula festivissima*." See *The Modern Language Review*, vol. IV, no. 2, pp. 268-9.

the first three scenes of act I and scene 3 and parts of scenes 2 and 4 of act IV. But that the play is the *Club Law* acted at Clare is proved by the constant introduction of the phrase, and by the general character of the comedy.

In an unconventional dramatic framework, wherein "Commike rules," as confessed in the epilogue, are not observed, the playwright gives an animated though bitterly partisan picture of the relations between university and town in the closing years of the sixteenth century. The chronic hostility between them arose from the peculiar privileges granted to the university by a series of royal charters and by parliamentary enactment. These privileges included powers of interference with the trade of the town, of searching the houses of citizens and of punishing them in the university courts. Every mayor on his accession to office had to take an oath to preserve the privileges of the university—an obligation which aroused the keenest resentment.

Of all these circumstances, the Clare hall dramatist makes skilful use. Two graduates of Athens (Cambridge), Musonius and Philenius, egged on by a waggish younger scholar, Cricket, determine to make the "muddy slaves," the rebellious citizens, "feele our stripes for their disobedience and renewe the ancient Club-lawe." At the same time, the newly chosen burgomaster (mayor) Niphle announces to the electors that he "will rout out the whole generation" of academicians, "they shall not nestle with us in our streets, nor out brave us in our owne dunghills." And he afterwards arranges a plan of campaign against them, including the retaliation of "their owne Clublawe." There are traitors, however, in the citizens' camp; Mrs. Niphle and Mrs. Colby, wife of a leading "headsman," to win the good graces of Musonius and Philenius, reveal the plot, and give the scholars directions for appropriating the clubs which were to be used against them. Meanwhile, the burgomaster has been caught out in a midnight visit to a courtesan at the house of his sergeant, the Welshman Tavie; and Colby has been detected in the act of carrying away corn in sacks supposed to contain coal. Both are sent to jail by virtue of the rector's (vice-chancellor's) authority, and bills of "discommoning" are issued, prohibiting scholars from having any dealings with prominent members of the corporation. It is this measure, whereby their means of livelihood are cut off, that brings the citizens to their knees, even more than their rout in a street skirmish by the "gentle Athenians" armed with the purloined clubs. A deputation headed by Niphle, who has been released from jail, comes to proffer submission to Musonius and Philenius.

> Wee crave pardon, and craving pardon we tender our supplication, that it may please you to letts live by you, and recover our old estats, that is, to reape what benefits we may by you, which if it please you to grant, I being the mouth of the rest doe promise for the rest hereafter to be obedient to you in any reasonable demand.

But it is not till the promise is confirmed by an oath that the scholars hold out to the suppliants a prospect of the renewal of their former privileges. The play hangs loosely together, and the satire is so acid and unrelieved throughout that it goes beyond the limits of dramatic plausibility. The author's knock-down blows are themselves a species of "club law." But he has a remarkable command of idiomatic and racy vocabulary, which gives pungency to the dialogue. The broken English of Tavie, the Welshman, and of Mounsier Grand Combatant, a French braggadocio, and the north-country dialect of Rumford, one of the corporation, give further evidence of the writer's quick ear for characteristic modes of speech.

Broadly contemporary with *Club Law* is the *Parnassus* trilogy, which, in originality and breadth of execution, and in complex relationship to the academic, literary, theatrical and social life of the period, ranks supreme among the extant memorials of the university stage. Both the first and second parts of the trilogy remained in manuscript till 1886, when they were published by W. D. Macray. The third part had appeared in quarto in 1606, with the title *The Returne from Pernassus: Or the Scourge of Simony: Publiquely acted by the Students in Saint Johns Colledge in Cambridge.* Internal evidence proves that this third part must have been written before the death of Elizabeth, and indicates Christmas, 1602, as the probable date of the performance. On similar evidence, *The Pilgrimage to Parnassus*, and *Part I* of *The Returne from Parnassus* (as the recovered plays have been named), may be assigned, respectively, to 1598 and 1601. The writer of the trilogy is unknown, for, though he throws out tantalising clues in the prologue to *Part I* of *The Returne*, they are not sufficient to identify him. The ingenious argument in support of the authorship of John Day is open to serious chronological and other objections. But, whoever he may have been, the St. John's playwright was a man of singularly penetrating intelligence, acute observation and wide reading. His mordant wit disdained to flow in the conventional academic channel of Italianate comedy, where a "lisping gallant" and his "wench," or a "sire" acknowledging "his lost son," were the stock figures. He struck out on a path of his own, with increased vigour and boldness at each stage.

The Pilgrimage is an allegory, in dramatic framework, of the difficulties and temptations that beset the scholar in his pursuit of learning. Two cousins and fellow students, Philomusus and Studiosus, are plodding to Parnassus by the well worn track of the *trivium*. In Logic land, "muche like Wales, full of craggie mountains and thornie vallies," they encounter Madido, a votary of the wine cup, who tells them that "Parnassus and Hellicon are but the fables of the poets: there is no true Parnassus but the third lofte in a wine taverne, no true Hellicon but a cup of browne bastard." Thence they pass to the "pleasant land of Rhetorique," where "shrille Don Cicero" sings sweetly, and where they are overtaken by Stupido. He is a type of the narrowest puritanism, who declaims against the "vaine arts of Rhetorique, Poetrie and Philosophie; there is noe sounde edifying knowledg in them. Why they are more vaine than a paire of organs or a morrice daunce." But the fiercest trial is in the land of Poetry, where Amoretto, a voluptuary, who perverts the muse into an agent of sensual passion, bids them "crop the joys of youth," and allures them for a time from their path. But, before it is too late, they realise that wantonness is "sourelie sweete," and they press on to the land of Philosophy. Here they meet an old schoolfellow, Ingenioso, who is hurrying away "in a chafe," and who cries to the pilgrims "What! I travell to Parnassus? why I have burnt my bookes, splitted my pen, rent my papers, and curst the cooseninge harts that brought mee up to noe better fortune." These words, and others that follow, are taken, with some modification, from Nashe's pamphlet *Pierce Penilesse* (1592), in which he bewailed the miseries of the life of a man of letters. The bitter cry of so gifted a member of the college must have come home to the St. John's audience, some of whom may have been present at the performance of *Terminus et non terminus* in the previous decade. But the pilgrims turn a deaf ear and fare blithely on to the "laurell mounte," where, for a time, they lie with "Phoebus by the muse's springes."

In *Part I* of *The Returne*, the playwright is in more sombre mood, and his satire is more incisive. He drops almost entirely the allegorical scheme, and, in a series of realistic genre pictures, portrays the miserable shifts to which scholars, when their course is completed, are reduced to earn a living. Philomusus goes through pitiful experiences as a parish clerk and sexton till he is dismissed for incompetency. Studiosus, who tries to find consolation in the moral commonplaces of Senecan tragedy, leads a dog's life as tutor to an idle and unruly "dandipratt" in a vulgar household. But he is sent packing, because he will not yield precedence to a servant at table, and the two friends, as a last hope, resolve to seek their fortunes under another sky, at "Rome or Rheims." Here, however, they fare as ill as at home and they hurry back, feeling

> That it's as good to starve mongst English swine
> As in a forraine land to beg and pine.

But the adventures of Philomusus and Studiosus furnish only one of the themes in this part of the trilogy. Another is found in the relations of Ingenioso to Gullio, a vainglorious pseudo-patron of letters, modelled in part on Nashe's portrait of "an upstart" in his *Pierce Penilesse*. Gullio, who is "maintaining" Ingenioso in most niggardly fashion, bids him personate his mistress, Lesbia, that he may rehearse amorous speeches afterwards to be addressed to her. These speeches are mainly variations on lines in Shakespeare's *Venus and Adonis* and *Romeo and Juliet*. Gullio afterwards commissions Ingenioso to write specimen verses for his lady "in two or three divers vayns, in Chaucer's, Gower's, and Spenser's and Mr Shakspeare's." He quotes the opening lines of *Venus and Adonis* as the preferable model, and cries sentimentally:

O sweet Mr Shakespeare! I'le have his picture in my study at
the courte.

When Ingenioso submits his poetical exercises for approval,
the lines in "Mr Shakspeare's vayne" are instantly preferred:

Ey marry, sir, these have some life in them! Let this duncified
worlde esteeme of Spencer and Chaucer, I'le worshipp sweet M^r
Shakespeare and to honour him will lay his Venus and Adonis
under my pillowe.

But the lines, accompanied by a Latin epistle of Gullio's own
composition, fail to move Lesbia, and Ingenioso is dismissed
by his indignant patron.

It is certainly not with complimentary intent that the
author makes Shakespeare the favourite poet of the shallow and
affected courtier. Further light is thrown on his attitude in
act I sc. 2 of *Part II* of *The Returne*. In this famous scene,
the Cambridge dramatist, under the thin disguise of Judicio,
reviews the merits of a number of the contemporary poets from
whom selections had been included in Bodenham's *Belvedere*, an
anthology issued in 1600. Shakespeare is briefly dealt with:

> Who loves not Adons love, or Lucrece rape?
> His sweeter verse contaynes hart throbbing line,
> Could but a graver subject him content
> Without loves foolish lazy languishment.

The critic, while recognising the beauty of language and versification in Shakespeare's two early poems, evidently considered
that he was misusing his talents in producing luscious studies
of amorous passion, though they might move Gullio and his
kind to sentimental raptures. His qualified tribute to the
actor-poet contrasts with his panegyric on Spenser and his
generous praise of Drayton, Nashe and other writers of the day.

In the later scene of *Part II* of *The Returne*, the St. John's
writer again deals with Shakespeare, not as a poet, but as a
dramatist and an actor. The references, doubtless, are inspired
by reminiscences of a recent visit of the lord chamberlain's
company to Cambridge. Owing to the competition of the
boy actors at the Blackfriars theatre, Shakespeare and his
fellows had had to go on tour probably in 1601. That they

visited Oxford and Cambridge, we know from the title-page
of the first quarto of *Hamlet* (1603), where the play is said to
have been acted "in the two Universities." With its scholar-
hero, and semi-academic atmosphere, the surmise is plausible
that it was adapted from Kyd's earlier play with a special
view to its being acted in the university towns. It was a
fresh mortification to the St. John's dramatist, embittered by
the woes of scholars, to see low-born actors from the capital
make a triumphal entry into Cambridge.

> England affords those glorious vagabonds
> That carried earst their fardels on their backes,
> Coursers to ride on through the gazing streetes,
> Sooping it in their glaring Satten sutes,
> And Pages to attend their Maisterships:
> With mouthing words that better wits have framed,
> They purchase lands, and now Esquiers are namde.

It is thus in a spirit of fierce mockery that he represents Philomusus and Studiosus, by way of a last resource, becoming can-
didates for the professional stage, and being tested by Burbage
and Kempe, who make merry over the deficiencies of scholars
both as actors and as dramatists.

KEMPE. The slaves are somewhat proud, and besides it is a
good sport in a part to see them never speake in their walke, but
at the end of the stage, just as though in walking with a fellow we
should never speake but at a stile, a gate, or a ditch, where a man can
go no further. . . .

BUR. A little teaching will mend these faults, and it may bee
besides they will be able to pen a part.

KEMPE. Few of the University [men] plaies well, they smell
too much of that writer *Ovid*, and that writer *Metamorphosis*, and
talke too much of *Proserpina* and *Juppiter*. Why heres our fellow
Shakespeare puts them all downe, I and Ben Jonson too. O that
Ben Jonson is a pestilent fellow, he brought up Horace giving the
poets a pill, but our fellow Shakespeare hath given him a purge
that made him bewray his credit.

The whole purport of this well known passage is misunder-
stood unless it be recognised that it is written in a vein of the
bitterest irony. The gownsman is holding up to scorn before
an academic audience the judgment of illiterate boors who

think that *Metamorphosis* is a writer, and that their fellow Shakespeare puts to shame the university playwrights, and has had the upper hand in a duel with Ben Jonson, the protagonist of classical orthodoxy in dramatic art.   With the relations of Shakespeare and Jonson in "the war of the theatres" we are not here concerned; but it is profoundly significant that the anonymous author of the *Parnassus* trilogy, perhaps the ablest of all the academic dramatists, should have singled out Shakespeare in his mid-career for his satiric shafts.   The foremost representatives of the academic and the professional stage stand revealed in this brief illuminating flash, sundered by an impassable gulf of class-prejudice and divergent ideals of art. Nor could the scholar-playwright have been expected to see that the supreme master of irony, Time, would turn back his ridicule with crushing effect upon himself.

In other scenes of *Part II* of *The Returne*, which account for the sub-title, *The Scourge of Simony*, the feud between town and gown finds as bitter expression as in *Club Law*.   But the satire is now particularly directed against Francis Brackyn, deputy recorder of Cambridge, who had taken a leading part in asserting the claims of the burgesses against the university. The feeling against Brackyn was intensified by the fact that he stood for common law, while the academic jurists, at this time, were striving to revive the influence and authority of civil law.   Under the name of the Recorder, Brackyn figures in the play as one of a confederacy who out of greed and spite, bestow the cure of souls on moneyed blockheads instead of on poor but deserving scholars.   The other members of the gang are Sir Frederick, a dissolute and rapacious patron of livings, and his son Amoretto, an affected braggart.   Academico, who has been a college contemporary of Amoretto and used his talents on his behalf, asks him for his good offices with his father.   But Immerito, the boorish son of a country bumpkin, is preferred to the benefice because his father can give one hundred "thanks" in current coin.   The Recorder approves the patron's choice, and seizes the occasion for a malignant outburst against the scholars and their colleges:

> But had the world no wiser men than I,
> Weede pen the prating parates in a cage;

> Knights, Lords, and lawyers should be log'd and dwel
> Within those over stately heapes of stone
> Which doting syres in old age did erect.

But, later, the scholars prove themselves the Recorder's match
in vituperation, and we get a forestaste of the yet more overwhelming ridicule of Brackyn in *Ignoramus*.

To us, the *Parnassus* trilogy is without an equal among
academic plays in the combined intimacy and breadth of its
appeal. But contemporary taste seems to have been hit more
successfully by another Cambridge drama, *Lingua, or The
Combat of the Tongue and the five Senses for Superiority*. This
comedy, first printed in 1607, went through six editions before
the Restoration. Its date is uncertain, though it must be later
than 1602, which is mentioned in one of the scenes. Its author,
as we learn from a memorandum by Sir John Harington, a
high authority on the university plays of his day, was Thomas
Tomkis of Trinity college, who graduated in 1600-1, and
whose name appears on the title-page of *Albumazar*, acted
before James I, at Trinity in 1615. *Lingua* falls in with the
contemporary fashion of personifying or allegorising the parts
and faculties of man, which finds its chief expression in Phineas
Fletcher's *Purple Island*. The scene "is Microcosmus in a
Grove," and the plot is concerned with the attempt of *Lingua*,
the tongue, to vindicate her claim to be a sixth sense. To
breed strife among the five recognised senses, she leaves in
their path a crown and a royal robe with the inscription:

> He of the five that proves himself the best,
> Shall have his temples with this coronet blest.

Tactus first finds the royal emblems, and invests his "brows
and body" with them. Thereupon, the other senses dispute
his sovereignty, and make preparation for deadly combat.
But Communis Sensus, the vicegerent of queen Psyche, under-
takes "to umpire the contention" and orders them "their
arms dismissed to appear before him, charging everyone to
bring, as it were in a shew, their proper objects, that by them
he may determine of their several excellencies." Visus's show
includes Lumen, Coelum, Terra and Colour, whom he "mar-
shaleth about the stage, and presents before the bench."

Auditus afterwards leads in Tragedus and Comedus, whose likeness and unlikeness are delineated in words of admirable critical insight. Olofactus presents "the mighty emperor Tobacco, king of Trinidado, that, in being conquered, conquered all Europe, in making them pay tribute for their smoke." Gustus has in his train Bacchus and Ceres; but Tactus has to appear alone, because his show was to have included "a nice gentlewoman," and in five hours a dozen maids have not had time to attire a boy for the part. Finally, Communis Sensus delivers judgment. On not very cogent grounds, he assigns the crown to Visus and the robe to Tactus, while the three other senses are consoled with appointments to high offices under queen Psyche. Lingua's claim to be a sense is rejected—with a significant reservation:

The number of the Senses in this little world is answerable to the first bodies in the great world: now, since there be but five in the universe, the four elements and the pure substance of the heavens, therefore there can be but five senses in our Microcosm correspondent to those . . . wherefore we judge you to be no sense simply: only this much we from henceforth pronounce, that all women for your sake shall have six Senses, that is, seeing, hearing, tasting, smelling, touching, and the last and feminine sense, the sense of speaking.

Lingua, enraged at being proclaimed "half a sense," revenges herself by making the senses drink a drugged wine at a supper to which Gustus invites them. Their wits become deranged, and strife threatens to be renewed among them; but Somnus charms them, and the mischief-maker Lingua, into sleep. In her sleep, Lingua confesses her trickery,[1] and is punished by being committed "to close prisin, in Gustus's house . . . under the custody of two strong dons, and . . . well guarded with thirty tall watchmen, without whose licence she shall by no means wag abroad."

It is not, however, in the plot, ingeniously worked out as it is, that the chief attraction of the play lies. Its distinguishing excellence is the style, or variety of styles, in which it is

[1] In *The Modern Language Review*, vol. IV, no. 4, pp. 518–520, the present writer has suggested that this episode is probably a parody of the sleep-walking scene in *Macbeth*.

written.   In the prose scenes, Tomkis proves himself a master
of polished and flexible dialogue, which has often a curiously
modern note.   The wit is sparkling and unforced, but lacks
the Aristophanic pungency of *Club Law* and the *Parnassus*
plays.   In the few verse passages where the author aims at a
serious effect, he writes with scholarly grace.   But most of the
metrical speeches are in a vein of burlesque, or are parodies of
lines in plays of the day.   Thus, there are intentionally ludicrous imitations of famous speeches in Kyd's *Spanish Tragedie*,
besides what appear to be caricatures of phrases or situations
in several Shakespearean dramas.   A hundred and one incidental allusions show the width of the author's reading, and the
remarkably detailed stage directions prove his interest in
matters of costume and heraldry.   The statement made in
1657, and elaborated by later tradition, that Oliver Cromwell
acted in the play, is, probably, a bookseller's figment, but
might, conceivably, be true if a revival took place about 1617,
when the third edition of the work appeared.

The last decade of Elizabeth's reign, which was very
fruitful in Cambridge plays, has left few memorials of dramatic
activity at Oxford, which seems to have been more dependent
on the external stimulus of royal visits.   But, at St. John's
college, which, from the beginning of the seventeenth century,
rivals Christ Church as a centre of academic stagecraft,
there was produced in 1602/3 the "twelfe night merriment,"
Narcissus.   The prologue declares that "the play wee play
is Ovid's own Narcissus," and it is true that the plot is taken
from book III of the *Metamorphoses*.   But the story is considerably expanded and treated throughout in a burlesque vein.
Thus, Tiresias, "the not seeing prophet," adorned "in bysh-
oppes rochett," is introduced to tell the fortune of the beautiful
youth from the "table" of his hand; and the trickery of the
mischievous nymph Echo leads to mock tragedy.   Throughout,
the author shows a remarkable command of out-of-the-way
phrases and grotesque rimes, and, in its farcical treatment of
a classical legend, *Narcissus* is curiously akin to the interlude
of *Pyramus and Thisbe* in *A Midsummer Night's Dream*.

Two and a half years later, in the summer of 1506, St.
John's took part with Christ Church in the series of entertainments provided for king James on his first visit to Oxford.

The king, accompanied by the queen and Henry, prince of Wales, made his entry on 27 August. Special preparations had been made for the festivities. In Christ Church, where the king and queen lodged, a stage had been

built close to the upper end of the Hall, as it seemed at the first sight. But indeed it was but a false wall fair painted, and adorned with stately pillars, which pillars would turn about, by reason whereof, with the help of other painted clothes, their stage did vary three times in the acting of one Tragedy.

That the actors in the various plays might be suitably apparelled, a number of costumes and properties were supplied by the office of the revels. Lists of these are preserved in the university archives.

The success of the performances seems, however, to have been scarcely on a level with the magnitude of the preparations. On the first evening, a pastoral play *Alba* was presented. "In the acting thereof they brought in five or six men almost naked which were much disliked by the Queen and Ladies." It needed the entreaties of the chancellors of both universities to prevent the king leaving "before half the comedy had been ended." On the following night, James saw *Ajax Flagellifer*. James would have done well to imitate his predecessor in countermanding,[1] as he "was very weary before he came thither, but much more wearied by it, and spoke many words of dislike." Nor did matters fare much better on the third evening, when *Vertumnus sive Annus Recurrens*, by Matthew Gwinne of St. John's, was performed on the Christ Church stage. Though it was well acted by a company consisting chiefly of St. John's men, the king fell asleep in the middle. But the play produced on the following evening "made amends for all." It was *The Queenes Arcadia* of Samuel Daniel, memorable as the first English pastoral drama written for the academic stage.[2] Guarini's *Il Pastor Fido* had been acted a short time previously at King's college, Cambridge, in a Latin version, *Pastor Fidus*. *Parthenia*, a similar version of Luigi Groto's *Pentimento Amoroso*, preserved in manuscript at

[1] Cf. *ante*, p. 336.
[2] For a brief sketch of the progress of the pastoral drama in England see the following Chapter (XIII).

Emmanuel college, Cambridge, is of uncertain date. Daniel,
as was natural, followed the general lines of Italian pastoral
drama; but the statement of a contemporary Cambridge
visitor to Oxford, that "it was drawn out of *Pastor Fidus*,"
is misleading. So far as Daniel's play owes a direct debt to a
foreign original, it is to Tasso's *Aminta* rather than to Guarini's
work, while the conception of the plot, though not of a number
of episodes, must be put down to the English poet's own credit.
It deals with the entanglements and evils produced in Arcadia
by the machinations of sophisticated representatives of the
outer world. Chief among these are Colax, "a corrupted
traveller," and Techne, "a subtle wench of Corinth," who,
by their nefarious schemes, delude the shepherd Amyntas into
the belief that Cloris, whom he wooes in vain, is a wanton.
In despair, he tries to take his own life, but, in an episode
imitated from *Aminta*, is rescued by Cloris, whose heart has,
at last, been touched by love. The arch evil-doers, after plotting not only against the hero and heroine but against other
Arcadian lovers, are banished for ever. Subordinate, but more
amusing, mischief-makers are Lincus, a pettifogging lawyer,
and Alcon, a quack doctor, into whose mouth is put a description of tobacco as

> a certaine herbe wrapt up in rowles
> From th' Island of *Nicosia* where it growes:
>
> And this he said a wondrous vertue had,
> To purge the head, and cure the great catarre.

This, of course, was intended to tickle the ears of the author of
A Counterblaste to Tobacco. But the permanent attraction of
Daniel's play lies not in its topical references or even in its
plot and characterisation, but in the lyrical sweetness of its
verse and the limpid grace of its diction and imagery. Its
production at Christ Church is amongst the most memorable
records of the Oxford stage. Probably, however, none of the
Christ Church plays gratified the king so much as a more
informal open-air interlude which took place in front of St.
John's college on the day of his entry into Oxford. Three
young scholars, dressed as nymphs, suddenly appeared in his
path. They announced that they were the sibyls who had

formerly foretold to Banquo the rule of his descendants, and
that they had come again to prophesy all happiness to James
and the perpetuity of Banquo's stock upon the British throne.
They then saluted the king in turn with a triple *salve*, and
greeted similarly the queen and prince Henry. James "did
very much applaude" the "conceipt," which was devised by
Matthew Gwinne, and it is possible that some account of it
reached the ears of Shakespeare and suggested the writing of
Macbeth in the following year.

The stimulus of the royal visit to theatrical activity at
Oxford, especially at St. John's college, seems to have lasted
for some time afterwards. To this, we have remarkable testimony in a unique memorial of the academic stage preserved in
the St. John's library. It is a manuscript written by Griffin
Higgs, a member of the college, who successively became fellow
of Merton and chaplain to Elizabeth of Bohemia, and entitled
*A true and faithfull relation of the risinge and fall of Thomas
Tucker, Prince of Alba Fortunata, Lord St. Johns &c., with all
the occurrents which happened throughout his whole domination.*
No extant document, not even Gager's letter to Rainolds, lets
us so completely behind the scenes of the collegiate theatre,
or brings home to us so intimately the hopes and fears, the
labours and difficulties, connected with the performances.
The manuscript is an account of a series of festivities which
lasted from All Saints' eve (31 October), 1607, till the first
Sunday in the following Lent.[1] On All Saints' eve, Thomas
Tucker, a bachelor of arts (later, a fellow of the college and
canon of Bristol) was elected "Christmas Lord or Prince of the
Revells . . . to appoint & moderate all such games and
pastimes as should come." Two "bills" were, therefore, sent
out to the masters craving allegiance to his authority and
"money & maintenance." Among those who contributed were
Laud and Juxon, each assessed at ten shillings. But, in
order to raise an adequate sum, Tucker (like a true Stewart
ruler) had to levy a further requisition on ex-fellows and com-
moners and on college tenants. Sufficient provision thus made,

---

[1] The narrative part of the manuscript and one play *The Seven Dayes of the
Weeke* were printed in 1816, with the title *The Christmas Prince*. The present
writer has been given facilities for consulting the manuscript, and the account of
the other plays is here printed for the first time.

he was publicly installed on St. Andrew's day by means of a
Latin "devise," *Ara Fortunae*. In this, the prince, with his
leading councillors, visits the temple of Fortune and is assured
by her priestess of the favour of the goddess. He accordingly
announces that he no longer reigns by popular favour but by
divine right, and that he is preparing "pomps and triumphs"
for the entertainment of his faithful subjects.

On Christmas day, the prince sat at high table in the vice-
president's place, and a boar's head was carried in as "the
first messe" by the "tallest and lustiest" of his guards, to the
accompaniment of a brisk carol. In the evening, a short
Latin interlude, *Saturnalia*, was performed, introducing a
Dominus and a *Servus* in the inverted relation peculiar to the
Roman festival, and afterwards Hercules, who, by interpreting
aright an equivocal Delphic oracle, shows that waxen lights
and not human sacrifices are the offerings enjoined at this
anniversary. As the season of the Saturnalia coincided approximately with Christmastide, these waxen lights, it is hinted,
are the source of Christmas candles; and, in a prose epilogue,
an ingenious parallel and contrast are drawn between the
pagan and the Christian festival.

The same sense of classical and Biblical analogies dictated
the choice of a play for Innocents' day. A Senecan tragedy
on the story of Philomela was written for the occasion, as it
was thought that the subject "well fitted the day, by reason
of the murder of Innocent Itis." But the performance had to
be postponed for a day because the carpenters were "no way
ready w.th the stage." Then a further mishap occurred.
"The Prince himself who was to play Tereus had gott such an
exceeding cold that it was impossible for him to speake,
or speaking to be heard." However, with the unnamed
author of the tragedy in reserve as an understudy should he
be "constrained to leave," the resourceful Tucker got through
his part with credit. "The whole play was wel acted and wel
liked," a more favourable verdict than had been pronounced
on Calfhill's tragedy on the same story acted before Elizabeth
at Christ Church in 1566.

It is characteristic of the academic taste of the time that
Philomela was much more appreciated than an English play
Time's Complaint acted on New Year's day as part of "the

princes triumphs." The failure of this piece, which received only "two or three cold plaudites," was partly due to the blunders of amateur actors, of which Higgs gives amusing details, and to the overcrowding on the stage. But, doubtless, the fault also lay largely in the plot, which combines awkwardly a semi-allegorical tale of Time's attempt to recover his daughter Veritas, kept in thraldom by Opinion and Error, and a farcical series of mistakes and entanglements arising out of the theft of goodwife Spigott's goods by a drunken cobbler, Swallow. Yet, *Time's Complaint* is far from being without interest. It contains genre pictures of characteristic Elizabethan types, such as the dispossessed countryman, the cashiered soldier and the professional beggar. It introduces, also, in Studioso, the poor and embittered scholar, and in Philonices, the grasping pompous lawyer and justice, two figures akin to those in the *Parnassus* plays.

The spirits of the St. John's actors, which had been grievously depressed by the cold reception of *Time's Complaint*, were revived by the success of an amusing show, *The Seven Dayes of the Weeke*, acted at the president's lodging on Sunday, 10 January, and repeated by special request before the vice-chancellor and other dignitaries a week later. Equally successful was a Latin comedy *Philomathes*, mingling abstractions with Plautine characters. After its performance "the stage & scaffold were pul'd downe wch had stood from Cristmas"; but they were set up again on Shrove Tuesday for the prince's resignation. This, like his public installation, was solemnised in the form of a play, *Ira seu Tumulus Fortunae*. The goddess has now grown angry with the prince because he has not paid her sufficiently constant homage. His ministers resign their symbols of office and desert him. In vain he visits again the altar of Fortune, and seeks to placate her wrath. He, therefore, strips himself of the emblems of sovereignty, and lays them in a sepulchre in her temple, dedicating himself henceforth to the service of Minerva.

Thus ended the memorable reign of Thomas Tucker; but, as the stage and scaffolds had been re-erected, and, as an English tragedy on the story of Periander, tyrant of Corinth, had been prepared, it was decided to perform this on the following Saturday. It attracted such a concourse that hundreds could not find room in the hall. They "made such an hideous noice, and raised such a tumult wth breaking of windows all about the colledge, throwinge of stones into the hall, and such like ryott" that the officers of the college had to rush forth, "wth about a dozen whiflers well armed and swords drawne." The rioters then ran away, but some of the ring-leaders were arrested, and imprisoned in the porter's lodge till the play was over.

Curiously enough, about a week later, on 20 February, there was a similar riot at Cambridge, when there was "foul & great disorder committed at the time of a comedy in King's College," probably a lost play by Phineas Fletcher. In the same month, four years later, there was a yet more serious disturbance at Cambridge, when the St. John's men, angry at being excluded from a comedy acted at Trinity college, began an affray outside the Great Gate, which led to proceedings in the vice-chancellor's court. In sharp contrast to these tumultuous proceedings was the scene in the hall of Trinity on 2 March, 1613, when prince Charles and Frederick, the elector palatine, saw Samuel Brooke's comedy called *Adelphe*, and when the elector slept during the greater part of the performance, which lasted from seven in the evening till one. On the following evening, the princes were again provided with solid entertainment by the performance of *Scyros*, a Latin version by Brooke of Bonarelli's pastoral drama, *Filli di Sciro*.

On 7 March, 1615, James himself, with prince Charles, came to Cambridge, and stayed at Trinity for four nights. As the sovereign had not visited the university since Elizabeth's "progress" in 1564, elaborate preparations were made to celebrate the event. The days were devoted to learned disputations and the evenings to plays. The first piece, *Aemilia*, a Latin comedy written by Edward Cecil of St. John's, was not very successful; but ample amends were made on the following evening when, in the hall of Trinity, *Ignoramus* was launched on its triumphant career. Its author was George Ruggle, fellow of Clare hall, who had formerly been a scholar of Trinity, and the actors were chosen from various colleges, difficulty being found in filling suitably the female parts. On one side, *Ignoramus* is linked with the group of Latin adaptations of Italian comedies mentioned above, for it is founded on G. della Porta's *Trappolaria*. But Ruggle transformed his original by extensive additions, and by a fundamental change in the central character, converting him out of a soldier into the lawyer who gives his name to the play. Thus metamorphosed, the typically southern comedy became the climax of Aristophanic attacks by gownsmen upon the town and its officials. The title part is a merciless caricature of the detested recorder, Brackyn, who had already been ridiculed in *The Returne from Pernassus, Part II*. The animus against him as a common lawyer had been intensified by public events. The law dictionary *The Interpreter*, published in 1607 by John Cowell, regius professor of civil law, had been suppressed on the demand of the House of Commons, because its tendency was to exalt the royal prerogative at the expense of common law. The civilians of the university and the king himself were, therefore, delighted when Ruggle brought upon the stage a burlesque figure talking a barbarous jargon of bastard Latin and the technical terms of common law. It is the novelty of this conception and the gusto with which it is developed that give the play its unique character. In the course of its intricate plot, Ignoramus goes through a variety of humiliating and painful experiences. On a visit to Bordeaux, he falls in love with the heroine, Rosabella, and engages to pay 600 pieces of gold for her hand. But, through the stratagems of Antonius, the favoured suitor of the girl, Ignoramus obtains possession instead of the heavy-handed virago, Polla, who belabours him soundly. Amazed at his incomprehensible outcries, she thinks he is bewitched and goes to fetch her husband and a monk, who, in a scene of richly farcical humour, exorcise the evil spirits out of him and carry him off, shrieking, to a monastery for his final cure. Rosabella, of course, is finally united to Antonius, and a mystery attaching to her birth is cleared up.

Ignoramus, with its mixture of learning and horseplay, was exactly suited for captivating James. The play presented on the following night, *Albumazar*, though adapted by Tomkis, author of *Lingua*, from another comedy of della Porta, *L'Astrologo*, was less successful. But it contains two amusing characters in Albumazar, the rascally astronomer, and Trincalo, the rustic whom Albumazar "transforms" into his absent master, Antonio, with ludicrous consequences when the latter unexpectedly returns home. In its printed form, the play was fortunate enough to attract both Dryden and Garrick, both of whom revived it on the London stage. But, on its production, it seems, from a contemporary account, to have been less appreciated not only than its predecessor, *Ignoramus*, but than its successor on the following evening, *Melanthe*, a Latin pastoral drama from the pen of Samuel Brooke, whose *Adelphe* and *Scyros* have been mentioned above. The king could not stay to see the last play prepared for his entertainment, *Sicelides*, by Phineas Fletcher; but it was acted a few days later. He thus missed seeing the first English "piscatory" on the stage, as he had already seen at Oxford, in 1605, the first English pastoral drama. The main plot of *Sicelides*, dealing with the romantic love stories of Perindus and Glaucilla and Thalander and Olinda, is, apparently, original, though episodes and motives are derived from classical and Italian sources. One underplot centres round Cosma, the typical "light nymph" of "Messena," and the other round Cancrone and Scrocca, low-comedy fishermen whose talk is largely a farrago of "malapropisms" and topical allusions. The machinery of the play is unduly intricate and perplexing, and the characterisation is not vivid. But the work has real charm in its delicate delineation of emotions, in the graceful imagery of its descriptive passages and in the lyric sweetness of its choruses.

James was so delighted with *Ignoramus* that he revisited Cambridge in May to see it a second time. Its triumph marks the close of the most vital period of the university drama. Henceforward, no new type was evolved, and the distinctively academic element dwindles. Allegorical plays became increasingly popular with college dramatists, though *Lingua* remained unrivalled for wit and *verve*. Thus, in February, 1618, *Technogamia or The Marriage of the Arts*, by Barten Holiday, was acted at Christ Church "with no great applause"; but it was repeated before the king at Woodstock in August, 1621. Though James seems to have found the piece very dull, it is not without merit. The action shows how some of the arts and sciences endeavour to enter into unnatural unions. Thus, Poeta seeks to win the hand of Astronomia,

but is finally allied to Historia and promises that his love shall
follow her "more inseparably than the Hexameter the Penta-
meter." Closely related to *Lingua*, to which it contains
direct references, is *Pathomachia or The Battell of Affections*,
published by "a Friend of the deceassed Author," in 1630, and
"written some years since." It deals with the revolt of the
Affections against Love and Hatred, "whom heretofore they
counted their King and Queene." Love and Hatred are
aided by the Virtues, headed by Justice, while the rebels have
the support of the Vices disguised as Affections or Virtues,
and commanded by Pride. Justice, however, unmasks them,
and sends them to confinement, whereupon the Affections
tender their submission and are pardoned. The work is in
prose throughout, and contains interesting passages and many
allusions to recent events, but lacks dramatic movement
and vivacity.

Religious satire is another predominant element in the
later university plays—a foretaste of the dread conflict that
was fast approaching. *Loiola*, by John Hacket, acted at
Trinity before the university on 28 February and before
James on a third visit to Cambridge on 12 March, 1623, is an
entertaining Latin comedy, which attacks impartially Roman
Catholics and Calvinists, the former in the person of Loiola,
"an unscrupulous Jesuit," the latter in that of Martinus, a
canting elder of Amsterdam, where the scene is laid. To the
same year belongs the semi-allegorical *Fucus Histriomastix*,
wherein the title *rôle*, that of a hypocritical puritan minister,
was played by Robert Ward of Queens' college, who was
probably the author of the piece. Fucus, who hates all plays
and amusements, seeks to prevent the marriage of Philomathes
and Comoedia, otherwise, the production of an academic
comedy. The arguments he uses are the same as those of
Rainolds in his controversy with Gager, and seem derived from
his book. But his intrigues are foiled, and he also comes off
badly in a feud with the merry-making countryman, Villanus,
who is in love with Ballada, an illegitimate sister of Comoedia.[1]

---

[1] See *Fucus Histriomastix*, edited by Moore Smith, G.C. (1909), introduction
and notes, pp. 98–9. The editor suggests that the play may have been partly
inspired by an attempt, recorded by Chamberlain, to suppress the performance
of *Loiola*.

Another actor in *Fucus* was Peter Hausted, afterwards
fellow of Queens', who, when Charles and Henrietta Maria
visited Cambridge in March, 1632, wrote in their honour the
singular play *The Rival Friends*. This is linked to the comedies
satirising religious hypocrisy by its caustic portraiture of the
wooers of the deformed and foolish Mistress Ursely, whose
hand carries with it an "impropriate parsonage." More
realistically humorous personages are Stipes, the shepherd of
the simoniacal patron, and his wife and daughter, all
genuinely rustic figures without the customary pastoral ve-
neer. From Hausted's preface to the play when it was
published, it is evident that his low-life portraiture had been
adversely criticised as unbefitting the royal presence. But to
modern taste this appeals much more strongly than does the
pseudo-romantic main plot. The two friends, Lucius and
Neander, rivals for the love of Pandora, vie in their readiness
to abdicate in each other's favour, and carry their altruism so
far that the lady gives her affections, at first in pretence,
afterwards in reality, to a third wooer. The popularity,
however, of such fantastic themes was evidenced by the successful production at Trinity, during the same royal visit, of
Thomas Randolph's *The Jealous Lovers*. Randolph, a distinguished *alumnus* of Westminster and Trinity had already
written two short academic "shows," *Aristippus or The
Joviall Philosopher* and *The Conceited Pedler*. *The Jealous
Lovers* was his first complete play, and the rapturous welcome
accorded to it does little credit to either the university or the
court. Randolph's inventiveness and rhetorical fluency cannot redeem the essential falsity of the main plot. Tyndarus
is insanely suspicious of the faithfulness of his beloved Evadne,
and Techmessa similarly mistrusts her devoted Pamphilus.
The two "jealous lovers" go through a mock funeral (which
gives occasion for an imitation of the gravedigger's scene in
Hamlet) as a final test of the constancy of the seemingly bereft
pair. But, after this ordeal has proved their loyalty unswerv-
ing, Hymen forbids the proposed unions, and it transpires
that Tyndarus is the brother of Evadne, and Techmessa the
sister of Pamphilus. Interwoven with these pseudo-romantic
episodes is an underplot of gross humour.

The royal pair, accompanied by their nephews, the palatine

princes, paid a second visit to Oxford in August, 1636, when
the last important series of academic plays was produced in
their honour. William Strode, public orator, welcomed the
king to Christ Church with a speech, and with an allegorical
drama, *The Floating Island*, which was staged with great
elaboration, and furnished with music by Henry Lawes. The
title and general conception of the work in which the island
represents the human mind afloat on the sea of the passions,
was, doubtless, suggested by Phineas Fletcher's *The Purple
Island or The Isle of Man*, published at Cambridge in 1633.
But Strode develops the theme on lines of his own, and with
the added spice of political and religious satire. A conspiracy
is formed by Audax, Irato and others against the rule of king
Prudentius and his counsellor, Intellectus Agens. Prudentius
resigns his crown, and Fancy is proclaimed queen, her only
law being "that each man use his proper humour, be it vice
or virtue." Discord and tumult are the result, and Prudentius is finally implored to resume the crown, after each of
the plotters has declined it in turn. The implied lesson on the
evil results of rebellion, and the castigation of Prynne, in the
person of Melancholico, a play-hating puritan, helped to
recommend the play to the royal favour. Equally successful
were the two dramas produced on the following day. One of
these, *Love's Hospitall*, by George Wilde, fellow of St. John's,
was performed in the afternoon at that college at the expense
of Laud, who, as chancellor of the university, was present to
welcome the king and queen. The piece is an entertaining
comedy of humours, in almost farcical vein, and is in no way
characteristically academic. This is also true of William
Cartwright's *The Royall Slave*,[1] acted in the evening at Christ
Church. An Ephesian captive, Cratander, in accordance
with an old custom among the Persians is granted for three
days before his execution the full insignia and privileges of
kingship. During this period, he displays such nobility of soul
that heaven intervenes in his favour, and he is spared to
become the wearer of a real crown. This theme is handled
by Cartwright with genuine rhetorical effectiveness, and his
drama was furnished with special scenic effects by Inigo Jones
and incidental music by Lawes. So delighted was the queen

[1] See, as to Cartwright's plays, *ante*, Chap. IX.

with the performance that she afterwards borrowed the costumes and scenery for a repetition of the play by her own company at Hampton court.

The academic stage was to number yet one more illustrious recruit in Cowley, whose *Naufragium Joculare*, based on classical sources, was acted at Trinity college, Cambridge, in 1638, and was followed in 1642 by his satirical comedy. *The Guardian*, remodelled after the Restoration into *Cutter of Coleman Street*. But the royal visit to Oxford in 1636 marks the close of these elaborate university displays, which had begun with Elizabeth's coming to Cambridge in 1564. Even in the traditionally loyal community on the banks of the Isis, there were ominous symptoms of the rapidly growing resentment against the autocratic rule of Charles and Laud. As the king and queen rode away from Christ Church, the streets, according to custom, were lined with "Scholers of all degrees," but "neither they nor the citizens made any expression of joy, nor uttered, as the manner is, *Vivat Rex*." When Oxford, some seven years later, again opened its gates to Charles, it was not to entertain him with "masques and triumphs," but to afford him shelter in his stern conflict with his parliamentary foes.

The civil war and the commonwealth mark a period of deep cleavage in English stage history. With the Restoration, came new men and new methods, and a forgetfulness of all but the greatest dramatists of "the former age." It was virtually the work of the nineteenth century to rediscover the lesser Elizabethan writers for the popular stage. The university drama, bilingual in utterance, and with its memorials not easy of access, has had to wait for yet tardier recognition. It had, of course, patent faults. It produced much that was artificial, amateurish and unduly imitative, and its moral standard was as unexacting as that of the London theatre of the day. But it had behind it truly formative influences, in the renascence ardour for classical lore and delight in pageantry, in the gownsmen's haughty resentment of the buffets of fortune to which they were exposed, and in the traditional hostility between scholars and townsmen by Isis and by Cam. Hence sprang that special type of Aristophanic comedy, unique in this period of the drama, represented by *Pedantius* and *Igno-ramus*, *Club Law* and the *Parnassus* trilogy. And, in addition to these distinctively topical university plays, we owe to the academic stage a number of dramas moulded and coloured by the peculiar conditions of their origin. Such are the semi-Senecan plays on religious, historical and mythological sub-jects, like *Archipropheta*, *Richardus Tertius* and *Ulysses Redux;* comedies like *Laelia* and *Hymenaeus;* allegorical pieces like *Lingua*, *Fucus* and *The Floating Island;* pastorals like *The Queenes Arcadia* and *Sicelides*. In these and kindred pro-ductions, noted in this chapter or merely recorded as "comedy" or "tragedy" in college account-books, the university human-ists preserved elements of classic and neo-classic culture which would otherwise have been almost entirely lost to the stage. From Oxford and Cambridge, these influences permeated to the capital. For, sharp as in general was the division, social and intellectual, between academic and professional play-wrights, the latter and larger class was constantly being recruited from graduates who had gained their earliest dra-matic experience as spectators, actors, or, in some cases, authors of college "shows." The royal visits to the univer-sities helped further to extend the range of influence of the amateur stage. And they did something more. Under the personal rule of the Tudors and Stewarts, the centre of national life was not fixed in Westminster, as at present; it moved with the movements of the sovereign. And thus, the university plays, as the principal magnet which drew Elizabeth, James and Charles with their courts to Oxford and Cambridge, per-formed a more important function than has been usually recognised. They helped materially for nearly a hundred years to keep the two seats of learning in contact with the throne, from which radiated, for good and for ill, the dominat-ing forces of the age.

CHAPTER XIII

Masque and Pastoral

THE Elizabethan drama, being without scenery and elaborate stage apparatus, made its appeal to the mind rather than to the eye, and used language as the main instrument by which the imagination of its audience was aroused and satisfied. This familiar fact goes far to explain the essentially intellectual character of the Elizabethan drama, and the wonderful literary power of the great dramatists. But we should misinterpret the facts very seriously if we allowed ourselves to suppose that the Elizabethan age was indifferent to the appeal of the eye, or to imagine that, because the Elizabethan playgoer was without the elaborate scenery and staging of the modern theatre, he was disdainful of spectacle, and unwilling to spend time and money on gorgeous shows in which the master art of pageantry combined music, singing, painting, dancing and architecture in united effort to charm and delight his senses.

The Elizabethan, for all his intellectual energy, was intensely sensuous. In this respect, he represents the end of the Middle Ages rather than the beginning of modern times. We cannot here consider the meaning of that reaction against pageantry which was an important part of puritanism, but we may note that the modern student does not see the Elizabethan age as it saw itself; for he overlooks as childish those things which it most cared for. The drama meant, broadly, the introduction into popular entertainment of a new intellectual element, which gradually discredited pageantry, so that it ceased to be the art of the educated and refined. But, all through the Elizabethan age and until the closing of the theatres in 1642, masque and pageantry held their place in

the public eye, and in the public interest, as the most important
and honourable and magnificent of the arts. The masque at
court and among the nobility, and the pageant among the
citizens, were practised with an energy that, for the time being,
made them the most obvious, if not the most characteristic,
of the national activities, the means by which corporate and
national feeling most readily expressed itself. This old world
splendour of masque and pageant has, for the most part,
perished. Neither antiquarian researches nor modern adaptations can make it live again, but, before it died, the intellectual
power of the new dramatic art came to the rescue and infused
into the Elizabethan masque a literary element, which has
been a preservative against decay. The leading dramatists
were pressed into the service of masque and pageant, and
contributed an element to the spectacle which, in many cases,
has survived. The words supplied to pageants and masques
by Munday and Middleton, by Campion, Chapman, Beaumont and Brown and, above all, by Jonson, form a small, but
very interesting, appendix to the many volumes of the drama.
The extant masques have considerable literary merits, and
they lead on to Milton's *Comus*, in which masque expands
into pastoral: with pastoral, generally, they have an important
connection. But, in studying masques as a literary form, we
have to bear in mind that we are not dealing with essential
masque. Even Ben Jonson's words are not much more than
the stick of the rocket after the firework has flamed and faded.
Essential masque was the appeal of the moment to the eye and
the ear, the blaze of colour and light, the mist of perfume, the
succession of rapidly changing scenes and tableaux, crowded
with wonderful and beautiful figures. All the gods of Olympus,
all the monsters of Tartarus, all the heroes of history, all the
ladies of romance, the fauns, the satyrs, the fairies, the witches
—all these were presented to the eye, while every kind of
musical instrument charmed the ear, and eye and ear together
were delighted by an elaboration of dance and measured
motion which has never been known since. We have put
away these childish things: but our maturity has elaborated
no art equally joyous and whole-hearted. The actual remains
of the masque with the careful description of the scenes,
written, afterwards, in cold blood by the deviser, even though

that deviser were Jonson himself, are but broken meats of a banquet that is over.

The curious modern reaches a direct and adequate conception of the vanished splendour and joy, and is enabled to comprehend clearly the medieval instinct, only when the medieval passion for masque and pageant receives imaginative expression in the work of a great descriptive poet. Such a poet there was, but he was not a dramatist. Spenser came before the drama. The masque was not drama; in many respects, it was the antithesis of drama. Dramatists who wrote while the masque was still alive often, in some metaphor or description, thrill us with a touch of its glamour. Shakespeare, for instance, regards the masque as a symbol of the evanescent. This world and all its inhabitants

> shall dissolve
> And, like this insubstantial pageant faded,
> Leave not a rack behind.

The words express negatively the delight of the spectator in the show by exhibiting his dismay that it must stop—"Our revels now are ended." But we require a positive description, in which the masque is not what it must be to the dramatist, unreal and unsatisfying; rather, on the contrary, the expression of life's wonder and joy. This positive description is given us with extraordinary power and fulness in Spenser's *Faerie Queene*, especially in the first three books, which were published in 1590, before English drama had developed its strength.

But, before we touch upon the relation of Spenser's art to the masque, we must attempt to summarise the history of masque and pageant before his time. The masque, like the drama, runs back into remote antiquity, and we must make an effort to conceive of masque as it was practised in England during the fifteenth and sixteenth centuries, if we are to understand clearly what a masque was, and what modifications it underwent while, in Ben Jonson's hands, it was the main amusement of the English court and nobility. Out of numerous accounts of masques that have come down to us, we may take two as typical of the kind of entertainments which, by their combination, finally produced the true masque. For the first, we will go back to the fourteenth century.

Edward III died on 2 January, 1377. On the second of February following, being Candlemas day, "the Commons of London made great sporte and solemnity" in honour of his successor, prince Richard, who was lodged with his mother and the leading nobles of the realm at the palace in the royal manor of Kennington, which had been a favourite residence of the Black prince. "At night and in the night," a cavalcade of 130 men "disguizedly aparailed and well mounted on horsebacke to goe on mumming," rode "from Newgate through Cheape" over London Bridge to Kennington. They went "with great noyse of minstralsye, trumpets, cornets and shawmes, and great plenty of waxe torches lighted." First came 48 esquires, two and two, "in cotes and clokes of red say or sendall, and their faces covered with vizards well and handsomely made"; next followed 48 knights, "well arayed after the same maner"; then a single figure, "as he had bene an emperor"; then another single figure, "as a pope"; after him, 24 "arayed like Cardinals"; and, last, 8 or 10 "with black vizardes like devils, nothing amiable, seeming like legates." On reaching the palace, all alighted and entered the hall, into which presently came the prince, his mother and the leading nobles, whom "the said mummers saluted"; the mummers then proceeded to play with a pair of prepared dice with the prince and other gentry for valuable gifts. When the gifts had all been won, "the prince and the lordes danced on the one side and the mummers on the other a great while," and then they drank and took their leave and departed to London.

In this account, we have what is probably the oldest and simplest form of what is afterwards the masque.[1] It is called "a mumming," and the performers are "mummers." The word means that the disguised performers say nothing that would betray their identity. They dice in silence, using only dumb show where they wish to signify their meaning. But they are all disguised with vizards, the old word for mask; they are accompanied by musicians; they dance together among themselves when their "mumming" business is over and torch-bearers conduct them on their way. Simple as their scheme was, the entry of masked mummers with blare of trumpets and

---

[1] We shall use this spelling for the spectacle, and "mask" for a vizard.

blaze of torches into the great banqueting hall must have been highly picturesque. The impressiveness of the moment is splendidly given by the dramatist:

> Night, like a masque, is entered heaven's great hall,
> With thousand torches ushering the way![2]

In this particular "mumming," the vizarded procession represented the emperor and pope as coming with attendant knights and cardinals to greet the uncrowned king. When a "mumming" was regarded from the point of view of the dress assumed by the "mummers," it was called a "disguising"; and, by the sixteenth century, this name quite superseded the other, as, in the seventeenth century, it was itself superseded by "masque"; so that Ben Jonson, in 1622, makes Notch aver, "Disguise was the old English word for a masque, Sir"; to which the groom of the revels answers, "There is no such word in the office now, I assure you, Sir; I have served here, man and boy, a prenticeship or twain, and I should know."[2]

"Mumming" came to be applied particularly to the custom, practised usually at Christmas time, of going round in masking habit from house to house and gaming with dice; the game itself was called "mumchance." There are many allusions to it in the Elizabethan dramatists. Finally, we may notice in this example of a disguising, the "8 or 10 with black vizardes, like devils, nothing amiable"; these are the germ of the Jonsonian antimasque.

For our second typical instance, let us go to the reign of Henry VII in the year 1501. The marriage of prince Arthur to Katharine of Arragon was celebrated in London with great magnificence. The walls of Westminster hall were "richly hanged with pleasant clothes of arras," and, in the upper end, had "a Royall and great Cupboard" erected, upon which was displayed a "goodly and rich treasure of plate." The king and queen took their seats "under their Clothes of Estate," and all the nobility "were ordered in their Roomes." To this great assembly entered a "most goodly and pleasant disguising convayed and shewed in pageantes proper and subtile": of

---

[1] *The Insatiate Countesse*, at end.   [2] *The Masque of Augures.*

which "the first was a Castle right cunningly devised sett uppon certaine wheeles and drawne into the said great hall of fower great beastes with chaines of gold." The beasts were two lions, a hart and an ibex, personated, each one of them, by two men. In the castle were "disguised VIII goodly and fresh ladyes looking out of the windowes of the same," and, in the turrets, "fowre children singing most sweetly and harmoniously." The castle was drawn into the hall and up to the king's state,[1] and then set on one side to allow of the entry of a second car, this time "a shippe," having "her mastes toppes sayles her tackling and all other apperteynances necessary unto a seemely vessel as though it had been sayling." The ship cast anchor in front of the king, next the castle. On board the ship was a lady, in apparel like to the princess of Spain. Hope and Desire go from the ship to the castle as ambassadors from the knights of the mount of Love; but the ladies in the castle will have nothing to say to the knights. "Incontinent came in the third Pageant," a mountain, with eight knights upon it to whom the ambassadors recounted their ill-success with the ladies. Thereupon, the knights make a great show of assaulting the castle, and the ladies surrender. The cars are wheeled back, and the knights and ladies "daunced together divers and many goodly dances." The cars then came back for the masquers and took them away; after which, prince Arthur and his bride and other distinguished people in the audience danced, including young prince Henry and his sister Margaret. This "disguising" was succeeded on the following evenings by three others, nearly as elaborate as the first. The whole display makes it quite clear that the early sixteenth century had not much to learn from the early seventeenth. The splendour of these shows reached a high water mark in the reign of Henry VIII, and then, again, in the reign of James I, when the mechanical and artistic genius of Inigo Jones introduced new contrivances and a more elaborate arrangement of scenery, suppressing almost entirely the processional character of the masque and the early car.

Our second example of a masque has added to the first the

---

[1] The royal seat.

important item of the pageant or car. This, of course, suggests a connection between the "disguising" and the medieval miracle-plays, which were performed on the movable waggon called a pageant. It is easy to see how the grandeur of the cavalcade would be increased if the emperor and pope were put in cars. In the British Museum, there is a design by Albert Dürer, dated 1522, of a triumphal car for Maximilian, which may serve as an illustration of the way in which a car would become a "pageant"—an elaborate structure to hold masquers. This pageant, as the above example shows, is capable of very varied developments. But, as the car becomes more elaborate, it cannot easily form part of a long procession; to draw it the length of the hall taxes the ingenuity of the carpenters; and, finally, it becomes stationary, suggesting something approximating to the modern stage at one end of the hall. The car, moreover, when it is a ship or a lanthorn or a "herbour," requires some explanation; and an exposition of the device of the car is added to the original dance of the masquers. This is the masque in its simplest outline—certain men or women disguised, who arrive in some setting which corresponds to their dress, and which has to be explained before they dance their measures; they retire as they came.

The disguisings had an extraordinary vogue under Henry VIII, and they found a historian whose prose descriptions have hardly received the attention which their great merit deserves. Edward Hall was a lawyer and a politician. His parents were in sympathy with advanced reformers. He affords, therefore, a remarkable instance of the passion for pageant displaying itself in a hard-headed political trimmer, bred up in a sober and serious middle-class family. Pageant was Hall's one passion. His English style takes on a new distinction when he begins to describe the splendid succession of festivities which distinguished the reign of Henry VIII. His masterpiece is, perhaps, his account of the Field of the Cloth of Gold; but, everywhere, thanks to his enthusiasm, his accounts of masques and entertainments are gorgeously coloured and wonderfully full of movement.

He is the writer who notes the coming of the word "masque." On the evening of Epiphany, 1512, the kyng with a XI other wer disguised, after the maner of Italie, called a maske, a thyng not seen afore in Englande; thei were appareled in garmentes long and brode, wrought all with gold, with visers and cappes of gold, *and* after the banket doen, these Maskers came in, with sixe gentlemen disguised in silke, bearing staffe torches, and desired the ladies to daunce, some were content, and some that knewe the fashion of it refused, because it was not a thyng commonly seen. And after thei daunced, and commoned together as the fashion of the Maske[1] is, thei toke their leave and departed, and so did the Quene and all the ladies.[2]

This passage raises problems which are still under discussion. What was the "thyng not seen afore in Englande?" What was the "thyng not commonly seen," which made some of the ladies refuse to dance? In short, what was the difference between the "disguising," familiar in England for centuries, and this innovation "after the maner of Italie, called a maske"? The probable answer is that there was a difference in dress which was connected with a difference in procedure. The masquers not only danced with one another but, after their own dance, they chose partners among the spectators. This introduced into the masque a new element of courtship and intrigue. For this device to maintain its proper piquancy, the disguise of the masquer must be complete; his costume must, like a domino, conceal any peculiarities of mien and shape which might betray him if he wore a more closely-fitting disguise. Whether this sufficiently explains Hall's language must be considered a question still under discussion; but two points are clear. There is a common conviction, both in France and England, that, in some of its characteristic aspects, the masque was Italian. Ronsard says that "masquerade" came from the Italians, and mentions "*ses vestemens, ses mœurs et ses façons*," as the things which were copied. Reyher, after quoting Ronsard, suggests that this borrowing from Italy took place *au moment des expéditions françaises de la fin du XVe et du début du XVIe siècle*. In our own literature, Marlowe's "I 'll have Italian maskes by night"[3] is familiar. But, secondly, the motive of intrigue, whatever its derivation, was a most

---

[1] The edition of 1550 reads "Masques."

[2] Hall (1548), f. 16r°. For the views that have been expressed on the passage, consult Reyher's first appendix, in *Les Masques Anglais*.

[3] *Edward II*, act 1, sc. 1.

important addition to the masque's attractiveness. Clearly,
it was much appreciated by Henry VIII. It is a breath of
natural drama introduced into what is essentially undramatic.
Because it is natural drama, it is often the means by which the
masque gets a place in dramatic literature. The masque in
Love's Labour's Lost[1] is delightfully dramatic, and it is an
excellent comment, so far as it applies, on the passage in Hall.
It is in a masque that Romeo loses his heart to Juliet;[2] and,
more interesting still, Henry VIII conceives his passion for
Anne Boleyn, in the same way, in the masque of the first act
of the play. Many other instances[3] occur in the dramatists,
where this dramatic moment in the masque is utilised. But,
in the masque itself, this item remains an episode upon which
the deviser of the masque never lays his hands; in Henry VIII's
reign, the undramatic character of the masque shows no sign of
changing.

When we reach the reign of Elizabeth, Spenser's poetry,
even more adequately than Hall's prose, reflects and revives
the glory of the medieval masque and pageant. His genius, in
some of its most characteristic aspects, was exactly fitted to
describe and appreciate the world just beyond the real world
with which the masque dealt. The masque of the Seven Deadly
Sins[4] and the masque of Cupid[5] are magnificent examples of
the processional masque. The former shows that the antimasque is implicit in the masque from the beginning. The
house of Temperance and the attack upon it[6] recall the knights'
onslaught on the castle of the ladies described above. Such
famous descriptions as the cave of Mammon[7] and the bower
of Bliss[8] are like the set pieces which Inigo Jones tried to make
real to the eye when the masque became a fixture at the end
of the great hall. There are cantos in The Faerie Queene in
which we seem in spirit to follow the procession until it reaches
the hall where the full device is displayed before us in all its
intricacy. Spenser's abstractions, Coelia, Fidelia, Speranza,

---

[1] Act v, sc. 2.   [2] Act i, sc. 5.
[3] Reyher gives a list of plays with masques inserted; Les Masques Anglais,
p. 497.
[4] Bk. i, canto iv.   [5] Bk. iii, canto xii.
[6] Bk. ii, cantos ix. and xi.   [7] Bk. ii. canto vii.
[8] Bk. ii, canto xii.

Charissa, the porter Humiltá of the house of Holiness[1] and scores of others, are just such as meet us in masques; but a line of description like "bitter Penaunce with an yron whip," calls up the figure before us more effectually than Jonson's most exact prose; and Spenser's poem abounds in similar vivid lines and stanzas. The poem, again, like almost every masque, is an elaborate compliment. Its relation to Elizabeth is precisely that of Jonson's masques to James or Charles. Spenser's poem, it should be remembered, greatly influenced Ben Jonson and other writers of masque—Ben Jonson in especial.

Elizabeth's frugality prevented the masque from developing in her reign. It was in frequent use, but the queen had not the special taste for it which made it prominent as an amusement of the aristocracy in the courts of Henry VIII and James I. But "entertainments," during the queen's numerous progresses, were plentifully produced. The entertainment was the masque out-of-doors, and consisted of some kind of welcoming device or function arranged for greeting the queen on her arrival, or "discovered" afterwards, as she was conducted round gardens and park. The entertainment had more dramatic possibilities in it than the masque, because it depended less upon scenery, but the English climate kept it always short and slight. One, by Sir Philip Sidney, of considerable merit, has survived—*The May Lady*,[2] presented in May, 1578, when the queen visited his uncle, the earl of Leicester, at Wanstead. Jonson's reverence for Sidney makes it likely that he did not overlook Sidney's work when he composed the entertainments which were the beginning of his masque work. But it seems more probable that *The May Lady* guided Jonson's views on pastoral than that it influenced his conception of masque, and it remains by itself as a short out-of-doors scene of pastoral comedy, not without influence upon Shakespeare's early comedy. The schoolmaster, master Rombus, is, obviously, an ancestor of Holofernes, and the play's likeness to masque lies in its complimentary character. Some of Lyly's plays, also, have affinities with the masque. They are elaborate compliments; their ideas are not concerned with the real world of men and women;

---

[1] Bk. I, canto x.   [2] Called, also, *The Lady of the May*.

their characters are mythological.[1] But perhaps their most important connection with the masque is their influence upon Jonson's *Cynthia's Revels*.[2] This play magnifies at all points Lyly's limited strength to such a degree that the reader may easily fail to notice its debt to Lyly. But its connection with Jonson's masques is obvious. In *Cynthia's Revels*, a great realist, the author of *Bartholomew Fayre*, succeeds in making us understand how he came to write masques. We see his mind becoming absorbed in the particular art and method of which the masque was an expression.

But, before we pass to Jonson's masques, one Elizabethan play must be mentioned which was neither a masque, nor a pastoral, nor a drama, but partook of the character of all three. It is, perhaps, the most elaborate and beautiful entertainment extant, and the brilliance of its total effect makes us regret that such a delightful type of renascence art did not receive fuller development. Peele's *Araygnement of Paris* comes before the development of the masque, as Milton's *Comus* comes after it, to suggest to us that in the method of the out-of-door entertainment or pastoral there is inherent a truer breath of poetry than is to be found in that of the indoor masque, in which scenery and carpentry and music and dance were always tending to smother and suppress the poetical soul.[3]

The first court masque after king James's accession was produced on 8 January, 1604, at Hampton court, because plague was prevalent in London. It was *The Vision of the Twelve Goddesses*, in which the masquers were queen Anne herself and eleven of her ladies. By the recommendation of Lucy countess of Bedford, Daniel was chosen to design and write the masque. An indiscreet printer presumptuously brought out an unauthorised account, and this obliged Daniel in self-defence to print a description "of the whole form thereof in all points as it was then performed by a most magnificent Queen, whose heroical spirit and bounty only gave it so fair an execution as it had." Daniel thinks that "these ornaments and delights of peace" deserve to be remembered; and,

---

[1] See Vol. V, Chap. VI.   [2] Cf. *ante*, Chap. I, p. 20.

[3] As to *The Araygnement of Paris*, see Vol. V, Chap. VI, and cf. Chap. XI of the present volume.

therefore, he relates how he devised his twelve goddesses to represent the blessings enjoyed by the realm under king James. Night ascends from below and awakes Somnus, who is sleeping in his cave, that he may conjure up the visions which are to delight and entertain the spectators. By the waving of the white horny wand of Somnus, the spectators are enbled to see the temple of Peace, elaborately constructed, where a sibyl stands as priestess,

> Preparing reverent rites with holy hand.

To her, comes Iris from a mountain raised at the lower end of the hall, to announce the coming of a "celestial presence of Goddesses," who are leaving their ancient haunts to visit Britain, "the land of civil music and of rest." Iris hands Sybilla a "prospective" through which to view the goddesses: and Sybilla proceeds to describe all the twelve, one after the other, in four-lined stanzas. Of these, that descriptive of Flora is best:

> Then cheerful Flora all adorned with flowers,
> Who clothes the earth with beauty and delight
> In thousand Sunday suits, whilst shining hours
> Will scarce afford a darkness to the night.

The stanzas read like faint echoes of Tennyson's descriptions in his *Dream of fair Women*, except that the last line is not shortened. After being thus described, the goddesses descend from the mountain, in threes, ushered by the three graces, with their torchbearers, also in threes, separating them. As they come down, "the cornets sitting in the concaves of the Mountain, and seen but to their breasts; in the habit of Satyrs, sound a stately march." This is the entry of the masquers. The company halt before the temple, and "the consort music begins"—the musicians being concealed in the cupola of the temple. Meanwhile, the goddesses, one after another, ascended to the temple and delivered their presents to Sybilla, while the graces sang. Then came the dance of the masquers, to the music of viols and lutes placed on one side of the hall. It was performed "with great majesty and art, consisting of divers strains framed into motions circular, square, triangular, with other proportions exceeding rare and full of variety." This ended, the graces sang again, in order to rest the ladies; after which, the masquing ladies "prepared to take out the Lords to dance; with whom they performed certain measures, galliards and corantos." Iris then came now to say that the deities must return, and, after her speech,

they fell to a short departing dance and so ascended the Mountain, whilst the cornets taking their notes from the ceasing of the music below, sounded another delightful march.

From this description, we can gather what the masque was in its outward features. A band of masquers assume an impressive and magnificent disguise. Some sort of explanation must be given of the nature and meaning of the disguise culminating in the entry of the masquers, which should be as sudden and impressive as possible. After the entry, the main or chief dance is performed by the masquers alone. Then, the masquers "take out" partners from among the spectators—lords if the masquers are ladies, but, more usually, ladies, the masquers being lords. With these partners, slow dances, called by Daniel "certain measures," are performed; and then quick dances—"galliards and corantos." It is to these quick dances that the title "the revels" is properly and strictly given.[1] After the revels, the masquers make their exit, usually with some preliminary dance by themselves. In Daniel's account of his masque, we see clearly how large a part of the interest was absorbed by spectacle, music and dance. The poet has his opportunity only when Sybilla pretends that she can see through her prospective or spy glass the masquers who are presently to march in, and describes them that they may be understood when they appear. The poetry for which occasion is thus found has some touch of the quiet grace of Daniel's best work, and the pure English of his prose and poetry alike is delightful to read. But this masque would seem to have survived in order to mark Ben Jonson's superiority. Daniel's contemplative temperament is contented to keep the masque undramatic, without either briskness or fire,

---

[1] The derivation of the word, according to Skeat, is neither from *réveiller*, to awaken, nor from *rêver*, to dream, but from O. F. *revel*, meaning rebellion, disorder, sport, and coming from Latin *rebellare*, to rebel.

and undifferentiated, without any contrast of its parts. In other words he does not in the least realise the possibilities of the art he is practising. By his own rashness in the publication of *Philotas*,[1] he lost favour at court, and the queen's next masque was written by Jonson.

But, before we consider this, we must examine some slighter pieces by Jonson, which preceded his first court masque.[2] In June, 1603, the queen and prince Henry, when they first came into the kingdom, were received by Sir Robert Spencer at Althorpe, and Jonson composed the entertainment[3] which welcomed them. As the queen came through the park, certain cornets sounded, whereupon a satyr "advanced his head above the top of the wood," wondering at the solemnities and, after a short strain on his pipe, jumped down to look close at the queen and prince, declaring,

> That is Cyparissus' face!
> And the dame hath Syrinx' grace!
> O that Pan were now in place—
> Sure they are of heavenly race.

He runs off in a fit of shyness and "to the sound of excellent soft music," a bevy of fairies come tripping up the lawn attending on Mab their queen. The fairies dance in a ring, and queen Mab begins to welcome queen Anne, when the satyr peeps out of the bush again and interrupts:

> Trust her not, you bonnibell,
> She will forty leasings tell;
> I do know her pranks right well.

The fairies try to catch the satyr, while he runs about singing in riming eight-syllabled couplets a graphic account of Mab's traditional pranks. Finally, he is caught and well pinched, but escapes again into his bush. Then the style changes from gay to stately, while a song of welcome is sung to Oriana— *quasi Oriens Anna*, Jonson explains in a note; this song is not quite the poet's best. But it is in such a setting as this

---

[1] As to the supposed reference in *Philotas* to Essex's plot, cf. Vol. V, Chap. XIV, p. 414, and see *Ward*, vol. II, p. 619.

[2] For some general observations on Jonson's masques, cf. *ante*, Chap. I, p. 13.

[3] Gifford calls it *The Satyr*.

that Jonson produces exquisite lyrics. Suddenly, he heightens his style, while the movement and merriment cease, and, for a moment, all ears listen. After the song, Mab presents the queen with a jewel, the fairies "hop away in a fantastic dance," and the satyr runs out again with his saucy octosyllables. After some references to Sir Robert Spencer, he fetches out the eldest son, attired and appointed like a huntsman, who is presented to the service of the prince along with some more gifts:

> The bow was Phoebe's, and the horn
> By Orion often worn;
> The dog of Sparta breed, and good,
> As can RING within a WOOD;
> Thence his name is: you shall try
> How he hunteth instantly.

At this, the whole wood resounded with the noise of cornets, horns and other hunting music, and a brace of choice deer were driven up and "fortunately killed, as they were meant to be, even in the sight of her majesty."

Nothing could be better in its kind than this vivacious entertainment. It is not too long; it is full of movement, being broken up into dialogue, song and speeches, all written in easy rimes. The satyr is own brother to Fletcher's satyr in *The Faithfull Shepheardesse*. Jonson expands him into a charming antimasque in *Oberon the Fairy Prince*.

It is surprising to find Jonson, who often gives us too much, and sows with the whole sack, restraining his hand thus artfully. It would seem as if he were able to put off his satiric and moralising instincts only when he conceives himself to be called upon for mere amusement. Perhaps, the awe of royalty natural to an Elizabethan held him in. Next year, on 1 May, 1604, he composed a second entertainment,[1] when the king and queen visited Sir William Cornwallis at Highgate. It is not so happy as the first; but it is quite new in its invention. The Penates or household gods, correctly attired, receive the king at the porch, addressing him in eight five-lined stanzas. The Penates lead the royal party into the house, where Mercury receives them in a prose speech which has more breath of

[1] Called, by Gifford, *The Penates*.

poetry in it than the stanzas. Mercury takes them through the house into the garden, where are various goddesses— Maia, Aurora, Flora and others. Three of the goddesses, when Mercury's speech is ended, sing a three-part song, beginning, "See, see, O see, who here is come a maying." Maia then recites some graceful octosyllabic verses of welcome. This is the morning's entertainment. After dinner, the king and queen are, once more, taken into the garden, when Mercury again accosts them. He explains that "a certain son of mine, whom the Arcadians call a god, howsoever the rest of the world receive him," is at hand: "yonder he keeps, and with him the wood nymphs." This is Pan. Mercury apologises for Pan's uncouth appearance and behaviour, but asks the royal guests to accept from him a cup of "a lusty liquor, that hath a present virtue to expel sadness," and is flowing from the fountain of Bacchus in the middle of the lawn. Pan then accosts the king, and, in rollicking verses, hopes he will let a god be his skinker.[1] When the king has drunk, the lords and ladies are served. A last word of apology for Pan's familiarities follows from Mercury, "and thus it ended." The fancy of all this is sprightly and the execution adequate. What is especially to be noticed is Jonson's effort to get some contrast into his show, first, by means of the satyr, and, secondly, of Pan. The entertainment is not to be mere spectacle; the tableaux are not to be merely explained; they explain themselves. A breath of the drama gives them life. The entertainment lent itself to this semi-dramatic treatment more readily than the masque, which was a lengthy evening function in a large hall.

But Ben Jonson, having written these two entertainments, was less likely to let his masque be mere spectacle enlivened only by tedious description. He was commanded to supply queen Anne's second masque, *The Masque of Blacknesse*, "personated at the Court at Whitehall on the Twelfth-Night, 1605," in which, again, the queen and her ladies were the masquers. It lacks the light touch of the two entertainments; it is a first attempt, and, evidently, the effort to devise an ingenious, splendid and impressive spectacle has made too absorbing a demand on Jonson's attention. How ingenious ·

---

[1] Drawer of wine or ale.

this spectacle was may appear from a short summary of Jonson's graphic description. Oceanus, presented in human form, the colour of his flesh blue, and Niger, in form and colour of an Aethiop, riding on two great sea-horses, with attendant tritons and sea-maidens, seem to advance out of the sea, which is artfully made to shoot forth as if it flowed to the land. This cavalcade "induces" the masquers, who are twelve nymphs, negroes and daughters of Niger, attended by twelve Oceaniae, who are their lightbearers. The masquers are all placed in "a great concave Shell, like mother of pearl, curiously made to move on those waters and rise with the billow"; the torch-bearing Oceaniae are on the backs of "six huge sea-monsters," disposed round the great shell. Cunningly placed lights raise the whole elaborate show to the highest point of brilliance. The "lines of prospective" of this show were planned with exact reference to the state at the upper end of the hall. "So much for the bodily part which was of master Inigo Jones's design and act." When the shell came to a standstill, a triton and two sea-maidens sang a song— a tenor and two trebles. Then, Oceanus enquires of Niger why he is far out of his course here in the west. Niger explains that his daughters, having heard the fable of Phaëton, are discontented with their blackness, and have seen a vision which ordered them to seek a land whose name ends in the syllables "tania." They have tried Mauritania and Lusitania and Aquitania; can Oceanus help them to any other? Oceanus answers that they have arrived at Albion, named after his own son; but, at this point, a vision of the moon, "discovered in the upper part of the house," as a beautiful queen on a throne, makes Niger "interrupt Oceanus with this present passion": "O see, our silver star," he begins. The Aethiopians, of course, worshipped the moon as Aethiopia; and this is Aethiopia herself come to tell them that this is the land they are seeking. It is ruled by a sun

> Whose beams shine day and night and are of force,
> To blanch an Aethiop and revive a corse.

King James is the sun:

> His light sciential is, and, past mere nature,
> Can salve the rude defects of every creature.

Then comes the main dance of the masquers. When it is finished, and the masquers are about "to make choice of their men, one from the sea was heard to call them with this Charm, sung by a tenor voice." The song very aptly bids the sirens of the sea beware of the sirens of the land. After the measures and corantos with the men, which are "the revels," the ladies "were again accited to sea with a song of two trebles whose cadences were iterated by a double echo from several parts of the land." The echo song over, Aethiopia gives a receipt for removing "this veil the sun has cast Above your blood"; and the masquers "in a dance returned to sea where they took their Shell, and with this full song went out."

We have said that this is not one of the best of Jonson's masques. The general conception is richly poetical; but he writes the heroic couplet awkwardly, the rimes are very harsh and the addresses of Oceanus and Niger are stiff. The arrangement of the songs is admirable; but their effect must have depended more upon the music and singing than the words. There is a lack of charm in the workmanship when we compare it with later work, or even with the earlier entertainments; but this makes only more apparent the contrast in method between this masque and Daniel's. The latter, in the main, is a description of the masquers; Jonson perceives the absurdity of describing to the audience what they can see for themselves. Since he has no elaborate description, he must invent some incident, and, accordingly, we have Niger's journey, his colloquy with Oceanus and the appearance of Aethiopia—all ingeniously contrived to compliment king James. For the use of those who did not see the masque, a prose description of the "*landtschape*," the dresses of the masquers and the scenic arrangements—a fine piece of terse English—is prefixed to the actual words; and we are told in a short foreword that "it was her majesty's will to have the masquers blackmoors at first."[1] This curious desire of the queen and her ladies is the starting-point of Jonson's scheme of Niger, whose people "are the blackest nation of the world."[2]

[1] "At first" must not be taken to mean "in the first part of the masque." This would introduce an antimasque too soon; we must paraphrase, "it was originally her majesty's will."

[2] For other sources of Jonson's ideas, see Reyher, p. 161.

There were no court masques in the beginning of 1606 and 1607; but Jonson was a second time requisitioned for the masque of 10 January, 1608. The queen wanted the daughters of Niger again, with "their beauties varied according to promise," and four ladies added to their number. *The Masque of Beauty*, therefore, is a continuation of *The Masque of Blacknesse*. Master Thomas Giles "made the dances," which were exceptionally elaborate, and personated the river Thamesis. The six steps before the throne were occupied by the torchbearers—"a multitude of Cupids, chosen out of the best and most ingenious youth of the Kingdom, noble and others." Here, unconsciously, the device of the antimasque is anticipated. As in some other masques, the torchbearers wear a distinctive dress, which makes them at once a kind of antimasque. Moreover, *The Masque of Beauty*, in itself, is a contrast to *The Masque of Blacknesse*, and their relation must have helped Jonson to reach that theory of the antimasque which is fully developed in his third court masque, *The Masque of Queens*. But, before going on to this, we have to consider two masques written for weddings.

Jonson's share in the solemnities which celebrated the marriage[1] of the earl of Essex, Robert Devereux, and Frances Howard,[2] on 5 January, 1606, was the masque *Hymenaei*, printed with a careful account of the whole arrangement of the dresses and spectacle in the same year. This, therefore, is the first full-grown masque as distinguished from an entertainment which he published. The introductory note shows the high ideals with which Jonson took up the composition of masques. It braced and encouraged his genius to feel that he was producing work to be presented by the highest notabilities of the realm, the queen herself taking the lead.

"It is a noble and just advantage," he says, "that the things subjected to understanding have of those which are objected to sense; that the one sort are but momentary and merely taking; the other impressing and lasting: else the glory of all these solemnies had perished like a blaze, and gone out, in the beholders' eyes:

---

[1] It was dissolved on the ground of nullity, and the lady was married again to the favourite of James, Robert Carr, earl of Somerset.

[2] The earl of Suffolk's second daughter.

so short-lived are the bodies of all things in comparison of their souls."

This consideration has made "royal princes and greatest persons, who are commonly the personators of these actions," not only "studious of riches and magnificence in the outward celebration or shew," but, also,

curious after the most high and hearty inventions to furnish the inward parts, and those grounded upon antiquity and solid learning; which though their voice be taught to sound to present occasions, their sense or doth or should always lay hold on more removed mysteries.

This is an admirable statement of what we find in Jonson's earlier masques.   The splendour and ingenuity of the spectacle set forth some central idea, the characters are taken mainly from classical literature, and the details of their dress and equipment are all minutely accurate—that is to say, Jonson is ready to quote the passage which sanctions his choice.   Six masques—the three already named, the second wedding masque, *The Masque of Queens* and *The Masque of Augures*— are elaborately annotated by him.[1]   In the dedication of *The Masque of Queens* to prince Henry, we are told that the prince[2] asked for this annotating and, accordingly, it is in this instance that Jonson is most copious.   It has, he says, proved "a work of some difficulty to me to retrieve the particular authorities to those things, which I writ out of fulness and memory of my former readings."   We can hardly believe, though Jonson would seem to hint as much, that he composed these masques without a most diligent ransacking of all the classical authors within his reach; but, after making this deduction from his claim, his annotations remain astonishing, and of special and unique interest as an exhibition of the scholarship of an Elizabethan man of letters.   Jonson did nothing carelessly; and these notes set a standard of style and establish annotation as a branch of English literature.   It is hardly necessary to add that they throw a flood of light upon the culture of the time.

[1] He supplied notes, first of all, to his account of the coronation entertainment in London, which he and Dekker devised.

[2] Jonson also mentions the fact in his autograph address to the queen, written in the copy presented to her, now in the British Museum library.

The introduction to *Hymenaei* denounces the folly of those "who squeamishly cry out that all endeavour of learning and sharpness in these transitory devices, is superfluous." This, doubtless, is a gird at Daniel, who, in his *Twelve Goddesses*, had spoken slightingly of "whosoever strives to shew most wit about these punctilios of dreams and shews." Jonson insists that the masque is to draw its types and personages from classical mythology, and considers "a few Italian herbs, picked up and made into a sallad" a meal much too light for a scholar. *Hymenaei* begins with a bridal procession, very carefully arranged according to ancient Roman ritual, and conceived as a sacrifice of the bride and bridegroom to the goddess Juno or Unio. It is ushered in by Hymen, who is said to have been personated by Jonson himself.[1] Hymen, having addressed the royalties seated in the state, "the first masque of eight men," appears out of a microcosm or globe marvellously planned in its movement and adornment. These nobles personate the four Humours, and the four Affections, who propose to disturb the marriage ceremonial; whereupon, Hymen invokes Reason's aid to curb the rudeness of the masquers. They are, therefore, a kind of antimasque. Reason descends from the summit of the globe, and, at his admonition, the Humours and Affections sheathe their swords. Then, the upper part of the scene, "which was all of clouds and made artificially to swell and ride like the rack," began to open. Juno is discovered with eight of her nuptial powers, each bearing one of her surnames, as used by classical writers. The eight nymphs dance out in pairs led by Order, who is Reason's servant. These ladies form the second masque. After dancing alone, they pair with the men masquers, and the whole sixteen dance, "with this song provoked":

> Now, now begin to set
> Your spirits in active heat,
> And since your hands are met,
> Instruct your nimble feet,
> In motions swift and sweet,
> The happy ground to beat.

---

[1] Fleay's conjecture; because Pory, describing the masque, says that "Ben Jonson burned the globe of earth standing behind the altar."

Jonson had prepared an epithalamion of fifteen eight-lined stanzas, admirably translated from Catullus; but "only one staff was sung," the company being exhausted by the length and elaboration of the performance. The poet, however, "sets it down whole" when he prints—"and I do heartily forgive their ignorance whom it chanceth not to please."

While this masque does not reach the highest level of Jonson's achievement, it is yet a beautiful and dignified composition, only less charming than his next marriage masque, produced for the marriage of lord Haddington[1] on 9 February, 1608, at which Venus, instead of Juno, is the presiding goddess. She appears in her chariot at the top of the scene, and, descending on foot with the three graces, declares that Cupid has disappeared and that she must have him cried, "and all his virtues told." The verses in which the three graces "cry" Cupid, "Venus' runaway," are the perfection of grace and lightness: a sprightlier opening to a masque could hardly be imagined. As the verses end, Cupid discovers himself, "attended with twelve boys, most antickly attired, that represented the Sports and pretty Lightnesses, that accompany Love." Cupid gives the order to his "little jocund Sports"—"with your revel fill the room"; whereupon

they fell into a subtle capricious dance to as odd a music, each of them bearing two torches, and nodding with their antic faces, with other variety of ridiculous gesture which gave much occasion of mirth and delight to the spectators.

But these boys are not the masquers. In the forewords of his next masque—*The Masque of Queens*—Jonson calls them "an anti-masque of boys"; but his first conception of them made them a dance of antics, who perform no true measures but a "revel" of "ridiculous gesture." A dance of antics, in which the performers wore absurd or monstrous masks, was not unknown in Elizabeth's time.[2] This, however, means only that Jonson does not reach a full realisation of the antimasque until *The Masque of Queens*. The torch-bearing Cupids of *The Masque of Beauty*, the contrast between this and *The*

---

[1] Called, by Gifford, *The Hue and Cry after Cupid*.

[2] In Munday's *John a Kent and John a Cumber* there is "a merry antique showe, in which four antics dance" (Collier's edition, pp. 31–34).

Masque of Blacknesse, the contrast of the two sets of masquers in the masque *Hymenaei*, and, finally, the twelve boys in antic attire of *The Hue and Cry after Cupid*, are the gradual steps by which the idea of the antimasque was reached in Jonson's mind. After the dance of the twelve boys, Cupid is about to explain what he has been doing when Hymen intervenes and introduces the king to Venus as the modern *pius Aeneas*, relating how the bridegroom of this great wedding has saved his monarch's life,[1] and expatiating upon the virtues of the bride. Venus is further overwhelmed by the appearance of Vulcan, at whose command the red cliff[2] at the end of the hall is cloven apart, revealing the wonderful globe in which are the masquers as the twelve signs of the zodiac. All the twelve are ingeniously explained as

> Sacred powers
> That are presiding at all nuptial hours.

Inasmuch as in the 18th book of the *Iliad*, Vulcan's gifts for Thetis were "twenty tripods or stools with golden wheels to move of themselves miraculously," Jonson, regarding this passage "a most elegant place and worthy the tenth reading," makes the dances of the masquers signify the magic stools of Vulcan. Two Cyclopes, as the masquers danced, "beat a time to them with their hammers." An epithalamion of seven verses comes at the end; and, this time, the poet insured the recitation of the whole of it by the device of putting four dances by his masquers "full of elegancy and curious device" between the verses. "The two latter dances were made by Master Thomas Giles, the two first by Master Hier. Herne," who were the Cyclopes. "The tunes were Master Alphonso Ferrabosco's. The device and act of the scene Master Inigo Jones's." The epithalamion is a noble lyric, which prepares our ears for the more wonderful music of Milton. Again and again, in the verse of Jonson's masques, we find workmanship afterwards elaborated and improved upon by Milton, between whom and the Elizabethans Jonson is the true link. His ardour and idealism prepare us for the deeper spiritual sublimity of the puritan poet. These two wedding masques have a

---

[1] At the time of the Gowrie conspiracy.

[2] The bride was lady Elizabeth Radcliffe, daughter of the earl of Sussex.

special charm of their own, and the second of them is the finest of its kind in the language.

We come now to *The Masque of Queens*—the third masque written for queen Anne—in which, as we have said, the idea of the antimasque is fully reached by Jonson and definitely stated by him in his commentary.   It was presented at Whitehall on 2 February, 1609, and immediately printed by prince Henry's command.   The dedication to the prince is worthy of comparison with the dedication, two years earlier, of *Volpone* to the universities.   The same lofty note is struck; "poetry, my lord, is not born with every man, nor every day"; and the poet goes on to explain that because "the nobility of the invention should be answerable to the dignity" of the persons taking part in the masque, he

chose the argument to be *A celebration of honourable and true Fame, bred out of Virtue*, observing that rule of the best artist,[1] to suffer no object of delight to pass without his mixture of profit and example.

This combination of the moralist and idealist is characteristic of Jonson in all his art, but it forms the very soul of his masques and gives meaning and dignity to all their glitter and mechanism.   He now gives us his definition of the antimasque.

And because her majesty (best knowing that a principle part of life in these spectacles lay in their variety) had commanded me to think on some dance or shew that might precede hers and have the place of a foil or false masque, I was careful[2] to decline, not only from others, but mine own steps in that kind, since the last year I had an anti-masque of boys; and therefore now devised that twelve women in the habit of hags or witches, . . . the opposites to good Fame, should fill that part; not as a masque but as a spectacle of strangeness.

To make a band of witches the foil or opposite of a band of heroines is a striking thought, and interesting from the light it throws upon the general conception of the witch in Jacobean

---

[1] Horace's maxim is meant, *Omne tulit punctum qui miscuit utile dulci, Ars Poet.* 343.

[2] Fleay is certainly right in explaining "Careful to decline" as = "afraid of declining" (*English Drama*, vol. II, p. 4).   See "Careful, 5," in Oxford Dictionary.

times.   The idea took a strong hold of Jonson's mind and, in
his masque, he worked it out with energy.   The witches of the
masque hold their own beside even the weird sisters of *Macbeth*.
They are the witches of popular superstition, and Jonson's
exceptionally elaborate annotations show the close agreement
between these superstitions in ancient and modern times.
Jonson's witches "with a kind of hollow and infernal music
came forth" from "an ugly Hell."   There were eleven, with
their dame.   After a dance, each one relates her misdeeds to
the dame, who proposes that they shall try to blast with their
wicked incantations the glory of the masque that is beginning:

> Darken all this roof
> With present fogs: exhale Earth's rot'nest vapours,
> And strike a blindness through these blazing tapers.

They fall into "a magical dance, full of preposterous change
and gesticulation." [1]   The loud music of the real masque
interrupts them, driving the witches back into hell and disclosing the magnificent house of Fame in which the twelve true
masquers are seated.   Heroic Virtue, "in the furniture of
Perseus," explains the heroines, who are twelve great queens,
beginning with Penthesilea and ending with Bel-Anna.   The
lyric at the close, "Who Virtue can thy power forget," influenced the ending of *Comus*.   In the witch scene, Jonson's
wonderful power of specialising as a dramatist—of "getting
up" a particular trade, or profession—is shown to perfection.
Elsewhere, we occasionally miss in him the fire of imagination
required for blending the accumulations and observation of
his intellect into a vitally artistic product; but, in the present
instance, his imagination is at its height, and he puts out his
full strength.   The third charm conveys powerfully the horrid
thrill that was the soul of the witch superstitions, and that
depended for its force upon all things ugly and foul in nature.

> The owl is abroad, the bat, and the toad,
> And so is the cat-a-mountain,

---

[1] It must have been impressive.   The witches do all things at their meetings
"contrary to the custom of men, dancing back to back, and hip to hip, their hands
joined and making their circles backward, to the left hand, with strange fantastic
motions of their heads and bodies.   All which were excellently imitated by the
maker of the dance, Master Hierome Herne."

The ant and the mole sit both in a hole,
    And the frog peeps out o' the fountain;
The dogs they do bay and the timbrels play,
    The spindle is now a turning;
The moon it is red, and the stars are fled,
    But all the sky is a burning:
The ditch is made and our nails the spade,
    With pictures full, of wax and of wool;
Their livers I stick with needles quick;
    There lacks but the blood, to make up the flood,
Quickly, Dame, then bring your part in,
Spur, spur, upon little Martin.[1]

Jonson, having reached a clear idea of the antimasque, did not go back upon it. But this antimasque quite eclipses its masque. The queens are mere wax-works after the witches. Jonson's imagination concentrated itself upon the first half of his work. Perhaps he left it to Inigo Jones to supply, by the magic of his scenery, the necessary contrast; in Jonson's own work, certainly, this is not done. If the second part had been carried out with the imaginative intensity of the first, this masque would have formed the prototype of an artistic species of great and enduring significance.

In 1610, Daniel supplied the masque for the court, and his *Tethys' Festival* shows no advance upon *The Vision of the Twelve Goddesses*. In 1611, Jonson is again at work: on 1 January, 1611, he produced *Oberon* at Whitehall for prince Henry, and, in the beginning of February, *Love freed from Ignorance and Folly* for queen Anne. *Oberon* is a most delightful masque. The opening is written in dainty octosyllabic verse and elaborates into a charming antimasque the part of the satyr in the entertainment already described. This antimasque made a distinct impression upon the literature of the day.[2] *Oberon* may be taken as an almost perfect example of the first kind of Jonsonian masque, in which the antimasque is not so much "a foil or false masque" as an antic-masque, something lighter and less dignified than the main masque,

---

[1] "Their little Martin is he that calls them to their conventicles. They find him in the shape of a great buck goat upon whom they ride to their meetings."

[2] See Reyher, *Les Masques Anglais*, p. 324. It is conjectured that the three dancers of *The Winter's Tale*, act IV, sc. 4, 329, had been among Jonson's satyrs.

but in keeping with it rather than in contrast, and not yet, in any true sense, dramatic. The grace, balance and finish of the whole composition are beyond praise. Unfortunately, this is the last masque annotated by Jonson for the 1616 folio; his notes stop in it halfway, before he reaches prince Oberon. The only later masque which he annotated was *The Masque of Augures*, specially printed as the first masque presented in the new banqueting hall at Whitehall. *Love Freed* is a companion piece to *Oberon*, but inferior to it in conception and workmanship.

If January, 1612, be the date of *Love Restored*, it is important for the student of the masque. Jonson innovated again on previous practice. The masque proper is preceded not by an antimasque, but by a scene of excellent comedy. The scene is the development in a new style of the part of the presenter, and still gives to that character the larger part of the dialogue, which is in prose. Just as the satyr of the first entertainment was the germ of the antimasque of *Oberon*, so the prose of Pan and his dialogue with Mercury in the second entertainment may have prompted this scene. The king and court being ready, Masquerado enters to declare that there can be no masque, "the rogue play-boy, that acts Cupid, is got so hoarse, your majesty cannot hear him half the breadth of your chair." But Plutus, "as Cupid," here interrupts, ordering Masquerado off. "What makes this light, feathered vanity here? Away, impertinent folly! Infect not this assembly." Plutus objects to the expense of the masque: "I tell thee I will have no more masquing; I will not buy a false and fleeting delight so dear: the merry madness of one hour shall not cost me the repentance of an age." But, here, Plutus is interrupted in his turn by Robin Goodfellow, who is aghast at the news of there not being any masque. He declares,

I am the honest plain country spirit, and harmless; Robin Goodfellow, he that sweeps the hearth and the house clean, riddles for the country maids, and does all their other drudgery, while they are at hot-cockles: one that has discoursed with your court spirits ere now; but was fain to-night to run a thousand hazards to arrive at this place: never poor goblin was so put to his shifts to get in to see nothing.

Plutus will not listen: "Your rude good-fellowship must seek some other sphere for your admitty." Robin's answer is a triumph of comic description. It puts before us all the crush and crowding, all the tricks and pretences, which were a part of the fierce competition to get a place at these great court masques. Robin has been hit over the head by the porter, and shoved off a ladder by one of the guards; then he tried "the carpenters' way," but "the wooden rogues let a huge trap-door fall on my head." He thought of getting in in a trunk, "but that I would not imitate so catholic a coxcomb as Coryat." So he tried disguises. "I was an engineer and belonged to the motions"; then, "an old tire-woman"; then, "a musician —marry, I could not shew mine instrument and that bred a discord"; then,

a feather-maker of Blackfriars, . . . but they all made as light of me, as of my feathers; and wondered how I could be a Puritan, being of so vain a vocation; I answered, We are all masquers some-times.

At last, "with my broom and my candles," he was himself, "and came on confidently, giving out I was a part of the Device." This admirable speech exhibits Jonson's comic power in its most genial and, therefore, most delightful vein. When Plutus goes on protesting against the expense of masques as "superfluous excesses," Masquerado and Robin detect him for an impostor—"Plutus, the god of money, who has stolen Love's ensigns." At this point, the real Cupid enters in his chariot "guarded with the Masquers, in number ten," who, says Cupid, were "the spirits of courts and flower of men." But, here again, the masque, as it has come down to us, is quenched by its antimasque. That antimasque, quite frankly, is a dramatic scene, although the long harangue of Robin Goodfellow may be called only a modification of the presenter's oration, and the colloquy is suggested rather by what was customary at an entertainment than by the new idea of the antimasque.

In Jonson's remaining masques, there are many similar scenes, and they are all admirable. But their right to a place in the masque may be called in question. They represent the intrusion of drama into masque, and it may be contended that Jonson never succeeds in evolving a type of masque which really absorbs them. The plays of Aristophanes afford an example on the grandest scale of the kind of artistic product that is aimed at, and Jonson, in the scene we have criticised and in other places in his masques, is Aristophanic in his combination of robust naturalism with imaginative fancy. Another consideration must be kept in mind. The masquers themselves were always the highest notables of the land, and, therefore, of course, amateurs in everything but dancing. The nobleman could dance exquisitely, but he might not act. This fact, of itself, prevented the development in a dramatic direction of the real masque. But the presenters and the allegoric personages who explained the masque were, usually, professionals, and the antimasque, when it came, was performed very largely by professionals. This is why the development of the antimasque in a dramatic direction was easy, and why the real coherence of masque and antimasque when the dramatic element intruded was impossible.

The development of the Jonsonian masque is now complete, although we have not yet considered half his work. Broadly speaking, there are two types of Jonsonian masque: the masque proper, in which the antimasque is a foil to the masque; and the masque improper, in which the antimasque is a dramatic scene. But the masque proper may be said to include two species; that in which the antimasque is an antic-masque, and that in which it is a true foil or opposite of the masque.

The date 1612, which we have now reached, offers a suitable occasion for considering shortly the work of certain other masque writers, since Jonson wrote no masque for the January and February of 1613.

The death of prince Henry in November, 1612, plunged the nation into great grief. Nevertheless, in three months' time, it welcomed, as an excuse for throwing off its gloom, the marriage of the princess Elizabeth to the elector Palatine. The festivities on this occasion were of an unparalleled magnificence and cost. It was arranged that, on the evening of the wedding, being Sunday, 14 February, the courtiers should present the first masque, known since as *The Lords' Masque*, and written by Thomas Campion, and that, on the two following evenings, the inns of court should present masques. So exhausted were the king and court generally by the elaborate proceedings, that

the third masque had to be put off till the 20th of the month.
The second masque—*The Masque of the Middle Temple and
Lyncolnes Inn*—was written by George Chapman, and the
third—*The Masque of Grayes Inne and the Inner-Temple*—by
Francis Beaumont. Jonson said to Drummond that "next
himself only Fletcher and Chapman could make a masque."[1]
Probably, he had Beaumont's masque in his mind, as we have
no record of a masque by Fletcher. But Campion, rather than
either Chapman or Beaumont, deserves the next place—*longo
intervallo*—to Jonson.[2] *The Lords' Masque* has an antimasque
of "Frantics." These are such characters as the lover, the
self-lover, the melancholic man, the schoolman overcome with
fantasy, the over-watched usurer, with others that made an
absolute medley of madness. These "Lunatics" danced "a
mad measure fitted to a loud fantastic tune," after which the
music changed to a solemn air, which drove out the "Frantics."
Prometheus displays eight stars shining and dancing—a kind
of second antimasque of stars. "The stars moved in an
exceeding strange and delightful manner, and I suppose few
have ever seen more neat artifice than Master Inigo Jones
shewed in contriving their motion." Campion's own songs,
which accompany the scenic effects, have that special charm
of melody and natural grace which make his lyrics more than
any other man's typically Elizabethan. The stars, vanishing,
become the eight masquers, "in their habits, which were
infinitely rich, befitting states."[3] To accompany these knights,
sixteen pages, "like fiery spirits," break from the earth with
torches, and "The Torchbearers' Dance" follows, making the
second antimasque. When the time came for the masquers to
take partners from the audience, "first of all the princely bridegroom and bride were drawn into these solemn revels." The
revels are interrupted by a second "set-piece" of elaborate
splendour, from which a "high vast obelisk dedicate to Fame"
is drawn out by Sybilla, who, in choice Latin verse, prophesies
prosperity to the wedded pair.[4]

---

[1] *Jonson's Conversations with Drummond* (ed. Laing, D.), p. 4. It is curious
that Jonson gives *The Faithfull Shepheardesse* to Fletcher *and* Beaumont.

[2] For a general account of Campion's life and work, see *ante*, Vol. IV, Chap. VIII.

[3] *i.e.* noblemen, as these all were.

[4] The gist is: *Additur Germaniae*
      Robur Britannicum: ecquid esse par potest?

It will be seen, from this imperfect summary of a masque remarkable for its elaboration, that Campion depends more upon Inigo Jones than does Jonson. Jonson instinctively feels for some situation which he must explain and which has in it a logical development involving some slight dramatic interest; Campion merely adorns the stage carpenter's ingenuities with beautiful songs and poetic recitative. Nevertheless, Campion's songs are very charming, and his masque has a poetic beauty in its conceptions as sweet and splendid as any of Jonson's. But it does not join to poetic beauty his moral impressiveness; melody and beauty are the ingredients of Campion's magic. We may add that Campion's account of his work is written in prose of which the ease and charm are not less remarkable than are the vigour and exactitude of that of Jonson's notes; while, in his references to his fellow-workers, Campion reveals himself as a man of a generous personality, eager to praise his friends. His three masques and single entertainment survive, as they deserve; they are all of them remarkable for the melody of their lyrics and the beauty of their conception. He would stand beside Jonson as a masque writer if he had written as many masques.

Chapman's masque is in pleasant contrast to Campion's. It is full of semi-dramatic matter and of quaint, picturesque, fantastic detail quite different from the purely beautiful detail of the first masque. It is interesting, also, because the cavalcade or procession from the rendezvous in Chancery lane to Whitehall was a special attraction of the show, and is carefully described by Chapman. The masque is very topical. It is founded, mainly, upon the current interest in the attempt to colonise Virginia,[1] the chief masquers being Indian princes, while their attendant Phoebades, or Virginian priests of the sun, form a second antimasque. The first antimasque satirises the globe-trotting propensities of Englishmen. The main items of the cavalcade were, first, "a mock masque of Baboons horsed with asses and dwarf palfreys, with yellow foot cloths, casting cockle-de-moys about in courtesy by way of largesse"; then, in a car, the twelve Phoebades, "chief musicians of our kingdom"; then, the twelve chief masquers riding in Indian

---

[1] Already, in *Eastward Hoe* (act III, sc. 2), Chapman puts into the mouth of captain Seagull a graphic account of Virginia's wonders.

habits, as Virginian princes; and, finally, another car driven by Capriccio with Honor and Plutus on the top, and their attendants Eunomia and Phemis beneath them. Capriccio, who has a pair of bellows on his head, describes himself as a "man of wit"; he is a parallel figure to Jonson's Fencer in *Pan's Anniversarie* or to his Christmas in *The Masque of Christmas*, where a single character takes the part of a presenter. When the hall is finally reached, he has a lively opening dialogue with Plutus,[1] who replies to his contemptuous invective:

Sinful? and damnable? What, a Puritan? Those bellows you wear on your head shew with what matter your brain is puffed up, Sir; a religion-forger I see you are and presume of inspiration from these bellows; with which ye study to blow up the settled government of kingdoms.

Chapman spells "antemasque" with an *e* and speaks of his prose dialogue as a "low induction"; his baboons' dance, he tells us, was "anticke and delightful." His conception of the antimasque, therefore, makes it rather like the farce in a modern theatre. It is to be noted, also, that his torchbearers have a dance—they descended and "performed another antemasque dancing with torches lighted at both ends." Chapman's work, obviously, is influenced by Jonson; but he has not grasped the principles of balance and composition which his master employs.[2] It is delightful, however, to find him in his explanatory narrative echoing exactly Jonson's arrogant note. He inserts a page "to answer certain insolent objections made against the length of my speeches and narrations," in which he shews himself the true mate of Ben, the only other Elizabethan who matches his pride in his poetic craft.

Beaumont's masque is a worthy third to the first two. The Inner Temple and Gray's inn made Winchester house, on the south bank of the river, their rendezvous, and their procession was by water. Unfortunately, Beaumont does not describe this with the fulness with which Chapman describes the cavalcade by land of the previous night; but we know, from other sources, that it was very elaborate. The gentleman-masquers

---

[1] There seems here a clear reference to the Plutus of Jonson's *Love Restored* (*ante*, p. 396).

[2] Cf. *ante*, Chap. II.

"were placed by themselves in the King's royal barge, with the rich furniture of state, and adorned with a great number of lights, placed in such order as might make the best show." They were "led by two Admirals," and a multitude of barges and galleys attended upon them, "with all variety of land music and several peals of ordnance." The king and the prince and the newly married couple watched the landing at Whitehall; but the hall of the palace was found to be too small for the performance. This is the reason Beaumont gives for the postponement till Saturday. We learn, however, from a private letter, that the king's fatigue was the real cause of the delay:

> Sir Francis Bacon ventured to entreat his Majesty that by this disgrace (*i.e.* the postponement) he would, as it were, bury them quick: and I hear the king should answer, that they must bury him quick, for he could last no longer.

But the masquers were reconciled to the delay by getting permission to use the banqueting house instead of the hall on Saturday.

Beaumont's masque is remarkable for the high quality of its blank verse, which has in it a hint of Miltonic music, and for the beauty of the lyrics, which, however, are few and short. The words of the masque are quite subordinate to the elaborate music, dances and scenic effects. Beaumont is at pains to point out that his antimasque is "not of one kind or livery (because that had been so much in use heretofore) but as it were in consort like to broken music." This innovation tended further to disintegrate the masque and break it up into a variety entertainment. For the second antimasque, Iris, "in token that the match shall likewise be blessed with the love of the common people," calls to Flora to bring in "a May dance or rural dance, consisting likewise not of any suited [1] persons," but of a pedant, May lord, May lady; servingman, chambermaid; a country clown, country wench; a he-baboon, she-baboon; a he-fool, she-fool; these rush in, dance their measure and as rudely depart. "The music was extremely well fitted," says Beaumont; "but the perpetual laughter and applause was above the music." The king was so pleased that he called

---

[1] Persons dressed alike.

for the second antimasque again at the end, and also, for the first, "but one of the statues by that time was undressed."

We have now to notice in Jonson's work the rapid growth of dramatic interest. Passing over the graceful and original *A Challenge at Tilt* and the realistic *The Irish Masque*, both produced in December, 1613, we find that, for four successive years, Jonson wrote the Twelfthnight masque at court and, in 1617, added a second, produced in February, as well as *The Masque of Christmas*, of the previous 25 December. *Mercury Vindicated from the Alchemists*, 1615, is the first of these. The antimasque, broadly, is in the style of *Love Restored*. Mercury delivers two admirable addresses in prose, worthy of a place beside the harangues of Robin Goodfellow. The scene is "a laboratory or alchemists' work-house, Vulcan looking to the registers," with a Cyclope tending the fires. The Cyclope begins with a beautiful song, "Soft, subtile fire, thou soul of art." Mercury then peeps out "at the tunnel of the middle furnace," whereupon Vulcan cries to hold him—"Dear Mercury! Help. He flies. He is scaped. Precious golden Mercury, be fixt: be not so volatile!" Mercury, after running "once or twice about the room, takes breath," and begins a long relation of his troubles—

Now the place and goodness of it protect me. . . . I will stand close up anywhere, to escape this poult-footed philosopher, old Smug here of Lemnos, and his smoky family. . . . The whole household of them are become Alchemists.

The comic invention of this opening is in Jonson's happiest vein; and Mercury's speech worthily maintains it. In his masques, Jonson's prose is more uniformly strong and distinguished than his verse, and has not received the attention it merits. Mercury recounts all he has suffered:

It is I, that am corroded, and exalted, and sublimed, and reduced, and fetched over, and filtered, and washed, and wiped; what between their salts and their sulphurs, their oils and their tartars, their brines and their vinegars, you might take me out now a soused Mercury, now a salted Mercury, now a smoaked and dried Mercury, now a powdered and pickled Mercury: never herring, oyster, or cucumber past so many vexations.

And his account of what the alchemists claim to perform comes to an excellent climax:

> They will lay you an old courtier on the coals like a sausage, or a bloat herring, and after they have broiled him enough, blow a soul into him with a pair of bellows, till he start up into his galliard, that was made when Monsieur was here.

There are two antimasques: one, "a troop of threadbare Alchemists"; and the second, a troop "of imperfect creatures with helms of limbecks on their heads," which Vulcan and his alchemists by their art have created. These "ridiculous monsters" vanish at Mercury's command, and a glorious bower appears in which are Nature, Prometheus and the twelve masquers. The lyrics are melodious, but short, and their effect in the reading is insignificant, after the vigorous life of the first scene.

The Golden Age Restored, of 1 and 6 January, 1616, goes back to the lyrical style. It is a graceful and beautiful conception, but not very fully reported. For next Christmas, Jonson wrote *The Masque of Christmas*, which Fleay says was "not a mask proper." By the allusions to Burbage and Heminge, we gather that it was acted by the king's players, and, consequently, there is no real masque—it is all antimasque, and, in style and form, very like the opening of *Love Restored*. Christmas takes the place of Robin Goodfellow as presenter, but is not allowed speeches of such length. Nowhere in our literature is the old merry Christmas more graphically put before us: "I am old Gregory Christmas still, and though I come out of Pope's-head alley, as good a Protestant as any in my parish." He has brought a masque of his own making, "and do present it by a set of my sons, that come out of the lanes of London, good dancing boys all." . . . "Bones o bread, the King!" (seeing James). His sons and daughters enter, ten in number, "led in, in a string, by Cupid, who is attired in a flat cap and a prentice's coat, with wings at his shoulders." The family are, Misrule, Carol, Minced-Pie, Gambol, Post and Pair, New-Year's-Gift, Mumming, Wassel, Offering and Baby-Cake. Each has his torchbearer, and Jonson's magnificent knowledge of English ways and manners finds delightful scope in their attire, which is succinctly described. In place of the usual elegant lyrics, we have a rollicking song, sung by Christmas to drum and fife; but, before this can be delivered, there is a short scene of comedy. "Venus, a deaf tire-woman" presents herself; she is Cupid's mother; she dwells in Pudding lane; "yes, I can sit anywhere, so I may see Cupid act; I had him by my first husband, he was a smith, forsooth, we dwelt in Do-little-Lane then." "Will you depart," says Christmas, impatiently;

Ay, forsooth he 'll say his part, I warrant him, as well as e'er a play-boy of e 'm all. I could have had money enough for him, an I would have been tempted, and have let him out by the week to the King's players. Master Burbage has been about and about with me, and so has old Master Hemings too.

The old dame has to be silenced by the drum, but a slight delay occurs because some of the properties are forgotten—"Mumming has not his vizard neither." "No matter! his own face shall serve for a punishment, and 't is bad enough." Misrule's suit is too small! "The players have lent him one too little, on purpose to disgrace him." The song has eighteen verses, which give the names and addresses of the masquers:

> Next in the trace, comes Gambol in place;
> And to make my tale the shorter,
> My son Hercules, tane out of Distaff-lane;
> But an active man and a porter.

It is the first purely humorous lyric with which we have met in a masque, and it smacks of the soil, or, to speak more exactly, of the street. It is banged out on the drum with glorious energy, and, when we are breathless with the speed of it, Cupid is called upon to say his piece; but his mother interrupts and puts him out, so poor Cupid breaks down ignominiously and has to be taken away, Venus exclaiming, "You wrong the child, you do wrong the infant, I 'peal to his Majesty." It was, perhaps, the knowledge that his work was to be acted by skilled professionals that inspired Jonson in this fascinating little sketch. It has to be confessed that, when the dramatist in Jonson gets to work in his masques, we obtain results worth more as literature than all the non-dramatic lyrics and descriptive verse. And Jonson's humour in his masques is without the acrid, scornful element which, in his great plays, too often obtrudes itself. In this little show, he is with Shakespeare and Dickens in the hearty kindliness of his comic observation. On the Twelfthnight after this Christmas day, *The Vision of Delight* was presented. It is a notable masque, containing the beautiful lyric, "Break Phant'sie, from thy cave of cloud," and, in remarkable contrast, the long speech of Phant'sie in doggerel lines of four beats. There is no prose. But we must pass it over, as, also, the interesting *Lovers Made Men*,[1] in order to mention *Pleasure Reconciled to Vertue* presented Twelfthnight, 6 January, 1618, because this masque supplied Milton with the main idea of *Comus*.

It was prince Charles's first masque. The scene is the mountain Atlas, "who had his top ending in the figure of an old man." From a grove at his feet, comes "Comus, the god of cheer or the Belly, riding in triumph," with one in front bearing the bowl of Hercules. The companions of Comus begin with a "Hymn; full chorus";

> Room! room! make room for the Bouncing Belly
> First father of sauce and deviser of jelly,
> Prime master of arts, and the giver of wit,
> That found out the excellent engine, the spit.

After nearly thirty lines in this style, the bowl-bearer speaks a prose oration on the Belly, which introduces the first antimasque of "men in the shape of bottles, tuns, etc." Hercules, the "active friend of virtue," enters, to reclaim his bowl and denounce Comus and his crew; "Help, virtue! These are sponges and not men." He drives them off, asking, "Can this be pleasure, to extinguish man?" Then he lies down at the foot of Atlas, and the pigmies forming the second antimasque steal in and try to steal his club. At his rising, they run into holes, and Mercury descends to crown Hercules with poplar, because he has "the voluptuous Comus, God of cheer, Beat from his grove, and that defaced." So far, the idea is clear and well-balanced, and the moral that pleasure must be the servant of virtue is expressed with an intensity that, obviously, influenced Milton in his *Comus*. But it is interesting to contrast the gross homely Comus of Jonson, the Belly god, with Milton's

---

[1] Called, by Gifford, *The Masque of Lethe.*

dignified abstraction, and to note, that to match his Comus,
Jonson's dramatic instinct supplies, not Virtue, but Hercules.
There is fine poetry in the conception and workmanship of
Jonson's masque; but it loses coherence after the crowning of
Hercules. Hercules is told that, in James's court, the "cessa-
tion of all jars" between pleasure and virtue is to be found;
and, as a proof, twelve princes are brought forth, bred upon
Atlas, "the hill of knowledge." These, led by prince Charles,
are the true masquers. The chaplain of the Venetian ambas-
sador[1] has described the masque.

He says that, after many dances, the dancers began to flag,
"whereupon the King who is naturally choleric got impatient, and
shouted aloud, 'Why don't they dance? What did you make me
come here for? Devil take you all; dance!' On hearing this, the
marquis of Buckingham, his majesty's most favoured minion, immediately sprang forward, cutting a score of lofty and very minute
capers with so much grace and agility, that he not only appeased
the ire of his angry sovereign, but, moreover, rendered himself the
admiration and delight of everybody. The other masquers, being
thus encouraged, continued successively exhibiting their prowess
with various ladies; finishing in like manner with capers and by
lifting their goddesses from the ground."

Finally, James, delighted at the grace of the prince's dancing,
kisses him affectionately, and pats the marquis on the cheek.
The king caused the masque to be repeated, but with "addi-
tions." This, apparently, meant that his majesty did not
appreciate the opening part of the masque. Contemporary
critics asserted that Inigo Jones had lost his charm, and that
Ben Jonson "should return to his old trade of brickmaking."[2]
Jonson, therefore, rewrote it for its second performance on 17
February, making it elaborately complimentary to Wales.[3]
Mount Atlas now becomes Craig-Ereri, and we have a dialogue
between three Welshmen, which, like the dialogue in *The Irish
Masque*, is inferior in wit and vigour, but curious for the Welsh-
English. The Welshmen criticise the first device of Hercules
and the Comus rout—"there was a tale of a tub"—and the pig-

---

[1] Rawdon Brown's translation, quoted in Harrison's *England*, part II, Forewords, p. 58. (New Shakspere Society.)

[2] Brent to Carlton, *Cvl. State Papers, Dom.* vol. xcv, p. 12.

[3] Called, by Gifford, *For the Honour of Wales*.

mies, and we have, instead, a dance of men and a dance of
goats—"the Welsh goat is an excellent dancer by birth"—
as antimasques, with songs in Welsh-English; and then,
apparently, the real masquers with their dances and songs followed. Though the first part of *Pleasure Reconciled to Vertue*
seems to have been too serious for the taste of king James, it
was able to stir Milton to the composition of *Comus*.

A break now occurs in Jonson's masque writing. His
journey to Scotland took place in 1618, and Jonson was not in
London again till about May, 1619. The new banqueting
house at Whitehall was burnt down on 12 January, 1619.
Queen Anne died in March. Jonson's quarrel with Inigo Jones
was in progress. He produced no more masques till 6 January,
1621, when the court called upon him again, and the admirable
Newes from the New World discovered in the Moone was the first
of a series of eight masques, containing some of his best work
and ending in 1625 before his paralytic stroke. Every one of
these, except the imperfectly reported *Masque of Owls*, contains
dramatic work that brings before us contemporary London life
and manners, with a lighter and easier touch than Jonson uses
in his plays. In *Newes from the New World*, the printer, the
chronicler and the factor allow us a glance, tantalisingly brief,
at the lower walks of literature in London and the beginnings
of the London press; *Neptune's Triumph*, in a witty dialogue
between a cook and a poet, magnifies the art of Jacobean
cookery; the Fencer, in *Pan's Anniversarie*, is an amalgamation of all the old gamesters who swaggered in the Elizabethan
fencing ring; *A Masque of the Metamorphos'd Gypsies*, Jonson's
longest masque, "thrice presented to King James," is an
exhaustive study of gipsy manners and gipsy language, wonderful for scope and minuteness. It contains the ribald song of
Cocklorrel, another song of the street, almost Aristophanic in
lusty vigour. The ballad of the bearward, John Urson, in the
excellent *Masque of Augures*, is another lyric of the same
quality. This lyric of the gutter is found cheek by jowl with
the solemn Latin notes about augurs as if to reveal to us the
two sides of Jonson—the schoolmaster and the street arab.
Both characters in Elizabethan London were endowed with a
fuller humanity than their modern representatives. There is
no failure of poetical power in these later masques. *Pan's*

Anniversarie and *The Fortunate Isles* contain exquisite lyrical work, and there is hardly anywhere in the masques a finer song than the last "hunting chorus" of *Time Vindicated*, with its characteristic ending

> Man should not hunt mankind to death,
>   But strike the enemies of man;
>   Kill vices if you can:
>   They are your wildest beasts,
> And when they thickest fall, you make the gods true feasts.

Two masques, in 1631, conclude his series. It would seem as if Jonson's experience in 1618 convinced him that he could not rely upon the contrast between the fantastic and poetic to hold the attention of his audiences. Popular taste began to ask for sensational antimasque, and the multiplication of these threatened to reduce the masque to chaos. Jonson fell back upon the dramatic scene as a means of compelling the interest of his audiences, and, either by the wit of his comic invention or the truth of his comic characterisation, succeeded nearly always in rising above mere farce.

Jonson has been called a prose Aristophanes.[1] In his masques, taken as a whole, he may be recognised as more truly Aristophanic than any other English writer. His serious lyrics are Horatian in their restraint and classic dignity and have none of the splendour of the imaginative choruses of Aristophanes. Nevertheless, in the lyrical and descriptive parts of the masques, Jonson's fancy, elevated as it is by his moral intensity and his sense of the poet's dignity, continually produces a total result which is more than fanciful—which, in a high sense, is imaginative. But, on the side of full-blooded humanity, of intense appreciation of the joy of life in the coarsest and commonest types, of wonderful knowledge of contemporary men and manners, Jonson matches even Aristophanes. Moreover, in the rollicking energy of his lyrics of the gutter and his long prose harangues, the challenging insolence and swagger of the Aristophanic *parabasis* is more than suggested. Jonson's gusto, his vigour and virility, are the most natural and unforced part of his genius. They were cramped

---

[1] *Jonson n'est pas seulement un Labiche ou un Scribe qui aurait du style; c'est pour ainsi parler, un Aristophane en prose,* Castelain, *Ben Jonson,* p. 353.

in the masque.   They were cramped even on the Elizabethan
stage.   An Athenian Dionysiac festival might have given them
scope.   Jonson, therefore, expresses this side of himself in his
masques only in fragments, and cannot be called Aristophanic
unless his masques are taken as a whole.

Jonson, as a masque writer, had no successor.   The two
great sensations of Charles's reign, Shirley's *Triumph of Peace*
and Carew's *Coleum Britannicum*, both produced in 1634,
are aptly characterised by Schelling: "as to form, Shirley's
masque is chaos in activity, Carew's chaos inert."   D'Avenant's
Salmacida Spolia, in which the king and queen took part in 1640,
has so large a number of successive "entries" in the antimasque
as to make it very like modern pantomime.

But, in 1634, *Comus* was produced at Ludlow castle.   We
have pointed out that Milton took suggestions from Peele's
Araygnement of Paris and from Jonson's *Pleasure Reconciled to
Virtue*, but his main inspiration came from Fletcher's *Faithfull
Shepheardesse.   Comus* must not be classed as a masque because
there is no disguising and no dancing.   It is a species of outdoor entertainment, and, therefore, akin to pastoral.   There
is a natural tendency for the outdoor entertainment, if
it be lengthy, to approximate to the pastoral; and pastoral
resembles the masque, because, by its conventions, it is
undramatic.

It may, therefore, not seem inappropriate to consider the
pastoral drama along with the masque.   The one is an off-
shoot of the legitimate drama for indoor use, the other for outdoor.   Both, in the main, may be described as efforts made
by amateurs to bring the theatre into their own halls or parks.
But it is not until the professed poet and dramatist come to the
help of the amateur that any great art results.   Jonson and
Milton, so far, have been examples of this fact, which becomes
even more apparent when we turn to pastoral drama in its
fullest manifestation.

Pastoral poetry is without a place among the greater forms
of literary art, because it is essentially a reaction.   Its two
motives are a longing for simplicity of thought and feeling and
a longing for country as opposed to town.   This latter longing
is innate in man, because his original home was the field or the

forest, and is the soundest and best part of pastoral art. The
desire for simplicity, on the other hand, has in it an element of
weakness and disillusionment. The pastoral poet is not strong
enough to confront and master his own age and find in it the
materials for his poem; his own age is too complicated and
sophisticated. He, therefore, takes refuge in Arcadia—in an
Arcadia of feeling and thought, which has the defect of being
visionary and unreal. It is not the life the poet knows, but
his refuge from that life. The Elizabethan drama was so
firmly rooted in present realities of passion and thought that it
swept pastoral poetry, for a time, out of sight. The prose of
Sidney and the verse of Spenser, noble as they were, were
superseded by the new art of drama, and it was only after the
dramatic impulse had spent itself that the exhausted dramatists
accepted pastoral as a sufficient exercise for their energies.

Theocritus and Vergil are the two fathers of pastoral poetry.
Of the two, Theocritus is commonly preferred as less artificial
than Vergil. The clear, bright naturalism of Theocritus, which,
in fact, is the perfection of art, makes Vergil's *Eclogues* seem
artificial; but these must not be considered apart from his
Georgics. The Italian farmer was very real in Vergil. He
was less of an artist but more of a man than the Greek, and,
spiritually, he is far above Theocritus. All his work is touched
and glorified by his natural piety, the wistful sincerity of his
religious feeling and his contemplative intensity. On its
dramatic and realistic side, pastoral poetry owes most to
Theocritus; on its contemplative and visionary, to Vergil.
Usually, both influences co-operated.

When the renascence begins in the fourteenth century,
pastoral composition follows three main lines of development.
First, there is the eclogue proper, beginning with the Latin
eclogues of Petrarch and the Italian eclogues of Boccaccio and
producing, in 1498, the extraordinarily popular twelve eclogues
of Mantuan. In English literature, this type is represented by
The Shepheards Calender of Spenser.[1] Secondly, there is the
mixture of prose pastoral story and poetical interlude of which
Boccaccio's *Admeto*[2] is the prototype. Boccaccio developed
from it his own *Decameron*, and Sannazaro's less potent genius,

[1] *Ante*, Vol. III, p. 250.
[2] In 1341. Boccaccio calls it *Commediia della ninfe fiorentine*.

regularising the prose and verse sections, produced, in 1481,
his *Arcadia*, which, in Spain, prompted the *Diana*[1] of George
of Montemayor, printed about 1560. The Spanish romance
added to the pastoral and classical elements of the Italian
writers a new chivalrous element. In English literature, these
works inspired Sidney's *Arcadia*.[2] The third type is the pastoral play, of which two famous examples were published in
Italy about the same time—Tasso's *Aminta*, in 1581, and
Guarini's *Il Pastor Fido*, in 1590. *Aminta* is distinguished by
its sensuous charm, its poetic grace and its emotional sweetness: *Il Pastor Fido* by its intricate and ingenious plot.
Both works were printed in London in 1591, in which year
Fraunce translated *Aminta* into English verse. But the direct
influence of this third kind of pastoral on English dramatic
literature is not apparent till the beginning of the seventeenth
century. The second kind reaches English writers earlier.
It has a great influence through the prose romances of Sidney,[3]
Lodge and Greene, but, before this begins, Peeles *Araynement
of Paris* and Lyly's dramas—especially his *Gallathea* and *Love's
Metamorphosis* exhibit an English type of pastoral so original
in its mixture of pastoral, mythology, allegory and satire, that
some critics have denied that it is pastoral at all. And when
Shakespeare, in *As You Like It*, uses Lodge's romance, *Rosalynde*, his play is closer to English traditions[4] of Robin Hood
and Sherwood forest than to anything Italian. Among the
lesser dramatists of the end of Elizabeth's reign, Munday, in
his use of the Robin Hood stories, offers, on his own low level,
an English kind of pastoral similar to Shakespeare's. The
feature of this dubious pastoral of Peele, of Lyly,[5] of Shakespeare and of Munday is that it is joyful, fresh and irresponsible.
It comes at the beginning of a literary epoch instead of at the
end, and the exhausted passion and elaborate artificiality of
the court of Ferrara are replaced by the heedless gaiety and

---

[1] *Los siete libros de la Diana de Jorge de Montemayor.* Bartholomew Young,
translated it into English in 1583, but his translation was not printed till 1598.

[2] For Sidney's *Arcadia*, cf. *ante*, Vol. III, p. 400.

[3] For plays founded on Sidney's *Arcadia*, see *ante*, Vol. III.

[4] For the formation of pastoral traditions in England, consult Chap. II of
Greg's *Pastoral Poetry and Pastoral Drama*.

[5] *The Maydes Metamorphosis*, a good play, of doubtful authorship, should be
included in this group.

robust life of Elizabethan England. *The Shepheards Calender* and *The Fairie Queene*, as well as *The Countess of Pembroke's Arcadia*, are examples of an appropriation of influences from Italy, France and Spain, which resulted in distinctive types of art. The new romance type was produced by the noble-minded idealism which characterised the genius of both Spenser and Sidney. In the plays, a parallel manifestation of the free and careless Elizabethan spirit produces again a new type of art.

It is curious that Daniel should have been the writer who attempted to reproduce in English the Italian pastoral play of Tasso and Guarini, as he had tried to reproduce the Senecan drama of Garnier. In 1602, he prefixed a sonnet to a translation of *Il Pastor Fido* in which he claimed acquaintance with Guarini and, in 1605, he wrote for queen Anne at Oxford *The Queenes Arcadia*, which he calls "a Pastorall Trage-comedie." In 1614, his second pastoral tragicomedy for the queen, *Hymen's Triumph*, was performed at Somerset house at the marriage of lord Roxborough. These plays are not without interest and charm. The satirical element in the first and the scholarly workmanship of the second are worthy of attention. But they have neither the freshness of Peele nor the passionate sentiment of Tasso. Daniel is the schoolmaster in drama; his plays are never more than praiseworthy exercises in composition. The effort of copying Garnier or Guarini was sufficient to extinguish his small dramatic gift, and his dramatic experiments did not produce any results of importance. As the virile Elizabethan drama softened and degenerated, pastoral revived, and meritorious plays were produced, such as *The Careless Shepherdess* of Thomas Goffe and *The Shepherd's Holiday* of Joseph Rutter.

But, before this decline came about, pastoral drama was three times essayed by men of genius, with the consequence that the Elizabethan and Jacobean period has left three plays which are the best that the language has produced in the pastoral kind, and are almost masterpieces. These are *The Faithfull Shepheardesse* of Fletcher, *The Sad Shepherd* of Jonson and Thomas Randolph's *Amyntas*. These three plays stand out conspicuously from the generally feeble and formless work of the pastoral drama; and, therefore, we shall leave on one side many works of minor importance, and endeavour shortly to indicate the interest, and estimate the value, of these three best specimens of their kind.

These three plays are alike attempts by dramatists to put pastoral poetry upon the boards. They are not, like Milton's *Comus*, written for outdoor presentation. In all three cases, the dramatist is consciously original. He is trying to see whether the conventions of the pastoral drama can be used with advantage on the London stage and be made to satisfy a London audience.

Fletcher, unmistakably basing his effort on Guarini's *Pastor Fido*, was the first to try, and his attempt failed. He tells us that the public, "missing Whitsun-ales, cream, wassel, and morris-dances, began to be angry." They did not understand that pastoral deals with shepherds who own their flocks, and not with "hirelings," who would be reasonably expected to behave as rude rustics. Such "owners of flocks," says Fletcher,

are not to be adorned with any art but such improper[1] ones as nature is said to bestow, as singing and poetry; or such as Experience may teach them, as the virtues of herbs and fountains, the ordinary course of the sun, moon and stars, and such like.

His characters were to be unsophisticated, but not vulgar, country people; and his play was to be a tragicomedy; there were to be no deaths, but "some were to come near it." It is impossible to read this note "To the reader" without feeling that Fletcher, as yet, has no practical experience as a dramatist. His effort is not to create men and women but to observe certain rules of pastoral tragicomedy. As a drama, the play fails; the plot is crude, and the characters are without life. But Fletcher has taken it for granted that his play must take us out of doors, and he has put so much exquisite description of nature into it that his dramatic failure hardly matters. Swinburne claims justly that *The Faithfull Shepheardesse* "is simply a lyric poem in semi-dramatic shape, to be judged only as such, and as such almost faultless." The liquid melody of the verse, too, has the natural sweetness of the songs of birds,

---

[1] Not proper, not peculiar, general.

and the rustle of leaves, and the flow of waters.[1] There is no laboured description of nature; but green grass and cool waters are everywhere in the play; the poet has the spring in his heart, and his poetry blossoms like the flowers of April and bubbles like the brook; there is no natural magic to compare with it until we come to Keats; and, even in *Endymion*, there is something hectic, something strained, when it is read along with Fletcher's play. In *A Midsummer Night's Dream* and *As You Like It*, we get descriptions of nature which, in our literature, are the nearest in their quality to Fletcher's work in *The Faithfull Shepheardesse;* but Fletcher is both more copious and more concentrated than Shakespeare just because his art fails on the dramatic side; whereas Shakespeare succeeds, and nature, in his dramas, is duly subordinated to human character. As a work of art, therefore, *The Faithfull Shepheardesse* is like *Comus*. Neither is dramatic; although it is probable that, in both cases, the writers aimed at a kind of drama. But, in both poems, we find, instead of drama, descriptive poetry of extraordinary richness and beauty, the first full expression of the young writer's genius. But, here, a contrast begins. Fletcher is Elizabethan; his self-consciousness is unruffled and unaware of the spiritual emotion stirring vehemently in Milton; while, on the other hand, this self-consciousness of Milton puts him out of touch with nature—which, for two centuries, was to recede into the background in English poetry. In *Comus*, the beautiful descriptions of nature are incidental; in no sense are they the reason or aim of the poem. And Milton's spiritual imagination is everywhere, ousting Pan and installing Apollo. But Fletcher's unembarrassed, happy enjoyment of Pan's Arcadia, in its natural greenness and freshness, is the abiding merit of his poem.

But a word must be said on the dramatic question. Fletcher has some plan of describing various types of love—for there is a "modest shepherd," a "wanton shepherd," a "holy shepherdess" and a "wanton shepherdess." Having his mind fixed on some special grade of propriety or impropriety in love, he does not give us men and women. If we do not ask for men and women, there is much in his work that is beautiful. The conception of Clorin, who has "buried her love in an arbour,"

---

[1] As to the verse of *The Faithfull Shepheardesse*, cf. *ante*, Chap. v, p. 132.

and has her mind fixed on holy things, except in so far as she pursues "the dark hidden virtuous use of herbs" for the relief of the sick—that being an "art" with which a shepherdess may be adorned—has much imaginative beauty and charm. The satyr, again, the wild creature tamed by a dim perception of spiritual beauty, and stedfastly loyal to that perception, is exquisite in its simplicity. But what can we say of Cloe, "a wanton shepherdess"? If she were a woman, she would be endurable, however wanton; but an abstraction illustrating wantonness in shepherdesses is unendurable, except when Fletcher forgets about the wantonness, and makes her talk pure poetry, as when she says to Thenot:

> Tales of love,
> How the pale Phoebe, hunting in a grove,
> First saw the boy Endymion, from whose eyes
> She took eternal fire that never dies;
> How she conveyed him, softly in a sleep,
> His temples bound with poppy, to the steep
> Head of old Latmus, where she stoops each night,
> Gilding the mountain with her brother's light,
> To kiss her sweetest.

This particular problem, as to how a young girl thinks of love, is particularly delicate and difficult for a young poet, whether the girl be good or bad. He reads his own mind into the woman's, and the result has an unnaturalness something like that which must have been the drawback of the acting of women's parts by men on the Elizabethan stage. This unnaturalness passes over from Fletcher's pastoral into Milton's *Comus*. There, it is the young Milton, disguised as a maiden, who utters, with some self-consciousness and bashfulness, the famous encomium on chastity. The speech is essentially undramatic—what neither the man nor the maiden would have said in their own persons.

Our second pastoral is Jonson's *Sad Shepherd*, which is almost as fine an achievement as Fletcher's *Faithfull Shepheardesse*. Of Jonson's work, something has already been said in an earlier chapter.[1] The work suggests a most perplexing problem of literary criticism. It was published after Jonson's

---

[1] *Ante*, Chap. i, p. 12.

death, and thus purports to be a work of his last years left unfinished because of his death. But this last effort of the partially paralysed poet is distinguished by a vigour of style and freshness of imagination that seem to mark it as a work of his prime. After reading Jonson's last masques and plays, in which a certain stiffening and flagging of his powers are clearly to be discerned, it seems impossible to ascribe *The Sad Shepherd* to the same date. Moreover, we hear of a work by Jonson called *The May Lord*, composed before his visit to Edinburgh, which has disappeared. The title may have been suggested by Sidney's *The May Lady*, in which case, Jonson's poem, probably, was some kind of pastoral play. Was *The May Lord* the first title of *The Sad Shepherd*, when Robin Hood was intended to be the central figure of the play? In that case, Æglamour's part would be a later edition. But Æglamour, in some respects, is the most remarkable of all the characters. He strikes the true romantic note, which is conspicuously absent in Jonson's main work. What could be finer in cadence and romantic suggestion than the first lines of the play, when Æglamour appears for a moment?

> Here she was wont to go! and here! and here!
> Just where those daisies, pinks, and violets grow:
> The world may find the spring by following her.

Even if we suppose that Jonson borrowed this opening from Goffe, we have not got over the difficulty, because Æglamour's speeches are consistently and strongly romantic in tone. It is easier to connect them in style and spirit with the additions to *The Spanish Tragedie* than with anything else written by Jonson. The man who wrote those additions and *The Sad Shepherd* might have been a great romantic. Castelain[1] has pointed out that the prologue divides itself into two parts. The first thirty lines are the real prologue to *The Sad Shepherd*. They are beautiful in feeling, and the silent passing of the Sad Shepherd over the stage in the middle of them seems absolutely right in imagination, if we omit the second thirty-six lines about the heresy "that mirth by no means fits a pastoral." These last lines might have been a prologue for *The May Lord*, but our problem is to decide when the first lines were written

[1] See the note in his *Ben Jonson*, p. 459.

which form an admirable prologue to *The Sad Shepherd*. As to this, we must note that, in spite of the "forty years" of the first line, the succeeding statement, that the public have "at length grown up to him," must refer to the vogue enjoyed by Jonson from 1605 to 1615, and cannot mean that he has forgiven the rejection of *The New Inne*. Another fine romantic motive in the play is Karolin's kissing of Amie under the mad Æglamour's compulsion. It compels us to revise all our conceptions of Jonson. He treats it with a sureness and delicacy of touch that Shakespeare could hardly have bettered; while, at the same time, he proves his authorship of the episode by the absurd list of "lovers' scriptures" and by putting into innocent Amie's lips the reference to

> the dear good angel of the spring,
> The nightingale.

But, so far, we have only touched upon one side or aspect of the play. We must add that the part of the witch is realised with great power. Alken's speech beginning "Within a gloomy dimble she doth dwell," and his later speech which describes the

> spanlong elves that dance about a pool,
> With each a little changeling in their arms,

are both in blank verse, marked by a freer movement than Jonson usually permits himself, and they also convey the old world idea of the witch with a force to be paralleled only in Jonson's own *Masque of Queens*, presented in 1609. One would wish to place these speeches of Alken within measurable distance of that date. Finally, the presentment of Robin Hood and Marian, while not so fully romantic as Æglamour's part, is such sunny sweet realism as touches upon romance; and may have led Jonson to add a fully romantic note to a play originally intended to prove that mirth befitted pastoral. Puck-Hairy or Robin Goodfellow appeared in the masque *Love Restored*, which we have dated 1612; again, we desire to put the Puck-Hairy of the play and all its Robin Hood scenes not too far from the splendid Robin Goodfellow of the masque. But the Scottish dialect, which is the only serious drawback to the artistic effect of the play, must, surely, have been introduced

after the poet's visit to Scotland in 1618.[1]   That visit may
have stimulated Jonson to compose *The Sad Shepherd* as we
have it; our fragment began, perhaps, as *The May Lord*, for
which the last thirty-six lines were originally intended as prologue.   Its composition should be placed both before and after
the visit.

The doubtful question of the date must not divert our
attention from the merits of Jonson's play.   *The Sad Shepherd* reads as if the poet had forborne to write out his play in
prose, as he tells us was his custom, and had set down his first
sketch in verse, rapidly, with his impulse fresh upon him.
Perhaps, he found he could not finish it by his usual methods.
Perhaps, he was disconcerted by the unfamiliar features of this
surprising child of his imagination and was half-ashamed of it.
It is strongly dramatic, and the breath of Jonson's realism gives
it substance, but it is touched by a romantic grace which is
almost romantic passion; and, therefore, it stands alone among
Jonson's dramas and will always have a special fascination for
his readers.

The third and last pastoral on our list does not require so
full a consideration as the first two.   It is not a poem like
Fletcher's, nor unfinished like Jonson's; but it belongs to a new
order of art, which has not the full humanity or high imagination of the Elizabethan era.   Randolph does not attempt,
like Fletcher and Jonson, to cast the pastoral into a new
mould.   His *Amyntas or the Impossible Dowry* follows the
conventions of Tasso and Guarini, and its plot is deliberately
artificial, removed from any contact with life's realities.   His
style recalls the work of John Day, and has a scholarly finish
and point that raise the play above the other pastorals of
Jacobean times.[2]   It is in curious contrast to *The Muses
Looking-Glasse*.   In that play, the force of the writing, and a
touch of dramatic reality in the sketch of the puritan onlookers,
are remarkable.   In *Amyntas*, Randolph's muse is strangely
subdued and gentle.   He develops a very individual type of
pathetic and ironical fantasy in his delineation of the mad
Amyntas, which seems very far removed from the boisterous

---

[1] Compare the Irish of *The Irish Masque*, December, 1613, and the Welsh of
For the Honour of Wales, February, 1618.
[2] As to Randolph's university plays, see *ante*, Chap. XII.

fun and rollicking rimes of *Aristippus*. This mellowing and
softening of Randolph's spirit extends to the comic scenes of
the play, and gives us the Latin rimes of the orchard-robbing
elves—the

> *beata Fauni proles*
> *Quibus non est magna moles.*

Few such Latin rimes have been written since the Middle Ages.
There are sweet and tender passages of poetry continually
occurring in the careful blank verse in which most of the
pastoral is composed, but they are so unemphatic and quiet in
tone that some familiarity with the poem is necessary before
the reader becomes aware of them. Fletcher impetuously
injects into his artificial plot and characters the fire of his
poetic genius; Randolph, with wonderful art and restraint,
keeps his true vein of poetry always in the right key—his
play is a more complete and coherent production than either
Fletcher's or Jonson's, but it is essentially artificial; its excellence is all in the handling and embroidery. It was, presumably, the last work of Randolph, and it raises our opinion both
of his art and of his genius.

CHAPTER XIV

The Puritan Attack upon the Stage

SEEING that the stage has always been intimately associated with religion, we can scarcely be surprised to find it the subject of vehement controversy at the two most important periods of religious revolution known to history—the rise of Christianity and the dissolution of the medieval ecclesiastical system. The latter event, being less fundamental and less universal than its predecessor, was, also, less disastrous to the stage, and in England alone, where the forces for and against the drama were most evenly matched, was there any real struggle. This struggle possessed many of the characteristics of that which had gone before; and indeed, at first sight, the puritan attack upon the Elizabethan theatre seems little more than a distant echo of the great battle which had raged around the Roman *spectacula*. Yet the stage was hated as sincerely and as bitterly in the sixteenth and seventeenth centuries as it was in the third and fourth, and for reasons strikingly similar. These reasons were both theological and ethical; and it will be instructive to consider them separately by way of introduction.

The Roman stage was essentially a pagan institution and remained such, in spirit, long after the triumph of Christianity. The early church hated it, therefore, first and foremost for its idolatry. It represented the old religion in a peculiarly alluring and ineradicable form, and it was the most dangerous of those "pomps" which every Christian renounced at baptism.[1] So long as the Roman theatre existed, it was felt to be a rival of the church, and not until the dramatic elements inherent in the catholic ritual had given birth to the religious drama of the

[1] Tertullian, *De Spectaculis*, § 4. See also, bibliography *s.v.* **Prynne.**

Middle Ages was a temporary reconciliation between church and stage brought about. From that time forward, the stage was included in the ecclesiastical machinery and was freed from the attacks of all save heretics and reformers.[1] In the fourteenth century, for example, there was produced in England *A tretise of miraclis pleyinge*,[2] in all probability by one of Wyclif's followers, which condemns the miracle on the score of its profanity. The reformation itself, however, was at first not at all, and never completely, hostile to the stage. Fired by the renewed interest in the classical drama and conscious of the convenience of the religious play as a controversial weapon,[3] reformers, among whom Melanchthon stands conspicuous, were, in the first half of the sixteenth century, setting themselves, all over Europe, to bring the stage into the service of the reformation. England, like Germany, had her protestant dramatists, chief of whom were John Bale and, strange as it may sound, John Foxe, both working under the direct influence of the Lutheran drama; while, at Cambridge, the movement found its theoretical exponent in Melanchthon's disciple, Martin Bucer, whose *De honestis ludis*,[4] was published about 1551. Precept and example, however, were alike soon forgotten in England, and this for two reasons. First, the English stage was destined by force of circumstances to become secular. The frequent religious changes in the middle years of the sixteenth century made it dangerous for the government to allow the theatre to be used for partisan purposes, and, accordingly, one regulation after another was passed to prevent the handling of matters of religion or state upon the stage, culminating in the proclamation of 16 May, 1559, whereby Elizabeth provided for the strict licensing of the drama. Secondly, the reformation was itself rapidly changing its character; and, as Geneva became its centre of authority instead of Wittenberg, the realm of anti-Christ was mapped out with greater precision and was

---

[1] The most important of these, before Lollard days, were Gerhoh of Reichersberg and Robert Grosseteste. See *Chambers*, vol. II, pp. 98–100.

[2] *Hazlitt's English Drama and Stage*, p. 73.

[3] Chambers, *op. cit.* vol. II, pp. 216 ff.; for the part played by the drama in the Scots reformation, see *ante*, Vol. III, pp.138, 159, 181, and, for the whole topic of the Protestant and humanistic drama, see *Creizenach*, vols. II and III.

[4] *Scripta Anglicana*, 1577, pp. 141–6; Symmes, *Débuts de la critique dramatique*, app. A.

found to embrace many spheres of activity which had hitherto been considered honest.[1]   When protestants became puritans, they were not long in discovering that the drama, which they had been forbidden to utilise for their own purposes, was without authority in holy writ, and before long, that it might not be suffered in any Christian commonwealth.   It was natural, also, that they should hark back to the early fathers for their arguments: for the puritans had the same *casus belli* as the fathers, though in a stronger form.   The Elizabethan drama was, in a measure, the direct heir of the medieval miracle-play: probably, the contemporaries of the later growth scarcely realised the fundamental differences between the two.   And the medieval miracle-play was, in origin, half liturgy and half folk-play: in other words, it was twice damned, since, like the maypole, it was heathen, and, like the mass, popish.   "Idolatry," Cyprian had declared, "is the mother of all public amusements"; the puritan could add a second parent— popery.   As William Crashawe, father of the poet, put the case in a sermon at Paul's cross:

> The ungodly Playes and Enterludes so rife in this nation, what are they but a bastard of Babylon, a daughter of error and confusion, a hellish device (the devils own recreation to mock at holy things) by him delivered to the Heathen, from them to the Papists and from them to us.[2]

As a "bastard of Babylon," the stage which Shakespeare trod was, in the eyes of his puritan contemporaries, more than immoral: it was unholy.   When this is realised, we catch and understand the note of passion in tracts which at first sight seem academic essays in polemic borrowed from early Christian divines.

In other and more obvious ways, also, dramatic performances conflicted with the religious prejudices of puritans.   For example, there was a conscious rivalry, frequently referred to in the literature of the subject, between the pulpit and the stage.   The function of the latter, until quite recently, had been almost entirely didactic; and, as we shall see, its defenders maintained that it was so still.   But the protestant preacher,

---

[1] Calvin himself was reluctantly brought into conflict with the stage by the zeal of his disciples. See Stähelin, *Calvin* (1863), vol. I, pp. 392–4.

[2] *Sermon*, 14 February, 1607. See, also, Selden, *Table Talk* (1892), p. 134.

with the newly-opened Bible in his hand, would brook no competition. At the mere thought of comparing a play with a sermon, he raised the cry of "blasphemy intolerable"; or he admitted the comparison, only to declare that "enterludes weare the divells sarmons."[1]   Again, the actor's practice, also derived from medieval tradition, of performing on Sundays[2] and holy days did not tend to soften the exasperation of the godly, who listened with indignant horror to the sound of the player's trumpet passing the open door of the church and mingling defiantly with the peal of the bells. Finally, the actor, as the early fathers had discovered and every puritan was careful to point out, was bound by the very necessities of his craft to infringe the divine law which forbade one sex to wear the costume of the other; and the point was a particularly telling one in an age when it was customary for boys to act female parts.[3] All things considered, it was natural that the stage should appear to rest under the peculiar displeasure of God. Lists of divine judgments meted out to sinful players or those who visited the theatre are a common feature in the tracts of the period. An earthquake, the fall of a scaffold or, indeed, a public disaster of any kind, also, seemed to the devout primitive intelligence of the time to indicate the Almighty's wrath at the continued existence of playhouses. Few things of this kind made a greater impression than London's grim annual guest—the plague. As one of the earliest writers against the stage unanswerably put the matter: "the cause of plagues is sinne, if you look to it well: and the cause of sinne are playes: therefore the cause of plagues are playes."[4]

[1] Harington, *Nugae Antiquae*, vol. I, p. 191, quoting a puritan objector. Osmund Lake, *A Probe Theologicall*, 1612, declares that God's blessing cannot rest upon the Scriptural play "because he hath ordained the Preaching, and not the Playing of his word," pp. 267–272.

[2] Furnivall (*Stubbes's Anatomy*, part I, pp. 296–301) brings together many interesting passages in reference to Sunday sports and Sabbath-breaking.

[3] *Deuteronomy* xxii, 5. Ben Jonson thought the matter so important that he asked Selden's advice upon it. The antiquary's letter in reply, dated 28 February, 1615, is interesting as an early example of biblical criticism. See *Opera Omnia* (1726), vol. II, pp. 1690–6; also, *De Venere Syriacâ (Opera*, vol. II, p. 365) and *Table Talk, u. s.*

[4] Thomas White, *Sermon*, 1576, p. 47; and the lord mayor remarks, in 1585, that to play in plague time increases the plague by infection, to play out of plague time calls down the plague from God. See *Malone Society Collections*, part I, p. 173.

Turning from the theological to the moral aspect of the matter, we may notice that here, too, puritans were walking in the steps of the early fathers. Roman shows and Elizabethan stage plays were both denounced as sinks of iniquity. Led into many absurdities by his theological prejudices, the puritan reformer, nevertheless, was at one with the best tendencies of his age in his attack upon "abuses." A considerable literature upon this subject has come down to us from the sixteenth century, the most famous example being Stubbes's *Anatomie of Abuses*. A perusal of this and similar productions shows us that puritanism was largely a revolt against medievalism; for a great number of the evils denounced were medieval practices and observances, folk festivals and such like, often innocent enough in themselves but commonly tending to rioting and wantonness. And, in singling out the theatre from among these as the special object of his abhorrence and invective, the puritan was not actuated by theological reasons alone. Undoubtedly the stage was the main channel through which what may be called the saturnalian elements of medieval life emptied themselves into the broad stream of the renascence. Furthermore, the rise of a secular theatre was one of the many problems created by the break-up of the medieval world which were engaging the attention of popular writers all over Europe in the sixteenth century. It is remarkable that, with hardly an exception, they condemned it as a sinister development, and gave moral reasons for excluding the player from the commonwealth. When a man like Montaigne, in one essay, classes "enterlude-players" with "harlots and curtizans,"[1] and, in another, describes them as "vagabond objects," we are not surprised to find Jean Bodin expressing the strongest disapprobation of plays in his *Six livres de la Republique*,[2] and the well known Jesuit publicist Mariana, in a chapter on "Spectacles" in his *De Rege et Regis Institutione* (1599), denouncing the evils of the theatre and recommending its strict regulation.[3] Not a few of these continental writers were translated into English and so came to influence the development of puritan

---

[1] See *Essays* (Florio's translation), bk. I, chaps. XLII and XLIII.

[2] English edition, 1606, bk. VI, chap. I, pp. 645, 646.

[3] Bk. III, chap. XV. Cf., also, his *Contra los Juegos Publicos* (*Obras*, vol. II, pp. 413–462).

opinion. It is interesting, for example, to notice that two of
the most popular translations of the Tudor period, North's
version of the Spaniard Guevara's *El Relox de Principes* (1557)
and Sandford's rendering of the German Cornelius Agrippa's
De incertitudine et vanitate scientiarum (1569), contain unfavourable references to the stage. Puritans, however, did not have
it all their own way. In 1559, William Bavand produced a
translation of a Latin treatise, this time, appropriately enough,
from Italy, under the title: *A Woorke of Joannes Ferrarius
Montanus touchynge the good orderynge of a common weale*, which
is important as being the first book in English to offer a defence
of the secular drama, assigning it a place in a well ordered state
on the ground that it "doth minister unto us good ensamples."[1]
This was exactly the line of argument that all subsequent English defenders of the drama adopted. Equally important on
the other side is Sir Geffraie Fenton's *Forme of Christian pollicie
gathered out of French*.[2] In his treatment of stage plays and
enterludes, the unknown French writer anticipates in a few
pages all the principal arguments of the puritans, and his book,
translated in 1574 just before the attack began in England,
exercised an appreciable influence upon Northbrooke and was
read and quoted by the author of the *Third Blast*. Other
examples, also, might be added to our list, such as a translation
from Petrarch by Francis Twynne,[3] who introduces into his
original an unfavourable comment upon the newly erected
Theater and Curtain.

The puritan opposition to the English stage did not burst
forth in any violence until about 1576; but there are indications of its existence, apart from the translations just noticed,
long before this date. English humanism, for example, though,
for reasons already given, inclined to look favourably upon the
drama, was in this as in many other respects laying down the
lines upon which puritanism developed later. Roger Ascham
was no puritan; yet his famous outburst against the popular
romances of the day is remarkably similar in tone and feeling
to the invectives launched by subsequent writers against plays

---

[1] Bk. v, chap. VIII.
[2] Yet Fenton, in his *Tragicall Discourses* (1567), employs the same arguments
in support of the novel as were used later by apologists for the drama.
[3] *Phisicke against Fortune* (v. bibliography).

which, to a large extent, were nothing but dramatised versions
of these very romances. The connection between the humanistic attack upon the Italian novel and the puritan attack upon
the romantic drama comes out most clearly in the case of
William Alley, bishop of Exeter, whose condemnation of
"Wanton Bookes" in *The Poore Man's Librarie* (1565) expressly
embraces plays. Alley appears to have been the first in
England, since Lollard days, to take up the pen against the
stage; he was the first Englishman, also, to cite with approbation the example of the ancient city of Marseilles, which
"kept so greate gravitie" that it would never allow a player
within its walls. A classical precedent of this kind was so well
adapted to the case of the city of London that it was eagerly
seized upon by later writers and reappears in almost every
pamphlet written against the stage. Another remarkable
indication of the prevalence of the anti-dramatic spirit at this
comparatively early period is to be found in the prologue of
Lewis Wager's *Life and Repentance of Marie Magdalene*, first
printed in 1566 but probably acted considerably earlier, which
shows us a dramatist not only already on the defensive but
employing the same arguments as were used, afterwards, by
Lodge, Gager and Heywood. But perhaps the most tangible
proof of the rising puritan flood was the quiet but persistent
suppression by bishop, preacher and zealous mayor of local
plays and pageants throughout England during the middle
years of the sixteenth century, as no longer seemly in "this
happie time of the gospell." [1] London, almost the only city in
the kingdom with its own stage when the cleansing process was
completed, was to be the scene of the great struggle between
puritan and player.

The puritan forces advanced against the London stage in
three lines: preachers, pamphleteers and civic authorities. In
the nature of the case, it is impossible to do more than indicate
here the incessant denunciation of the stage from the pulpits,
and especially from the famous rostrum at Paul's cross. The
work of the preachers was to sound the note for battle and to
urge the godly forward in the war; but, save for one or two
sermons which have found their way into print, few traces of

[1] Chambers, *op. cit.* vol. II, pp. 110–113; *Laneham's letter,* Furnivall, pp.
26–28.

their contribution to the controversy have come down to our day. With the pamphleteer it was different; his weapon was the book, and the book has a tendency to endure. It will be well, however, to defer our consideration of this aspect of the campaign until we have examined the efforts of the corporation of London to drive players out of the city; for, in its opening phases at any rate, the literary attack was of secondary importance as compared with the administrative. Indeed, to some extent, it seems to have been prompted and controlled by the lord mayor himself.

The city merchant had reasons, other than those already mentioned, for hating the player. The customary processions through the streets, before playing, interfered with traffic. Public performances were a possible source of disturbance. As for the actor himself, he and his like, as the lord mayor informed the privy council upon one occasion, were "a very superfluous sort of men."[1] He was either the retainer of some nobleman, in which case he was supported by his master, instead of being left to make his living at the public expense,[2] or he was by law a rogue and a vagabond and ought to be dealt with accordingly. He lived for and by pleasure alone, grew rich by beguiling the simple poor of their money and, hereupon, aped the manners and habits of gentlefolk, swaggering about the city in dress so extravagant and costly as to be positively offensive to the eye.[3] In short, his profession, as it seemed to the civic mind, represented a definite and constant drain on the national resources. In the language of the day, he was a "caterpillar of the commonwealth."

The player, therefore, could expect no mercy from the city authorities; but, fortunately for the development of the English romantic drama, he found a rock of defence in the queen and her courtiers. Elizabeth liked to be provided every Christmas with theatrical amusements, but refused to be responsible for the entire maintenance of a special company. The privy council, accordingly, was instructed to satisfy both her love of pleasure and her passion for economy by seeing that the "common players" were allowed full opportunity, not

---

[1] *Malone Society Collections*, part I, p. 46.
[2] *A Second and Third Blast*, Hazlitt, *op. cit.* p. 133.
[3] *School of Abuse*, Arber, p. 39. *Anatomy of Abuses*, Furnivall, p. 1;6.

merely of practising for Christmas festivities, but of earning
sufficient to maintain themselves at other seasons. The privy
council was not sorry to have an excuse for interfering with the
city's internal policy; but there was no reason why without
special royal injunctions, it should have lifted a finger to
succour the stage. Throughout its whole career, the Elizabethan theatre, though essentially popular in origin and
character, depended for its very existence upon the patronage
of the court, and the quarrel which we are now to consider was
an early trial of strength between the same forces which, later,
broke up England into two hostile camps. Apart from other
considerations, the legal status of the actor would have been
sufficient of itself to produce a conflict. It was defined by two
regulations: the proclamation of 16 May, 1559, issued to prevent the handling of religious and political questions upon the
stage, which forbade performances in any town without a
licence from the mayor; and the statute of 1572, which imposed
the penalties of vagrancy upon any player not in the service
of some nobleman.[1] In other words, acting companies, while
placed under the direct protection of great lords at court, were
not allowed to produce plays without the express permission
of the lord mayor. Thus, the stage was subject to two authorities, not only different in character but rivals in policy and
interest. The lord mayor was perpetually trying to put his
legal powers into force and so to clear the city of actors; the
court party, on the other hand, as perpetually intervened
through the privy council, or overrode the mayor's authority
by royal patents and other expedients of a similar nature. In
the end, the stage succeeded in freeing itself from the grip of the
city, but found itself, *ipso facto*, more than ever dependent
upon the court, and under the particular sway of the master of
the revels.

A detailed account of the struggle would be scarcely possible
in the present state of our knowledge—so meagre, fragmentary
and tantalising is the evidence hitherto brought to light upon
the subject. The normal course of the controversy may,
however, be followed in the correspondence between the privy
council and the lord mayor, to be found in the council's register

---

[1] Cf. as to these regulations, *ante*, Chap. x; and see Hazlitt, *op. cit.* pp. 19, 21.

and in the city archives known as *Remembrancia*.[1] The letters are amusing enough. The city's trump card, played with wearisome monotony, was the plague, almost as inevitable in Shakespeare's London as smoke is in ours. While the sickness raged, the privy council was as ready to close the playhouses as was the corporation.[2] But, ordinarily, the plague was only a summer visitor. In the autumn, therefore, the lord mayor would receive a letter from the council reminding him that the queen must have her Christmas amusements, and requiring him to allow the actors an opportunity of practising their art. The city usually resisted these recommendations with all the power and ingenuity at its command.

Matters remaining in this constant state of tension, an occasional crisis was inevitable; especially when an unusually severe epidemic gave the lord mayor an excuse for attempting to suppress the stage altogether. The documents at our disposal give us the particulars of three such crises, two of which had an appreciable influence upon the character and number of the tracts we are to examine later. We even catch a glimpse of a possible fourth at the time of the great plague in 1563, when Grindal, then bishop of London, is found writing to Cecil to advise a year's inhibition of all plays in the city and for three miles round, adding, significantly, "and if it were for ever it were not amiss."[3] Our records, however, do not begin till 1572 when, as Harrison tells us, with approval, in his *Chronologie*,[4] players were expelled because of the plague; and it seems that the lord mayor refused to re-admit them, if we may judge from the letters of the privy council on their behalf in 1573 and, again, in the spring of 1574.[5] These letters, evidently, were of no avail; for, on 7 May, 1574, the court party found it necessary to take out a royal patent in favour of the earl of Leicester's company, giving it express permission to play

---

[1] See *Acts of the Privy Council*, ed. Dasent, T. R., and *Malone Society Collections*, part 1, the latter of which gives all the letters from the *Remembrancia* and the *Burghley Papers*, dealing with the stage. Unfortunately, there is a gap in the register from June, 1581, to Feb., 1586, and in the *Remembrancia*, from March, 1584, to Jan., 1587.

[2] Cf. *ante*, Chap. x.

[3] *Remains of Grindal*, Parker Soc. Publications, pp. 268, 269, *Malone Society Collections*, part 1, p. 148.

[4] Furnivall, *Harrison's Description of England*, New Shaksp. Soc. part 1, p. liv.

[5] *Acts, op. cit.* vol. VIII, pp. 131, 132, 215.

within the city notwithstanding any orders to the contrary, and
eluding the consequences of the proclamation of 1559 by stipu-
lating that its performances should be licensed by the master
of the revels.[1] This is the beginning of the policy of sub-
ordinating the stage to the revels' office. Its immediate effect
was to force the city to open its gates; but, later in the same
year, the lord mayor retaliated by procuring an order of the
common council requiring that all playhouses, companies and
plays should be licensed by the corporation, and enumerating
in a preamble all the "great disorders and inconvenyances"
occasioned by the drama; which proves beyond doubt that the
city's attitude was largely influenced by puritanical convictions.[2] At this juncture, our information becomes insufficient
to follow the sequence of events. But the upshot of the conflict
is clear. Certain players, finding the city obdurate and unwilling to submit to its severe regulations, began to look about
them for some means of carrying on their business out of reach
of the mayor's authority. Thus, while the innyards of the city
continued to be used for dramatic purposes, in 1575, the
foundations of the first permanent playhouse in London were
laid "in the fields to the North of the City," and, in 1576,
or the following year, the buildings were completed.[3] The
puritan watched with horror the rise of these "houses of purpose, built with great charges for the maintenance of them and
that without the liberties, as who shall say: there, let them say
what they will, we will play";[4] but he could not do anything
save vent his rage in sermons and tracts.

The second crisis appears to have centred round the great
plague of 1582–3, though there are signs of its approach
several years earlier. In 1578, we find Fleetwood, the city
recorder, referring to certain standing orders by Burghley for
dealing with plays;[5] and, in the correspondence of 1580, it is
evident that a campaign is on foot for the abolition of the stage
not only in the city but also in the fields.[6] An earthquake in
April that year, celebrated in a contemporary ballad beginning:

---

[1] Hazlitt, *op. cit.* p. 25.

[2] Hazlitt, *op. cit.* p. 27; *Malone Society Collections*, part I, p. 175.

[3] Cf. *ante*, Chap. x.

[4] Stockwood, *Sermon*, 1578, p. 134.

[5] Wright, *Elizabeth*, vol. II, p. 88; *Malone Society Collections*, part I, p. 157.

[6] *Malone Society Collections*, part I, pp. 46–49.

Comme from the plaie, comme from the playe:
the house will fall so people saye:
the earth quakes lett us hast awaye,[1]

probably did much to strengthen the city's cause, and the
plague came to its assistance in 1581, so that the playhouses
were shut all through the summer.   Then began the customary struggle over the players' re-admission.   In December, we
find the privy council, in answer to a pitiful petition from the
acting companies, obliged to renew in a stronger form its usual
reminder to the lord mayor that the Christmas festivities were
approaching.[2]   And, on 24 December, the master of the revels
was granted by royal patent certain wide, if vague, powers over
the whole stage which seem to have been intended to counterbalance, if not to override, the powers of the lord mayor.[3]   It
was probably this patent which called forth, as an answer from
the city, the famous undated act of common council for the
permanent prohibition of plays in the city which has been
usually, but, as has now been proved, erroneously, ascribed to
the year 1575.[4]   London had followed in the wake of Marseilles; the filthy player had been expelled.   At the beginning
of 1582, the privy council pleaded with the mayor to invoke his
late "inhibityon,"[5] but in vain, and further discussion was
stopped for that year by the plague.

It was not until the autumn of 1583 that the plague abated
sufficiently to allow of a renewal of the dispute.   But, in the
meantime, two events of great importance had taken place; the
first probably doing more than a thousand learned treatises to
stamp the stage as an unholy institution.   On Sunday, 13
January, 1583, great crowds were gathered to watch the bear-
baiting at Paris garden, a pleasure resort outside the juris-

---

[1] Arber, *Stationers' Register*, vol. II, p. 167 b.   Cf. passage from Gardniers'
Doomesday Booke, 1606, quoted in Halliwell-Phillipps, J. O., *Outlines*, vol. I,
p. 343, and Stubbes's *Anatomie*, part I, p. 180.

[2] *Acts*, vol. XIII, p. 269.

[3] Chambers, *Tudor Revels*, pp. 62, 72, 75.

[4] *Orders appointed to be executed* (Singleton), Art. 62.   For the question of
date v. Chambers, *The Academy*, 24 August, 1895, and *Malone Society Collections*,
part I, pp. 168-9.

[5] *Malone Society Collections*, part I, pp. 52-54; *Acts*, vol. XIII, p. 404.   There
is evidently some confusion of dates here.   The letter of the privy council is
given 11 April in the *Remembrancia* and 25 April or May in *Acts*.   These are not
different letters, as is stated in *Malone Society Collections*, part I, p. 54.

diction of the city, when a wooden scaffold on which many were seated collapsed, killing a few and injuring many more.[1] It seemed a direct fulfilment of the prophecies of puritans, a "judgment" which not even the most abandoned playgoer could disregard. Yet the court hardened its heart like Pharaoh, for, on 10 March, it once more stepped in on the players' behalf. At Walsingham's suggestion and under the direction of the master of the revels, "a companie of players for her Majestie" was formed.[2] This, obviously, was intended as a move against the lord mayor, though it led, also, to important consequences for the stage. As in the case of the Leicester company ten years before, the city was forced to yield for the moment, and, by arrangement with the privy council, the royal company was admitted into the city from the autumn of 1583 till the following Shrovetide.[3] When, however, her majesty's players sought re-admission in the autumn of 1584, they were met with the absolute refusal of the lord mayor. He had been tricked the season before, for all the playhouses had been filled with men calling themselves the queen's players. The company could do nothing beyond appealing to the privy council. The text of this appeal, together with a detailed answer from the city and certain other documents connected with it, has been preserved for us among the Burghley papers;[4] but we are completely ignorant of the events that followed. In much the same tantalising fashion, we catch a glimpse of an attempt upon the Theater and the Curtain in the same year. The lord mayor's letters of 1580 tell us that he was then already preparing to stretch forth his hand against the impudent Jerichoes in the fields; and, in 1583, we find him pleading with Walsingham that they should be closed. In June, 1584, he actually seems to have accomplished his purpose; for, apparently, by reason of a brawl outside the Theater entirely unconnected with actors or their craft, he managed to procure an order from the privy council for the destruction of the houses.[5] Again the curtain falls at the most exciting point.

[1] *Malone Society Collections*, part I, pp. 59, 61, 65, 159, 161, 171 for references to this incident.

[2] *Tudor Revels*, p. 62.

[3] *Malone Society Collections*, I, pp. 66, 67.

[4] *Ibid.* p. 168.

[5] *Ibid.* pp. 164–6. Cf. as to this brawl, *ante*, Chap. x.

We do not even know whether the order was ever carried out.

The year 1584, evidently, was a very critical one in the history of the English stage; yet we cannot doubt that the players successfully weathered the storm. Certainly, plays did not cease to be acted in London; nor do the houses in the fields appear to have suffered any material damage. Meanwhile, the stage drifted more and more under the control of the revels' office, until, in 1592, we find the lord mayor, apparently on the advice of archbishop Whitgift, proposing that the master, Edmond Tilney, should be bought over to the city's point of view by an annuity.[1]

The third, and, so far as we know, the last, serious crisis in the relations between the city and the stage occurred in 1597. Thomas Nashe, writing to a friend in 1596, complains that

the players . . . are piteously persecuted by the Lord Mayor and the Aldermen; and however in their old Lord's time they thought their estate settled, it is now so uncertain they cannot build upon it.[2]

The "old Lord" here referred to was lord Hunsdon, lord chamberlain, a staunch supporter of the players' interests in the privy council. He died on 22 July, 1596, and was succeeded in office by the puritanically-minded lord Cobham.[3] We do not know to what measure of persecution in 1596 Nashe is here referring; but, on 28 July, 1597, we find the lord mayor addressing an interesting letter to the council and enclosing a statement of "the inconveniences that grow by stage playes," which we recognise as the basis of many earlier letters. The council was desired to take measures "for the present staie and fynall suppressinge" of plays both within and without the liberties,[4] and it immediately complied by sending an order to the justices of Middlesex for the dismantling of the Theater and Curtain "so as they maie not be ymploied agayne to suche

---

[1] *Malone Society Collections*, I, pp. 68–70; *Tudor Revels*, p. 78, for the skirmish between the authorities and the stage, in 1589, which arose out of the Marpreiate controversy, had nothing to do with the matter in hand. See above, Vol. III, of the present work, p. 445; *Malone Society Collections*, part II, p. 180; *Acts*, vol. XVIII, pp. 214–5; Collier, vol. I, pp. 275–7.

[2] Fleay's *Chronicle of Stage*, p. 157; Collier, vol. I, pp. 292–4.

[3] *Malone Society Collections*, part I, p. 39.

[4] *Ibid.*, pp. 78–80.

use."[1]   Once again, however, we are left in the dark as to the fate of the houses in the fields.   As a matter of fact, the Theater was closed this very month and year, but the cause appears to have been nothing more serious than a difficulty in renewing the lease.   Perhaps, the death of lord Cobham and the influence of the new lord chamberlain, another lord Hunsdon, may have weakened the force of the order.   In any case, the civic authorities do not seem to have gained much from a fight of over a quarter of a century.   Sunday performances were abolished, at least in theory; playing was forbidden in Lent; and certain other restrictions were placed upon the freedom of the actor. But the enemies of the stage had aimed at abolition, not regulation.[2]

It is now time to turn to the literary side of the puritan campaign and to speak of the bombardment which the pamphleteers kept up, while the city fathers made their repeated assaults upon the stage.   It will be remembered how the players had nonplussed the corporation by setting up their houses outside the walls of the city.   The question was now as to what could be accomplished by the voice of the preacher and the pen of the pamphleteer.   The erection of the Theater and the Curtain in 1576 and 1577 acted at once upon the already highly charged atmosphere and called down a veritable hail of sermons and tracts.   Of the former, only one or two, which are preserved for our edification in book form, need here be noticed.   There is, for example, the sermon of one Thomas White, delivered at Paul's cross on 9 December, 1576 and, apparently, repeated on 3 November in the following year, to which we are indebted for the syllogistic statement of the plague argument already quoted, and which, by its reference to "the sumptuous Theatre houses, a continuall monument of London's prodigalitie and folly" helps us to determine the date of their establishment.   Another divine who, by publication, sought a larger congregation than had assembled to hear him

---

[1] Halliwell-Phillipps, J. O., *Outlines* (7th ed.), vol. I, p. 356; *Acts*, vol. XXVII, p. 313.

[2] For the order against the theatres in 1600, which, curiously enough, the city did not carry out, perhaps because it had some reference to the Essex rising perhaps because the lord mayor of the year seems to have been himself in favour of plays, see Simpson, *New Shaksp. Soc. Trans.*, 1874, vol. II, pp. 386–9; Lee, *Life of Shakespeare*, pp.174–6, 212–3; Fleay's *Chronicle of Stage*, p. 161; Halliwell-Phillipps, J. O., *Outlines*, vol. I, pp. 307–9.

at Paul's cross was John Stockwood; his sermon, dated 24 August, 1578, laments the immorality of playhouses and the immense gains of players, and gives a very forcible expression to that feeling of rivalry between stage and pulpit to which we have referred.

From the printed sermon to the godly treatise is no great step. The honour of taking it belongs to John Northbrooke, a puritan clergyman residing near Bristol, who had suffered imprisonment at the hands of his bishop, apparently for some act of nonconformity. As his *Treatise, wherein Dicing, Dauncing, vain Playes or Enterludes with other idle Pastimes etc. commonly used on the Sabbath day, are reproved by the Authoritie of the Word of God and auntient Writers*, was entered for publication in the year 1577, it is natural to suppose that the erection of the playhouses was the immediate occasion of its appearance. Yet the book was rather a general arraignment of the "abuses" of the age than a special treatise on the subject of stage plays, to which scarcely more than a sixth of its space was given. Indeed, while its debt to Fenton's *Forme of Christian pollicie* is considerable, it became, in its turn, as regards both contents and dialogue-form, the model for Stubbes's *Anatomie of Abuses*. When he addresses himself to the subject of plays, it is the moral aspect of the question upon which Northbrooke lays especial stress, providing his readers with an appalling list of the vices which might be learnt at the theatre, while his remark that "it is better to be subject to a magistrate under whom nothing is lawful than under him to whom all things are lawful" indicates the remedy which commended itself to him and to most of his fellow puritans.

Quaint, simple-minded and long-winded Northbrooke remained a solitary pioneer. He has his special niche, of course, in Prynne's pantheon of stage haters, and Stubbes, as we have said, evidently read him and learnt from him; but his immediate successors either did not know of him or deliberately ignored his existence.[1] In 1579, the very year when a second edition of his book was appearing, a new writer was, with considerable ostentation, "setting up the Flagge of Defiance"

---

[1] That he was not forgotten altogether is clear from a reference to his book in *A true reporte of the death . . . of M. Campion* (1582) which, incidentally, affords a proof that this topic was interesting to Catholics as well as to puritans. See *The Modern Language Review*, vol. IV, p. 485.

to the prevailing abuses of the day, and claiming to be the one
to "found the schoole and reade the first lecture of all." [1]   This
fresh arrival in the lists was Stephen Gosson, one of the most
interesting and important of those who took up arms against
the stage.   Though not more than twenty-four years of age
when he published *The Schoole of Abuse*, he had already, if
Meres is to be believed, written pastorals which ranked among
the best of his age, though none of the specimens of his poetry
that have come down to us soars above the commonplace.
In addition to this, the style of his *Schoole* suggests that he
deserves almost as much credit as Lyly for giving to Euphuism
its final and complete form; both having been bitten with the
craze at Oxford, very possibly in company.   Like Lyly, also,
Gosson left Oxford for London, and took to the stage as both
actor and playwright.   At least three dramas were produced
by him, as he tells us himself: *Catalines Conspiracy*, which
appeared at the Theater, "a cast of Italian devices called
The comedie of Captaine Mario" and "a moral" entitled
Praise at Parting.[2]   From certain hints he gives us, we are
led to suppose that his theatrical career was neither prosperous
nor successful.   Whether for this reason or, as he would rather
have us think, because the nonconformist conscience was
already beginning to make the playwright discontented with his
surroundings, about the end of 1578 he left London and became
a private tutor in the country, where he prepared his *Pleasaunt
invective against Poets, Pipers, Plaiers, Jesters and such like
Caterpillers of a commonwelth*, which was entered at Stationers'
Hall on 22 July of the year following.

If *The Schoole of Abuse* was intended as a puritan palinode,
it certainly does not read like one.   Its worldly, flippant air,
very different from the sober dulness of Northbrooke, suggests
that this assault upon Parnassus was little more than a trick to
catch the public ear and to win something of the success of
Euphues, which had appeared a few months earlier.   Doubtless its author also hoped that his remarks upon the drama
would attract the favourable notice of London puritans.

---

[1] In the same year there appeared a pamphlet by "T. F.," entitled *Newes
from the North*, which complains of playhouses, and especially the Theater and
Curtain.   Ed. 1585 sig. F 4.

[2] See *The Schoole of Abuse*, ed. Arber, p. 40, and *Plays Confuted*, Hazlitt, *u.s.*
p. 165.

Among the letters at the end of the book is one addressed to the lord mayor and aldermen, applauding their policy with regard to the players, and touching the root of the matter in the remark that, "if their letters of commendation were once stayed, it were easie for you to overthrow them." As Gosson was one of the few anti-dramatic writers who possessed a first-hand acquaintance of the theatre, it is interesting to observe that there is very little he can find to advance against it. He is careful to point out that nothing of an unseemly nature ever went on within the precincts of the playhouse itself; that actors might even be "sober, discreete, properly learned honest householders"; and that there were several "good playes and sweete playes" to be seen in London, among which, of course, are those by Stephen Gosson himself.

The patron at whose feet Gosson laid this work was none other than that "right noble gentleman, Master Philip Sidney Esquier," who, as we learn on the authority of Spenser, was anything but flattered at the tribute.[1] Indeed, there can be little doubt that the famous *Apologie for Poetrie*, written in the autumn of 1581 though not published before 1595, was undertaken, in the first place, as a reply to Gosson; the disdainful reference to "that kinde of people, who seek a prayse by dispraysing others, that they doe prodigally spend a great many wandering wordes, in quips and scoffes"[2] being a palpable hit at him and his pamphlet.

Despite its affectation and folly, *The Schoole of Abuse* gained its immediate object. It was widely read, and met with a storm of opposition. Gosson refers to this in the introduction to his second book, *The Ephemerides of Phialo*, published in the autumn of 1579, making special mention of a tract, no longer extant, which assumed the curious title of *Straunge Newes out of Affrick*. Possibly this name, very similar to that of hundreds of news-pamphlets of the time, was intended to cloak the real nature of the publication from the eyes of the authorities. The author, whose name Gosson knew but did not disclose, has been conjectured to be Lyly, but without sufficient foundation.[3] At the conclusion of *The Ephemerides* appears *An*

---

[1] *Three proper and wittie familiar Letters*, by Immerito and G. H., 1580, p. 54.

[2] *Apologie*, Arber's reprint, pp. 48, 49. See *ante*, Vol. III, p. 340, for the place of the controversy in the history of literary criticism.

[3] Indeed, a favourable reference to *The Ephemerides* in *Euphues and his England*

Apologie for the Schoole of Abuse. Much of a piece with the work it sets out to defend—being, indeed, little more than a disquisition on the immorality of the pagan deities—this fresh contribution was undertaken in answer to a second champion who had come forward in defence of the arts. Gosson asserts that, after offering rewards at both universities to anyone who would write for them, the players had found a writer in London to comply with their needs. He had put forth a book, of which, at the time of writing, Gosson knew nothing save its title, *Honest Excuses*. This, there seems no reason to doubt, was the pamphlet by Thomas Lodge which has come down to us without a title-page.[1]

This tract, the earliest publication of the future author of *Rosalynde*, and usually described as *A Defence of Poetry, Music and Stage-Playes*, must have been written immediately after Gosson's *School* appeared, and printed in the late summer of 1579. It appeared surreptitiously, however; for it was refused a licence—a very striking indication of the power and determination of the puritan opposition. In other respects, there is nothing in any way remarkable about the book. A piece of very ordinary Elizabethan prose, full of classical allusions, and every now and then, attempting the euphuistic manner, it is yet in no way inferior to the work it attacks. After the controversial fashion of the age, it contains a considerable amount of personal insinuation, which, probably, bore some relation to the truth, since Lodge and Gosson, apparently had been contemporaries at Oxford and, undoubtedly, were acquaintances later in London. It is worth noticing, in view of Gosson's accusation that Lodge had been hired by the players, that the defence of poetry and music is quite as lengthy and serious as that of plays. The last topic is treated in a remarkably moderate tone. After a discussion of the antiquity and origin of play making, which anticipates the line of defence taken up later by Heywood, Lodge proceeds to consider the condition of the contemporary theatre. Here, he is ready to own, there is much room for improvement, and he admits that he wishes "as zealously as the best that all abuse of playinge were abolished"; but this, he adds, is no reason for abolishing

would seem to preclude the possibility altogether. See Bond, R. W., *Lyly*, 1902, vol. II, p. 99.

[1] See *The Modern Language Review*, vol. III, pp. 166–8.

the stage itself.   Such frank recognition of the claims of reform
makes the refusal to license his book all the more remarkable.

We must turn aside from Gosson and Lodge for the moment, to notice the entrance of another combatant.   The year
1580, which, as we have seen, was the beginning of the second
great struggle between the city and the court, also marks a new
development in the tactics of the pamphleteer.   Up to this
point, the stage had been attacked in company with other
"abuses"; but, late in 1580, there appeared for the first time a
book which devoted itself exclusively to the subject of stage
plays.   It was entitled *A Second and third Blast of retrait from
plaies and Theatres*, and, lest there should be any mistake as
to the source of its inspiration, it bore the arms of the corporation of London upon the reverse of its title-page.   No clearer
proof than this can be needed of the close connection between
the administrative and literary attacks.   The lord mayor
had evidently discovered the usefulness of the pamphlet
agitation, and the sudden increase in the output of tracts
during the next two or three years points unmistakably to
encouragement by the authorities.   In addition to all this,
the book is instructive as affording a fresh illustration of the
fact that the puritan attack was largely an echo of the old
conflict between the pagan theatre and the primitive church;
for the *Second Blast* (the first, of course, had been sounded by
Gosson) was a translation of Salvian's attack on the iniquities
of the Roman stage, which forms a section of his *De Gubernatione
Dei*.[1]   But a greater interest attaches itself to the work of
the other devout trumpeter whom the title proclaims, "a
worshipful and zealous Gentleman now alive."   Like every
other writer in the controversy, he borrows largely from his
predecessors, especially from Twynne and Fenton.   Being
under the patronage of the city, he is naturally chiefly concerned
with the administrative side of the problem.   The root of the
evil, he declares, as Gosson had done, is the support that
players receive from the nobility; and he even goes on to say
that, unable or unwilling to maintain their servants at their
own cost, noblemen allowed them to live at the expense or
charity of the general public.   These bold words could scarcely
have been uttered a year or two later when the queen herself

[1] The *editio princeps* of his works was published this same year at Paris.

had her company of actors. Yet, curiously enough, violent as the language of the tract is, it proposes no drastic measures of reform. The magistrate is advised to go slowly, and to begin by stopping all Sunday playing.

This tame conclusion, in all probability, may be put down to half-heartedness, or even insincerity, on the part of the author. Gosson, two years later, in his *Playes Confuted*, asserted that, beside himself, no playwright had written against plays "but one who hath changed his coppy and turned himself like ye dog to his vomit to plays againe."[1] As the author of the *Third Blast* himself informs us that he had previously "bene a great affector of that vaine art of Plaie-making," it is natural to suppose that it is he to whom Gosson refers. The present writer is of opinion that the apostate playwright in question was that Elizabethan Jack-of-all-trades, Anthony Munday, who had been deliberately hired for the purpose by the opponents of the stage.[2] If this theory, which is supported by a good deal of circumstantial evidence, be true, it throws a somewhat sinister light upon the tactics of the puritan party as having taken out a year's lease of a scapegrace actor's pen and paraded his sham conversion as a triumph for the cause of public morality.[3]

Meanwhile, the players had been seeking to discredit puritans in general and Gosson in particular. They had revived two of his plays, which, as he tells us, they "impudently affirmed" to have been written since the publication of *The Schoole of Abuse*. Moreover, on 23 February, 1582,[4] a drama in the manner of the old moralities was produced at the Theater under the title: *The Playe of Playes and Pastimes*, which Prynne, probably erroneously, ascribed to Lodge.[5] The

---

[1] Hazlitt, *op. cit.* p. 212.

[2] See Fleay's *Chronicle of Stage*, pp. 51, 52; *The Modern Language Review*, vol. IV, pp. 484–7. Cf. however, *ante*, Vol. V, p. 348, note.

[3] *A Treatise of Daunses* (1581), usually quoted as one of the pamphlets in the controversy, contains no reference whatever to the stage, the word "playes" on the title-page, which has misled the unwary, meaning games of chance.

[4] This date is given us by Gosson, *Plays Confuted*, Hazlitt, p. 189. Halliwell-Phillipps (*Tarlton's Jest*, Old Shakesp. Soc., 1844, p. xx) prints from "a manuscript in the possession of Mr. Collier" Tarlton's *Jigge of a horse loade of Fooles*, cf. *ante*, Vol. IV, p. 602, which brings in Gosson as a Puritan-fool, "for sure a hypocrite." If genuine (which, however, is a very doubtful assumption) the "jigge" was probably written about this time.

[5] *Histrio-mastix*, p. 700. Prynne was evidently confusing *The Playe of Playes*

play is not extant, and was probably never even printed; but we learn a great deal about it from Gosson who is ever very liberal in his accounts of his antagonists' movements. Its object was to show how dangerous Zeal, or puritanism, might become as the sole guide to Life. Only when "somewhat pinchte in the wast" and in company with Delight and Recreation was she tolerable, being then ready to allow the use of comedies, provided, of course, "that the matter be purged, deformities blazed, sinne rebuked, honest mirth intermingled and fit time for the hearing of the same appointed."[1]

For a long time, Gosson had been unable to procure a copy of Lodge's suppressed pamphlet. His rejoinder, therefore, promised in *An Apologie for the Schoole of Abuse*, did not make its appearance until 1528, and included an answer to the players also. *Playes confuted in five Actions*, as he calls his book, is unlike *The Schoole of Abuse* in every respect, and the complete change of tone, in all probability, may be attributed to the influence of the lord mayor, for we have little confidence in the sincerity of Gosson's sentiments.[2] Like the author of the *Second* and the *Third Blast*, he is now concerned with the stage alone, which has overshadowed all other "abuses" in his eyes. Plays "are not to be suffered in a Christian commonweale," for are they not "the doctrine and invention of the Devill"? Even Lodge cannot deny that they were originally dedicated to idols, or that the first theatre was erected to facilitate the rape of the Sabine women. And the style has changed with the matter. Euphuism and the classics are laid aside, and, in their stead, we are treated to divinity and the early fathers; there is no longer even a pretence at pleasantry in Gosson's invective. The book, probably, was written in haste, for, despite its division into "five actions," which anticipates the acts and scenes of *Histrio-mastix*, it has no intelligible arrangement of topics. Revenge is taken for Lodge's personalities in the dedication, which, this time, is addressed to Sir Francis Walsingham,[3] a scarcely more fortunate choice than Sir Philip

---

with Lodge's *Defence*. The controversial "morality" was also employed against the Martinists. See *ante*, Vol. III, pp. 446, 447.

[1] Hazlitt, pp. 201-3.

[2] The coarse *Pleasant Quippes for Upstart Gentlewomen* (1596), almost certainly by Gosson, could hardly have been written by a genuine puritan.

[3] Cf. the lord mayor's letter of 1583 (*Malone Society Collections*, pt. 1, p. 63). It

Sidney. Gosson declares that his antagonists had been "hunted by the heavy hand of God and become little better than a vagarant." Whether these words are merely an outburst of spleen or actually referred to a discreditable passage in the doctor-novelist's life, is not known. Lodge, at least, did not consider them worthy of any immediate reply, and, when, two years later, he recalled the controversy in the dedication of his *Alarum against Usurers* (1584), he charitably excused Gosson for his spiteful remarks, declaring that he bore him no grudge for them. Thus closed the earliest and most important of those hand to hand encounters which occasionally enlivened the course of the struggle.

The next tract we have to notice deals with the Paris garden disaster of January, 1583, which was too striking not to evoke something more permanent than the inevitable broadside ballad. Within a week of its occurrence, a small octavo of forty pages appeared from the press of the puritan printer, Robert Waldegrave.[1] It was the work of John Field, part author of the first *Admonition to Parliament* and posthumous contributor to the Marprelate controversy. He had long been known as an opponent of the stage, and, in a letter, dated 25 November, 1581, thanking Leicester for procuring his release from prison, into which he had been thrown for non-conformity, he actually takes occasion to chide his benefactor for his love of "these impure interludes and playes."[2] His *Godly Exhortation*, as he styled it, deals with the drama chiefly from the Sabbatarian point of view and contains the usual list of terrible judgments, among which the late disaster at Paris garden, naturally, took a prominent place. This interesting little tract is far better written than the majority of the series.

In the same year, 1583, a book was published which has an importance far beyond that belonging to it as a contribution to the controversy under discussion. This was *The Anatomie*

seems that, in spite of his action on 10 March, 1583, puritans had some reason for regarding Walsingham, in Gosson's words, as "a Hercules in the Court" to cleanse the Augean stables.

[1] Dated on the last page 17 Jan. Fleetwood notes its appearance in an entry in his diary under 19 Jan. (*Malone Society Collections*, part 1, p. 161).

[2] Collier, J. P., vol. 1, pp. 243–6. Another pamphlet on the same topic, Henry Cave's *Narration of the Fall of Paris Garden* (1588?), seems to have disappeared.

of Abuses, by the foremost of puritan social reformers, Philip Stubbes.   Practically, nothing is known of his life, and it is unfortunate that the only contemporary testimony extant concerning his character is a ribald story in the anti-Martinist tract, *An Almond for a Parrat*.   His literary activity, which covered a period of some thirteen years, seems to have begun about 1581, when he published a broadside ballad setting forth the fearful fate that had befallen "a lewde fellow usually accostomed to sweare by Gods Blood."   A second edition of this, containing another ballad of similar nature, appeared shortly afterwards.   Stubbes continued this practice of turning the public taste for horror to godly purposes in his fourth and most important work, by bringing together a formidable array of examples of divine judgments suddenly executed upon sinners of various kinds.   This book, the famous *Anatomie of Abuses*, the title of which, perhaps, was intended to suggest comparison with the fashionable *Anatomy of Wit*, was printed on 1 May, 1583, and, immediately becoming popular, passed through four editions in three years.   It was followed, a few months later, by a second part no less interesting, if less well known, than its predecessor.   Both were "made dialogue-wise" and consist of descriptions and condemnations, backed by scriptural text and the aforesaid terrible examples, of those evils in the commonwealth which needed abolition or reformation. In all this there was nothing original.   The records of the time are full of references to tracts against dicing, gaming, sabbath-breaking, usury and so forth.   Excellent as his intentions were, Stubbes's title to fame rests rather on the vigour and pictur-esqueness of his style, the shrewdness of his observations and, above all, the surprising knowledge he displays as to the manners and customs of his age.   *The Anatomie of Abuses* and Harrison's *Description of England*, which is dealt with elsewhere, are our two chief contemporary sources of information upon the social and economic conditions of the Shakespearean period.   The lengthy description which Stubbes gives of the extravagances of Elizabethan fashion is a unique storehouse of facts relating to late sixteenth century costume.   But this famous passage has tended unduly to obscure the merits of the rest.   The opening words of *The Anatomie* give us to understand that the author had been travelling up and down the country for "seven winters and more," collecting material for his book. Certainly nothing but the greatest patience and industry could have brought together all these details upon a great variety of subjects. The flippant Nashe, attacking Stubbes and his like in *The Anatomie of Absurditie,* declared that they "extend their invectives so farre against the abuse, that almost the things remaines not whereof they admitte anie lawfull use."[1] There is some truth in this; but, had Stubbes been less earnest and less sweeping, we should have had none of those interesting and curious allusions to church-ales, barbers, football, astrologers and a hundred other seemingly trivial matters. Moreover, there is much sound commonsense behind most that he writes. While pleading on almost every page for the rights of the poor, he has no sentimental pity for the idle vagrant. Rackrenting, prison reform and many other problems that still press for solution, are touched upon in a manner that would do credit to a modern socialist. *The Anatomie of Abuses* is a very remarkable book. It is essentially the work of an original thinker, and, in fact, is an early attempt to sum up the moral and economic forces of a nation in a fashion far removed, but not radically different, from that employed by the sociologists or political economists of the twentieth century.

Though confined to a short section of some five or six pages, entitled "Of Stage-Playes and Enterludes, with their wickedness,"[2] Stubbes's condemnation of the theatre is far the most uncompromising and intolerant that had yet appeared in England. Also, he was unmistakably sincere, which is more than can be said of any of his predecessors except Northbrooke and the preachers. The devilish origin of plays and their ghastly moral results are sharply and effectively driven home in Stubbes's hammerlike style, weighted by the authority of Scripture and the early fathers. There is no mincing matters; to patronise the theatre is "to worship devils and betray Christ Jesus," and, as for players themselves, they can only be earnestly exhorted to repent and so flee from the wrath to come, which, as Stubbes thought, was to come speedily. These trenchant observations, in a book which at once became

[1] McKerrow's *Nashe,* vol. I, p. 20, l. 7.
[2] Furnivall's edition, part I, pp. 140–6.

popular, must have gone to swell the rising puritan opposition.   Stubbes himself, it may be noted, rose with the tide;
for a conciliatory preface, admitting that some plays were
"honest and chaste" and, as such, "very tollerable exercyses,"
was omitted after the first edition, thus proving that his final
opinion on the matter was one of unqualified condemnation.[1]

In William Rankins, who, in 1587, published his pretentious
Mirrour of Monsters, we seem to have a case somewhat similar
to that of Munday.   The *Third Blast* rings weak and hollow
beside Rankins's strident denunciations of the "spotted
enormities that are caused by the infectious sight of Playes";
yet, in 1598, Henslowe lent his company £3 in order to purchase
one of Rankins's plays.[2]   So rapid a fall from the heights of
virtue creates suspicion.   Despite the violence of its language,
the *Mirrour* does not quite succeed in striking the note of
sincerity.   The voice is the voice of the godly; but the euphuistic style and the elaborate pageant "Of the marriage of Pride
and Luxury" with which the book closes suggest the flesh
pots of Egypt.[3]

The pamphlets we have hitherto considered cover a period
of about ten years, the agitation to which we owe them being
directly traceable to the erection of the playhouses in 1576.
But these houses, in spite of all the efforts of the city authorities,
were now firmly established, and, though puritan feeling against
them did not in any way decrease, the general public, we may
suppose, began to take considerably less interest in the discussion.   The failure, too, of the city's determined attack
of 1583-4 probably took the heart out of the pamphleteers.
Moreover, in 1588, a fresh topic of public interest arose in the
famous attack upon the bishops by Martin Marprelate, which,
indeed, made so large a stir as to throw into the shade for some
time to come all other aspects of puritanism.   Nor is it fanciful
to suppose that the great struggle with Spain, which belongs to
the same period, diminished the demand for pamphlets of this
nature.   Preachers, we cannot doubt, continued to denounce

---

[1] George Whetstone's *Touchstone for the Time*, published with his *Mirour for
Magestrates* (1584), and Thomas Newton's *Treatise, touching Dyce-play and
prophane Gaming* (1586), are two books, belonging to this period, which express
a desire to see the stage reformed but not abolished.

[2] *Henslowe's Diary*, part I, p. 96; part II, p. 198.

[3] For a curious letter, on the subject of stage plays, of the same date as Rankins's *Mirrour*, see Halliwell-Phillipps's *Illustrations*, part I, app. XVII.

the stage with unabated vigour.   Theologians, we know, did
not cease in the course of their treatises to warn their readers
against it.[1]   But such contributions to the controversy as
possess any importance, in the last fifteen years of Elizabeth's
reign, are almost entirely on the side of the players.   It was,
for example, doubtless by way of apology that Robert Greene
penned the "large digression" on "Playes, Playmakers, and
Players" in his *Francesco's Fortunes* (1590).[2]   Again, his
friend, Thomas Nashe, whose satirical pen was the most powerful that had yet been wielded against the puritans, in his earliest
work *The Anatomie of Absurditie*, the title of which, probably,
was intended to recall that of Stubbes's,[3] who, indeed, is
attacked by name, devotes considerable attention to the
writers upon "abuses," "who make the Presse the dunghill
whither they carry all the muck of their melancholicke imagi-
nations."[4]   And, in his *Pierce Penilesse*, published in 1592,
during which year, be it noted, the theatres had been closed
because of a riot,[5] he advances still further into the enemy's
quarters.   After "a bout" with those who presumed to attack
poetry, he here embarks upon a lengthy defence of plays.   He
declares that they are the salvation of idle men about town,
keeping them from worse occupations and giving them something upon which to sharpen their wits.   The playgoer has
not only an opportunity of learning the history of his country,
but the examples of the great and good of the past are set before
his eyes, while vice, in all its forms, is "most lively anatomized."
As for the attacks of the city, he asserts that they were made
solely in the interest of the

Vintners, Alewives and Victuallers, who surmise, that if there were
no Playes, they would have all the companie that resort to them,
lye bowzing and beere-bathing in their houses every afternoone.[6]

So telling an argument was not likely to be allowed to rust
for want of use.   A few months later, it did service in an enlarged form as Tarlton's defence of "the profession" in

[1] Among these may be mentioned bishop Babington's *Very Fruitful Exposition of the Commandments* (1583) which drew largely upon Stubbes. See
Furnivall, *Anatomy of Abuses*, pp. 75*–93* for copious extracts.

[2] Grosart's *Greene*, vol. VIII, pp. 129–133.

[3] But see McKerrow, *Nashe*, vol. IV, p. 3.

[4] *Ibid.*, vol. I, p. 20.   [5] *Acts*, vol. XXII, p. 550.

[6] McKerrow, *Nashe*, vol. I, pp. 211–215.

Chettle's *Kinde Hart's Dreame.*[1]   For any reply to these, however, or, indeed, for anything in the nature of a definite attack upon the stage, we may look in vain among the pamphlets published in London at this period.[2]   One more passage at arms took place before the end of the century; for this, however, we must turn from the capital to the universities.

As puritanism, in its origin, was intimately connected with humanism, it was only natural that the anti-dramatic spirit should have early penetrated to Oxford and Cambridge. Gosson asserted that "many famous men in both Universities have made open out-cries of the inconveniences bredde by playes." It is probable, however, that the number of these was never very large at a time.   In 1565, we hear of "two or three in Trinity College," Cambridge, who did not think that Christians ought to countenance plays;[3] and, in 1579, there broke out a "controversy between Mr. Drywood of Trinity, and one Punter a student of St. John's, Cambridge" on the same subject.[4]   Four years previously, at the same university, the privy council had forbidden all "common plays," with a view to keeping the youth of the nation undefiled.[5]   This and a similar order, in 1593,[6] seem to indicate that the council's real convictions, on these occasions, at any rate, inclined towards puritanism, and that its support of the stage in London was largely actuated by the wishes of the queen and, perhaps, by a desire to interfere with the city's authority.   Such orders, of course, did not touch academic or private plays, which, naturally, flourished at the seats of classical learning.   Most puritans, indeed, allowed them to be harmless.   At Oxford, for example, a certain John Case, in his *Speculum Moralium Quaestionum*, published in 1585, while utterly condemning the

---

[1] *Shakespeare Allusion Books*, part I, pp. 62–66 (New Shaksp. Soc.); McKerrow, *op. cit.* vol. IV, pp. 133–5.

[2] Sir John Harington's amusing *Treatise of Playe* (*Nugae Antiquae*, 1804, vol. I, p. 186), written about 1597, seems to show that the city's third attack revived a certain amount of public interest in the question.

[3] *Correspondence of Bp. Parker*, Parker Soc., p. 226.   This appears to be the earliest indication we have of the anti-dramatic spirit at the universities.   The case of *Pammachius*, in 1545, sometimes cited is that of a protestant controversial morality condemned by Gardiner, and, therefore, not to the point.

[4] *State Papers, Domestic*, 1547–80, p. 638.

[5] Collier, *op. cit.* vol. I, p. 223, quoting Lansdowne MSS., 71.

[6] For the order of 1575, and the long correspondence preceding the order of 1593, see *Malone Society Collections*, part I, pp. 190–202.

public or "common" play, not only allows, but goes out of his way to defend, the academic play. Yet Case's defence in itself shows that the matter was already under discussion in university circles; while his pointed reference to the Mosaic text, forbidding persons of one sex to wear the dress of the other, proves that the lines of the later controversy had been thus early laid down.

When, therefore, William Gager of Christ Church, a well known Latin dramatist, and John Rainolds, an eminent theologian, afterwards president of Corpus Christi, crossed swords, in 1592, on the subject of the propriety of the academic play, they were fighting over old ground. The duel, however, attracted considerable attention at the time owing to the reputation of the combatants. Never before had the drama a more learned opponent than Rainolds or a more accomplished defender than Gager. The dispute broke out over the performance of Gager's *Ulysses Redux*, a Latin tragedy, to which Rainolds had been invited by a friend. By way of covering them with ridicule, Gager, following a common practice among Latin dramatists of this age, had placed some of the puritan objections to the drama in the mouth of one of his characters. Unknown to Gager, Rainolds had used many of these very arguments in the letter in which he had refused the invitation, and he naturally supposed that their reproduction was intended as a personal insult to himself. A correspondence followed, in the course of which Gager sent his opponent a printed copy of his *Ulysses Redux* by way of self-justification. Rainolds's reply, which forms the first section of a volume entitled *Th' Overthrow of Stage-Playes* printed at Middleburg in 1599,[1] attacks both this and a comedy by Gager known as *Rivales*, at the same time setting forth at full length his objections to all forms of dramatic representation. Gager, like other stage apologists, had appealed to antiquity; Rainolds refers him to a Roman praetor's decree against actors. Gager's performers, moreover, had twice broken the divine law, first in playing on the Sabbath and, secondly, by donning women's clothes. The latter point, a stock argument in the puritan portfolio, is treated with overwhelming fulness. Gager's

---

[1] Collier, *Bibliographical Catalogue*, p. 246, suggests that it was printed in view of the projected erection of the Fortune theatre.

elaborate reply, dated 31 July, has never yet been printed and
was, indeed, practically unknown, until attention was called to
it two years ago.[1]   It is claimed as one of the most graceful
and convincing of the treatises in answer to the puritan attack.
Every argument of Rainolds is courteously but firmly met,
while, at times, the learned dramatist waxes eloquent in defence
of his art. Despite this urbanity and the request with which the
letter closes, that the dispute should be dropped, Rainolds was
in no mind to allow his adversary the last word. After a delay
occasioned by sickness, he produced, on 30 May, 1593, a very
lengthy reply in which, however, he did little more than
recapitulate and enlarge his previous arguments.[2]   Gager
received this fresh outburst in contemptuous silence, but his
friend Alberico Gentili entered the lists on his behalf and a
discussion in Latin followed, chiefly dealing with the legal
aspects of the dispute.

This Oxford controversy, it should be borne in mind, was of
a different nature from the discussion upon the merits of the
public stage which had been proceeding in London. Indeed,
one of the most interesting points about it is Gager's manifest
contempt for the professional side of his craft. While valiantly
defending himself and his young actors from the aspersions of
Rainolds, he admits the worst his opponent has to say about
"common playes." As an occasional recreation for learned
gentlemen, acting received his highest praise; as a regular
means of livelihood, it was regarded with scorn. This contempt of the gentleman for the rising class of actors, which had
only a remote connection with the loathing and abhorrence of
the puritan, was, undoubtedly, a factor in determining the
social status of Shakespeare and his fellows. The latter were
often, it is true, on terms of familiarity with the noblemen of
the day; but, however great a favourite he might be, and however respectable and wealthy he might become, the Elizabethan
common player was a "servant" in the eyes both of the nobleman to whose company he belonged and of everyone else.
Even Shakespeare's main ambition, apparently, was to become
a "gentleman." It is not difficult to understand the disgust

---

[1] By Boas, F. S., in *The Fortnightly Review* for August, 1907. The letter itself
is preserved among the manuscripts of Corpus Christi college, Oxford.

[2] This is also to be found in *Th' Overthrow of Stage-Playes*.

of those who amused themselves with the time-honoured academic play, at this intrusion into their sphere of persons whom they would deem base-born hirelings.

After Elizabeth's death, and under a new dynasty, a change came over the character and position of the stage.   In 1604, the right of noblemen to patronise players was virtually withdrawn by the repeal of the previous statutes exempting the members of their companies from the penalties of vagrancy.[1] This gave a formidable weapon into the hands of any provincial corporation and magistrates that wished to rid their community of the presence of travelling actors, as Sir Edward Coke carefully explained to the good people of Norwich on his circuit of 1606.[2]   On the other hand, by extending the policy introduced by Walsingham in 1583 and placing the great companies, one after the other, under the direct patronage of the crown, the position of the London stage was rendered practically impregnable.   Yet the theatre lost more than it gained.   It ceased to be a national institution and became a department of the revels' office; while its direct subordination to the court made it more unpopular than ever with the puritans, who were rapidly becoming the anti-court party.   The actor could scarcely be anything but royalist.   The dramatist could see but one side to those great questions which were sweeping England on to civil war.   But there was another side to this matter, which should not be overlooked.   While there can be no doubt whatever that, among the generality of puritans, the destestation of the stage was steadily on the increase at this period, wealthier citizens now began to look with more favourable eye upon theatrical performances.   The playhouses, in short, or, at least, the best known among them, by entering into close relations with the court added the finishing touches to the reputation for respectability which they had been slowly acquiring during Elizabeth's last years.   They lost, to a large extent, their popular character and became fashionable resorts which citizens and, more especially, citizens' wives found it both pleasant and socially advantageous to attend.   This fact helps to explain the almost complete cessation of the city's attacks and later pamphleteers, such as Rawlidge, do not

---

[1] Prothero, G. W., *Select Statutes*, p. 253.
[2] *The Lord Coke his speech and charge*, Nath. Butter, 1607.

hesitate to compare the more complacent citizens of Stewart London with "the religious senators" of a previous day.

Puritan anti-dramatic literature, with the exception of the sermon and the theological treatise,[1] was almost as scanty under James I as it had been during the last decade of Elizabeth's reign.   The first to revive the old controversy was a writer of the theatrical party.   In 1612, Thomas Heywood took upon him to defend his calling, apparently from some attack on the part of the authorities of which we have no knowledge.[2]   His tract was entitled *An Apology for Actors*. The poems by various of the author's friends with which it opens are not its least interesting feature.   John Webster's name figures among them; but his contribution is scarcely so entertaining as that by Richard Perkins, which makes some amusing hits at the hypocritical aspect of puritanism.   Heywood divides his book into three parts, which set out to display the "antiquity," the "ancient dignity" and the "true use" of his profession.   Much of his argument recalls that of Lodge, whose "patchte pamphlet," *A Defence of Stage-Plays*, doubtless he had studied.   Among new lines of defence may be noticed the observation that, though the classical stage was at its height at the time when Christ and His apostles were on earth, yet there is not a single text in the whole New Testament condemning it.   Great stress is laid upon the value of the drama as a moral tonic, and the puritan method of backing an argument with lists of divine judgments is cleverly adapted to the actors' purposes by a series of stories illustrating the strange and wonderful workings of a powerful play upon a guilty conscience.   The inevitable puritan reply appeared three years later and is conjectured to have been the work of one John Greene.   In *A Refutation of the Apology for Actors*, as it is called, Heywood is laboriously answered point by point.   The author borrows largely, and, at times, almost verbally, from Stubbes, while, in the methodical arrangement of his argument and in his tedious list of quotations from the fathers, he anticipates the work of Prynne.[3]

---

[1] See above, pp. 423, 424.   [2] *Apology*, ed. Collier, p. 14.
[3] A year after Heywood's *Apology*, appeared George Wither's *Abuses Stript and Whipt*, but, notwithstanding the familiar ring of its title and the unfavourable references to the stage which it contains, this slashing satire in verse is of a quiet different order from the ordinary puritan "abuse" pamphlet.

In 1614, a new literary fashion was started by the publication of Sir Thomas Overbury's *Characters*, and it was but natural that the controversy concerning the stage should be reflected in this and many similar publications. In 1616, for example, the author of *The Rich Cabnit furnished with a Varietie of exquisite Discriptions* devoted a chapter of his book to the character of a player. He is ready to admit that the actor possesses certain excellent accomplishments such as "dancing, song, ellocution, skill of weapon, pregnancy of wit"—a suggestive list of what was required of those who trod the Jacobean stage—but he can find no epithets strong enough to describe the immoral results of frequenting the theatre.

These character writers, however, hardly belong to the ranks of the regular combatants. We catch a better glimpse of the real strength of the feeling against the stage at this period, and of what the actor frequently had to suffer on its account, from an interesting letter, preserved among the *State Papers* for 1616, by Nathaniel Field, actor and playwright, to a certain "Mr. Sutton, Preacher att St. Mary Overs." Stung to the quick by the railings, frequently, it appears, spiced with personal allusions, which the worthy minister hurled at the heads of the members of the "Hope" company who formed part of his congregation, Field, at length, felt forced to take up the pen in self-defence. His letter, manly and independent in tone, protested in almost impassioned language against the puritan conception of an actor's mode of life, and appealed in pathetic terms to Heaven in self-justification. As the son of that doughty opponent of both bishop and stage, whose pamphlet in reference to the Paris garden disaster we have already noticed, Field was, doubtless, in a delicate position.[1] But, having been left an orphan a year after his birth, he had been brought up as one of the children of the Chapel Royal, and, if he had ever been troubled by any scruples about the profession for which fortune had fashioned him, a diligent study of the Bible, in which he found no "trade of life except conjurers, sorcerers and witches, *ipso facto*, damned" had long removed them. However, it was a case of mutual irritation; for if, as Field's letter shows, the pulpits resounded with invectives against that monster of vice and minister of sensuality, the

---

[1] John Field's other son Theophilus, it is interesting to notice, became a bishop.

actor, the audience at the theatre daily shook its sides over the antics of that ludicrous compound of nasal piety and furtive hypocrisy, the puritan.   Lucy Hutchinson, writing of the treatment which puritans suffered at this period, declares that

> every stage, every table and every puppet play belched forth profane scoffs upon them, the drunkards made them their songs and all fiddlers and mimics learned to abuse them, as finding it the most graceful way of fooling.[1]

The drama of the age is full of references to puritans, and, as time went on, these became more and more contemptuous and insulting.   Lucy Hutchinson's words and Nathaniel Field's letter, both brimming over with passionate resentment, give us more insight into the real exasperation of the two parties than treatises stuffed with patriotic and classical lore.

The foolish and short-sighted policy of the first two Stewarts was not likely to diminish, in any way, this bitter feeling against the unholy amusement which they favoured and protected. Instead, it raised up a fresh engine of reform before which both court and stage, eventually, went down.   In 1625, the year of Charles's accession, an anonymous puritan opened a new, and, in the light of subsequent events, an ominous line of attack.   It was hopeless to ask the crown to cleanse the Augean stables, and the city had long since given up the task in despair; he, therefore, addressed himself to parliament, round which the hopes of all reformers were beginning to cluster.   His petition, calling itself *A Short Treatise against Stage-Playes*, is a brief and exceedingly businesslike enumeration of the chief arguments against the drama.   In these twenty-eight pages may be found the whole gist of *Histriomastix;* indeed, the tract reads so much like a first draft of its unwieldy successor that the suspicion is forced upon us that it was either written by Prynne himself, who as we know, began to collect his materials in 1624, or taken by him from another writer to be made the basis of his book.[2]

---

[1] *Memoirs of Colonel John Hutchinson*, ed. 1885, vol. i, p. 115.

[2] The Brit. Mus. Cat., on what grounds is not apparent, attributes it to Alexander Leighton, whose cause and character were very similar to those of Prynne.   In 1628, Richard Rawlidge, in *A Monster lately found out and discovered or the Scourging of Tipplers*, wrote unfavourably of the theatre.   His bitter

When we of the twentieth century hold in our hands the cube of printed matter known as *Histriomastix*, and turn over its eleven hundred pages, in which marginal notes and references to authorities, for the most part, long since forgotten, often take up more room than the text itself, we find it very difficult to realise just what the book meant in its own day. To us, it seems half pathetic and half ridiculous, a gigantic monument of misplaced energy and zeal, a pyramid left gaunt and useless on the sands of time. To a great extent, the work was the outcome of a peculiar personality. Prynne was a fanatic of that indomitable and most intolerant kind—the moral enthusiast. Apparently with very little of the milk of human kindness in his composition, he burned with an internal flame of righteous conviction, and this alone could have sustained him, not merely in his sufferings, but, also, in those untiring labours which his pen produced, over and above the immense *Histriomastix*. Yet, at the same time, he was thoroughly representative, his idiosyncrasies being extreme developments of, rather than departures from, the normal characteristics of his fellow reformers. If it be ever possible for one man to sum up a movement in his own person, Prynne summed up puritanism. And, since his book epitomises, likewise, the whole puritan attack upon the stage, a consideration of author and book together form a suitable close to the present study.

The story of its publication and of his cruel punishment is too well known to require lengthy treatment here. Nor is this the place to go into the vexed question as to whether he was technically guilty of seditious libel. After more than seven years' labour, and after several fruitless attempts to procure a licence, he managed at last, in 1632, to get his great work through the press. About the time when the last sheets were being worked off, queen Henrietta Maria and her women were engaged in rehearsing a pastoral play for a performance at Whitehall, which, apparently, did not actually take place until the book was in circulation. The idea of women appearing on the stage was new and shocking to English spectators. In 1629, a company of French actresses, at the invitation of the

language is rendered all the more remarkable by his obvious commonsense in other matters. His book, which refers to Whetstone's *Mirour*, must rank with that as one of the secondary contributions to the controversy.

queen, had attempted to give a performance at Blackfriars and had been "hissed, hooted and pippen-pelted from the stage." Prynne referred to this incident in great glee and, whether in ignorance of the impending pastoral or of set purpose, inserted in the table of contents at the end of his book an expression stigmatising women actors as "notorious whores." He was immediately summoned before the Star-chamber; and, though it is not clear what was the exact charge, there can be no doubt that his chief offence was the accidental or intentional application of these words to the queen's person. The upshot was that he was condemned to stand in the pillory, a penalty he underwent on two separate occasions, to lose both his ears, to be branded as a seditious libeller on both cheeks, to pay a fine of £5000 and to be perpetually imprisoned. Perhaps, the loss of his Oxford degree and his expulsion from Lincoln's inn were not the lightest part of the punishment to a man of Prynne's habits and temperament. His life sentence was afterwards cancelled by parliament; but he suffered the remainder of the sentence in patience and serenity. Prynne was a narrow-minded, dry-hearted, fierce fanatic; but, could he stand before us now, with his cropped ears and the letters S. L. burnt into his cheeks (*Stigmata Laudis* he interpreted them, in a rare burst of humour), we should acknowledge that the narrow-mindedness and fanaticism were not all on one side.

Despite its enormous length, there is nothing new in *Histriomastix, The Player's Scourge or Actors Tragedie*,[1] except, perhaps, the extraordinary fierceness of its denunciation. Prynne's knowledge of the stage was of the scantiest description. He owns, indeed, with shame, that, when a "novice," he had been enticed by evil companions to attend "foure severall Playes"; but, with these exceptions, he seems to be completely ignorant of the dramatic literature of the age, his only reference to our greatest dramatist being the indignant observation that "Shackpeers Plaies are printed in the best Crowne paper, far better than most Bibles." But, if Prynne knew little of contemporary drama, his seeming knowledge of anti-dramatic literature was astounding. Laud asserted that,

---

[1] For the full title, which, if given above, would occupy a whole page, see bibliography. A very useful analysis of the contents of the book is to be found in *Ward*, vol. III, pp. 241–3.

merely to read the works cited by Prynne would take sixty years of an ordinary man's life. The truth was that Prynne could not have read a tithe of his authorities; and he quotes, for the most part, not from the authors themselves, but from the quotations of previous puritan writers. During a campaign of over sixty years, carried on by a large number of eager seekers for chapter and verse, half the accessible writers of antiquity, and most of those since the beginning of the Christian era, had been ransacked for even the slightest hint of anti-dramatic feeling, which, when discovered, was pounced upon and pigeonholed under its special argument. The same points, too, were made by puritan after puritan with scarcely a change of word, and in sublime innocence of the sin of plagiarism. Thus, the stream of argument and quotation went on swelling from year to year, until, at last, it emptied itself into Prynne's great reservoir.[1] In his case, such a method was extremely dangerous; for his was the pursuit of proof, not of truth. A single statement from an author in dispraise, or apparent dispraise, of plays is allowed to outweigh the testimony of the writer's whole life and character. Thus, Plutarch, Horace and Cicero are found in company with the early fathers as abhorrers of stage plays. This must not be taken as an impeachment of Prynne's honesty. He was honest enough; but he often quotes at second hand, and, even when he had the original before him, he was blinded by the force of zeal to anything that conflicted with his argument—as what controversialist is not?

Perhaps the most original thing about the book is its arrangement. It is divided into two parts, and these, in turn, are subdivided into acts and scenes with an occasional chorus. This dramatic setting, curious in a book written against the stage, was intended to carry out the idea of *The Actors Tragedie* suggested on the title-page; but, also, it was an extremely convenient form for the purposes of the argument. The first act, for example, naturally deals with the satanic origin of the theatre, while, in the seventh, Prynne triumphantly marshals his mass of authorities in seven different squadrons or scenes, according to period or character, the whole being crowned

---

[1] Thus the Table (40 pp.) at the end of *Histriomastix*, forms, perhaps, the best index to the whole controversy.

with a chorus in which he announces that none can withstand his "all-conquering troopes." This plan of arrangement may owe something to Gosson's *Playes confuted in five Actions;* but the execution and the details were all Prynne's.

His book is the last of the series which we have to note. Its size and elaboration, the supposed insult to the queen, the celebrated trial and the sufferings of the author, must have brought the topic of stage morality very much to the fore and have greatly increased the bitterness of the puritan party. But *Histriomastix* had no imitators. It had completely exhausted the subject. Besides, it was now dangerous to write against the theatre, since this involved the risk of offending royalty and of thus falling into the inexorable hands of the high commission. Further than this, events were fast drifting towards revolution, and the minds of men were filled with other and greater matters than the stage.[1] Whether, as has been suggested, Prynne's attack did anything to reform the stage, it would be extremely difficult to determine; and, in any case, the question is a somewhat idle one. Of greater importance is the fact that the theatre was in a far from prosperous condition immediately before its suppression, as is clear from a curious little tract printed, in 1641, under the title *The Stage-Players Complaint*.

Monopolers are down, Projectors are down, the High Commission Court is downe, the Starre Chamber is downe, and (some think) Bishops will be downe and why should we then that are farre inferior to any of these not justely feare that we should be downe too?

Such is the burden of the author's tale, and the atmosphere of impending disaster which pervades the tract appropriately culminates in the concluding words: "From Plague, Pestilence and Famine from Battel, Murder and Suddaine Death—Good Lord deliver us." Few contemporary documents give a better picture of the gloom and sense of coming catastrophe that had come over a large part of the nation at this juncture in our history. But the words of the Litany were applicable to present needs and sorrows as well as to future fears. The

---

[1] This, probably, also accounts for the fact that Prynne's book, apparently, remained unanswered until 1662, when Sir Richard Baker published his *Theatrum Redivivum*.

plague had been more than usually violent since 1630, and, in consequence, the playhouses had been shut for the greater part of each year. The net result of these various factors in the situation was that the ordinance of 2 September, 1642, for the total suppression of stage plays was received, not only without surprise, but almost without attention. In estimating parliament's reasons for this step, political considerations should not be left out of account. The actor was now hated, not only on account of his profession, but, also, as the minion of the despot, and the passage just quoted shows that he realised the fact well enough. Moreover, the stage, obviously, was too dangerous an institution to be tolerated by any anti-royalist government. Players were "malignants" almost to a man, and, however efficient the censorship might be, the performance of an apparently harmless play might easily develop into a demonstration in favour of the king. Yet, for all this, we cannot doubt that the main intentions of the act were moral. The stage was swept away by the tide of puritan indignation and hatred, of which we have been watching the rise.

It was not to be expected, however, that so drastic a measure could be carried out without difficulty. Parliament found it necessary in 1647 and, again, in 1648 to pass further and more stringent ordinances against the stage, ordering all players to be apprehended and publicly whipped, all playhouses to be pulled down and any one present at a play to pay a fine of five shillings. Protests were not wanting against this policy. In 1643, two tracts appeared: one, *The Actors Remonstrance*, a humble request for the restoration of acting rights in return for sweeping reforms, which, incidentally, gives an interesting glimpse of what went on behind the scenes of theatrical life; the other, *The Players Petition to the Parliament*, a piece of satirical verse, which mocked at the Rump under pretence of appealing to it. The sauciness of the latter, however, was nothing to that of an unknown person who, at the beginning of 1649, actually published a book called *Mr. William Prynne, his defence of Stage-Playes or a Retraction of his former book*. Needless to say, the indignant victim of this effrontery at once issued a denial of the charge.[1]

[1] The fortunes of the players under the Commonwealth may be followed in some detail in James Wright's *Historia Histrionica* 1699 (reprinted in *Hazlitt's*

We have now enumerated and described the chief documents and events relating to the puritan campaign against the stage, culminating in the victory of 1642. The controversy has never really died out. It burst forth again in all its old vigour and with all its characteristic pedantry at the end of the seventeenth century. Curiously enough it was a high Anglican non-juror, Jeremy Collier, upon whose shoulders the puritan mantle fell; and his example was followed, thirty years later, by yet another Jacobite, William Law, the author of *A Serious Call*. Even modern writers have found it difficult to discuss the Elizabethan stage without ardently defending the puritans who attacked it. Yet the influence which the early fathers, like distant planets, seemed to exert upon every puritan in turn, the wholesale manner in which each borrows the arguments and expressions of his predecessor and, above all, the almost complete ignorance displayed by a large proportion of the assailants as to the real character of the institution they were attacking, combine to give the whole discussion an air of academic unreality. This impression, perhaps, is partly due to controversial methods which appealed forcibly to the Elizabethan intelligence, but which, by exasperating the modern reader, blind him to the genuine feeling that lies under their antiquated and absurd forms. For there can be no doubt whatever that puritan antipathy amounted to a fierce loathing, of whose strength a generation living in blander times cannot have any conception. In a word, the whole movement, from the outset, was not one for reforming the theatre but for abolishing it. Proposals for reform came rather from those who wrote in defence of the theatre, and whose attitude, it may be observed, was, in one sense, singularly in accord with that of their opponents. In the modern sense of the word, at least, they were puritans to a man. The stage-hater stoutly maintained that the drama did not and could not fulfil any ethical function. On the other hand, Bavande, Wager, Lodge, Gager, Nashe and Heywood, one and all, regarded the drama, first and foremost, as an engine for moral instruction. That such a man as Heywood should express himself thus, proves

---

Dodsley (vol. xv), and in Whitelocke's *Memorials*. It is, perhaps, worth noticing here that, in 1658, William Cartwright found courage to reprint Heywood's *Apology*, under the title *An Actor's Vindication*.

that he had scarcely more understanding than Stubbes and Prynne of the real nature of the drama which he represented. No one can pretend that Shakespeare and his fellow playwrights troubled themselves about theories of conduct. The defenders of the stage made pitiful attempts to justify their craft upon moral principles; but, in admitting the subordination of art to ethics, they had yielded their whole position. Had puritans only studied the theatre more and the early fathers less, they might, starting with the premisses which their antagonists gave them have made out a much better case for prosecution. They had all the logic on their side. On the side of the apologists, was all the common-sense—if they could only have seen it!